THE EXPLORER'S GUIDE to
DEATH VALLEY
NATIONAL PARK

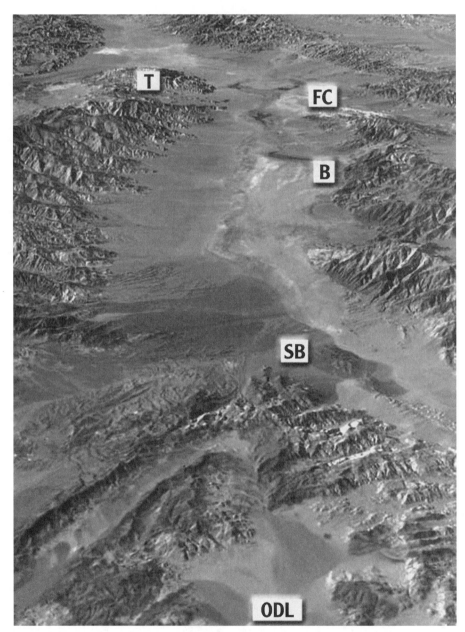

A virtual oblique northward view of south-central Death Valley. The labels indicate: T, Tucki Mountain; FC, Furnace Creek Ranch; B, Badwater; SB, Shoreline Butte; ODL, Owl Dry Lake.
(Digital image by Michael J. Rymer, U.S. Geological Survey)

THE EXPLORER'S GUIDE TO
DEATH VALLEY
NATIONAL PARK

Third Edition

T. SCOTT BRYAN AND
BETTY TUCKER-BRYAN

UNIVERSITY PRESS OF COLORADO

© 2014 by the University Press of Colorado

Published by the University Press of Colorado
5589 Arapahoe Avenue, Suite 206C
Boulder, Colorado 80303

 The University Press of Colorado is a proud member of
the Association of American University Presses.

The University Press of Colorado is a cooperative publishing enterprise supported, in part, by Adams State College, Colorado State University, Fort Lewis College, Mesa State College, Metropolitan State College of Denver, University of Colorado, University of Northern Colorado, and Western State College of Colorado.

∞ The paper used in this publication meets the minimum requirements of the American National Standard for Information Sciences—Permanence of Paper for Printed Library Materials. ANSI Z39.48-1992

Library of Congress Cataloging-in-Publication Data

Bryan, T. Scott.
  The explorer's guide to Death Valley National Park / T. Scott Bryan and Betty Tucker-Bryan. — Third edition.
     pages cm.
  ISBN 978-1-60732-340-2 (pbk.) — ISBN 978-1-60732-341-9 (ebook)
1. Death Valley National Park (Calif. and Nev.)—Guidebooks. I. Tucker-Bryan, Betty, 1927– II. Tucker-Bryan, Betty. III. Title.
  F868.D2B79 2015
  917.94'8704—dc23

                      2014034889

Design by Daniel Pratt

23   22   21   20   19   18   17   16   15   14   10   9   8   7   6   5   4   3   2   1

Contents

List of Maps   **ix**

List of Tables   **xi**

Foreword to the First Edition by Superintendent Edwin L. Rothfuss   **xiii**

Acknowledgments   **xv**

INTRODUCTION: An Introduction to Death Valley National Park and Vicinity   **1**

Part I. Geological, Human, and Natural History

CHAPTER 1. Geologic History   **9**

CHAPTER 2. Native American Cultures   **21**

CHAPTER 3. Explorers, Prospectors, and Miners   **27**

CHAPTER 4. Tourism and the National Park   **39**

CHAPTER 5. Plantlife   **47**

CHAPTER 6. Wildlife   **65**

Part II. The Death Valley Environment

CHAPTER 7. The Desert Environment: Climate, Precautions, and Regulations for Explorers of Death Valley   **97**

Part III. Exploring Death Valley National Park by Foot and Bicycle

CHAPTER 8. Hiking and Backpacking in Death Valley   **107**

CHAPTER 9. Bicycling in Death Valley   **123**

Part IV. Trip Route Road Logs

CHAPTER 10. An Introduction to the "Trip Route" Road Logs   **131**

CHAPTER 11. Southern Death Valley   **143**
Trip Route S-1—Jubilee Pass Road, Ashford Junction to Shoshone   **143**
Trip Route S-2—Harry Wade Road, Ashford Junction to Harry Wade Monument   **149**
Trip Route S-3—State Highway 127 South, Shoshone to Harry Wade Road   **160**
Trip Route S-4—Ibex Valley Road, State Highway 127 to Harry Wade Road   **164**

CHAPTER 12. South-Central Death Valley   **169**
Trip Route SC-1—Badwater Road, Furnace Creek to Badwater   **169**
Trip Route SC-2—East Side Road, Badwater to Ashford Junction   **178**
Trip Route SC-3—West Side Road   **181**

CHAPTER 13. Eastern Areas and Amargosa Valley   **201**
Trip Route E-1—State Highway 190 East, Furnace Creek to Death Valley Junction   **201**
Trip Route E-2—Dante's View Road, State Highway 190 to Dante's View   **214**
Trip Route E-3—Greenwater Valley Road   **217**
Trip Route E-4—Death Valley Junction to Devil's Hole   **225**
Trip Route E-5—State Highway 127, Death Valley Junction to Shoshone   **227**
Trip Route E-6—Lee Ghost Town   **229**
Trip Route E-7—Indian Pass Road   **231**

CHAPTER 14. North-Central Death Valley   **235**
Trip Route NC-1—State Highway 190 Central, Furnace Creek to Stovepipe Wells Village   **235**
Trip Route NC-2—Beatty Cutoff Road   **245**
Trip Route NC-3—Mud Canyon Road and Daylight Pass Road   **249**
Trip Route NC-4—Monarch Canyon Road and Chloride Cliff Road   **254**
Trip Route NC-5—Titus Canyon Road   **257**

CHAPTER 15. Western Areas, including the "Wildrose Country"   **263**
Trip Route W-1—Cottonwood Canyon Road   **263**
Trip Route W-2—State Highway 190 West, Stovepipe Wells Village to Darwin Road   **266**
Trip Route W-3—Emigrant Canyon Road and Wildrose Roads   **271**

CHAPTER 16. Panamint Valley Areas   **287**
Trip Route PV-1—Panamint Valley Road and Trona-Wildrose Road   **287**
Trip Route PV-2—Indian Ranch Road   **292**
Trip Route PV-3—Wingate Road and Goler Wash Road   **295**

CHAPTER 17. Northern Death Valley   **303**

    Trip Route N-1—Scotty's Castle Road, Sand Dunes Junction to Scotty's
    Castle   **303**

    Trip Route N-2—Bonnie Claire Road, Scotty's Castle to U.S. Highway
    95   **311**

CHAPTER 18. Big Pine Road and Eureka Valley   **313**

    Trip Route BP-1—Big Pine Road, Ubehebe Crater Road to Big Pine   **313**

    Trip Route PB-2—South Eureka Road to Eureka Sand Dunes   **322**

CHAPTER 19. Racetrack Valley and Hunter Mountain   **325**

    Trip Route RH-1—Racetrack Valley Road and Hunter Mountain Road,
    Ubehebe Crater to State Highway 190   **325**

CHAPTER 20. Saline Valley Road, including Lee Flat   **345**

    Trip Route SV-1—Saline Valley Road   **345**

CHAPTER 21. Nevada Triangle   **365**

    Trip Route NT-1—Phinney Canyon Road and Strozzi Ranch Road   **365**

    Trip Route NT-2—McDonald Spring Road   **370**

    Trip Route NT-3—Mud Summit Road   **373**

Appendixes

    A. Ghost Towns and Mining Camps   **377**

    B. Railroads of Death Valley   **401**

    C. Visitor Services and Activities   **415**

Suggested Reading   433

About the Authors   437

Index   439

Death Valley Wilderness and Backcountry Stewardship Plan of 2013   455

Maps

MAP 1. Introduction, Main Points of Interest   **2**

MAP 2. Death Valley Fault Zones   **16**

MAP 3. Southern Death Valley   **144**

MAP 4. South-Central Death Valley   **170**

MAP 5. Eastern Areas and Amargosa Valley   **202**

MAP 6. Furnace Creek Wash Detail   **204**

MAP 7. Indian Pass Road   **232**

MAP 8. North-Central Death Valley   **236**

MAP 9. Western Areas, including Wildrose   **264**

MAP 10. Panamint Valley Areas   **288**

MAP 11. Northern Death Valley   **304**

MAP 12. Big Pine Road and Eureka Valley   **314**

MAP 13. Racetrack Valley and Hunter Mountain   **326**

MAP 14. Saline Valley Area, including Lee Flat   **346**

MAP 15. Nevada Triangle   **366**

MAP 16. Ghost Towns of Death Valley   **378**

MAP 17. Railroads of Death Valley   **402**

MAP 18. Scotty's Castle   **419**

MAP 19. Death Valley Campgrounds   **421**

MAP 20. Furnace Creek Area   **425**

MAP 21. Stovepipe Wells Village   **429**

Tables

TABLE 1. Geologic Time Scale for Death Valley   **11**

TABLE 2. Biological Environments of the Death Valley Region   **64**

TABLE 3. Death Valley Temperature and Rainfall Records   **99**

TABLE 4. Death Valley Roads and Trails: Descriptions and Map Symbols   **133**

Foreword to the First Edition

In the summer of 1983 I accepted the superintendency of Death Valley National Monument. During my previous twenty-four years with the National Park Service I had worked in some pretty spectacular national parks—Glacier, Grand Canyon, Everglades, and Canyonlands to name a few. I did not know Death Valley at all, and like many who have not visited the area I naturally expected the area to be hot, dry, flat, sandy, and perhaps boring. I was challenged, however, with the assignments of removing the alien burros that were competing with the native bighorn sheep for forage and water, and of dealing with the mining companies still active within the monument—an anomaly in a park. With my preconceived ideas, I was in for a surprise!

I found Death Valley to be intensely complex (geologically as well as administratively), beautiful (sometimes bold and brash and other times and places very subtle), full of life (if you know where to look, and as you would expect a desert after the spring rains), and with a rich history of man (from the first Native Americans to the early explorers to visitors). With such a large and magnificent area compared with many of the earlier parks I had worked in, I wondered why Death Valley was not a full national park rather than "just" a national monument. Surely park status must have been someone's dream. Briefly, I wondered, what is the story behind it?

In 1890 Stephen Tyng Mather, who worked with the *New York Sun* newspaper, suggested to his co-reporter John Spears that Spears might want to go to California to do a story on a vast and beautiful desert—Death Valley—where Steve's father, Joe, was working for Pacific Coast Borax. John did visit the area, and his book *Illustrated Sketches of Death Valley,* published in 1891, became immensely popular and brought the Death Valley beauty and lore to the American public.

In January 1927 Pacific Coast Borax invited Mather, by then the director of the National Park Service, and his assistant Horace Albright to Death Valley to see the company's new Furnace Creek Inn, scheduled to open the next month. Also on the agenda was a discussion of the possibility of making Death Valley a national park.

All concurred that it was the right thing to do and that the area deserved national park status, but they also felt the political timing was wrong and the area was still open to mining. Death Valley would have to wait.

Horace Albright soon became director of the National Park Service, and he still hoped Death Valley would become a national park. In the final days before leaving office, he got outgoing President Herbert Hoover, who was his good friend, to sign the proclamation establishing Death Valley National Monument on February 11, 1933. It was a start, but for Horace and all of us who have worked in Death Valley and grown to love it, the dream continued. Over the decades there were occasional efforts to elevate the area to a full national park. The Mining in the Parks Act of 1976, which closed Death Valley to mineral entry, removed one of the serious obstacles to its attaining national park status.

The California Desert Protection Act was introduced before Congress in 1986. After eight years of debate, the bill came to a happy conclusion on October 31, 1994, when President Bill Clinton signed the bill that established Death Valley National Park. The long dream of many was fulfilled. Death Valley, the nation's fifty-third national park, was increased in size to almost 3.4 million acres, making it the largest national park area outside of Alaska.

Scott Bryan and Betty Tucker-Bryan had a dream, too. Both were very familiar with Death Valley from having lived, worked, and spent years exploring and studying the area. Their dream was to put out a guide to this magnificent national park. This book is their result. I think you will enjoy reading it as you plan your trip to Death Valley. I know you will find it useful as you explore the park. Enjoy, good reading, and have a good time exploring my favorite national park.

EDWIN L. ROTHFUSS
Superintendent, Death Valley National Park
August 1983–November 1994

Acknowledgments

This book would not have been possible without the extensive help of many National Park Service, Bureau of Land Management, and other interested people. We acknowledged them in the first edition, and here we thank all of them again.

Above all, we must again thank former Superintendent Edwin L. Rothfuss, who in 1994 encouraged the initial production of this book, authorized our use of a trailer site in the government housing area, read and commented on the manuscript, and wrote the foreword to the first edition; and Esy Fields, former managing director of the Death Valley Natural History Association, who also encouraged our original work and coordinated additional National Park Service and DVNHA reviews of the manuscript.

Many members of Death Valley's interpretive staff contributed their knowledge of the park environment and public programs. Rangers Charlie Callaghan and Alan VanValkenberg added information for the second and third editions, especially regarding backcountry and wilderness use regulations.

Linda Greene, of Death Valley's resource management division, kept us informed of administrative policy plans and changes. Carre Shandor forwarded to us the park's GPS database, and Terry T. Fisk provided the 2006 inventory of spring and other water source locations and discharges.

Blair Davenport, Death Valley's Museum Curator, provided historic photographs from the park archives for all three editions.

Roberta Harlan, Museum Assistant at the Eastern California Museum, and Dan Davis, Historical Archivist at the Merrill-Cazier Library of Utah State University, produced additional historic photographs for the second and third editions.

As before, information has also been received from many individuals who love to explore Death Valley, including those who anonymously post items to the "Death Valley Talk" Internet chat pages. We appreciate all the help.

■ PUBLISHER'S NOTE

Regulations and conditions regarding road and trail use change frequently. Before undertaking any of the trips outlined in this guidebook, please check for the latest information with the Death Valley National Park headquarters located in the park at Furnace Creek.

THE EXPLORER'S GUIDE TO
DEATH VALLEY
NATIONAL PARK

An Introduction to Death Valley National Park and Vicinity

In 1957, famous naturalist Dr. Edmund C. Jaeger wrote: "The complete natural history of Death Valley will never be written. . . . [It] is a subject too vast." That might well be true, for Death Valley National Park encompasses an immense area that is unique in its diversity.

- The park is nearly 150 miles long from north to south, about 60 miles wide from east to west, and covers 3,399,000 acres (or 5,311 square miles). In addition, considerable portions of the adjacent mountains and valleys are culturally and biologically part of Death Valley.
- The park's elevations range from desiccated salt flats 282 feet below sea level near Badwater, where the average rainfall is less than two inches per year, to pine-clad peaks higher than 11,000 feet above sea level in the Panamint Range, where heavy snow falls in the winter.
- Death Valley's life zones follow the changes in elevation, ranging from the Lower Sonoran life zone, through the Upper Sonoran and Transition life zones, to the Canadian life zone; the very highest peaks qualify for the Arctic (or Boreal) life zone.
- Summer temperatures on the valley floor routinely reach over 120°F (50°C), and there is nothing unusual about winter days as cold as 0°F (−18°C) in the higher mountains.
- More than 1,000 species of plants, at least 16 of which are endemics found nowhere else, inhabit the park along with at least 440 species of animals.
- Death Valley includes hundreds of archaeological sites, most of which have never been fully documented but some of which may be more than 9,000 years old.

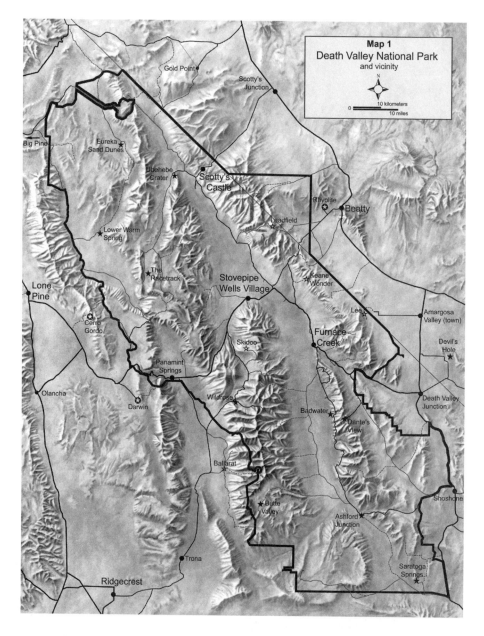

- The park's geology encompasses everything from recrystallized metamorphic rocks at least 1.8 billion years old to salt crystals that grow larger as you watch them.

- Mining for precious metals, borax, and talc led directly to Death Valley's discovery, fame, tourist industry, and the creation of the national park itself.

- The park contains 260 miles of paved highways and over 1,000 miles of dirt roads, everything from major state highways to four-wheel-drive routes of poor quality.

Obviously, it takes time and effort to fully experience the variety that Death Valley has to offer. This book provides information for all of Death Valley's visitors, from first-time travelers just learning about the area to those who are able to return for in-depth explorations.

FORMAT OF THIS BOOK

This book is divided into five sections.

Part I (Chapters 1 through 6) discusses the geology, human history, plantlife, and wildlife of the park.

Part II (Chapter 7) deals with the desert environment—Death Valley's climate and, with that, the precautions that explorers should take before venturing into the park. This includes the National Park Service regulations that all park visitors should keep in mind.

Part III (Chapters 8 and 9) provides ideas for day hiking, backpacking, and bicycling in Death Valley.

Part IV (Chapters 10 through 21) first introduces and then describes the entire park in eleven sections of detailed mile-by-mile road logs that cover every road within and several roads outside the national park boundary.

Part V (Appendices A, B, and C) provides historical information about Death Valley's ghost towns and railroads and the modern interpretive services, lodging and camping facilities, and special events. There is also a suggested reading list for sources of further information.

LAND CLASSIFICATION

National Park Service. Most of the land described in this book lies within Death Valley National Park, which is a unit of the National Park Service (NPS) of the U.S. Department of the Interior. Land-use regulations within the park are more stringent than they are on most of the public lands outside the park boundary. Especially worth noting is that most of the national park is wilderness, and the wilderness boundary is just 50 feet from the centerline of nearly all backcountry dirt roads. By permit required starting in 2015, only foot or horseback travel is allowed within the wilderness areas. Also, no collecting of any kind—plant, animal, fossil, mineral, or archaeological artifact—is allowed within the national park. The headquarters for the park is adjacent to the Furnace Creek Visitor Center.

Bureau of Land Management. Much of the land immediately surrounding Death Valley National Park is administered by the Bureau of Land Management (BLM), which is an agency of the Department of the Interior. Land-use regulations here are generally less stringent than are those of the NPS, but much of this land is wilderness where off-road travel is not allowed. The collecting of mineral specimens for personal, noncommercial use is permitted in most areas. Detailed regulations are available at the offices of the BLM Desert District in the town of Ridgecrest, California, and at and the Eastern Sierra Interagency Visitor Center just south of Lone Pine, California.

U.S. Forest Service. Relatively small areas bounding the northwestern part of the national park lie within Inyo National Forest, a unit of the U.S. Forest Service (USFS), an agency of the U.S. Department of Agriculture. Again, land-use regulations here are somewhat less stringent than they are within the national park, but they are also significantly different from those that apply to the BLM areas. The national forest's offices in Bishop and Lone Pine and the Eastern Sierra Interagency Visitor Center have detailed information and use regulations.

Indian reservations. The Timbisha Shoshone Village adjacent to the Furnace Creek Ranch and the Indian Ranch in Panamint Valley are private areas that are off-limits to entry except by invitation or unless the Indians are holding an advertised public event.

Military ground. The land bordering the extreme southwestern part of Death Valley National Park is within the Mojave Range B of the Naval Air Weapons Station–China Lake, and the land only a short distance south of the park's southern boundary lies within the Fort Irwin Army National Training Center. These areas are fenced and well-marked, and entry into them is strictly forbidden.

Private property. There is very little private property within Death Valley National Park. Most of these places are patented mining and related millsite claims that date to the late 1800s and early 1900s, before the establishment of the original national monument. Most of this land is unoccupied and undeveloped, and much of it may be quitclaimed to the NPS in the near future. There are, however, still a few private inholdings scattered in those areas that were added to the park by the 1994 expansion, and these may be posted against trespass. In addition, the grounds of the Furnace Creek Inn and Ranch Resort and those of the Panamint Springs Resort are private properties.

ROAD CLASSIFICATIONS

Death Valley's roads fall into four use categories.

Paved routes. Paved all-weather roads accessible to any vehicle. Some of these roads are narrow and may have broken asphalt and unmarked sharp curves.

High-clearance routes. Dirt roads on which vehicles with high clearance are recommended. Although some of these roads are graded on occasion and then can be driven with caution in any vehicle, they are subject to washouts and also may be extremely rough, making high-clearance vehicles desirable if not outright necessary.

Four-wheel-drive (4WD) routes. Unimproved dirt roads on which 4WD, high-clearance vehicles are often required and therefore strongly recommended; this does *not* include all-wheel-drive automobiles. These roads typically have areas of loose sand or gravel, high centers, sharp pitches, steep grades and so on (often in combination).

Severe or questionable routes. Roads that are extremely rough and narrow and in such poor condition that driving them is not recommended except by experienced drivers accompanied by others.

As of spring 2014, all of the roads described here are open to use. This could change, however. Explorers are always encouraged to check with the Park Service for any updates about a road's status and condition, as well as about any changes in backcountry-use regulations.

■MAPS

All of the maps used in this book have been produced from public domain base maps available online from the National Park Service, Harpers Ferry Center (www.nps.gov/carto/MAPS). The shaded-relief background was a jpeg file obtained from the same site. The originals were downloaded as large-format Adobe Illustrator files that were cut into smaller areas as appropriate. Symbols to indicate points of interest and road classifications were superimposed onto the base maps. All were produced at full, original scale but then were variously resized to fit this publication. The distance scales therefore vary from one map to another, but all show accurate layouts.

■ROAD LOG MILEAGES AND GPS LOCATIONS

Mileages. Each route that is described in Part IV of this book has viewpoints, specific places of interest, and road turnoffs referenced according to car odometer readings. These must be taken as approximate only because trip odometer readings are often different from trip to trip, even when driven in the same vehicle; this is especially true on dirt roads. Also, most modern odometers are digital and only record the distance every 1/10 mile so that one "click" to the next represents more than 500 feet.

Global Positioning System (GPS) coordinates. Especially in Death Valley's backcountry but also from time to time along the main roads, there are road intersections or points of interest that are unmarked and difficult to find. These places are noted by their geographic locations using coordinates that are easily checked using any handheld or vehicle GPS unit. In this book, latitude-longitude coordinates are used because that is the system employed by Death Valley National Park in its park maintenance database (which was used to double-check coordinates determined in the field or from topographic maps). All GPS coordinates in this book are considered accurate to within 50 feet.

PART I

Geological, Human, and Natural History

CHAPTER ONE

Geologic History

■ THE SETTING

Death Valley National Park has an extraordinarily long and complex geologic history. Its most ancient rocks are more than 1.8 billion years old, whereas its youngest are forming today. They have been folded, faulted, and recrystallized in every imaginable way, inundated by volcanic lava and ash beds, and deeply sliced by erosion. The result is a wonderland that represents both the driest part of the Great Basin and the most extreme portion of the Basin and Range.

The Great Basin is a geographic region that covers parts of Oregon, Idaho, Wyoming, Utah, Nevada, and California. It is defined by its climate and hydrology. Heavy rain and snow may fall in the mountains, but the intervening valleys are dry because of the storm-blocking "rain shadow" effect of its mountain ranges. Streams draining the slopes simply soak into the ground or evaporate. None of the rivers reaches the ocean. In the spring and early summer there is sometimes enough run-off to form small lakes on the valley floors, but they soon dry up in the summer heat, leaving behind shimmering playas—barren lake beds of salt and clay.

The Basin and Range is the geologic province that formed the Great Basin's mountains. The crust of the earth was uplifted and stretched under severe tension, and large-scale fault zones broke it into a series of parallel north-south-trending valleys and ranges that march east one after another from the Sierra Nevada Mountains in California to central Utah, north into Idaho and Wyoming, and south through Arizona into Mexico.

The Basin and Range is geologically young—less than 65 million years old. Its development began in Utah. As time went on the action gradually migrated westward and produced greater relief. Because it is nearly westernmost in the province, the Death Valley region boasts some of the youngest and most extreme topography of all the Basin and Range. Its mountains are still growing taller, and the valleys are becoming deeper. Rock exposures are fresh and reveal nearly every variety of stone that exists. The rocks in one mountain range are often completely different from those a few miles away, and sometimes the age difference can vary a billion years in only a few inches. Great earthquakes and volcanic eruptions have torn the surface. Ice Age lakes filled the valleys with hundreds of feet of water and left behind wave-cut terraces, beaches, and salt beds. Wind has stripped the surface bare in some places and piled up sand dunes in others. The result is a geological paradise.

What we see today is only the latest development in a region that contains many complex ingredients that have gone through countless processes. A little understanding about rocks and time helps make sense of Death Valley National Park's otherwise incomprehensible hodgepodge of geology.

■ PRECAMBRIAN TIME

Geologic time is divided into four major parts based mostly on the types of life that existed during each era. The fossil record indicates that life had somehow developed on Earth nearly 3.5 billion years ago, but from then through most of the next 3 billion years there was little change. Life existed entirely as single-celled forms such as archaea, bacteria, and cyanobacteria. These cells reproduce by simple cell division, and there is little evolution because the offspring is genetically identical to the parent. Colonies of bacteria sometimes caused mounded mineral accumulations called stromatolites to grow around them, but only rarely were the cells themselves preserved as fossils. Because of this lack of preserved cells, and also because rocks this old have almost always been recrystallized during later mountain-building episodes, very little is known about the first 4 billion years—87 percent—of the Earth's history. All of this vast time span, from the creation of the entire Earth 4.7 billion years ago up to "only" 700 million years ago, is commonly lumped together as *Precambrian Time*.

Death Valley's Precambrian rocks are divided into three main sections. Oldest are high-grade metamorphic materials that make up much of the bedrock in Death Valley's mountain ranges. Little can be said about these rocks but, because of their original composition of sand and silt, we know they were deposited as sediment on a gentle floodplain about 1.8 billion years ago. Later they were severely metamorphosed during major mountain building. Those mountains were stripped away by erosion long before the end of the Precambrian. These rocks are exposed at the surface in relatively small areas. Two places where they can be easily seen are the cliffs above Badwater and along lower Wildrose Canyon below the campground.

Later, a series of sedimentary rocks known as the Pahrump Group was deposited. These formations—the Crystal Springs, Beck Spring, and Kingston Peak—were laid down mostly in a shallow marine environment. Later metamorphism affected them too, but it was less intense and the original sedimentary structures often remain visible. The most important aspect of these rocks is that sometime much later they were intruded by an igneous rock called diabase. Where it

Geologic Time Scale for Death Valley

Era	Period	Rock Formation	Events in Death Valley
Cenozoic	Quaternary	none specifically named except Ubehebe Volcanics	Holocene Epoch-modern alluvial fans, playas, salt pans, and sand dunes form; Pleistocene Epoch–Lake Manly
	Tertiary	Mormon Point Funeral Nova Furnace Creek Artists Drive Timber Mountain and other volcanics Titus Canyon	Opening of modern Death Valley Development of the Basin & Range province with major regional volcanism, lakebed sediments in localized basins Oligocene Epoch–localized deposits
Mesozoic	Cretaceous	miscellaneous igneous intrusions such as Skidoo Granite and Hunter Mountain Granodiorite	Nevadan Orogeny mountain building and volcanic activity; thrust faulting and regional uplift in Death Valley; ocean withdraws from area
	Jurassic		
	Triassic	Butte Valley	Localized shallow marine deposition
Paleozoic	Permian	Owens Valley	Long inundation by tropical ocean begins to end as deposits contain progressively more silt and sand
	Pennsylvanian	Keeler Canyon Tihvipah Rest Spring	
	Mississippian	Lee Flat Perdido Tin Mountain	Long period of sediment deposition on stable continental margin. Most sediment is limestone and often is highly fossiliferous; occasional interruptions with withdrawl of the ocean and deposition of non-marine sand and silt
	Devonian	Lost Burro	
	Silurian	Hidden Valley	
	Ordovician	Ely Spring Eureka Barrel Spring Pogonip	
	Cambrian	Nopah Racetrack Bonanza King Carrara Zabriskie Wood Canyon Zabriskie Wood Canyon	Thick wedge of coarse sand and silt shows the opening of a new ocean basin

continued on next page

Geologic Time Scale for Death Valley (*continued*)

Pz	Cambrian	Zabriskie	
		Wood Canyon	
Precambrian	Vendian (Ediacaran)	Stirling Johnnie	Dominated by sand and silt indicating rifting of the continent
		Noonday	Shallow marine limestones of a tropical environment
		– – – – – – unconformity (gap in the geologic record) – – – – – – – – – –	
	Proterozoic	Kingston Peak	Coarse grained sediment including glacial debris
		Beck Spring	Shallow marine sediments, locally converted to talc within Crystal Springs
		Crystal Springs	
		– – – – – – unconformity (gap in the geologic record) – – – – – – – – –	
		unnamed assemblage of igneous and high-grade metamorphics	Death Valley's "Basement Rock," at least 1.8 billion years old
	Archean	Rocks of these periods (older than 1.8 billion years) are not exposed anywhere in the Death Valley Region	
	Hadean		

encountered the dolomite (calcium-magnesium carbonate) of the Crystal Springs Formation, large deposits of talc were formed.

Again, there was a hiatus before the deposition of sedimentary rocks resumed. These last Precambrian rocks are commonly assigned to the Vendian (or Ediacaran) Period, a time transitional to the Paleozoic Era. Trace fossils, such as burrows and feeding trails but not fossils of the animals that made them, are occasionally found in these rocks.

■ THE PALEOZOIC ERA

The abrupt appearance of complex multicellular life between about 700 million and 540 million years ago marks the end of the Precambrian and the start of the *Paleozoic Era*. In time, shallow ocean waters teemed with mollusks (clams and snails), echinoderms (starfish, urchins, and crinoids), arthropods (trilobites), brachiopods, and bryozoans. Many of the Paleozoic formations contain abundant fossils. Since the geologic time scale is based mostly on the fossil record, it is in the Paleozoic that time is first divided into spans shorter than eras. From oldest to youngest, these periods are called the Cambrian, Ordovician, Silurian, Devonian, Carboniferous-Mississippian, Carboniferous-Pennsylvanian, and Permian. Each period is represented within Death Valley National Park.

During the Paleozoic, the entire West Coast of North America was a quiet continental shelf. The setting was much like that along the East Coast of modern North

Most rocks in Death Valley's mountains are Precambrian or Paleozoic sediments. These in the Last Chance Range near Eureka Dunes are dominated by the striped Bonanza King Formation of Cambrian age.

America. There was dry land to the east, about where the Rocky Mountains are now, and gentle rivers flowed to the sea to deposit layers of sand, silt, and clay along the seashore. The water was clear and tropical most of the time, and extensive limestone platforms and reefs formed a short distance offshore. These layered rock formations make up most of the exposed rock in the Funeral, Grapevine, Panamint, Cottonwood, and Inyo mountains.

People often think of catastrophes when they consider geology, but the real stories of geology involve slow, uniform events. A total of more than 25,000 feet of sediment was deposited in this region during the Paleozoic Era. However, the era lasted 450 million years. Put together, this means that the sediment was deposited at a net average rate much less than one one-thousandth of an inch per year! Time was responsible for the vast accumulation of rock.

◼ THE MESOZOIC ERA

Conditions abruptly changed at the end of the Paleozoic Era as the passive continental margin became part of an active igneous belt that was building a range of mountains. The unifying theory for geology is called plate tectonics. Masses of continental and oceanic rocks move as plates of crust on top of a deeper, semifluid material called the asthenosphere. It is a simple process. During those quiet Paleozoic years, North America was being carried eastward. At the end of the Paleozoic, it abruptly reversed its direction toward the west, causing a process called subduction.

Subduction occurs when a slab of oceanic crust is forced to slide beneath a plate of continental crust, such as North America. Some of the subducted plate melts, and magma rises up into the overriding material. During this particular mountain-building episode, called the Nevadan Orogeny (from *oros*, "mountain," and *genes*, "birth"), this region must have looked quite a lot like today's Cascade Range—rolling hills studded with volcanoes similar to Mt. St. Helens, Mt. Rainier, or Crater Lake's Mt. Mazama.

The start of the Nevadan Orogeny marks the beginning of the *Mesozoic Era*. Comprising the Triassic, Jurassic, and Cretaceous periods, it covers the geologic time span from about 250 million to 65 million years ago. The quiet sedimentary setting of earlier times was completely disrupted. (The only known Mesozoic sedimentary rock in the Death Valley region is the Butte Valley Formation, exposed in a limited part of the southern Panamint Mountains.) Intrusions of magma penetrated into the older rocks, cooling and solidifying as granite thousands of feet below the surface. The older sedimentary rocks were deformed and often recrystallized at high temperatures and pressures into a miscellany of metamorphic rocks, and solutions percolating through them created ore deposits of gold, lead-silver-zinc, and copper. Compression forced huge chunks of rocks to slide horizontally along thrust faults, superimposing the sequences of sedimentary formations on top of one another. At the surface, volcanoes erupted and laid down ash beds and lava flows.

It is only by chance that the Nevadan Orogeny occupied the entire Mesozoic Era. Elsewhere around the world this was the "Age of the Dinosaurs," but you will not find dinosaur remains in Death Valley. The environment was not suitable; there was very little dry land, and most of what did exist was on the slopes of the active volcanoes.

The volcanic rock eroded away long ago, since it was originally perched on top of everything else. Intrusive rocks can be found in many places, such as around the ghost town of Skidoo, on Hunter Mountain, in the Owlshead Mountains, and in other areas where high uplift and deep erosion have revealed what once were deep-seated materials.

■ THE CENOZOIC ERA

The Mesozoic Era and Nevadan Orogeny ended nearly simultaneously as time entered the *Cenozoic Era*. During this era the Basin and Range Province began to form, a process that started 65 million years ago and continues to this day. The Earth's crust was stretched by tension. Estimates are that the east-west distance across the entire Basin and Range Province has increased by at least 150 miles. To accommodate the stresses, the rocks fractured in a series of north-south faults along each of which the block of rock on one side moved up relative to the block on the other side. This kind of vertical movement produces what is called a normal dip-slip fault. The down-dropped valley blocks like Death, Panamint, and Saline valleys are grabens, whereas the intervening uplifted mountains such as the Panamint and Funeral Ranges are horsts. These alternating down-up-down-up fault blocks are the basins and ranges of the province. (In the Death Valley region each of the valleys has had much more fault activity along one side than the other, and the faults flatten into horizontal planes at depth. Technically, these modified normal faults are called listric faults, and the valleys are halfgrabens.)

As the valleys were pulled open, some of the rocks were twisted and bowed upward into broad curving forms. Where hard igneous and metamorphic rocks were overlain by softer sedimentary materials, the younger rocks literally slid off of the older. Pulled by gravity down into the valley via detachment faults, they quickly eroded away to expose curving turtleback surfaces of Precambrian basement rock. A series of turtlebacks is found in southeastern Death Valley, and the jumbled rocks of the Amargosa Chaos near Jubilee Pass show where another detachment fault began but did not complete the process.

As the mountains are thrown up relative to the valleys, erosion tries to strip them away. The debris is deposited as new sediment on the valley floors and hides much of the true geologic structure. The highest point in the Panamint Range at Telescope Peak reaches 11,049 feet above sea level. Directly below it, near Badwater, are the two lowest points in North America, both 282 feet below sea level, as measured by the U.S. Geological Survey. (Recent unofficial reports of an elevation of −289 are officially considered to be "misinformation.") That change of elevation is

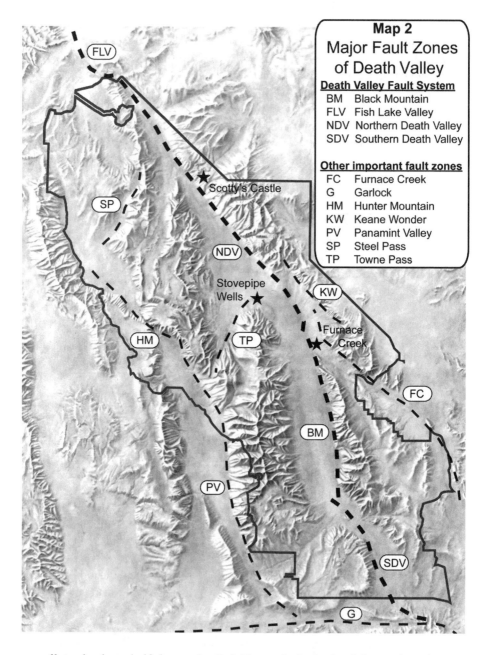

Map 2

Major Fault Zones of Death Valley

Death Valley Fault System
BM   Black Mountain
FLV   Fish Lake Valley
NDV   Northern Death Valley
SDV   Southern Death Valley

Other important fault zones
FC   Furnace Creek
G   Garlock
HM   Hunter Mountain
KW   Keane Wonder
PV   Panamint Valley
SP   Steel Pass
TP   Towne Pass

Scotty's Castle

Stovepipe Wells

Furnace Creek

actually only about half the total relief. To reach the bedrock beneath Badwater, one would have to dig through nearly 9,000 feet of sand, gravel, and salt. The true amount of vertical fault offset has been more than 20,000 feet.

This basin and range faulting is only part of the structural story. The national park is also cut by strike-slip faults. On these most of the movement is horizontal.

In effect, dip-slip faults create the mountain blocks, and strike-slip faults slide them past one another. The total offset along the Northern Death Valley Fault Zone through central Death Valley north toward Nevada may be as great as 50 miles. In a similar manner, the Southern Death Valley Fault Zone has generated as much as 20 miles of movement. Fully as important, probably, is the fault zone that links the Panamint Valley and Hunter Mountain faults into a single system perhaps 150 miles long.

These faults and uncountable others have slashed Death Valley's rocks into thousands of pieces. Each has been moved a bit differently than the others. Some are tilted on end, others severely folded, and a few are completely upside-down. The details are exceedingly complex, and geologists working with these exposures have recently reinterpreted many of their meanings. The complete story is far from being fully understood.

The geologic creation of Death Valley National Park is still underway. Every time a fault ruptures, the result is an earthquake. Reasonably fresh fault scarps formed by prehistoric shocks are visible along Badwater Road south of the Furnace Creek Inn, parallel to Scotty's Castle Road, and along the east side of Panamint Valley. Several earthquakes of significant size have occurred within the park area during the twentieth century. One on November 4, 1908, had a Richter magnitude of about 6.0 and was probably centered somewhere in the Panamint Mountains, possibly near Butte Valley. Another quake stuck south of, but near, Death Valley on November 15, 1916, with a magnitude of at least 6.1. And on May 17, 1993, a quake of magnitude 6.2 struck Eureka Valley. The largest earthquake to have actually occurred within the national park area in recorded time, this 1993 quake caused minor damage in Owens Valley but was not quite strong enough to form a new scarp. Finally, several small tremors were recorded at Harrisburg Flat in 1994, and there was a series of small (up to magnitude 4.4) quakes in the Slate Range near Trona in early December 2008. It is certain that more earthquakes, some of large scale, will take place in the future.

◼ FIRE AND ICE

The tension that caused the faulting also thinned the crust throughout the Basin and Range Province. Continental crust is usually about 25 miles thick, but below Death Valley it might reach down as little as 12 miles. Faults can serve as conduits for magma to rise toward the surface, especially in thin crust areas, so the park has been the site of geologically young volcanic activity. About 28 million years ago, the entire region was blanketed with ash from huge eruptions within what is now the Nevada Test Site. In places, this ejecta was piled in layers over 1,000 feet deep. Much of the rock in the Black Mountains, in the Saline Range between Saline and Eureka valleys, and in the Argus Mountains west of Panamint Valley is composed of lava flows and ash beds formed between 12 and 4 million years ago. Still younger are cinder cones in southern Death Valley and in Saline Valley. Especially remarkable is the Ubehebe

A small normal fault in Johnson Canyon.

Ubehebe Crater is the pit of a maar crater, that is, a crater formed by a steam explosion caused by volcanically heated groundwater that apparently occurred only about 300 years ago.

Crater complex of volcanic explosion pits, sixteen maar craters that completed their development not more than 300 years ago when Ubehebe Crater blanketed 15 square miles of the surroundings with as much as 150 feet of volcanic ash and cinders.

During the Ice Age glacial episodes, there was much greater runoff out of both the Sierra Nevada to the west and the local ranges. The Owens River twice reached as far as Panamint Valley and Death Valley. Panamint Lake was as deep as 900 feet—it is amazing to realize that those terraces high above the ghost town of Ballarat were verdant lake shores about 130,000 years ago. The Amargosa River was a large and permanent stream that flowed through Lake Tecopa and into Death Valley where Lake Manly was 640 feet deep, up to 8 miles wide, and more than 90 miles long. Other lakes occupied Panamint, Saline, and Eureka valleys at the same time. Smaller temporary lakes have existed many times since then, and the evaporation of each one left behind salt beds such as the Devil's Golf Course and Saline Salt Marsh on the valley floors. The process continues as new salt is added with every spring runoff and flash flood.

We do not usually notice the slow but uniform events that make geology work, but there is constant change. It is difficult for anyone to understand what the span of geologic time really means. Geologists toss around billions and millions of years as if they were nothing, but time is everything. Somebody once remarked that in geology the impossible becomes possible, the possible is probable, and the probable is certain. Nowhere are the seeming impossibilities of geology better revealed than in the realities of Death Valley National Park and vicinity.

It must be emphasized that collecting rock, mineral, fossil, and archaeological specimens is prohibited within the national park. Mineral collecting remains legal in many areas surrounding the park, provided that the location is on public land and not on a valid mineral claim. The collection of fossil specimens is a matter subject to revision, confusion, and debate. A strict interpretation of the Paleontological Resources Protection Act of 2009 (signed into law in March 2009) implies that there can be no fossil collecting of any kind on any public land without a permit from the Department of the Interior. However, a Bureau of Land Management brochure distributed since the passage of the act states that limited collection of invertebrate and plant fossils is allowed, provided that the specimens are for personal use only; such specimens cannot be bartered or sold. Collectors are strongly advised to check with the appropriate agency for current regulations.

CHAPTER TWO

Native American Cultures

■ PALEOINDIANS

During the Wisconsin Glacial Period, the last major episode of the Ice Age, glaciers covered much of the northern hemisphere. Sea level was hundreds of feet lower than it is now, and the Bering Land Bridge connected Siberia to Alaska. Animals migrated in both directions, and humans, who lived as hunters and gatherers, followed them. As they spread south through North America they encountered a variety of environments. One of these was the Great Basin. Now a desert land, the Pleistocene setting had great rivers and deep lakes. A cooler climate with plentiful rainfall supported grasslands, marshes choked with rushes and shrubs, and forests of juniper, pine, and oak. Wildlife was more abundant and diverse than it is today.

Semi-nomadic people camped along the shores of the lakes. These Paleoindians, the forerunners of modern Native Americans, occupied Death Valley more than 9,000 years ago. A campsite at Deception Knoll, a few miles south of Death Valley within the U.S. Army's Fort Irwin, is at least 9,800 years old; similar ages have been determined in several other places, including Death Valley's Greenwater Canyon. These earliest residents are known as the *Nevares Spring Culture*. The Wisconsin Glacial had ended by then, but there was a remnant of Lake Manly, and springs and other water sources were still reliable.

The Nevares people led a simple subsistence life. They built stone circles to support temporary brush shelters and pits to store the bounty of good harvests. When hunting, they used leaf-shaped stone knives, choppers, scrapers, and projectile points of the sort attached to throwing sticks, or atlatls. Evidence of their lifestyle is sparse, however. They wandered throughout a bountiful country and seldom stayed long at any one place.

In time, the land became more arid. The lakes disappeared, and many of the springs went dry. Grasses and browse shrubs were sparse, and the herds of large game animals were gone. Around 5,000 years ago, a climatic episode sometimes called the "Great Drought" made this region uninhabitable. For two millennia, Death Valley was completely abandoned.

When people returned they settled in places that had reliable food and water. The new *Mesquite Flat Culture* was much like the earlier Nevares population, and many of their remains are similar—stone circles and miscellaneous stone tools found near water sources. Unlike before, however, the Mesquite Flat people probably lived as loose communities of independent families that tended to remain in a home area. They used mortars and pestles to grind seeds, and they relied heavily on insects for vitamins, minerals, and protein. Regional trade brought in beads of shell and stone, and obsidian for toolmaking.

By AD 500, conditions in Death Valley had become about the same as they are now. Drinkable water was scarce, and the arid desert could support fewer people. The *Saratoga Spring Culture* made its appearance. The remaining population spread out into the higher mountains. The Saratoga Spring people were culturally more advanced than their predecessors. Food seeds were ground on portable millstones rather than in the more awkward mortar. For what little hunting could be done, accurate weapons were needed, so the bow and arrow were devised. The people made their own pottery bowls, water jugs, and pots for domestic purposes and had clay figurines for religious or simple decorative uses. They traded with the Anasazi people of the Colorado Plateau for bowls with black-on-white and black-on-red designs. The people decorated themselves with beads made from seashells, carved schist pendants, and brightly colored feathers that may have come from Mexico. They also decorated the world around them, producing a wide assortment of petroglyphs, pictographs, and geoglyphs.

More migrations occurred. Populations grew and shifted, languages intermixed, and villages were established. Family members were often separated by great distances. Permanent settlements consisting of cooperative family units were developed at Furnace Creek, Surveyors Well, Mesquite Spring, and Grapevine Springs in Death Valley, at Goldbelt Spring in the Cottonwood Mountains, and near Hunter Canyon in Saline Valley. Seasonal camps were used each year at Saratoga Springs, Panamint Valley's Warm Sulphur Springs, and on Hunter Mountain. These people, who again led a semi-nomadic subsistence lifestyle, were the ancestors of the modern Native Americans.

■ NATIVE AMERICANS

A number of different tribal affiliations met in and around Death Valley. The Northern (or Owens Valley) Paiute lived to the north and northwest. The Ute occupied areas east of Death Valley. Southern Paiute, or Chemehuevi, were to the south across the Mojave Desert to the Colorado River. Kawaiisu ranged into the Panamint Valley; known to the Paiute as the Panümünt, they lent their name to the valley and mountain range. The related Coso (or Koso) foraged in the mountains to the west. Surrounded

Low rock walls served as hunting blinds for the Indians of the Saratoga Springs Culture.

by these other tribes and occupying Death, Panamint, and Saline valleys were the Timbisha Shoshone (historically also called the Desert, Death Valley, or Panamint Shoshone). All of these tribes were in place by around AD 1000.

The Timbisha Shoshone hunted sheep and antelope, held community rabbit drives, and sought small game, but they were primarily gatherers. In season, they gathered bean pods from the honey and screwbean mesquite trees on the valley floors. Forays into the mountains sought Joshua tree buds and pinyon pine nuts. They would roast the "apples" of prickly pear cacti, gather grass and primrose seeds, harvest chia and other sage crops, and pick fresh greens from around the springs. The fall harvests were followed by festivals during which there were feasts, gambling, circle dances, and annual mourning observances.

Today most of the Indian villages are gone. There were sixty-five Timbisha in Saline Valley in 1938, but now there are none. A few people occasionally occupy Indian Ranch in Panamint Valley, and around fifty Timbisha remain at Furnace Creek's Indian Village. In 1983 they received full recognition as the Timbisha Shoshone tribe, and the modern people have tentative plans to establish their own resort facilities and a cultural center in Death Valley. The era of the Indian culture is disappearing, but their history left behind a rich archaeological legacy of sleeping circles, storage pits, hunting blinds, baskets, tools, trails, stone alignments, and rock art.

■ THE ARCHAEOLOGICAL HERITAGE

Thousands of archaeological sites have been identified within Death Valley, and thousands more are found in Greenwater, Panamint, Saline, and Eureka valleys.

Pictographs, designs painted onto rock surfaces, are rare. They have been found in only three remote locations within Death Valley National Park.

Campsites are most common, marked by stone circles, fragments of pottery and jewelry, tools, and other artifacts. There are also extensive areas of rock art.

Petroglyphs—designs pecked into the dark, weathered surface of desert varnish on rock faces—are widespread in the Death Valley region. They can be seen in places like Cottonwood and Titus canyons, where there are permanent water sources. Some of the designs are obviously pictures of bighorn sheep, lizards, and people. Most of the diagrams, however, are enigmatic sets of abstract zigzags (trails?), wavy lines (water?), crosshatches (settlements?), circles, squares, and miscellaneous squiggles.

Pictographs are comparatively rare. They were painted onto protected rock surfaces in caves and beneath overhanging canyon walls. They often include a number of different colors made by grinding minerals or staining clay with vegetable dyes. Pictographs appear to be panels that tell a definite story about an event such as a battle, a successful hunt, or a special celebration, but as with petroglyphs, many are complete mysteries.

Rock alignments are probably the most common. Typically they are long, straight (occasionally serpentine) alignments of equal-sized rocks that extend across the alluvial fans. Some are several hundred feet long, and a few appear to be

Alignments of loose rocks are common but somewhat mysterious. Some may have served as map-like guides to water sources and storage caches, but in some cases there may have been a religious connotation, too.

color-coded to match the surrounding topography. Perhaps these served as maps or guideposts, as they often seem to point from the valley into the mountains where there are freshwater springs.

Geoglyphs are rare and have been seen by few people, since they are best viewed from the air. They are large tracts of ground on which patterns have been created by moving some rocks into position and clearing others away to expose the bare earth beneath. On a steep slope in Saline Valley is a series of stone circles much too large to have been used for shelter, and also in Saline Valley, at a spot far from the roads, is a human "stick figure" near an equilateral triangle. Other geoglyphs are known in Panamint Valley below Wildrose Canyon.

Only a few of Death Valley's archaeological sites have been thoroughly documented by archaeologists. This book, therefore, gives specific locations for only a handful of them, all of which have been professionally excavated and mapped and which are also visible from the roads, marked on published maps, or identified by National Park Service interpretive brochures and signs. If you encounter undisturbed sites while hiking, remember that they are irreplaceable and protected by the Antiquities Act of 1906 and the Archaeological Resources Preservation Act of 1979.

CHAPTER THREE

Explorers, Prospectors, and Miners

■ THE 49ERS

Mexicans explored the Death Valley region long before American settlers arrived. They discovered a number of mines at least as early as the 1830s, and they attempted agriculture near some of the springs. Occasionally there were hostilities with the Southern Paiute; however, the Mexicans left few stories of hardship. To them, the desert was just a land to be worked as well as they could.

The United States won possession of California at the end of the Mexican War in 1848. Gold was discovered in the Mother Lode of the Sierra Nevada that same year. A few settlers had arrived earlier, but when word of the gold reached the East Coast, hoards of people, few of whom had any wilderness experience, began the journey west. Some of these wagon trains reached Salt Lake City in the fall of 1849. If the pioneers stayed with the California Trail, they would have to spend the winter in Nevada, for to tackle the Sierra snow would tempt a fate similar to that of the Donner Party of 1846, whose travails in the snowy Sierra were already well-known. Many, therefore, chose to avoid the long winter wait by going south from Salt Lake City.

Led by Captain Jefferson Hunt, the "Sand Walking Company" (the name was a corrupt version of the San Joaquin Company) of 110 wagons and more than 400 people easily moved south along the Spanish Trail through Utah. Along the way the company was overtaken by a group of packers, twenty-year-old Captain Orson K. Smith among them. Anybody who professed knowledge could be called a "Captain," and extensive experience clearly was not necessary. Smith had a map that showed a cutoff directly westward and through the mountains. Go that way, the travelers were told, and they would get to the gold country more quickly.

Hunt had been over the trail before and argued against taking the cutoff. Those who took his word and stayed on the Spanish Trail all the way to San Bernardino, California, reached the mines first. But some believed Smith. The gold was to the

The first view the 49ers had of Death Valley's floor and the rugged Panamint Mountains beyond was a shocking disappointment.

west, and that is where they would aim. Along the way many (including Smith) realized their error and again turned south, but twenty-six wagons with 100 people did not.

These people were related only by their travels. In time they constituted a scattered stream of wagons and hikers more than 100 miles long from front to back. The first of the group reached Death Valley in early December, the last not until the middle of the month. (Convention has it that the Brier family reached Travertine Springs on Christmas Day that and the Bennett-Arcan party arrived on December 27, 1849. Those people's own journals, however, describe arriving there under dim starlight without any visible moon. There was a bright waxing gibbous moon on Christmas, so some historians now believe that the 49ers' arrival at Travertine Springs was actually as early as December 10–12.) One group after another, these argonauts blundered down Furnace Creek Wash into the driest of deserts. Only two of their wagons made it out of the valley.

When they encountered the barren floor of Death Valley, the various parties began to split into their own companies. The Jayhawkers, Mississippians, and other groups—a total of eighty single men plus the Reverend Brier with his wife and three children—went north, where they encountered the Georgians who probably crossed the mountains at Indian Pass. Their oxen were dying of starvation and exhaustion and obviously could not tackle the mountains beyond the valley. With no other choice, they abandoned their wagons in central Death Valley, near Salt Creek at a place now called Burned Wagons Point. After they butchered some of the animals and dried the flesh into jerky, they hiked past the site of modern Stovepipe Wells Village and along the present route of State Highway 190 to the vicinity of Emigrant Junction. The Georgians chose to go over Tucki Mountain, only to reach the easier route taken by the others on the opposite side. Splitting into still smaller parties, some escaped Death Valley through Emigrant Canyon, others by Jayhawker Canyon, and more over Towne Pass. All these people eventually made it to civilization, except for two who died of exhaustion in the Slate Range near modern-day Trona. (The story of one large party being slain by Indians near Owens Lake was apparently untrue or, at least, never proven.)

Meanwhile, after resting for a few days at Travertine Springs near the mouth of Furnace Creek Wash, seven wagons with 19 men, 3 women, and 8 children crossed the valley and moved south from one water hole to the next. They paused at Tule Spring before pushing on to either Eagle Borax Spring or Bennett's Well. They thought they could cross the mountains above there, but a two-day attempt was unsuccessful, and they turned back too tired to go on. They decided that the best course would be for two of the younger men, William Lewis Manly and John Rogers, to travel on by foot in hopes of reaching help. Manly and Rogers left the next day.

Within a week, the Wade family decided to push along rather than wait for the return of Manly and Rogers. Traveling through Wingate Pass and then south, they successfully made it to the Mojave River, rested, and escaped the desert in three weeks. A few days later, the Earhart family followed the Wades. Those two were the only wagons to escape Death Valley. One by one, most of the other families and single men left on foot too.

Only the Bennett and Arcan (or Arcane) families were left at Bennett's Well. Strong in their faith, they were rewarded after 26 days. Manly and Rogers had found help at Rancho San Francisco (near modern Saugus) and returned with supplies. In another two days everything that could be carried was packed and ready. The last party of 49ers left the valley on February 17, 1850. (As above, this chronology is questionable, and the departure from the valley might have been as early as February 1). The next 250 miles of desert proved to be a trial equal to that of Death Valley, but the Bennetts, Arcans, Manly, and Rogers finally reached the security of Rancho San Francisco.

It is ironic that the Spanish Trail, the route abandoned in Utah, actually crosses the extreme southern end of Death Valley. Captain Hunt and those who stayed with him discovered the gold of the Salt Spring Mine as they passed within fifty miles of Bennett's Well a full month before the 49ers reached there, and some of Hunt's group had returned to the desert to work the mine even while some of Death Valley's 49ers were still struggling toward civilization.

◼ THE NAME

Who named Death Valley? The answer comes in several versions. Some authorities contend that Death Valley was named by Juliet Brier, the minister's heroic wife who traveled with the Jayhawkers. More likely, somebody with the Bennett and Arcan families came up with the name as they crossed what is now called Rogers Pass in the Panamint Mountains, and there is no question but that Asa Bennett and Lewis Manly promoted the name while searching for a lost gold mine in late 1860. Regardless of who deserves the credit, the tale always sounds the same: somebody turned around at the last view and said "Goodbye, Death Valley."

But why would they do so? Only one 49er—Captain Richard I.A. Culverwell—is known to have died inside Death Valley. Two others passed away in the Slate Range near Searles Lake. Two members of a group of eleven who split off from the Jayhawkers were rescued by Indians near Owens Lake. The other nine have been listed as victims, but even if they did die (and they probably did not), it was far outside Death Valley.

In any case, although it is certain that the name Death Valley originated with one of the argonauts, it was not used as a formal place name until it appeared in the *Los Angeles Star* newspaper on March 18, 1861, and then on a map published later that year. The name quickly took hold.

■ PROSPECTORS AND MINERS

On the way out of Death Valley, one of the Georgians, named Jim Martin, replaced a broken gunsight using a heavy but soft piece of rock. It has been said that he had no idea it might be high-grade silver ore (or possibly pure silver) until it was seen by an assayer months later. Some authorities counter that he and the other Georgians knew what it was but that the escape from Death Valley was more important. (They are also said to have buried $2,500 in gold coins in the same area, a supposed treasure that has never been found.) As with most lost-mine stories, the tale of the "Lost Gunsight Lode" comes in many versions.

Years later, some of the 49ers and others who had heard about the valuable gunsight returned to Death Valley to locate the Gunsight Lode. Unfortunately, neither Martin nor any of the other Georgians ever did so. Only they could have known the true location, so the prospectors had to rely on secondhand accounts. The Gunsight Lode was said to be on "Silver Mountain," which was "in Death Valley." Some took Silver Mountain to be today's Tucki Mountain. Although the Georgians climbed over Tucki Mountain, only a little high-grade silver ore has ever been found on it. Perhaps the lost lode is on Pinto Mountain, which rises above Emigrant and Jayhawker canyons. And maybe it is not within Death Valley at all—much more silver was found in the Argus Range, west of Panamint Valley, and both the Georgians and Mississippians passed right through the rich New Coso Mining District at Darwin.

Numerous silver deposits were eventually found throughout the region, but none had ore that matched Jim Martin's gunsight. The continuing search for it opened the area, with a series of mining booms separated by busts.

Panamint City in 1875. Located high in Surprise Canyon of the Panamint Mountains, the city underwent a spectacular boom when the mining district's population reached more than 2,000.
(U.S. Borax [Rio Tinto] Collection, courtesy National Park Service, Death Valley National Park)

■ SILVER BOOM

The silver boom came first, perhaps simply because the prospectors were looking for the silver of the Lost Gunsight Lode rather than other metals. The earliest discovery was at Coso in 1860. Cerro Gordo was found in 1867, the fabulous deposits of Panamint City in 1873, Darwin in 1874, and the Modoc in 1875, all places near (but none actually within) Death Valley National Park.

At each of these sites a lawless town was born. None had richer ore than Panamint City. Some of the rock was worth over $4,000 per ton—and that is in 1873 dollars—and a ton would not even fill a standard wheelbarrow. Sorted ore sometimes contained 10,000 troy ounces of silver in each ton—40 percent silver metal by weight. However, it was all "supergene ore" in which low-grade primary rock was highly enriched in metals by geologic leaching and redisposition during erosion. Paying values were confined to a few feet near the surface. By 1877 the Panamint deposits were virtually worked out, and what had been a city of 2,000 people was abandoned.

None of these silver towns lasted long except for Darwin. Large-scale commercial mining continued there into the 1950s, and as many as fifty people still live in the town.

■ BORAX BOOM

Borax was discovered at about the same time the rich silver deposits were found. The first of several discoveries of borax in the California desert was at Searles Lake in 1862. Details of the early mining operations there are unclear, but some production at Searles Lake occurred in 1874, and the Saline Valley Borax Works was operating as early as 1875. Later, Frederick Conn and Edward Trudo established a more sophisticated and profitable borax works in Saline Valley in 1889. It operated into 1907, employing thirty men and sometimes yielding as much as forty tons of pure borax per month. As many as five other smaller Saline Valley plants operated intermittently in the 1880s and 1890s.

However, Death Valley's borax deposits have always been better known. They were first identified in 1871, and Isadore Daunet found additional Death Valley deposits in 1875. Then in 1881, Aaron Winters, a prospector living in Ash Meadows, Nevada, was told about borax discoveries at Teel's Marsh, Nevada, and how to test for borax. The test is simple: take a sample, dissolve it in sulfuric acid, add alcohol, and touch a flame to it. If borax is present, the flame will be green. Aaron tried it on samples from Death Valley. "She burns green, Rosie! We're rich, by God!" he shouted to his wife.

Winters's discovery started the borax boom. He sent word of his discovery to the two most important borax men in the country, William Tell Coleman and Francis Marion Smith. Together they organized the Greenland (later Harmony) Borax and Salt Mining Company, with claims covering 4,000 acres of the salt flats northwest of Furnace Creek. Winters then sold his share to Coleman for the handsome sum of $20,000.

Because of the attention generated by Winters's discovery, Daunet decided to try production from his deposits. He established the Eagle Borax Mining Company on the west side of Death Valley, built a processing works, and started the operation in late 1882. Everything worked well until the heat of summer in 1883 forced the plant to shut down. When production restarted that fall there was competition and other producers were offering lower prices. Daunet could not compete. Bankrupt, he ended his misery by committing suicide in May 1884.

At first, things went better for Coleman and Smith. Their company built the Harmony Borax Works in Death Valley and also the Amargosa Borax Works near modern Shoshone during 1883 and 1884 and immediately began production. The first shipments left by wagons pulled by eight mules. Faced with the low-price economics of borax, these small wagons were quickly replaced by larger twelve-mule versions purchased from the defunct Eagle Borax Mining Company. Seeking still more efficiency, a foreman familiar with freighting oversaw the building of a set of ten huge wagons. Grouped in pairs and accompanied by 500-gallon water tanks, these were successfully pulled by teams of eighteen mules and two horses. (The horses, the two "wheelers" immediately in front of the wagons, were needed for control when turning; teams of twenty mules were rare despite their later fame.)

One of the famous 20-mule teams was photographed at Harmony Borax Works in 1886. (Courtesy U.S. Borax [Rio Tinto] Collection, courtesy National Park Service, Death Valley National Park)

The operation was a huge success, with Harmony producing borax in the cool of winter and Amargosa during the summer. Five teams with wagons trekked back and forth across the desert between Death Valley and the railheads at Daggett and Mojave, California. Each carried up to twenty-eight tons of borax and completed a round trip in twenty days. Net production was more than 2 million pounds per year.

But the company's success also led to its demise. Deposits of a new borate mineral, colemanite, had been discovered in both the local Furnace Creek Wash and Mule Canyon of the Calico Mountains near Barstow. Mining at the new town of Borate in Mule Canyon, only 11 miles from the railroad at Daggett, doubled borate production but simultaneously caused the price of borax to crash. Coleman's enterprise could not control the situation, and his empire collapsed. The Harmony and Amargosa borax works closed permanently in 1888.

Coleman died a broken man in 1893, and Smith took control of Pacific Coast Borax. He bought all of Coleman's holdings for only $150,000. Stephen Tyng Mather, whose father had helped Smith arrange the purchase, was hired to promote the borate products, and his "20 Mule Team Borax" trademark has remained famous to this day. With these moves, however, the reorganized Pacific Coast Borax Company turned the Calico mines into the only significant producer of borax in the country.

The Cashier Mill worked ore from the Cashier and Eureka mines at Harrisburg between 1909 and 1914.

Death Valley was largely abandoned until mining returned after Mule Canyon was worked out in 1906.

■ GOLD AND COPPER BOOMS

In the interim years, rich silver deposits, somehow missed decades earlier, were discovered at Tonopah, Nevada, in 1900. The fabulous gold of Goldfield, Nevada, was found in 1902, and moderately rich mines near Ballarat in the Panamint Valley had been worked since 1897. With these back-to-back discoveries, the mountains were suddenly crawling with prospectors.

Two of the prospectors were Frank "Shorty" Harris and Ed Cross. In August 1904 they found tremendously rich ore on a low hill east of Death Valley. The rock was greenish and lumpy, something like a bullfrog. It was studded with "jewelry-rock" gold that assayed as high as $3,000 per ton. The Death Valley gold boom, the last great gold rush in North America, was on. Within a year, the town of Bullfrog had a population of more than 1,000, and the nearby city of Rhyolite was home to 6,000 residents. Other mines were found and towns established at Harrisburg, Skidoo, Lee, Schwab, Gold Valley, and more. The entire world took notice.

In addition to the gold strikes, copper was also located. Promoters said the Greenwater mines were richer than those at Butte, Montana, which were then felt to be the best copper properties in the world. The town of Greenwater was platted with streets 150 feet wide and soon had two newspapers and a magazine called the *Death Valley Chuck-Walla*. At the same time, the discovery of copper, lead, and zinc triggered the Ubehebe and Loretto rushes to northern Death Valley.

Railroads crossed the desert to service the mines. The Bullfrog Goldfield reached Rhyolite from the north. The Las Vegas & Tonopah came up from the south. Last was the Tonopah & Tidewater, built by borax king Francis Smith. And then, in October 1907, the nation was hit by a financial panic (precipitated, at least in part, by the San Francisco earthquake of April 1906). Mines closed throughout the west. As had been the case with the earlier silver strikes, the gold and copper deposits were primarily shallow supergene ore. At times the deposits had been meager at best, and little remained by 1907. More than $250 million worth of stock was issued on the Greenwater copper mines, but the total value of ore shipped from them was only $2,625.09. By the time of the 1910 census, the population of Rhyolite was less than 700; in 1922 it was reported to be exactly one person. The only railroad traffic came from people passing through or away from the area.

Ed Cross is perhaps the only prospector who achieved success as a result of the boom he started. He sold his shares in the Original Bullfrog Mine for $125,000. Cross retired to a farm he already owned near Lone Pine and later to a ranch near Escondido, California, where he died in 1958. Shorty Harris had once said that he would not be happy if he had $10 million. "I wouldn't know what to do with it. But don't you know? It's the chase, man!" He sold his Bullfrog shares for a paltry sum, blew the money during a wild party, and returned to the hills. He later discovered more gold as well as copper and tungsten. A "single blanket jackass prospector" content with his way of life, he died in 1934 at age seventy-seven and was buried in Death Valley alongside his friend Jim Dayton.

■ SECOND BORAX BOOM

"Borax" Smith built his Tonopah & Tidewater Railroad (the T&T) in hopes of making a fortune from the Tonopah, Goldfield, and Rhyolite booms. He was too late—the Bullfrog Goldfield and Las Vegas & Tonopah railroads both reached Rhyolite several months before the T&T—but nonetheless the rail line was in place and had the benefit of Death Valley's borate deposits. The railroad ran north across the Mojave Desert from Ludlow, California, and through the Amargosa Valley just east of Death Valley. By this time, too, the mines in the Calico Mountains had been worked out. The railroad survived, although only barely, on borax shipments from new Death Valley mines.

Initial production was from the Lila C. Mine at the town of Ryan, just west of Death Valley Junction. Bigger and richer deposits were known farther west in the Funeral Mountains, and the Lila C. was only a temporary measure. By 1915 it had produced more borate ore than all of Death Valley's previous mining operations combined. But Smith, like Daunet and Coleman before him, went bankrupt. Real estate investments elsewhere did not work out, and he lost control of the mines. Years later he reentered the borax business, but he was never again a major player in the industry.

A reorganized and renamed Pacific Coast Borax Consolidated continued. To reach the better deposits over the mountains of Death Valley, the Death Valley Railroad was constructed 17 miles from Death Valley Junction to the site of "New Ryan." "Old Ryan" and the Lila C. were abandoned. Over the next dozen years extensive mining was conducted in the Biddy McCarthy, Widow, Grand View, Lizzy V. Oakey, and Played Out mines. By 1927 the production had totaled more than $30 million.

Also by 1927, new, amazingly rich deposits of pure mineral borax had been discovered at Kramer (now Boron) on the Mojave Desert, immediately next to a transcontinental railroad. Significant production of borax was also taking place at Searles Lake. The Death Valley operation could not compete, and the mines closed that October.

■ OTHER MINERALS

Many other minerals were mined at the same time, the most important of which was talc. The talc of Death Valley, Saline Valley, and the Talc City Hills near Darwin is of exceptional purity, some of the best quality from any source in the United States. Talc was first mined in Death Valley in 1912. Production in Death Valley continued into 1981, and mines in Saline Valley are still being worked on a small scale. In total, talc ranks second in Death Valley mineral production value, behind only borax and well ahead of "precious" gold, silver, and other metals.

Pure salt and borax had been found in Saline Valley at least as early as 1874. Although borax was produced into 1907, attempts to mine the salt were futile until 1911. In that year the Saline Valley Salt Company contracted for the construction of a tramway that would run from the salt flats, up tortuous Daisy Canyon, over the Inyo Mountains, and down to a terminus next to Owens Lake. The tram was expensive and took longer to build than was planned, but the first shipments of salt took place in 1913. Production continued intermittently until 1933.

Extensive deposits of salt, gypsum, and celestite (strontium sulphate) were located in the Noble Hills at the south end of Death Valley. The Avawatz Salt and Gypsum Company proposed a railroad in 1912 but quickly realized that with or without rails, no profit was to be made there.

Sodium and potassium nitrate minerals occur on the floor of Death Valley. These minerals are needed for explosives and fertilizer, and considerable promotion of the deposits began in 1909 and peaked with the start of World War I. The nitrates proved to be limited and of poor quality, and not a single shipment of ore was ever made.

Antimony veins that contained silver had been discovered in Wildrose Canyon back in 1860. Silver mining was never successful, but during World Wars I and II the

Death Valley's famous Frank "Shorty" Harris (right) *continued to prospect into the late 1920s. Here he shared lunch with an unidentified friend next to a 1926 Dodge Brothers automobile.* (Special Collections & Archives, Merrill-Cazier Library, Utah State University)

production of antimony metal from the Christmas Gift Mine amounted to more than a million dollars.

A Los Angeles florist tried to develop a deposit of Epsom salts near Wingate Pass. To transport the product he built a monorail, of all things, down through Panamint Valley, up over the Slate Range, and down again and across the salt flats of Searles Lake. Technologically advanced though it may have been for 1924, the scheme never really worked. The mine and monorail were abandoned in 1927.

Pure sulfur in ancient hot spring formations was discovered at Crater in the Last Chance Range in 1917, and between 1929 and 1940 over 150,000 tons of 99 percent pure sulfur was shipped to market. More activity took place in the 1950s (until an explosion of sulfur dust blew up the mill), and renewed mining that included mercury metal production took place during the 1980s and 1990s.

◼ FINAL PROMOTIONS

Nearly every case of mining in Death Valley occurred because mineral deposits valuable enough to justify commercial exploits had been located. However, some people can always be tricked into foolish investments. The last two of Death Valley's mining rushes were based primarily on promotion.

Extensive but low-grade lead deposits were found in Titus Canyon, and the town of Leadfield was established in 1925. In February 1926 Charles C. Julian became the major stockholder and he dreamed of making the Western Lead Company into an international power. Leadfield was highly promoted and the town boomed. The

Titus Canyon Road was built to serve the district, lots were sold, stores and a post office opened, and mines were dug. But ore values were not sufficient, and Leadfield was abandoned by the end of January 1927.

The town of Skookum had a little more reason to exist. A few pounds of high-grade, hand-sorted gold ore were found on Chuckawalla Hill in the Last Chance Range. The ore was too sparse to support much of a town, but for a short time there were four wooden buildings and two dozen tents at Skookum and a store and gas station conducted business 10 miles away at Sand Spring.

Nearly every aspect of Death Valley's exploration and development was tied to mining in some way. By the 1920s, however, it was clear that mineral rushes were a thing of the past. Yet the railroads, mines, and people remained in Death Valley, and in the booming economy of the Roaring Twenties they needed money. If money is not coming from the ground, where do people turn? To tourists, who had already been seduced by the romance of the desert.

CHAPTER FOUR

Tourism and the National Park

■ PROMOTION

The idea of promoting Death Valley as a tourist attraction had been around for some time. A 1907 advertisement in Greenwater's *Death Valley Chuck-Walla* magazine suggested: "Would You Enjoy a Trip to Hell? Probably you would not [but] . . . You Might Enjoy a Trip to Death Valley, Now!" It had, read the ad, "all the advantages of hell without the inconveniences."

At almost the same time, the Great Automobile Race from New York to Paris via North America, Asia, and Europe started from Times Square on February 12, 1908. The racers passed through Rhyolite and Death Valley on March 21 accompanied by great publicity. (Ultimately, the race was won by a Thomas Flyer that reached Paris, France, after covering 22,000 miles in 169 days—a record that remains unbroken.) In short order auto manufacturers such as Thomas, Studebaker, and Dodge Brothers were using Death Valley in magazine sales promotions.

In fact, books and magazine articles had been pushing Death Valley since the 1890s—it did not matter that most of these were blatant mining company advertisements. Death Valley, 20 Mule Team Borax, the wonderful riches, and the mystery of the desert wilderness were all well entrenched in the minds of the American public.

The advent of movies visibly opened this wasteland. Zane Grey's *Wanderer of the Wasteland*—"ghastly gray through the leaden haze, an abyss of ashes, iron walled and sun blasted, hateful and horrible as the portal of hell"—was filmed primarily within Death Valley during 1923 and 1924. When released, the movie was Hollywood's first all-color feature film. It was a smash hit. Two years later a modern Western movie called *The Air Mail* used Rhyolite as "Ghost City"; Rhyolite's famous Bottle House was reconstructed for that film.

By that time, Pacific Coast Borax could see that the end was near for mining in Death Valley. The company realized that it was about to be left with equipment,

The theater poster for The Wanderer of the Wasteland, *which was filmed almost entirely in Death Valley in 1924. It was only the third film ever shot in Technicolor.*

buildings, and railroads, but no mines. In an attempt to make up the lost revenue, the company built the Furnace Creek Inn on a bluff at the mouth of Furnace Creek Wash, 15 miles below the mines at Ryan. It opened in February 1927. The plan was for people to ride the Union Pacific Railroad (UPRR) to its junction with the Tonopah & Tidewater. There they would transfer to the T&T for the ride to Death Valley Junction, where they would board the Death Valley Railroad (DVRR) for the ride into Death Valley. Buses borrowed from Zion National Park completed the trip to Furnace Creek Inn. After the mines closed in October 1927, the visitors had a second option of staying in the Death Valley View Hotel in remodeled buildings at Ryan, which was renamed Devar (later, Devair).

Many tourists made the trip, but the numbers were too small to satisfy the Union Pacific. The age of the automobile had arrived, and in 1930 the UPRR terminated its part of the trip package. The Tonopah & Tidewater and Death Valley railroads were left without passengers or any other sources of income. The DVRR was abandoned that year; the T&T managed to hang on until 1940. Some of the buildings at Ryan were moved to the Furnace Creek Ranch at the base of the slope below the Inn.

Although they are the best known, the Furnace Creek Inn and Ranch were not the first tourist facilities in Death Valley. In 1925 former Rhyolite prospector and miner Bob Eichbaum applied for a franchise to build a scenic toll road into Death Valley. A permit was granted by Inyo County that October. The road, with entrance gates at each end, ran 38 miles from Darwin Wash near Panamint Springs over Towne Pass to Death Valley's sand dunes. The fee was $2 per car plus 50¢ per person. The highway was completed in May 1926 with the enthusiastic support of the Automobile Club of Southern California, which had been erecting mileage signs and encouraging the governments to improve desert roads. Bungalow City, later called Stovepipe Wells Village, was built to serve tourists at the Death Valley end of the road. With twenty tent cabins, a restaurant, a store, and a gas station, the facility opened for business on November 1, 1926.

■ "DEATH VALLEY SCOTTY"

"Scotty's Castle" was never intended to be a public place. It was only a house at Death Valley Ranch, a millionaire's desert hideaway. It did not even belong to "Death Valley Scotty."

The millionaire was Albert M. Johnson, a Chicago insurance man. He loved the West and the romance of the prospectors, and for years he had financed their wanderings. Like others, he was conned into believing that Walter E. Scott, "Scotty," owned a fabulously rich gold mine at a secret place in southern Death Valley. Nobody had been able to figure out where it was, but Scotty always seemed to have money. The mine, of course, involved other people's bank accounts.

Scotty was one of the best self-promoters that ever lived, but by 1906 his financial friends were beginning to doubt the existence of his mine. To prove its

The construction of "Scotty's Castle" was highly publicized and added to the romance of Death Valley.

existence to Johnson, Scotty arranged a special tour. While traveling through Wingate Pass the party was attacked in a ruse intended to scare Johnson away. The "Battle of Wingate Pass" was a setup gone wrong. Gunfire erupted, and Scotty's brother Warner was wounded. Arrested and found guilty of fraud, Scott was released on a technicality—the crime took place within Inyo County, not in San Bernardino County where he was tried, and the Inyo authorities refused to prosecute.

Now called "the Death Valley Humbug," Scotty soon lost all financial support and went into "retirement." But in 1915 Johnson renewed their friendship simply because "Scotty repays me in laughs." Together they explored Death Valley for the perfect place to build the house that became Scotty's Castle. When construction finally began in 1922, the massive and opulent 8,000-square-foot scale of the mansion added greatly to the romance and wonder of Death Valley.

◼ THE NATIONAL PARK IDEA

With all of the attention Death Valley had received over the years, the idea of turning it into a national park was quite natural. First, the National Park Service had only been in existence since 1916, and new park units were being created regularly. More important, the same Stephen Tyng Mather who had invented the "20 Mule

Team" trademark also founded and served as the first director of the Park Service. His assistant, Horace Albright, was born and raised in nearby Bishop, California. In January 1927 Pacific Coast Borax invited the two to visit the new Furnace Creek Inn, where company officials presented the pair with the idea for a national park.

Mather resisted the idea. He was in favor of a park, but he also believed he might be accused of a conflict of interest because of his former borax company ties. He would not make a recommendation unless he perceived strong public support for the idea, and, in fact, he never publicly backed the proposal.

Mather died in 1929. Albright took over as director and immediately set about to create the national park. He drafted the boundaries, and an executive recommendation was signed by President Herbert Hoover in July 1930. The *Death Valley Days* radio program, sponsored by Pacific Coast Borax, began weekly broadcasts that September. The program lasted thirty-two years—fourteen years on radio and eighteen years on television—and some of the last episodes of its run were hosted by future president Ronald Reagan.

The operators of resorts and transportation systems rejoiced, but miners did not. Albright and the president had proposed that Death Valley National Park encompass everything from the middle of the Panamint Valley east to the Nevada state line and from Ubehebe Crater south to Wingate Wash. This was a huge area that encompassed many working mines. It also included Albert Johnson's Death Valley Ranch. Neither mining operations nor private property are allowed within the natural preserve of a national park without special dispensation. Also, full national park status can only be conferred by a congressional act.

Recognizing these problems, Albright revised the plans and downgraded the proposal to a national monument. One advantage of this plan is that a monument can be created by a simple presidential proclamation; it does not require congressional action. Furthermore, special legislation can restore mining rights and private property. Hoover signed the proclamation on February 11, 1933, and Death Valley National Monument became a reality. The bill to make allowance for the private property took longer, but Johnson happily purchased 1,500 acres surrounding Scotty's Castle for just $1.25 an acre in 1935.

Hoover left office only three weeks after signing the bill and was replaced by Franklin D. Roosevelt. Albright resigned from the National Park Service in order to take a job with U. S. Potash, a subsidiary of Pacific Coast Borax. Later in 1933, the borax company redesigned Furnace Creek Ranch using buildings moved from Ryan and the Gerstley Mine near Shoshone and cabins purchased from the construction camp at the just-completed Boulder Dam. The modern resort opened in 1934. That same year the state bought the rights to Eichbaum's toll road and merged the route with others into today's State Highway 190. The Civilian Conservation Corps worked through the Great Depression to build campgrounds, improve roads, and develop water systems. The "Nevada Triangle" of almost 306,000 acres was added by a proclamation of President Roosevelt on March 26, 1937, and some boundary adjustments and the addition of Devil's Hole to the park area were made by the

Mining continued long after the establishment of Death Valley National Monument in 1933. The Broken Pick millsite in Trail Canyon became a population center in the early 1950s during a brief tungsten boom.

proclamation of President Truman on January 17, 1952, bringing the total land coverage to over 2 million acres.

ANOTHER BORAX BOOM, THIS TIME WITH OPPOSITION

A third borax mining boom started in 1971 when the Boraxo, Sigma, and Billie mines were developed near the head of Furnace Creek Wash. These operations had tremendous production. The Boraxo alone yielded more than 10 million tons of pure colemanite ore. The Boraxo Mine also left behind an empty pit and unsightly waste dumps within the national monument.

Perhaps more than any other single mine anywhere, the Boraxo led to the passage of the Mining in Parks Act of 1976. The National Park Service was given the authority to examine mining claims for validity and to declare properties without significant mineral deposits null and void. In 1975 there were more than 4,000 mining claims within Death Valley National Monument. By 2009 the number had been reduced to just 183 claims within the enlarged national park. Many of these are patented borate properties in Furnace Creek Wash. There are also a few gold claims near Rhyolite, gold and silver properties on the west face of the Panamint Mountains, the worked-out Epsom salt deposits in the Crystal Hills, and several mineral and millsite claims scattered here and there within the lands involved in the 1994 expansion of the park.

In the early 1990s the borate companies relinquished title to some claims along Furnace Creek, but there was a tradeoff—they retained title and all rights to the patented claims in upper Furnace Creek. However, the Billie Mine shut down in 2005 and the mining company relinquished that title to the National Park Service. Even the old townsite of Ryan has been donated to the non-profit Death Valley Conservancy to possibly become an education center.

Someday there may be a fourth borax boom in Death Valley. Drilling explorations beyond the east boundary of the national park have shown the existence of some huge deposits of borate minerals, and they could support the region's largest mining episode ever. But if so, it will be outside of Death Valley itself, and outside of the national park.

■ THE CALIFORNIA DESERT PROTECTION ACT OF 1994

In 1934, Death Valley National Monument's first full year as a park area, the park had fewer than 20,000 visitors. In 1995 there were more than 1,000,000 visitors for the first time in the park's history. The crowds have mandated advance reservations for some campgrounds, and the lodges are booked for much of the time. Visitors from Europe now make the months of July and August as busy as mid-winter. Death Valley has changed a great deal since 49er Richard Culverwell died just 160 years ago.

The idea of making Death Valley into a full national park had never died, and the California Desert Protection Act was introduced to Congress in 1986. After eight years of debate, the bill passed and was signed into law by President Clinton on October 31, 1994.

The creation of Death Valley National Park was one of the major provisions of the act. The park covers 3,399,000 acres, or 5,311 square miles, making it the largest unit of the national park system south of Alaska. Although irregular in outline, the straight-line distance between the park's northern and southern extremes is nearly 150 miles, and the area is as much as 60 miles wide. With rugged mountain ranges separating deep valleys, the park seems much larger.

Death Valley National Park is one of the richest treasures of our national park system. A wonderland of history, nature, and scenery is sealed within its corridors, now preserved for the future.

CHAPTER FIVE

Plantlife

The environmental range of plantlife in Death Valley National Park has some of the most extreme climate and altitude changes imaginable. Plants have adapted to life where the ground temperature below sea level near Badwater has been recorded exceeding 200°F, and to Telescope Peak higher than 11,000 feet where below-zero weather is common in the winter months. The types of soil are as varied as the temperature. There are blindingly white salt and alkali pans, creamy sand dunes, soggy green oases, and gray alluvial fans spreading from the mountain canyons, combined with the slopes and peaks of the surrounding mountains. The biotic communities extend from the Lower Sonoran life zone (below sea level to 3,000 feet), where the ranges and intervening basins have high summer temperatures and very little rainfall, to the Boreal life zone (over 8,000 feet), where rain and winter snow are common. With the adaptations afforded by all these variables, more than 1,000 plant species have been identified within Death Valley National Park.

In the low elevations where the soil is predominately saline live the pickle-weed, salt grass, honeysweet, true greasewood, and iodine bush. As the elevation rises and the soil changes, the types of plants are different also. Now one finds brittlebush, several varieties of buckwheat, creosote bush, arrowweed, burrobush, shadscale, and desert holly. At the higher elevations of Hidden Valley, Lee Flat, White Sage Flat, and the Nelson Range of Saline Valley, Joshua trees are found. At even higher elevations are mountain mahogany, junipers, mountain maple, limber pine, and bristlecone pines. At damp canyon heads there are cottonwoods and willows.

Color is added to the desert by the yellow flowers of rabbitbrush, the purple pea-like blossoms of indigo bush, and the pure white of the sage blossoms. Desert mallow has strikingly beautiful apricot blooms. The beavertail cactus with its large magenta flowers adds bright patches to the tan desert floor. During the spring months, if the rainfall has been just right, the washes and fans are covered with the tall, swaying gravelghost, dainty white fleabane, and the magenta of sand verbena.

Not all plants are natives. Some trees have been introduced into the area. Most noticeable are the trees and tall shrubs of the *Tamaricaceae*, or tamarisk, family, native to the southern Mediterranean area. These trees were planted to provide fast-growing windbreaks and shade. Their roots have proven to be extremely thirsty, rapidly depleting groundwater. *Tamarix aphylla*, sometimes called salt cedar, grows thirty to forty feet tall. Greenish jointed branchlets give the tree its evergreen appearance. Where there are saline soils the tree will take on a grayish tinge that is caused by secretions of salt. *Tamarix ramosissima*, or five-stamen tamarisk, is a rank-growing shrub that can reach a height of fifteen to twenty-five feet. The tiny leaves are a pale blue-green. The plumes of pinkish to white flowers will almost cover the shrub.

The Deglet Noor date palms at Furnace Creek were planted in the 1920s by the Pacific Coast Borax Company and began producing dates in the 1930s. The harvest is no longer done, but when ripe in October, each bunch may have up to 750 dates. Birds and coyotes have carried and deposited the seeds to many places such as Travertine Springs, where nature (and man) did not intend.

▪ ENDEMIC PLANTS

Desert though it may be, Death Valley National Park is home to more than 1,000 species of plants. Among these are at least sixty-three Class I and Class II endemic plants (see following list).

Class I endemics occur only within the boundaries of the national park. **Class II** endemics have the majority of their known ranges within the park boundaries, but some localities also exist outside the park. **Class III** endemics are not listed here, as they are plants whose ranges mostly lie outside the national park area and sometimes extend far beyond its boundaries. An example is *Ephedra funerea*, the Death Valley joint fir, which would be a Class II endemic were it not for specimens found as distant as central Nevada.

Endemism and rarity often go hand-in-hand, but they are not equivalent. Endemic plants are those that live within restricted geographic or environmental areas, but within their range they may be very common. Many are rare, however, and one—rock lady—has been found only in Titus and Fall canyons and has a known population of only a few dozen plants.

All plants—endemic or not—are protected by law. It is illegal to collect or pick any plant within Death Valley National Park. Endemic species are further protected by California's Endangered Species Act, Native Plant Protection Act, Natural Communities Conservation Planning Act, and Environmental Quality Act. Inquire at the Furnace Creek Visitor Center for any recent update about newly identified endemics.

Class I

Plants known to occur only within the boundaries of Death Valley National Park (sixteen species).

Astralagus funereus	Black milkvetch
Astralagus lentiginosus micans	Shining locoweed
Cordylanthus eremicus eremicus	Desert bird's beak
Erigonum infractum	Napkinring buckwheat
Galium hilendiae carneum	Panamint Mountains bedstraw
Galium hypotrichium tomentellum	Telescope Peak bedstraw
Gilmania luteola	Golden carpet
Maurandya petrophila	Rock lady
Mimulus bigelovii panamintensus	Panamint monkey flower
Mimulus rupicola	Death Valley monkey flower
Oenothera avita eurekensis	Eureka Dunes evening primrose
Perityle villosa	Hanaupah rock daisy
Phacelia amabilis	Saline Valley phacelia
Polygala heterohyncha	Notch-beaked milkwort
Swallenia alexandre	Eureka Valley dune grass
Tetracoccus ilicifolius	Holly-leaved four-pod spurge

Class II

Plants with the majority of their known range within the boundaries of Death Valley National Park, but with some concentrations also known a short distance outside the park area (forty-eight species).

Anulocaulis annulatus	Death Valley sticky ring
Arabis pulchra munciensis	Darwin rock cress
Arabis shockleyi	Shockley's rock cress
Arctomecon merriamii	Bear poppy
Astralagus atratus mensanus	Darwin Mesa milkvetch
Astralagus funereus	Black milkvetch
Astralagus gilmanii	Gilman's rattleweed
Astralagus lentiginosis sesquimetralis	Sodaville milkvetch
Astralagus panamintensis	Panamint locoweed
Blepharidachne kingii	King's eyelash grass
Boerhaavia annulata	Death Valley sticky ring
Calochortus panamintensis	Panamint mariposa lily
Camissonia boothii inyoensis	Inyo evening primrose
Camissonia cardiophylla robusta	Heart-leaved evening primrose
Camissonia claviformis funerea	Death Valley brown-eyed evening primrose
Caulostramina jaegeri	Jaeger's caulostramina
Centaurium namophilum	Ash Meadows gentian
Cordylanthus eremicus eremicus	Desert bird's beak
Cymopterus gilmanii	Gilman's cymopterus
Dedeckera eurekensis	July gold

Dudleya saxosa saxosa	Panamint stonecrop
Enceliopsis covillei	Panamint daisy
Ericameria (Haplopappus) gilmanii	Gilman's goldenbush
Erigernon uncialis	Limestone daisy
Erigonum eremicola	Wildrose Canyon buckwheat
Erigonum gilmanii	Gilman's buckwheat
Erigonum hoffmanni hoffmanni	Hoffmann's buckwheat
Erigonum hoffmanni robustus	Robust Hoffmann's buckwheat
Erigonum microthecum panamintense	Panamint slenderstem
Erigonum rixfordii	Rixford's pagoda buckwheat
Lathyrus hitchcockianus	Bullfrog Hill's wild pea
Lupinus holmgrenanus	Holmgren's lupine
Lupinus magnificus magnificus	Magnificent Panamint lupine
Mentzelia longiloba	Panamint blazing star
Nama demissum covillei	Colville's purple mat
Nitrophila mohavensis	Amargosa nitrophila
Penstemon calcareus	Limestone penstemon
Penstemon fructiformis amargosae	Death Valley beardstongue
Perityle inyoensis	Inyo rock daisy
Petalonyx thurberi gilmanii	Death Valley sandpaper plant
Phacelia mustelina	Death Valley round-leaved phacelia
Physocarpus alternans panamintensis	Panamint ninebark
Salvia funerea	Death Valley sage
Sclerocactus polyancistrus	Mojave fish-hook cactus
Sibara rosulata	Death Valley rock cress
Sisyrinchium funereum	Death Valley blue-eyed grass
Sphaeralcea rusbyi eremicola	Rusby's desert mallow
Viguiera reticulata	Death Valley goldeneye

Note: this list was initially compiled in 1995 from a variety of unpublished government documents and the *Inventory of Rare and Endangered Vascular Plants of California*. Published by the California Native Plant Society, the *Inventory* was used as the authority for the scientific and common names of the plants, which may be different here than seen in other references. Endemics listed in a 2003 National Park Service document have been added. However, this list makes no claims as to completeness. New studies reveal additional endemics. For example, the Furnace Creek Water Management Plan, dated 2000, apparently found several completely new Class I endemics near Travertine Springs, and ongoing surveys resulting from the national park expansion are likely to reveal still more endemic plants.

■ PLANT SURVIVAL

Plants deal with the lack of water and extreme heat in a variety of ways. Some, like the mesquite, send taproots down into the earth perhaps 100 feet. Others, such as cactus, radiate out tiny filament roots just below the soil surface to capture every drop of moisture, which they store in their spiny bodies. The blackbrush drops leaves, looking almost dead in the hottest months. Other plants, like the turtleback, hug the ground, protecting their fragile root system much as a mother hen protects her chicks from the weather. As a rule, the desert plants cover more space underground than on top.

Because of the high salt and alkali content, halophytes (plants that grow in saline soil) predominate in the lower valleys. These plants are capable of removing some of the salts by an osmotic process, thus maintaining proper water balance.

Other protective measures include a plant being covered with scales (desert tea) rather than having leaves. There are tiny, thin, narrow leaves (mesquite), extremely fuzzy leaves (stingbush), and shiny leathery leaves (creosote). All of nature's protective measures are intended to deal with the problem of transpiration. Plants need to retain as much moisture as possible.

In spite of this harsh environment, after plentiful rains wildflowers cover the washes and slopes with such an array of color that visitors travel many miles to see them. Hikers will find their boots covered in yellow pollen. The photographer will be delighted. Those who simply drive along the road will be awestruck. From valley floors, up canyons, and on mountaintops, springtime puts on a fragrant display.

The following listing of plants is intended as a casual introduction to the plants you are most likely to encounter. A wildflower book will broaden your knowledge.

■ PLANTS OF LOWER ELEVATIONS

Four-wing saltbush. Atriplex canescens can be seen in the Furnace Creek area. This shrub is a rather erect, deep-rooted woody plant that grows to a height of 6 feet. The branches become scaly as they age, and the leaves are quite small. The name comes from the wing-shaped fruiting bracts that arch up from the seed's exposed face. The male flowers are tiny yellow spikes. The female forms a loose flower cluster up to 14 inches long from May to August. This is an important browse plant.

Desert broom. Baccharis sarothroides is very common throughout the American deserts, especially along sandy washes and on disturbed areas such as graded roadsides. Its vertical growth habit can reach 5 to 6 feet tall. The stems are green and the plants tend to be nearly leafless. Closely related is the seep willow or Indian water, *Baccharis salicifolia.* It has a more open form and requires more water than does desert broom; nearly pure stands grow in the southern reaches of Greenwater Valley.

Stingbush. Eucnide urens, also known as rock nettle and Velcro plant, is a low, rounded bush 1 to 2 feet high. The shiny green leaves are covered with stinging barbed hairs. If one is ever stuck on your clothing or shoe, you will never forget the introduction. Flowers are large and floppy in a silky, whitish-tan shade. Stingbush favors sheltered canyon floors from the 3,000-foot elevation to below sea level and is especially abundant in parts of Titus Canyon.

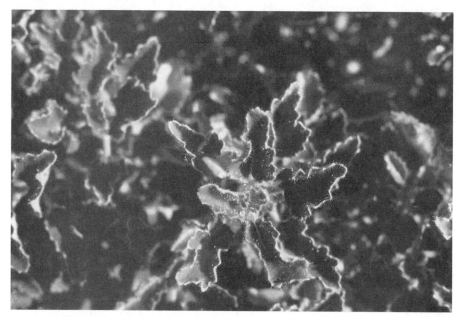

The foliage of stingbush bears irritating barbed hairs that cling to clothing and skin like a natural Velcro, leading to its alternate name "rock nettle."

Cheesebush. *Hymenoclea salsola* grows in the sandy washes of low elevations. Its lush, pale-green springtime foliage gives off an odor that some liken to spoiled cheese, yet other people cannot smell it at all. The flowers are tiny but surrounded by large, silvery bracts. During the dry season the plants lose their leaves and are not at all attractive. One of the densest stands in Death Valley is along the Ibex Valley Road near State Highway 127.

Desert fir. *Peucephyllum schottii* is also known as pigmy cedar and spruce bush because of the foliage that resembles conifer needles. It is, however, a member of the sunflower family and bears fuzzy yellow flowers in the spring. It is common along low-elevation washes where its rich green color contrasts with the gray of desert holly.

Pickleweed. *Allenrolfea occidentalis* can be found in most highly saline areas. It is one of the most salt-tolerant species in the United States. Almost leafless, the plant has elongated, succulent stems that form cylindrical joints resembling brownish-green baby's fingers. Pickleweed has an extremely long taproot that goes deeply into the damp salt pans. It is especially abundant along the Salt Creek interpretive trail. In nearby areas that are slightly higher and less saline is another succulent plant, *Suaeda moquinii*, sometimes called **inkweed** or **seepweed**; dark juice from its stems will stain the fingers yet its tiny seeds are highly nutritious.

Horsetail. Equisetum hyemale is a primitive, rushlike survivor of the Carboniferous Period. Up to 4 feet tall, the bright green, hollow stems are jointed. These joints are marked with black- and cream-colored rings. Spores are produced in cone-like spikes at the top of the stems. Horsetail can be found near springs and permanent streams, such as the one in Johnson Canyon.

Cooper rush. Juncus cooperi grows around springs and seeps on the valley floor. The surrounding areas of bleached gray soil might look unproductive, but the rushes in these desolate locations are lush and spreading. Almost 3 feet tall, the round, stiff stems bear papery tan flowers. Rush canes are used in basket making. Often living in the same marshes is **bulrush**, *Scirpus americanus*, which is taller and has triangular stems.

Honey mesquite. Prosopis glandulosa, depending on its location, can be considered either a tall shrub or a short tree because it can reach 20 feet in height. The branches are thick and spiny; the leaves are bright green. In the spring and early summer yellow catkins cover the tree, followed in September or October by long, brown bean pods. Not only is the mesquite valued for its sweet pods, which are eaten by many mammals, but the tree is also a prime water indicator. In the Furnace Creek area, the mesquites are dying as the tamarisk trees and people take their water; because of the lowered water table, seeds are not able to sprout and survive, and even some mature trees have lost their water supply.

Screwbean mesquite. Prosopis pubescens is a deciduous, small, fairly erect tree that grows to 20 feet. It is usually found in dense thickets. The branches are a dark brownish-red color. In the spring the tree is covered with closely clustered yellow catkins. These mature into tightly coiled 2-inch-long tan pods. Great stands of these trees can be found in Saline Valley. Although honey mesquite was preferred, dried screwbean pods were also harvested by the Indians, who ground them into flour for baking into a kind of bread.

Creosote bush. Larrea tridentata is an evergreen shrub that will grow to a lush 12 feet high and 8 feet wide if there is abundant water. In its normal under-watered state, the plant is generally around 4 feet tall. It generally is the most abundant plant on the alluvial fans throughout Death Valley. The creosote multiplies by sprouting vertically until it reaches a few inches in height, and then lateral branches develop. As the plant matures it sends up other basal shoots from its root crown, but always at the outer perimeter. Eventually the older inner stems die, leaving a ring of living plant. One of these gigantic growths ("King Clone," located near Old Woman Springs, California) measures 70 feet long and 25 feet wide and is believed to be 11,700 years old, making it the oldest living plant on Earth. Creosote has several protective skills. On the leaf surface, the resins decrease the amount of ultraviolet light and heat that can reach the leaf interior, where photosynthesis takes place.

Resins also limit the loss of water by transpiration. The plant is protected chemically from browsing animals and insects by at least forty-nine volatile oils. The black stripes on the branches are the crusty casings of the lac insect, *Tarcardiella larrea*. The lac has been used as a glue to repair everything from broken pottery to cracked engine blocks. (Note: many people refer to the creosote as "greasewood," but the true greasewood is *Sarcobatus vermiculatus*, the entirely different plant described below.)

Greasewood. *Sarcobatus vermiculatus* has light green foliage that shows brightly against its habitat background of grayish-white, salt-encrusted playas. It likes to grow where water is close to the surface. Directly the east of the Grapevine Mountains is the vast Sarcobatus Flat, so named because of the concentrated growth of this plant on alkaline, clay-rich dunes.

Arrowweed. *Pluchea sericea* is the plant of the Devil's Cornfield near Stovepipe Wells Village and the sand dunes. In this area windblown sand has scoured the ground around the slender, willowy plants, making them stand out like the corn shocks farmers once made in their fields after harvesting the corn. The stronger stems were used by the Indians to make arrow shafts, and the younger, more pliable stems were utilized in basket making. If underground water is fairly close to the surface, arrowweed grows in pure stands. The springtime blossoms are blue-violet.

Desert holly. *Atriplex hymenelytra* is most outstanding when viewed on the black lava slopes of Ubehebe Crater, but it grows in any area of moderate salinity. The small, rounded shrub, with its silvery-white holly-shaped leaves, grows up to 3 feet tall but is most often much shorter. A halophyte, this saltbush has large, membranous fruiting bracts that are a succulent light-green shade. Later in the year the white leaves take on a pinkish tint.

Honey sweet. *Tidestromia oblongifolia* is a white, wooly perennial. A member of the amaranth family, it is low growing, from 9 to 18 inches high, and spreads out like a mat. It likes the sandy washes and alkali flats where the hot sun and winds finger its sweet-scented yellow flowers, releasing an enticing fragrance. Honey sweet is especially common along the West Side Road south of Bennett's Well.

Desert trumpet. *Eriogonum inflatum* is only one of the many types of buckwheat that can be seen along the roadside throughout the desert. Desert trumpet has short, grayish leaves that lie flat on the ground. Emerging from the leaves is a tall, bulbous, or inflated, stem topped with slender, narrowly swollen branches. The plant bears tiny yellow flowers. A variety without the enlarged stem is *E. inflatum deflatum*.

Pagoda buckwheat. *Eriogonum rixfordii* comes into flower in the late summer. Its leaves flare upward, cupping slightly. The gracefully curved stems, with branchlets forming platforms, one above the other, are reminiscent of a Japanese pagoda. The plant grows to a height of 16 inches. This plant is a Class II Death Valley endemic but is prolific along the northern part of the Scotty's Castle Road and near Salsberry Pass.

Death Valley sage. *Salvia funerea* lives on hot, rocky slopes and on canyon walls. Ranging from 1.5 to 4 feet in height, this rounded shrub is densely branched and covered with a thick, white wool. The small flowers are violet, with the corolla protruding from the wooly calyx. The fuzzy wooly covering is protection from the blistering heat and strong, drying winds. Often listed as a Class I endemic and placed on the endangered species list, a few specimens have been found short distances outside the park.

■ PLANTS OF HIGHER ELEVATIONS

Cottontop cactus. *Echinocactus polycephalus* grows in 2-foot-high clumps of up to thirty heads. The central stems are dark red, fading to dark gray. Unlike most cacti, cottontop tends to bloom in late summer. The light-yellow flowers develop fruit nestled in thick cottony tufts of hair. The plant lives in the rocky areas of mountain slopes. Some can be seen in Titus Canyon on the right side of the road where the canyon walls narrow. Racetrack Valley and portions of Saline Valley have vast cottontop gardens.

Beavertail cactus. *Opuntia basilaris* is spectacular, with brilliant magenta flowers. The beavertail is aptly named because its pads or joints are so flat. The bluish-green stems are spineless but make up for this lack of protection with small, round cushions of spicules. At one time the Indians would dry the pads and then, when food was scarce, cook and eat them. Common throughout Death Valley, there is a large concentration on the alluvial fans near Navel Spring in upper Furnace Creek Wash.

Joint fir. There are several species of joint fir, or Ephedra, within Death Valley National Park. They are gymnosperms, related to the pines and firs. The long-jointed, stiff stems have small scalelike leaves, and the flowers on both the male and female plants are small cones. **Mountain**, or **green joint fir**, *Ephedra viridis*, forms shrubs found in the higher desert grasslands and sage country up to 6,000 feet elevation, where they stand out because of vertical, bright-green stems up to 4 feet tall. **Death Valley joint fir**, *E. funerea*, and **Nevada joint fir**, *E. nevadensis*, are difficult to tell apart; both are gray in color, and the shrubs are rounded and seldom more than 2 feet tall. Additional species may exist within the park. All of the joint firs grouped together are known as **Mormon tea**. The stems contain a large amount of tannin.

*The mound cactus (*Echinocereus mojavensis*) is locally common in some of the park's higher mountain canyons. It is also known as "claret cup cactus" because of its brilliant red flowers.*

A beverage with a medicinal taste can be made by adding one handful of the stems to boiling water, and Indians used the tea as a cure for intestinal ailments.

Chia. *Salvia columbariae* have basal leaves from which grows a fuzzy 8-inch- to 10-inch-long stem topped with a lavender-blue flower that looks somewhat like clover. But it is the tiny triangular seeds that make the plant special. In 1875, a report written by Dr. John T. Rothrock, surgeon-botanist of the Wheeler United States Geological and Geographical Survey, stated, "[A]n Indian, with but a hand-ful of [chia] seeds, can sustain himself on a 24-hour forced march." Not only is chia extremely high in protein, it creates a strong catalytic action on the body's digestive enzymes that aids in assimilation of the protein.

Sweet-leaf wildrose. *Rosa woodsii* is quite common in moist, protected places throughout Death Valley. It is, naturally, common in parts of Wildrose Canyon, but dense stands occur in many moist canyons and springs. Delicate pink (rarely, white) flowers appear in the spring and are followed by red seedpods (hips) that are eaten by many animals. Wildroses are notoriously difficult to identify by species, and it is possible that *Rosa californica* and *Rosa mojavensis* also occur within the national park.

Apache plume. *Fallugia paradoxa* is a member of the rose family. Partially ever-green, it grows up to 8 feet tall and about as wide. The branches are a light-tan shade with flaky bark. The leaves are small and clustered, with dark green on top and a rusty shade underneath. In late April and May the shrub is covered with small, white single flowers that later turn into fuzzy greenish fruits. As the fruits age the fuzz elongates and turns into pinkish or reddish feather-like forms (the plumes of name). Large plants are common around South Pass on the Saline Valley Road.

Lichen. *Thallophyte* family. The word lichen (LIKE-en) comes from the Greek *leichen*, meaning tree moss. It was so named when botanists considered it to be the lowest form of plant life. Then in 1867, lichenologist Simon Schwendener discov-ered that lichen are a combination of two entirely different organisms—fungus and alga—growing together in a symbiotic, mutually beneficial union. The moldlike fungus captures the microscopic green alga, and in the process a new, self-sufficient plant called a thallus is born. The chlorophyll-bearing alga uses sunlight to produce organic food that is absorbed by and sustains the fungus. The fungus in turn selec-tively parasitizes but does not kill its host. Mineral nutrients come from dew, rain, and dust. When it is moist, the lichen grow; when it is dry, they enter a dormant stage and can then endure long droughts. *Candelariella rosulans* has a habitat on granite, gneiss, and sandstone rocks. The color is lemon yellow. *Acarospora chloro-phan* likes acidic rocks such as granite for a home. It is a dark yellow. *Caloplaca cirro-chroa* is rather rare but can be seen widespread on lava outcrops. It is a deep-orange shade.

Cottonwood. *Populus fremontii* can be found at the head of many of the Panamint Mountain canyons where there is a riparian environment. With enough water this tree will grow to 80 feet tall, with large, spreading branches. The leaves are a shiny bright green. The flowers are reddish catkins that mature and fill the breeze with masses of white puffy seeds. This tree provides welcome shade in the hot desert.

Joshua tree. *Yucca brevifolia* is one of the most spectacular plant species in this area. The Joshua is a member of the *Liliaceae* family. Although it is known to reach as tall as 32 feet in Joshua Tree National Park, Death Valley's specimens are usually smaller. Death Valley's largest concentration is on Lee Flat. They can also be seen on White Sage Flat, between Ubehebe Crater and The Racetrack, in the higher reaches of Saline Valley, and along the Big Pine Road. It is possible that all Death Valley Joshua trees are the variety *Yucca brevifolia jaegeriana*. These have shorter leaves and a more singular manner of growth. The Joshua does not bloom every year, but when it does it produces creamy lily-like flowers followed by large seed-pods that hold several black flat seeds. The seeds sprout easily, but few survive since the new shoots are tender and favored by rabbits and ground squirrels. The Joshua sometimes reproduces from subterranean stems that grow out from the base of the trunk; new plants rise from these runners. Joshua trees are believed to live as long as 1,000 years.

Pinyon. *Pinus monophylla* is a slow-growing tree that may eventually reach a height of 25 feet. This black-barked tree is common on high desert ranges. There are small, dense forests of pinyon on the north slope of the Grapevine Mountains, in upper Wildrose Canyon, and on Hunter Mountain. The tree's limbs seem to lack organization, branching out every direction. The pinyon was a very important staple food source for desert Indians. When the cones ripened in September, the Indians would camp near the trees and, using long poles, beat the cones from the pinyon. The heat from campfires released the rich, oily nuts, which were used as a supplement to the Indians' diet.

Juniper. *Juniperus californica* and *J. osteosperma* both inhabit the upper reaches of the mountains, where one or the other is often more abundant than the pines of the pinyon-juniper forests. Neither is a particularly tall tree, at best reaching around 40 feet with a 15-foot spread. *J. californica* produces small, berrylike cones that turn from silver-blue to reddish when mature. The Indians ate the fruit fresh or ground the mature berries to make a floury meal. *J. osteosperma* is the Utah juniper. It is often host to a parasitic mistletoe that has adapted to living off this particular species. Juniper wood is highly flexible and was used by the Indians to make bows.

Mountain mahogany. *Cercocarpus ledifolius* is a small tree that can reach 12 to 20 feet tall. The namesake of Death Valley's Mahogany Flat and campground, it is common in the mountains above 7,000 feet. It is readily identifiable because of the

Joshua trees thrive in the higher valleys of Death Valley mountains.

thick, leathery leaves that are densely covered with white hairs on the underside. The small yellow flowers of spring are followed by seeds that bear long feathery plumes that are often twisted like a corkscrew.

Limber pine. *Pinus flexilis* grows above 8,000 feet in the Panamint Mountains. This tree is aptly named. The tough, pliant limbs are extremely flexible to withstand the high winds and the weight of winter snow. Growing to 50 feet with trunks 2 to 3 feet in diameter, it forms a rounded crown. The cones are yellow-brown, egg-shaped, and up to 6 inches long. The large seeds in the cones are an important food source for many kinds of wildlife.

Bristlecone pine. *Pinus longaeva* (sometimes listed as *P. aristata*) survives alongside limber pines on some of the highest windswept slopes of the Panamint Mountains, such as Telescope Peak; reports of a few specimens on Grapevine Peak and Tin Mountain are probably unfounded. The trees are always gnarly and twisted and appear to be mostly dead, but they are healthy and some specimens are at least 3,000 years old.

■ WILDFLOWERS

Mojave desert mallow. *Sphaeralcea pulchella* is a small, rounded perennial with deep-apricot flowers. It belongs to the same family as the hollyhock, cultivated cotton, and okra. The dark-brown stems and deep-green leaves are both covered with white hairs. The mallow grows in much of the desert. It is a favorite browse for rabbits, hares, and the desert tortoise.

Desert five-spot. *Malvastrum rotundifolium* grows in washes and desert pavement flats. It is always a pleasant surprise to find one of these "lantern flower" plants. They are sometimes fairly small, but given proper growing conditions they may reach heights of up to 2 feet. No matter what their size, the pinkish-rose petals look as if they have been painted inside by five strokes of a carmine-dipped fairy brush. The reddish-tinged leaves and flower buds are covered with stiff hairs.

Death Valley ghost-flower. *Mohavea breviflora* is a gorgeous flower that is often overlooked. Favoring sandy washes in early spring, the stems are only 2 to 6 inches high. The pale yellow flowers resemble the related snapdragons and reach as much as 1 inch long. In years of low rainfall, the plant's entire life may be as short as a few days.

Purple mat. *Nama demissum* grows as a flat circle of stems as much as 1 foot across. The reddish-purple flowers are borne near the ends of the stems and are as much as 0.5 inch across. In good years, plants will overlap one another and will bear numerous flowers, so that large areas of the alluvial fans are splotched with purple. In poor years, the plants are sparse and may bear only a single flower.

Panamint daisy. *Enceliopsis covillei* (or *E. argophylla grandiflora*) is also known as the large-flowered sunray. It is an extremely rare Class II endemic that is native to only a few Panamint Mountain canyons, but it often blooms near the road in lower Wildrose Canyon. The sunray grows to heights of 2 to 3 feet and bears yellow flowers up to 6 inches across. The leaves have a soft, feltlike surface.

Phacelia. Phacelias, also known as scorpionweed or wild heliotrope, are handsome plants with coarse foliage that is somewhat hairy and sticky to the touch. They are usually found growing within perennial shrubs that protect and support the phacelia. There are several species in the Death Valley region. **Death Valley phacelia**, *Phacelia vallis-mortae*, which grows among shrubs in the higher elevations of Death Valley, is abundant throughout the Great Basin as far east as Utah. The flowers are a pale purplish-lavender. The Class II endemic **round-leaved phacelia**, *P. mustelina*, has light-purple or white flowers and occurs in scattered locations throughout the park's mountains. Rarest is the Class I endemic **Saline Valley phacelia**, *P. amabilis*, which interestingly is rare in Saline Valley but common near Death Valley's Mud Canyon; it bears deep-purple flowers.

Desert chicory. *Rafinesquia neomexicana* loves the sandy washes. From 6 to 20 inches tall, the plant sports white rays of 1.5-inch flowers that are purplish on the underside. The leaves grow from the base and are pinnately divided into narrow lobes. This plant blooms from March to May.

Jimsonweed. *Datura stramonium* is also known as sacred datura. Extracts from this plant are narcotic and, in the wrong hands, can be deadly. It is said that some Indian tribes used a decoction of datura for ceremonial purposes. A strong, rank-growing plant that reaches heights of 5 feet, jimsonweed is often seen in disturbed areas along roadsides or in loose sand. The large, white trumpet-shaped flowers show nicely against the dark-green leaves covered with prickly hairs. The fruit is a round 1- to 2-inch tan ball covered with spines.

Dune primrose. *Oenothera deltoides* can be found on the dunes of Saline, Panamint, and Ibex valleys. This plant has large, white, sweet-scented flowers. The outer stems of the older plants turn inward, forming what look like bird cages. The white-lined Sphinx moth assists in pollination, after which its larvae feed on the leaves. The variety *O. d. eurekensis* is a Class I endemic that lives only on the Eureka Dunes.

Brown-eyed primrose. *Camissonia claviformis* has white flowers with dark centers. It is common throughout the national park but perhaps especially so in Saline Valley near the warm springs. Some of these plants are the variety *C. c. funerea*, a Class II endemic.

Sand verbena. *Abronia villosa* occurs in any sandy area but it tends to be most abundant on sand dunes where it often blooms along with the dune primrose. The

As viewed from Aguereberry Point, groves of mesquite trees grow around the base of the Furnace Creek alluvial fan. Furnace Creek Ranch is the square area at the far-left side of the photograph.

leaves are hairy and sticky. The rose-pink (rarely, white) flowers are unmistakable. They often virtually cover the plants, which in turn may completely cover large areas of the sand dunes, especially in southern Death Valley such as at the Ibex Dunes.

Pygmy blazing star. Mentzelia reflexa is a coarse-stemmed, branching annual 5 to 8 inches high. The flower is straw-colored and tinged with bronze. The plant particularly likes the salty soils of Death Valley. **Panamint blazing star**, *M. longiloba*, a Class II endemic, has light-yellow flowers and grows in the Panamint and Argus mountains.

Desert velvet. Psathyrotes ramosissima is a compact little plant that grows in a cushion-like form, lending itself to the common name of turtleback. The flowers are rayless, deep-yellow heads that hold themselves just above the light-gray velvet leaves. If crushed, the leaves have the odor of turpentine.

Desert dandelion. Malacothrix glabrata flowers somewhat resemble the common dandelion. The cheerful yellow flower has a small, bright-red dot in the center.

Often many flower heads are in bloom at the same time. During good wildflower years these plants form masses of color in the sandy areas of the western deserts.

Desertgold. *Geraea canescens* is one of the reliable annuals. Even when the rainfall is light, this tall (to 24 inches) sunflower springs up along the fans and rocky desert floor. The leaves and stems are covered with fuzzy white hairs (Gerea comes from the Greek *geraios*, meaning old man, a reference to the white hairs on the fruits.) The 2-inch-wide golden-yellow flowers bob at the ends of several branches, their fragrance attracting insects.

Indian paintbrush. *Castilleja linariaefolia* has scarlet bracts whose shape looks rather like a much-used paintbrush. The red color that catches your eye is not the flower itself but rather the bracts beneath each flower. Paintbrushes are semi-parasitic, dependent on host plants to supply water and nutrients. This slender, tall-stemmed perennial provides a welcoming touch of color along the south entrance roadside into Saline Valley. It is most profuse near springs or seeps but can also be seen in fairly dry soils.

Gravel ghost. *Atrichoseris platyphylla* has large ovate, brown- or purple-spotted leaves that lie flat on the ground (leading some to call it tobaccoweed). The canopy of large, white flowers that grows from a slender stem gives rise to the name, parachute plant. Others call it parachute plant because of the way the flowers seem to hover and sway in the breeze without support. Whatever the name, the plant is beautiful. A vanilla-like perfume drifts from the flowers. Following rains, it can be seen from February to May in the sandy washes or near the clay hills.

Biological Environments of the Death Valley Region

Habitat	Elevation Range	Representative Plants	Representative Animals
Salt flats—Barren, flat floors of the valleys where intermittent water evaporates to deposit layers of salt. Occasional permanent water such as Cottonball Marsh and Salt Creek.	valley floor	Barren on actual salt flats. Pickleweed, inkbush, saltbush, and saltgrass in areas of moderately salty water.	Pupfish in some permanent water; Badwater springsnail, brine flies, migratory birds.
Desert floor—Low and flat valley bottoms that are non-saline or only slightly saline. Not rocky, but soils generally sandy or silty and of poor quality so that vegetation is sparse.	below sea level to 1,500 feet	Arrowweed, desert holly, greasewood, indigo bush, creosote bush, annual buckwheats; mesquite and introduced tamarisk and palms in areas of near-surface water.	Coyote, kit fox, kangaroo rat, lizards.
Sand dunes—Areas of windblown sand, sometimes piled into high dunes but more often as a thin surface layer of loose sand. Infertile and constantly shifting, dunes support little plantlife but considerable wildlife (mostly nocturnal).	below sea level to 1,500 feet	Sparse growths of creosote bush and mesquite; some seasonal wildflowers such as dune primrose and sand verbena.	Kangaroo rat, jackrabbit, kit fox, sidewinder, gecko and other lizards, eleodes beetles.
Alluvial fans—Coarse sedimentary debris deposited between mountain canyons and the desert floor. Sandy, with large rocks.	sea level to 3,000 feet	Creosote bush, blackbrush, sagebrush, brittlebush, desert broom, rabbit brush, yucca, cacti, buckwheat, stingbush.	Coyote, bighorn sheep, rabbit, ground squirrel, kangaroo rat, ringtail, desert tortoise, chuckwalla, snakes.
Riparian—Places where there is abundant fresh springwater, sometimes seasonal but usually enough to support a year-round surface runoff stream or pool.	below sea level to 4,000 feet	Cottonwood, willow, wild grape, wildrose, ferns, herbs, reeds, and introduced palms.	Frogs, migrating birds, bats, butterflies; any wildlife will be attracted to the open water, making the riparian habitat critical for survival.
Mountain slopes—The lower faces of the mountains and the upper reaches of their canyons. Often rocky but with significant soil as a result of greater precipitation than in the valleys.	3,000 to 6,000 feet	Creosote bush, sagebrush, winterfat, blackbrush, desert broom, Joshua trees (local), cacti, Mormon tea, perennial buckwheat.	Bighorn sheep, mule deer, coyote, bobcat, mountain lion, packrat, jackrabbit, badger, snakes, golden eagle, hawks.
Mountain crests—Alpine regions confined to the highest reaches of the mountain ranges.	above 6,000 feet	Pinyon pine, juniper, limber pine, bristlecone pine, mountain mahogany, annual grasses.	Bighorn sheep, coyote, squirrels, golden eagle, hawks.

CHAPTER SIX

Wildlife

■ADAPTATION

As with plants, animal survival in the extreme conditions of Death Valley has required a long series of evolutionary adaptations. As a result, Death Valley National Park is home to at least 440 species of animals.

Some animals, such as the kangaroo rat, have developed systems that require no free water. Birds and reptiles resorb water from their urine, excreting an almost solid waste. Bats and two birds, the poorwill and nighthawk, aestivate or go into a state of dormancy. Other birds raise their wings to provide body shade and to allow the heat to escape. Mammals cool themselves by producing sweat, panting, or retreating to burrows. The temperature of a burrow 18 inches below the ground surface will fluctuate no more than 2°F, regardless of whether the temperature is hot or cold. Coloration is also a factor in survival. Many animals are a pale shade, which better reflects the sun.

In a land where the average annual precipitation is only 1.91 inches, the most important concern is getting and retaining water, because the real killer in the desert is dehydration. Frogs absorb water by sitting in mud. Coyotes dig into underground water sources, providing a drink not only for themselves but for other animals too. Many birds and animals live near small oases that contain a steady supply of life's essential liquid.

Never feed anything to any of these animals. Once fed, coyotes and foxes expect these offerings, creating danger for visitors' pets and themselves. Sometimes these animals must be taken away because they have become pests through no fault of their own. Feeding wild animals also upsets their healthy diet.

■ ENDEMIC ANIMALS

As with plants, Death Valley National Park and vicinity is host to a number of endemic animals. At least thirty-two have been described.

Class I

Animals known to occur only within the boundaries of Death Valley National Park (at least twelve species).

Aegialis sp.	unnamed beetle
Assimnea infirma	Badwater snail
Cardiophorus sp.	Eureka obligate beetle
Cyprinodon diabolis	Devil's Hole pupfish
Cyprinodon milleri	Cottonball Marsh pupfish
Cyprinodon nevadensis nevadensis	Saratoga Springs pupfish
Cyprinodon salinus	Salt Creek pupfish
Edrotes sp.	unnamed beetle
Horistonotus sp.	Eureka Dunes beetle
Tryonia margae	Grapevine Springs elongate tryonia snail
Tryonia salina	Cottonball Marsh tryonia snail

Class II

Animals restricted to Death Valley and the nearby surrounding areas (at least nine species).

Crotalus mitchellii stephensi	Panamint rattlesnake
Cyprinodon nevadensis amargosae	Amargosa pupfish
Dipodomys panamintinus panamintinus	Panamint kangaroo rat
Gerrhonotus panamintinus	Panamint alligator lizard
Pyrgulopsis amargosae	Amargosa springsnail
Pyrgulopsis microcussus	Oasis Valley springsnail
Thomomys umbrinus oreocus	Pygmy pocket gopher
Thomomys umbrinus scapterus	Panamint pocket gopher
Tryonia variegate	Amargosa tryonia snail

At least nine additional species of Class I or Class II snails have been identified, and the All-Taxa Biological Inventory, a program started in 2007, discovered several unidentified, probable-endemic insects in one of the first small study areas.

■ MAMMALS

Merriam kangaroo rat. *Dipodomys merriami* are dainty, coffee-cream-colored, silky-furred little creatures who emerge from their underground dens after dark. They fill their fur-lined cheek pouches with seeds that are later stored in their burrows. Kangaroo rats are farmers of sorts. They cache seeds for safekeeping, and those not eaten often sprout and grow, producing more seeds for the next year's use. The "Dipys" have extremely long hind legs, with big feet almost like snowshoes. When in a hurry they can leap up to 20 feet per second in two hops, the long tail acting as a rudder. But the most special thing about kangaroo rats is their abil-

Kangaroo rat. (Photo by George Harrison, U.S. Fish & Wildlife Service)

ity to exist without drinking water. Their urine is highly concentrated, requiring only a small amount of water to expel waste. They can also produce free water by metabolizing their food of seeds and plants. By means of a simple chemical procedure, water is formed in their bodies as nutrients are broken down into usable components.

Black-tailed jackrabbit. Lepus californicus are not jacks and they are not rabbits—they are hares. The difference is that rabbits are born helpless, blind, and hairless. By contrast, hares are born "street-ready," eyes open, fully furred, and ready to run. Hares are tall, standing almost 28 inches high, including their ears. Their overgrown legs can propel them at speeds up to 35 miles per hour. They can turn in the middle of a bound and come down running in the opposite direction. The long ears have millions of small vessels that bring the blood close to the surface and act as radiators during the long, hot summer months. Vibrating the ears creates a cooling effect. Breeding may continue year-around with several litters of two to four babies. The mother hides the young when she goes out to feed. During the day they lie crouched in a "form" worn into a clump of grass or a shrub by constant use. Hares are most active at night. They are considered such good food by predators that they seldom reach the age of two.

Coyote. Canis latrans pups are usually born in April, sixty days after breeding. They are raised by both parents, with the father assisting in their rearing after the

Black-tailed jackrabbit. (U.S. Fish & Wildlife Service photo)

first six weeks. Their home is at the end of an underground tunnel, probably borrowed from a badger. As they grow older their color changes from brownish-black to grayish-yellow, which helps them blend with their surroundings. By the middle of the summer the pups are ready to hunt with their parents, who teach them the canine way. The den is abandoned by August, when the pups go out on their own. When they are grown, coyotes look something like thin shepherd dogs. Adults usually hunt in pairs and will range for food from 10 to 100 miles if need be. They are very important in keeping down the rodent population. When alone, or if small game is scarce, coyotes will eat nuts, seeds, and even dates. The coyote remains the symbol of the desert. The coyote's high-pitched yapping voice, which ends in a yi-yi-yi, bounces off the desert mountains and into the hearts of visitors.

White-tailed antelope squirrel. *Ammospermophilus leucurus* are often mistakenly called chipmunks. Comic and clever in their actions, they are entertaining to watch. But life for ground squirrels is quite serious. They have the ability to fluctuate body temperature so it is a degree hotter than air temperature, which allows for cooling by radiation. Depending on the available food, the squirrels' forage area can be up to 15 acres. The quick little mammals have extraordinarily sharp eyesight, and they can see danger approaching from all angles. Mating begins in mid-February, and by the end of April up to ten young have been born. The squirrels live in very deep burrows that have several emergency exits. Life in the nest is crowded, so when the small squirrels are only half grown they are kicked out into the world to forage

Coyote tracks in the mud along Salt Creek.

Coyote. (Photo by R. H. Barrett, U.S. Fish & Wildlife Service)

for themselves. This less-than-motherly attitude cuts into the population, allowing only the quickest, smartest, and most alert to survive. As a result, ground squirrels are among the healthiest and most successful of the desert animals.

Round-tailed ground squirrel. *Spermophilus tereticaudus* has pinkish-cinnamon fur covered over lightly with a grayish shade. Their tails are pencil slim, not bushy as are most squirrel tails. Ground squirrels feed on insects and seeds. Perhaps the most interesting thing about them is their ability to enter a deep underground tunnel, curl into a ball, drop their metabolic thermostat, and enter a state of torpor. The squirrels can remain in this condition without food or water for up to six months at a time. This is advantageous because they can sleep during periods when the weather is too cold or too hot, or when food is scarce.

Kit fox. *Vulpes macrotis* are mostly nocturnal animals, about the size of small house cats, with big, dark, shiny eyes and a neat button of a nose. The foxes' coloration is a creamy white with a yellowish-buff mix with black-tipped overhairs on the tail and huge upright hair-lined ears. Even their feet are covered with furry hairs, which allows easy running on sand dunes. In the spring the otherwise solitary fox meets its mate. Together they appropriate a rodent's burrow and enlarge it to make nesting space. In February four to five pups are born. The young stay with the parents until they are two months old, by which time they have become proficient at hunting on their own. Their diet consists of lizards, insects, small rabbits,

Kit fox. (Photo by B. Peterson, U.S. Fish & Wildlife Service)

Bobcat. (Photo by Conrad Fijetland, U.S. Fish & Wildlife Service)

and the kangaroo rat. Tracks of their feeding efforts can easily be seen on the sand dunes where they dig out small rodents.

Bobcat. Lynx rufus, the most common wild cat in North America, is named because of its short, "bobbed" tail. The tawny fur is spotted on the body and stripped on the legs and tail. The face resembles that of an ordinary house cat, but adults can be as long as 4 feet and weigh nearly 30 pounds. Bobcats are solitary animals, associating with one another only during the late-winter breeding season. Kittens are usually born in May and, although weaned within two months, they stay with their mother until the following year while they learn to hunt their favorite food of rabbits and squirrels. Mostly nocturnal, bobcats hunt in areas where there is dense scrub brush and rocky outcrops, which provide hiding places during the day.

Mountain lion. Although extremely rare and known mostly from the tracks they leave in soft soil, a few mountain lions (*Felis concolor*, also called cougar or puma) live in the Panamint and Hunter mountain areas.

Bighorn sheep. Ovis canadensis nelsoni have ancestors that evolved during the early Pleistocene Epoch. By the end of this time they had migrated across the Bering land bridge and into North America. They live in the high reaches of the mountains and eat only the plant material that is too coarse and unappetizing for other herbivores. Even so, their territory has been threatened by the wild burros. Freed to

Bighorn sheep. (Photo by H. Engels, courtesy National Park Service)

fend for themselves after prospectors no longer needed them, the burros adapted readily to desert life. In the process they muddied the already-scarce water holes. The bighorn dislike even the presence of burros and refuse to eat or drink in places where the burros have been present. As the numbers of burros increased, the sizes of the bighorn sheep herds decreased. An active burro removal program has partially controlled this problem. At the present time an estimated 500 bighorn sheep are found in Death Valley National Park, and visitors are asked to report any sightings to the Park Service. A large animal, the male sheep weighs up to 220 pounds and the female up to 130 pounds. Both are brownish in color, with a creamy-white rump. The male, or ram, has massive coiled horns that he uses in battle with other males at rutting time. The female, or ewe, is adorned by much narrower horns with a shorter curl. Lambs—usually only one, but sometimes twins—are born in the spring.

Ringtail cat. The *cacomistle* of Spanish-speaking areas, *Bassariscus astutus* is also known as the miner's cat. After dark these cat-sized mammals leave their homes in the rocky ridges or abandoned mine shafts to hunt for small rodents, insects, birds, and berries. They are agile and intelligent animals and are usually found in pairs. Their fluffy white-and-black banded tails are 15 inches long—the same length as their head and pale yellowish-gray body combined. Ringtails have alert foxy faces, enormous round eyes, and rather large ears. Three or four white fuzzy babies are born in May and are weaned at three months. When they are young, the little ones

Ringtail cat. (Courtesy State of Arizona)

scamper and play like kittens. Throughout life, the ringtails are very active. Their gait has been described as "loping, humping along with tail straight out behind, drooping toward the end." Although not rare, they are shy and rarely seen except by night wanderers or people spending the night in an abandoned cabin.

Burros and horses. At one time, large numbers of wild (or feral) burros and a few wild horses populated Death Valley's mountains. Escaped from the early explorers and prospectors, they overgrazed many areas and fouled water sources. Therefore, a series of roundups were done in an effort to reduce if not eliminate the numbers of these non-native animals. Although this was largely successful, as many as 400 burros still roam parts of the southern Panamint Mountains near Butte Valley, southern Saline Valley and Hunter Mountain, Jackass Flats, and the Nevada Triangle. Wild horses are far less common, but a few live in the Cottonwood Mountains and the Nevada Triangle, and a semi-tame herd is routinely fed at Death Valley Junction. Note, too, that cattle grazing rights still exist on Hunter Mountain and Lee Flat.

Bats. Family *Chiroptera* are the only truly flying mammals. Bats are also the only major predators of night-flying insects; each bat eats up to 3,000 insects in a single night. Insects are captured in the basketlike sticky membrane of their wings

Wild burros are most likely to be seen in and near Saline Valley, and the Nevada Triangle but have been observed in all portions of the national park. (Courtesy Bureau of Land Management)

and tail as they hunt together in the early evening. Bats live in rock crevices, abandoned buildings, or wherever they can find protection and room. Once a roost is selected it will be used repeatedly for many years. Bats have been portrayed far too often as vicious or as blood suckers. Some people think bats will fly close enough to get caught in their hair. None of this is true. Bats can get rabies, as can dogs and cats, but the disease is rare. Actually, bats are fascinating creatures. They have fur and a warm body temperature, and they nurse their young. In spite of their tiny size they may live for up to thirty years. Two of the types of bats found in the park are listed here.

California myotis. *Myotis californicus* is probably the most common bat in the California deserts. Small in size, they have an erratic flight as they forage 5 to 10 feet above the ground. They are particularly fond of the pinyon-juniper, the arid desert scrub, and even the riparian situations. Seldom are these myotis found above 6,000 feet. Bats roost singly or in small groups in mine tunnels or rock crevices. They are fairly torpid during their winter hibernation, and any disturbance can deplete their fat stores and could endanger survival.

Western pipistrel. *Pipistrellus hesperus* is often referred to as a canyon bat. They weigh just one-fifth of an ounce and are ashy-gray or yellowish-gray in coloration. As with all bats, pipistrels have a zigzag flight that led the Germans to call bats *Fledermause*, or fluttering mice. They are most common at lower elevations, where they roost singly in rock crevices of canyon walls. At dusk the air becomes alive as hundreds of these tiny creatures emerge from their homes to feed over the creosote flats. These bats remain active during the winter, often hunting during the middle of the day. Birth usually produces two youngsters.

◼ BIRDS

Raven. *Corvus corax* is often confused with the crow. Not only is the raven larger, but it also has a wedge-shaped tail, whereas the crow's tail is straight across. When flying, the raven soars on flat wings; the crow's wings turn upward in flight. Ravens mate for life, and they are usually seen in pairs or with their young. They are scavengers and will eat almost anything they find, leading them to congregate near people who might have food. Their nest consists of a large mass of sticks, bones, shredded bark, and rabbit fur—the exact ingredients depend on whatever is available. After the four to seven pale-green eggs have been laid, the parents take turns during the three-week incubation. When the eggs have hatched, the young birds remain in the nest for a month, keeping both parents constantly on the hunt to satisfy the youngsters' voracious appetites. By the time the birds leave the nest, they are almost as large as adults. They continue to fly with their parents until breeding time arrives, when the young adults fly off to find their own mates.

Red-tailed hawk. *Buteo jamaicensis* is a large, thick-set hawk with a broad wingspan that reaches more than 4 feet wide. The red-tail is one of the desert's best-known birds of prey. When they are hunting they soar at great heights and then gracefully glide earthward. The hawks' keen eyesight enables them to spot the rats, mice, smaller birds, and reptiles that make up their diet. Their favorite nesting site is along ledges located high on an almost vertical cliff. Here the male and female

Ravens are intelligent birds, adept at opening things such as daypacks, camera bags and, above all, anything with food inside.

hawks build a platform of loose sticks. The female then lays two to four spotted eggs. Hawks mate for life, and the couple uses this same nest many times. When the young have hatched, both parents are kept busy feeding their white, down-covered little ones who constantly clamor for more food. The red-tail's call is a rather asthmatic but piercing keeeer-r-r.

Roadrunner. *Geococcyx californianus* is one of the most beloved birds of the desert. A member of the cuckoo family, roadrunners often act just that way: cuckoo. They run across the ground on long legs, leaving tracks that look as though they are going in both directions because of two long toes pointing forward and another pair of the same size aimed to the back of each foot. The roadrunner's face is narrow with a deep-slit mouth; the body is slim, brownish colored above and white with brown streaks underneath. Constantly raising and lowering their topknot, they peer around, seemingly delving into everyone else's business. *Paisano* (meaning "countryman"), as they are fondly called in Spanish, are rather comical to watch, if only because of their eating habits. With appetites as strange as their manners, they swallow horned toads, bumblebees, lizards, grasshoppers, mice, and some snakes, and for dessert devour cactus fruits and sumac berries. The female's nest is

Roadrunner. (Photo by Gary Kramer, U.S. Fish & Wildlife Service)

a slipshod affair of twigs, snakeskin, or anything else she might consider attractive. In the spring she lays three to eight white eggs.

Costa's hummingbird. Calypte costae look like sparkling jewels as they flit from one spot of nectar to another. Only 3 inches long, these pugnacious little birds will sip the juice from your glass. Sometimes they can be a bit pushy and must be shooed away. Their wings are the keys to their aerial prowess as they fly with a wing motion of eighty beats per second. They also rotate their wings at the shoulder, which enables them to hover, turn rapidly, or come to a complete stop. The gem-quality shine of hummers is caused by the iridescent green feathers of the back and purple gorget (long neck feathers). The intensity of coloration varies with the angle of light. Their nest is a finely woven cup that is often thatched with lichens or bits of leaves. They build their nests in a bush or a tree and will return to this nest for several years. In the spring two tiny eggs are hatched.

Phainopepla. *Phainopepla nitens* are slim, glossy birds about seven inches long. The male is jet-black and has a rather large, upright head crest, leading some to call it a "black cardinal." His white wing patches are noticeable when he flies. The less flashy female is more of a gray tone. These birds leave the hot desert during the summer months, returning in October when the weather cools a bit. Around January, serious courting gets under way. Depending on just how the female feels about it, this attempt to gain favor can last for up to four months, during which time the male builds a nest. If the female likes his craftsmanship, they mate. Although these

Gambel's quail. (Photo by Lee Karney, U.S. Fish & Wildlife Service)

birds eat insects, their favorite food is the berry of the parasitic mistletoe that grows on the mesquite trees, so this is where the nesting usually takes place. The baby birds fledge in five weeks. When the weather starts to warm up, the birds fly to a cooler climate where the courting, nest building, and egg laying start once again.

Gambel's quail. *Callipepla gambelii* are small birds with a charming black plume that curves upward from their heads. The male has a russet crown and a black patch on his belly, whereas the female is less boldly marked. Quail seem to get along fairly well in the desert, never straying far from water holes. They eat insects, seeds, berries, and flower buds. The quail travel in small coveys and this ensures a type of protective safety. If surprised by a predator, they make an explosive sound as they scatter and fly off in all directions. This action puts the attacker off guard and allows most, if not all, of the quail to escape. The female nests on the ground, where up to sixteen eggs are laid. Once they are old enough to leave the nest, the young trail in a line behind the mother looking like an animated pull toy. The call of the quail is a loud "ka kway-er."

Great horned owl. *Bubo virginianus* are the most widespread and successful of our large owls, multiplying in spite of human encroachments on their habitant. They are about twenty-three inches long and are a robust brown, with noticeable ear tufts and big yellow eyes. Soft, serrated feathers at the leading edge of their flight feathers eliminate the swishing sound made by most birds' wings. This adaptation gives owls an edge in hunting, as they can fly silently to their prey. They have excellent night vision but also rely heavily on extraordinary hearing. They hunt at night, and dinner consists of rats, frogs, snakes, large insects, rabbits, and even lizards. Their nests are often in trees, but they are sometimes found in rock crevices or even on the ground. Three white eggs are laid. The owl makes resonant hooting sounds in a series of up to eight hoots—"hoo, hoo-oo, hoo, hoo."

Bullock's oriole. Icterus bullockii are the most widespread orioles in the West. The male is a fiery orange and black with big white wing patches. He has a black crown and orange cheeks. The female is an olive-gray with yellowish color on the tail and throat. She has two white wing bars. Their nest is a finely woven pouch that is slung from a branch of a tree. They are particularly fond of small fruits, insects, and seeds. Orioles add a beautiful touch of color to desert surroundings. At higher elevations where there are Joshua trees, the brilliant yellow and black **Scott's oriole**, *I. parisorum*, is more common.

■ REPTILES

Desert tortoise. Xerobates agassizii represent the oldest type of living reptile, evolving around 200 million years ago. The desert tortoises are from the Gopher family of tortoises, subfamily *Testudininae*. They have brown, domed shells with prominent growth lines. Thick, sturdy legs—often referred to as elephantoid—end with flat feet and sturdy digging claws. The head is shaped like that of a big reptile, the mouth an unsmiling slit. When threatened, all appendages can be pulled under the safety of the shell. The tortoises live in creosote bush communities at around 3,000 feet elevation, where the soil is such that they can easily dig deep while constructing their burrows, which have half-moon entry openings. They usually dig both a summer burrow and a deeper, warmer winter home. They are known to "patrol" their territory, leaving pathways formed from constant use. In the spring the tortoises depend heavily on wildflowers for nourishment. Tortoises reach sexual maturity around age twelve, by which time they are about eight inches in length. The male has a concave bottom shell, or plastron, that aids in mating. The clutch of from two to twelve white golf-ball-shaped eggs takes from 70 to 120 days to hatch, depending on the soil temperature. Tortoises may live to be eighty years or older.

Zebra-tailed lizard. Callisaurus draconoides run across the hot ground by holding the forepart of their bodies fairly erect, using just the back legs for locomotion. They are slim-bodied lizards, with long, flat tails that have black bars, giving them their "zebra" name. The bodies in general are a gray shade with subtle darker stripes running across the back. The sides and belly are a pale-yellowish color. The lizards run the washes and smooth "desert pavements." Food consists of insects, spiders, smaller lizards, and the new tender growth of plants. Shortly after emerging from

Bullock's oriole. (Photo by Gary Kramer, U.S. Fish & Wildlife Service)

Desert tortoise. (Photo by Glen Clemmer, Nevada Natural Heritage Program)

hibernation, the male begins his courtship activities by showing the bright-black and metallic-blue patches on his underside. Within a few weeks two to six eggs are laid in a hole the female has scratched in the ground. The eggs are covered and abandoned. The babies emerge in about forty-five days.

Desert horned lizard. *Phrynosoma platyrhinos* has a very blunt snout with rather short horns and body spines. Protective coloration allows these lizards to blend with their habitat. This camouflage is necessary because the lizards' wide, flat bodies prevent fast escape from a predator. They live at the edge of sand dunes or on hardpan where blow sand is present, and when danger threatens the lizards simply press their bodies down into the sand. Their habitat ranges from the hot desert floor to as high as 10,000 feet in elevation. Ants, although a poor-quality food, are the meal of choice of the horned lizard. To accommodate these rations, through evolution the lizard's stomach has expanded to 13 percent of its entire body weight, larger than that of any other lizard. Following hibernation, courtship and mating take place. The female lays from six to thirty eggs from which half-inch babies emerge. Loss to predators is great.

Chuckwalla. *Sauromalus obesus* is easily identified by a thick tail; a wide, flat, dingy charcoal-colored eighteen-inch-long body; and a wrinkled "turtleneck." Although still torpid, chuckwallas can usually be seen on top of big rocks, basking in the early-morning sun. When frightened, they run into the protective shelter

Horned lizard. (Photo by Dave Geoke, U.S. Fish & Wildlife Service)

of a crevice or crack between rocks. Once there, the chuckwallas gulp in air, distending their bodies until they are tightly wedged between the rocks; Indians used pointed sticks to puncture and deflate chuckwallas so they could be removed and eaten as food. Herbivorous, they delight in daintily munching on wildflowers or the new growth on the burrobush, but the creosote bush furnishes the staple food. The female lays seven to ten eggs. The young have distinct yellow-and-black bands on their tails. If the tail is grabbed by a predator, it comes off, and the chuckwalla escapes alive. A new tail is grown. These are long-lived lizards. The males may reach twenty years old, and the females often live to age forty.

Banded gecko. Coleonyx variegatus can be found from below sea level to the pinyon woodlands above 4,000 feet. Chiefly rock dwellers, they also like to stay near the remains of old mining cabins. Geckos have soft skin with fine, granular scales and large eyes with vertical pupils and movable eyelids. Most other geckos do not have eyelids that move. The *variegatus* is a pink to pale-yellow color with chocolate bands. The undersides of the toes are covered with plates that bear numerous microscopic hairlike structures, with spatulate tips that allow them to cling to flat surfaces. Geckos look too tender and unprotected to live in such harsh surroundings, but they have several survival tactics. They are nocturnal; not only do they stay out of the hot sun, but by hunting at night they have no competition from other lizards. Fat is stored in their breakaway tails so that, if necessary, they can

Chuckwalla. (Photo by Glen Clemmer, Nevada Natural Heritage Program)

live in their underground tunnel for up to nine months, nourished by the stored fat. When they are stalked by a snake, they wave their tails as an enticing offering. The snake grabs the tail, the tail breaks off, and the snake is fed. The unharmed gecko simply reproduces another tail. Baby scorpions and spiders are the food of choice. Fastidious as a cat, the gecko licks its face clean after eating. The female buries two eggs in the soil and they hatch in about forty-five days.

Side-blotched lizard. *Uta stansburiana* is so named because of a dark spot directly behind each front leg. These small brownish lizards have dark V-shaped markings running down their backs from the end of each white eye stripe. The markings meet at the base of the tail, from which just one row continues to the end of the tail. These lizards are among the most common lizards in the arid West. They are active all year in the warmer deserts such as Death Valley. Extremely territorial, the male will establish what he considers to be his home ground. Any other male who enters this area will be aggressively challenged. Their food includes insects, scorpions, ticks, mites, sowbugs, and spiders.

Mojave rattlesnake. *Crotalus scutulatus* is a venomous serpent that grows to fifty-one inches in length. Large, hollow, movable fangs are located in the front of the upper jaw. During biting, these venom-filled fangs are moved forward and the victim is stabbed and poisoned at the same time. The venom yield is from fifty to ninety milligrams and is considered the most toxic of any snake in North America.

Mojave rattlesnake. (Photo by Mark Barton, Edwards Air Force Base, USAF)

The estimated lethal dose for an adult human is only ten to fifteen milligrams. Often called the Mojave Green, this rattler is a greenish, heavy-bodied snake with a broad triangular head. At the end of the tail are a series of interlocking horny segments, or rattles, which "rattle" when the snake is irritated. A new segment is added to the tail each time the skin is shed. If you hear the rattling sound, immediately stop movement. Locate the snake and carefully move away from it. This is generally safe, as the snakes can only strike a distance of about half their body length. Activity can occur at either day or night, depending on the climate. The snakes have a rather narrow temperature range and can sometimes be seen lying in a torpor, waiting for the early-morning sun to warm them. The snakes are most commonly found in areas of scrubby growth such as mesquite or creosote.

Sidewinder. Crotalus cerastes are best known for their sideways method of movement, which leaves a series of parallel, J-shaped tracks in the sand. The hook of the J points in the direction of the snake's movement. These snakes are narrow bodied, rough scaled, light-tan to creamy-colored, with no outstanding markings. The supraoculars, or tops of their eyes, are pointed and turned upward, giving them the appearance of having horns. Sidewinders live in areas where sand has piled up around mesquite and creosote bushes. This is also where one finds many rodent burrows, the homes of this snake's chief food supply. Sidewinders, like all rattlesnakes, are ovaviparous, which means the eggs develop inside the mother's body

Gopher snake. (U.S. Fish & Wildlife Service photo)

and the young are born alive. The female may bear anywhere from two to twenty young. Although this snake is poisonous, its venom yield is only twenty-five to thirty-five milligrams, and the estimated lethal dose for an adult person is thirty to forty milligrams.

Panamint rattlesnake. *Crotalus mitchellii stephensi* is usually listed as being a variety of speckled rattlesnake but sometimes also has been equated to the sidewinder. They are small snakes, seldom as long as eighteen inches, and very dark-brown in color. They live in rocky areas in the mountains usually higher than 3,000 feet in elevation. Like all rattlers, they are poisonous but, in this case, the toxin is relatively mild.

Gopher snake (bull snake). *Pituophis melanoleucus* grows to the impressive length of up to seven feet. They are cream-colored with reddish-brown dorsal blotches. Often seen during daylight in the spring, they basically feed at night during the hot months. Although nonpoisonous, their manner of expelling a great rush of air to make a hissing sound is alarming. Excellent climbers, the gopher snakes can sometimes be seen in trees, intent on robbing birds' nests. Other animals' burrows are also easy for this snake to enter. They feed on rodents, rabbits, and birds and birds' eggs. Killing is done by constriction, with the snake wrapping its long body about the prey and squeezing the victim to death.

Common king snake. *Lampropeltis getulus* has either rings of plain black or dark brown alternating with pale yellow or white along the entire body or a yellowish strip the length of the back. They use the method of hissing, vibrating their tails, and striking to frighten away predators. King snakes are true cannibals, eating their own kind. They can also kill a rattlesnake by coiling rapidly around the other snake, squeezing until all breath is gone and the rattler dies. King snakes are immune to the rattler's venom. During the spring, cannibalism is held at bay while mating takes place. The female lays her eggs in a rodent burrow and promptly forgets about them. Few of the babies survive.

■ FISH

During the Pleistocene Epoch the Death Valley area was part of a large system that contained many lakes and streams. The land bordering these waters supported mastodons, ground sloths, camels, horses, saber-toothed tigers, horses, and dire wolves.

About 20,000 years ago, during the latest stage of the Pleistocene, the glacial melt that caused these vast water systems receded for the last time. Although overall there was less water than before, Lake Searles, Lake Panamint, Lake Manly, and Lake Mojave were still interconnected and were fed by the Amargosa, Mojave, and the Colorado river drainages, which allowed fish to move among the lakes. These waterways are known as the Death Valley System because Death Valley was the sump for the drainage.

As the climate became even more arid between 10,000 and 4,000 years ago, most of the watercourses disappeared, leaving only a few intermittent streams. As the lakes and rivers receded the larger fish died, leaving mainly smaller fish of the killifish and minnow families. Today, these tiny fish, some of them isolated in highly select habitats for at least 10,000 years, have evolved into distinctive types. Nine species in the regional Death Valley System are thought to exist nowhere else on Earth—five species of pupfish (genus *Cyprinodon*) that occur within the national park, plus one species of killifish (genus *Empetrichthys*), two species of minnow (genera *Gila* and *Rhinichthys*), and one species of sucker (genus *Catostomus*) that exist within nearby waters.

All pupfish display almost the same characteristics. They are omnivorous, feeding on crustaceans, plankton, flying insects, algae, and the dead remains of their own kind. Pupfish are extremely aggressive toward each other when feeding, defending territory, or chasing down a mate. Once a willing female has been found, the pair goes to the bottom of the stream or pond where they spawn. She deposits her eggs among the algae and the male ejects his milt on them.

Salt Creek pupfish. *Cyprinodon salinus* are found in Salt Creek to the north of Furnace Creek. These are the most slender of the pupfish. The female is brownish with a silvery sheen. From gill to fin darker lateral markings are found. The male is

California king snake (ringed variety). (Courtesy California Academy of Sciences)

The Salt Creek pupfish are most likely to be seen during the spring breeding season, as shown here.
(Courtesy National Park Service, Death Valley National Park)

bluish with a purple sheen on the back. He has dark-gray lateral bars. People often have trouble seeing even a single fish in Salt Creek, but a visit during the late winter–early spring breeding season will reveal them in incredible numbers.

Cottonball Marsh pupfish. *Cyprinodon milleri* live in a system of pools that were once part of the Salt Creek system but are now isolated in an area that may reach nearly five times the salinity of ocean water. The main difference between this and the Salt Creek pupfish is their complete lack of pelvic fins. These fish are also smaller than the Salt Creek pupfish.

Saratoga Springs pupfish. *Cyprinodon nevadensis nevadensis* are found in Saratoga Springs in the south end of Death Valley. These are the first pupfish to have been described in Death Valley, in 1889. They are found only here and are a subspecies of the Amargosa pupfish. The male has the broadest body and its rich-blue breeding coloration is also the most intense of all the pupfish.

Amargosa pupfish. *Cyprinodon nevadensis amargosae* can be found in two permanent flows of the lower Amargosa River northwest of Saratoga Springs. They must live through extreme desiccation during the summer and flash flooding in the winter. The female is a dull-brown color. The male, during breeding, takes on a silvery shade layered over a blue background.

Devil's Hole pupfish. *Cyprinodon diabolis* are located in a limestone cavern along a fault in the side of a hill in Ash Meadows, Nevada. They live on a shallow limestone shelf where their very existence is threatened by any drop in the water level—this is believed to be the most restricted habitat of any vertebrate animal on Earth. These pupfish have probably been isolated longer than any other group, conceivably as long as 10,000 to 20,000 years. These are the smallest of the pupfish, and decidedly the rarest with a population of only a few hundred at the most. The adult has all of the characteristics of the juvenile with a large head and eyes, reduced pigmentation, and a long anal fin. The Devil's Hole pupfish has been placed on the endangered species list. Devil's Hole is a part of Death Valley National Park and can be visited, but the cavern itself is fenced and public access into the cave is not allowed.

■ SNAILS

The tiny springsnails of Death Valley surpass even the pupfish in their diversity and endemism. At least fifteen endemic species are known to exist today in the Death Valley ecosystem; see the Endemic Animals list at the start of this chapter for a partial list. Research has revealed the evolutionary changes made by the snails in order to accommodate the reduced aquatic habitat and resulting salinity of the water. They inhabit the wetlands and tiny springs, clinging to life during the drastic temperature changes wrought by the weather. Among these snails is *Assimnea infirma*, also known as the **Badwater snail**. It is the world's only known soft-bodied invertebrate animal to live in saturated salt water and has been listed as a candidate for the threatened or endangered list.

When visiting the various pools and seeps, remember that these tiny creatures live on the very edges of these watery habitats. Keep back so you do not mistakenly step on them and kill them. Also never remove any of these creatures from the water.

■ INSECTS AND OTHER ARTHROPODS

Desert tarantula. *Aphonopelma chalcodes* are neither dangerous nor deadly. The venom is only potent enough to subdue and digest prey. The male is a little over two inches in size; the female is twice as large with a leg span up to four inches. Both have heavy, hairy, dark-brown bodies. They have adapted to living in the desert by digging short underground tunnels. Their lairs can be identified by the webbed covering of the small entry holes. The tarantula's hunting tactic consists mostly of simply waiting for dinner to wander by; the victim is then grabbed and pulled into the burrow. Autumn is mating time. The male tarantula ventures forth just before sunset, searching for a female. When the male finds a female, he will chase her until she mates with him. Eggs are not laid until the following May or June. The female then deposits 500 to 1,000 eggs in almost any natural cavity, wrapping them in a protective silken covering. The mother stays with the eggs until the spiderlings hatch a month later. The male tarantula may live up to ten years. The female has been known to outlive the male by twenty years.

Darkling beetles. Members of the genus *Eleodes*, these inch-long, wide-bodied black beetles can raise their abdomens to an angle of about forty-five degrees. Because of this, they are sometimes called circus beetles: "Oh look, he is standing on his head and kicking his feet in the air." In fact, this elevating experience is a protective measure during which the beetle gives off an offensive odor, which explains why they are also known as stink bugs. Whatever their nickname, the evenly spaced, zipperlike tracks left by the beetles can be seen neatly trailing across the sand dunes.

Giant desert hairy scorpion. *Hadrurus arizonensis* are members of the class *Arachnida*. Among the most ancient terrestrial arthropods, scorpions have been traced back to the Silurian Period, more than 300 million years ago. Hairy and scary looking, this six-inch-long species of scorpion is not lethal, although its sting is similar to that of a bee. The scorpion's body is dark brown; the pincerlike pedipalps and legs are a pale yellow. Nocturnal, they are often preyed upon by owls. The young are hatched inside the female and then born live. She carries them on her back for up to fifteen days, or until they shed their first skin. After that the young scatter and are on their own. Campers note: these scorpions are common in the litter around the trees at the Furnace Creek Campground.

Centipedes. Class *Chilopoda* are long and wormlike. Their venom is mildly poisonous and is secreted by the first pair of clawlike appendages behind the head, which are used to paralyze their prey. Their bite can be most painful, and some people have a severe allergic reaction to them. Centipedes live in and around rotting wood, under debris at old mines and cabins, and under tree bark.

Tarantula hawk. *Hemipepsis* species are large digger wasps. Shiny dark blue with reddish-orange wings and long black legs, the tarantula hawks have a sting comparable to that of a bee. They are not interested in humans. The female wasp preys on tarantulas and other large spiders. When the perfect spider has been found, the wasp mounts the victim and injects her venom, leaving it paralyzed but not dead. She then drags the prey into a hole where she lays one egg on the body. This ensures that the young have fresh food for their entire larval period.

Tracks on the sand dunes, like the "zippers" left by Eloedes *beetles, are abundant during early morning hours.*

Midges. Family *Ceratopogoidae* are extremely tiny black flies that travel in compact swarms. They can be serious pests, as their bite raises welts and often causes severe swelling. Midges are found throughout this region, even in places seemingly

Painted lady butterfly. (Photo by Thomas G. Barnes, U.S. Fish & Wildlife Service)

far from the water they need for breeding. At least five species of **mosquitoes** have been described in Death Valley, too.

Rough harvester ant. Pogonomyrmex rugosus are reddish-brown ants that are usually found at the exact spot where you would like to put your chair or your food. They have a two-segmented "waist" between thorax and abdomen. They mate and together dig a small nest area in which to place their cluster of eggs. As the young are born, the worker ants enlarge the space to make room for developing larvae. These ants have nasty stings that are painful and can cause swelling.

Painted lady butterfly. Vanessa cardui invades the deserts in awesome northerly migrations (often up to 1,000 miles long) during February and March of wet years. These are two-inch, salmon-orange butterflies with black forewing tips spotted with white. The hind wings are crossed by small black-rimmed blue spots. The female's eggs are a barrel-shaped pale green; during her lifetime she may lay up to 500 eggs. Like all butterflies, they taste with their feet and breathe through their abdomens. The preferred host plant is the thistle (*Cirsium*), but they also feed on other composites and mallows (*Malvaceae*).

PART II
The Death Valley Environment

The Desert Environment: Climate, Precautions, and Regulations for Explorers of Death Valley

▨ DEATH VALLEY'S CLIMATE

An elevation range from the salt flats 282 feet below sea level to the highest peak 11,049 feet above sea level provides an extremely varied temperature range regardless of the time of the year. For the new desert visitor the most surprising variable is the daily temperature fluctuation—an 80°F day can be followed by a 40°F night because the lack of humidity and cloud cover permit the daytime heat to dissipate into the night sky. In spite of the nighttime temperature drop, Death Valley in summer is the hottest place on Earth, with a world-record high temperature reading of 134°F at Furnace Creek. Thermometers placed at ground level on the open floor of Death Valley have officially registered 201°F.

On the other hand, winter in Death Valley can be brutally cold. Temperatures below freezing are often recorded on the valley floor; the all-time low temperature recorded at Furnace Creek is 15°F. Readings colder than 0°F are not rare in the higher mountains, where snowfall can be significant.

Although this is a desert, it can also be devastated by storms. February is usually the wettest month, although even then rains that collect below sea level typically measure only 0.33 inches. A year's overall average is just 1.91 inches, and no rain at all was recorded during 1929 and 1953. When the rains do come, however, they are often torrential, sending earth-ripping flash floods down the narrow canyons. The lakebed in south-central Death Valley has been known to fill in recent years with enough water to support brief, but noteworthy, canoe launchings on "New Lake Manly."

At the higher elevations, snow often caps the mountain peaks into early June. Some of the higher roads, such as Hunter Mountain, the North and South passes in Saline Valley, and Upper Wildrose Canyon Road, are sometimes closed because of snow. The best time to visit the Panamint Mountains is after the snow melts in the

Despite Death Valley's famous summertime heat, the mountains receive significant snowfall in winter, something the explorer must prepare for.

Death Valley Temperature and Rainfall Records
recorded at Furnace Creek, 1911 through 2008

	January	February	March	April	May	June	July	August	September	October	November	December
Average High Temperature *(degrees Fahrenheit)*	67	73	82	90	100	110	116	115	106	93	77	65
Average Low Temperature *(degrees Fahrenheit)*	40	46	55	62	73	81	88	86	76	61	48	38
Record High Temperature *(degrees Fahrenheit)*	89	98	102	113	122	128	134	127	123	113	97	88
Record Low Temperature *(degrees Fahrenheit)*	15	21	30	35	42	49	62	64	41	32	24	19
Average Rainfall *(inches)*	0.27	0.35	0.25	0.12	0.08	0.04	0.11	0.10	0.14	0.11	0.18	0.19

- The wettest single calendar year (January–December) on record was 2005, when 4.73 inches of rain fell at Furnace Creek.
- The wettest single rainfall year (July–June) on record was 2004–2005, when a rain total of 6.44 inches was recorded.
- It was in 1913 that both the highest temperature (134°, on July 10) and the lowest temperature (15°F, on January 8) were recorded, and 1913 was also the second wettest calendar year, with 4.54 inches of rain at Furnace Creek.
- In 2001 there were 154 consecutive days with a high temperature greater than 100°F.

spring, when you can climb Telescope Peak and look down at the hot, shimmering valley below or just walk among the trees, reveling in the cool microclimate of a desert range.

And then there is the wind. The long and low valley floor surrounded by high mountains acts like a wind tunnel. The wind most often (but not always) blows either north or south and can come in the form of a gentle breeze, a zephyr, or what might be described as a sandy, blasting hurricane.

■ DESERT TRAVEL PRECAUTIONS

Before starting on a trip through the desert, always leave your agenda with someone reliable. Tell them where you are going and when you expect to arrive. Whenever you travel through the desert, whether by foot or by vehicle, keep in mind that you are on your own. There are few gas stations, medical facilities, or grocery stores, and there is even less shade and water. If your engine dies or your car overheats, you get stuck on a back road with no spare bike tire, your 4WD vehicle is wedged in a tight place, or you twist an ankle while hiking in the backcountry, you must be prepared to take care of the problem. If you tell a friend your travel plans, eventually you will be missed and someone will show up to help, but until that time (which might be two or three days) you will remain much calmer knowing you are prepared.

To this end, it is requested and recommended that you fill out a free backcountry registration form that is available at the Furnace Creek Visitor Center or any ranger station. On this you will indicate your plans and when you expect to return. If you do this, however, please be absolutely certain that you check back in at the end of your trip.

■ PASSENGER CAR AND HIGH-CLEARANCE VEHICLE

For travel on the highways and improved dirt roads, check your vehicle before going into the desert. Are your tires properly inflated, including the spare? Underinflated tires generate excessive heat and might explode. Check your oil level. Keep your gas tank filled, as there are many miles between stations.

What you need:

2 gallons of water for vehicle use only	first-aid kit
emergency flares	flashlight
matches	2 quarts of oil
wide-brimmed hat	jumper cables
blanket	jacket
1 gallon of drinking water per person per day	snacks that will stay fresh in the heat
	spare set of keys

When driving up long mountain grades, turn off your car's air conditioner. If your car heats up, the engine can be cooled by turning on the heater and driving slowly in a lower gear or by pulling off to the side of the road and turning your car so it is heading into any prevailing breeze. Do not stop your engine. If and only if it is absolutely necessary, run the engine at a fast idle speed and slowly pour water over the radiator core to help cool it. If you must add water to the radiator, do so only when it is fully cooled.

Never "lug" your engine on steep inclines. With both standard and automatic transmissions, shift to a lower gear.

In case of strong winds, try to pull off the road and park with the back of your car into the wind. This helps prevent sand from blowing into your engine or pitting your windshield.

If you develop car trouble, stay with your car. NEVER try to walk for help.

■ FOUR-WHEEL-DRIVE VEHICLE

Most of the 4WD roads have washboard surfaces and may be crossed by deep runoff gullies. In the mountain canyons high centers and large rocks are the rule. Drive slowly. It is easy to lose control, slide, or fishtail on curves.

When approaching deep sand, start with enough speed to keep you going and to maintain that speed. Never slow down or try to speed up in sand. If all fails, remove the boards mentioned in the list below, shovel in front of your tires and put the boards under two of the tires. Slowly but firmly drive onto the boards and, it is to be hoped, out of the sand. If you deflated your tires, be sure to reinflate them at once.

Be especially alert when traveling in canyons. Thunderstorms in the mountains can cause flash floods. Never set up camp in a wash, and never camp near a backcountry water supply.

What you need at a minimum:

2 gallons of water	gas in heavy plastic gas can
heavy-duty 12-volt tire pump	fix-a-flat tire sealant
quality, full-service spare tire	four 10" × 48" plywood boards
lug wrench	jack and small board to set it on
fire extinguisher	spare fuses
can of brake fluid	radiator "stop leak"
tow chain or nylon rope	small folding shovel
can opener	first-aid kit
cans of food	hat
knife	spoon
matches	backpacker's stove
flashlight	cook pot with lid
a good, basic tool kit containing	ground cloth
pliers, screwdrivers, Vise-Grip	sleeping bags
locking pliers, air-pressure gauge,	insect repellent
open-end wrench, hammer, and	sunscreen
electrical tape	

■ NATIONAL PARK SERVICE REGULATIONS

The following is a summary of the restrictions and regulations that apply to all areas within Death Valley National Park. Some of the trip routes include areas on other public lands (Bureau of Land Management or U.S. Forest Service) outside the national park, where the legal requirements may be different and less stringent. There are relatively few restrictions for casual visitors to keep in mind, but failure to abide by them can result in severe penalties. Because the new Death Valley Wilderness and Backcountry Stewardship Plan was approved in 2013, visitors should check with the visitor centers for changes in the regulations. Among other things, permits will be required for some backcountry uses starting in 2015.

Camping. In addition to the developed campgrounds, camping is permitted almost anyplace within Death Valley National Park, *provided* that the site is at least two miles from the nearest paved road, above sea level elevation, and at least 100 feet from any open water source (some places are posted and require a separation of 100 yards). Areas designated for "Day Use Only" are generally well marked and include all areas on the floor of Death Valley that are below sea level, Titus Canyon, Skidoo Road, Aguereberry Point Road, Wildrose Road, the first eight miles of Cottonwood Canyon Road, all parts of Racetrack Valley (excepting Homestake Dry Camp), and Big Pine Road south of Crankshaft Junction.

Campfires. Campfires are permitted *only* within a constructed campfire ring at a developed campground or where kept elevated off the ground within a portable barbecue or hibachi, in which case the dead coals must be removed for proper disposal. Collecting dead wood for a campfire is illegal; this includes any old lumber that might be found in a mining area.

Off-road driving. All of Death Valley's roads are designated as highways, regardless of condition, and all vehicle travel is confined to these roads. The term "vehicles" includes bicycles and all forms of motorcycles, dirt bikes, and all-terrain vehicles (ATVs), which must be licensed as street-legal. Old roads that have been closed to vehicles are open to foot travel only.

Specimen collecting. All collecting within the national park is strictly illegal. Everything is protected: minerals, rocks, plants, animals, archaeological artifacts, and historical debris. What may look like mining camp trash is an archaeological resource that is as fully protected by law as is the rarest plant. For this reason, the use of metal detectors is prohibited in all areas of the park.

■ CAUTIONARY NOTES

Water sources. The listing in this book of springs, streams, and other water sources does not guarantee that water is available in those places. Any water that is present may be unusable because of chemical and/or biological contamination. If you must use it, then it should be purified using a professional-grade filter or chemicals. Carry drinking water with you, at least one gallon per person per day in winter and more in summer, whenever you travel within any part of Death Valley National Park.

Closed roads. With the passage of the California Desert Protection Act of 1994 and the resulting expansion of Death Valley National Park, a number of old roads were closed to vehicle travel. All such routes are blocked off and/or posted, but some may still appear on maps or in old books. Also, additional closures may take place in the future. Always check with the National Park Service if in doubt about any route. All roads described in this book were open as of Spring 2014.

Mining areas. There are literally thousands of old mines and mineral prospects within the national park. Most of these are small but all are dangerous places. *Never* enter an old mine tunnel or shaft. All are legally closed by regulation because any supporting timbers have long-since decayed and cave-ins are likely, and because "bad air" can accumulate in mine recesses. And to repeat—even on old mine dumps, mineral and artifact collecting is illegal within the national park.

Communications. People have gotten used to having cell phone communications available almost everywhere, but this is not the case in Death Valley. As of Spring 2014, there was no service in most of the national park, and only limited service by some providers at Furnace Creek.

PART III

Exploring Death Valley National Park by Foot and Bicycle

CHAPTER EIGHT

Hiking and Backpacking in Death Valley

The tiny tracks in the sand, the belly flowers, the intricate mosaics of the dried mud playas—none of this can be truly seen or understood from a vehicle. Unless you get down on your knees, how can you peer closely into the hollow of a salt pinnacle? Unless you walk, you will miss the Gnomes' Workshop and the early morning tracks on the sand dunes. Desolation Canyon will remain an unknown, as will the rare and endangered pupfish at Salt Creek. An hour or two spent on a morning or evening walk will reward you with memories and a love for the desert.

Keep in mind that the desert holds beauty, but it also holds danger for those who do not respect it. You may have spent years strolling along beaches or up mountain trails, but you must reorient your thinking before hiking in the desert. Distances are deceiving. A hill that seems close could be more miles away than you want to travel. Keep personal safety in mind. *Hiking in the summer is never recommended.* Stay out of abandoned mines and open shafts or underground tunnels. There might be poisonous gases in the mines, and weak supports could suddenly cave in. A 100-foot drop into darkness is also a possibility.

Water is something we usually think about only when the newspapers urge us to conserve usage. But if you plan on being in the desert, you must give water top priority. Bread may be the staff of life, but water *is* life. You should always carry water with you, and you must also drink that water. Never wait until you feel thirsty. Your body dehydrates rapidly in the dry air. Long lists of air temperatures, wind velocity, cloud cover, and other fascinating facts have been printed to impress people with the very real need to drink water to stay alive. You need three to four quarts of water in some form (fruit juice, soft drinks) each day in the desert, even in cool weather. Alcoholic beverages, coffee, and tea act as diuretics, so save their consumption for another time.

Pets are not usually acclimated to the desert. Taking your small house dog on a long walk is putting extreme stress on that pet. The ground is often very hot, but we humans are buffered from the heat by the thick soles of our shoes. Test the ground with the palm of your hand before you expect your pet to take a walk. If you decide on a short walk, take a small bowl and give the dog water along the way. Better yet, take your dog on short, shaded jaunts and do the rest alone.

■ SHORT WALKS

The difficulty in describing a day hike stems from the fact that you can park your car and start walking almost anywhere. You need no plan or destination, just an experience. This entire park, away from inhabited spots, is beautiful in nature's stark way. For those who want to get started on these adventures, here are a few short walks. These are all easy and require no strenuous effort. Most people moving at a very slow pace can easily cover a mile in half an hour; those who are fleet of foot can do the same mile in fifteen minutes. Remember, the distance you travel when going must also be covered on your return, so do not overestimate your capabilities. Take your time. Visit with the plants and animals. Distance does not count; pleasure does.

What you need:

a small lightweight day or fanny pack	pocket knife
2 quarts of water	sunscreen
a hat that cannot blow away	sunglasses
identification book for flowers, etc.	insect repellent
identification (driver's license)	several Band-Aids
vehicle plate number and description of the vehicle	camera and film and/or batteries

Food is not a requirement. You will not starve on a short walk. Water is the only true requirement in the desert. If you want to take a snack, take an apple (carry out the core) and some trail mix of raisins, nuts, and chocolate candies. These are light and filled with energy.

Most people are fairly comfortable in whatever clothing they feel suits the weather. On a warm sun-kissed day, a white long-sleeved cotton shirt and light-weight long pants do the best job of protecting your skin from the sun's burning rays. Be sure to apply sunscreen. Never take a desert walk in sandals—wear protective foot covering, such as walking, running, or hiking shoes. Do not forget to wear your hat.

The following are the more popular of Death Valley's short walks.

FURNACE CREEK VISITOR CENTER TO HARMONY BORAX WORKS—3 MILES ROUND-TRIP

The asphalt walkway heads north along the west side of the highway to the Harmony Borax Works, which operated from 1883 to 1888 to process borax that was shipped by twenty-mule team to the railhead at Mojave, California, a distance of 165 miles.

THE HAYSTACKS—1 HOUR ROUND-TRIP

Distance is of no importance on this walk, but time is. Park at Harmony Borax Works and hike west onto the floor of the valley. The hike may be muddy and fairly rough, so plan on at least an hour. Out on the valley floor, the "haystacks" are mounds of marsh mud that was heaped up in the early 1900s to satisfy legal assessment work on borax claims. They have little historic significance, except to demonstrate how easily a mining patent could be obtained.

GNOMES' WORKSHOP—0.5 MILE ROUND-TRIP

Park along State Highway 190, 2.2 miles north of the Furnace Creek Visitor Center. From the highway, walk up the ridge to the south (right) of the small canyon, where sometimes there is a trickle of water within brilliant white salt deposits. A very short distance from the highway, to the south of an old road, is an Indian rock alignment that is perfectly straight, is about 170 feet long, has a short line of rocks extending eastward at one point, and ends with a rounded enlargement at the brink of a small canyon. In the canyon directly below, and probably related, is a small pit that may have been a storage cache. Please do not remove or realign the rocks.

Follow the old road to a trail that leads north the few feet into Gnomes' Workshop. On the canyon walls above and below a waterfall are oddly shaped salt formations. Most are muddy and brown on the outside, but inside they are nearly pure table salt. Similar growths exist all along this stream from below the waterfall to almost half a mile upstream. Please do not walk on these formations as they are brittle and easily broken—not only does it take decades for nature to replace them, but should you break through the crust you could easily break your leg.

ZABRISKIE POINT TO GOLDEN CANYON—5 MILES ROUND-TRIP

Take State Highway 190 to the Zabriskie Point parking area. This hike includes Gower Gulch and connects to and ends with the Golden Canyon Interpretive Trail. Morning is the best time for photography. Beginning at Zabriskie Point, this trail leads through the old lake beds of the Furnace Creek Formation that have been upended into yellowish mud hills. Take time to stand on top of one of these hills, where true desolation is in your grasp. Listen for the sounds of expanding and contracting earth as the temperature changes. Sit on a rock that has come to rest after a watery rush down the wash and look around at the stark beauty. This area has been used to depict moon shots in science-fiction movies.

As you approach Golden Canyon, the color deepens. Leaving the twisting canyon, the downhill route breaks into an open view of the deep, shimmering valley with its backdrop of the Panamint Mountains.

GOLDEN CANYON INTERPRETIVE TRAIL—2 MILES ROUND-TRIP

Located on the Badwater Road, five miles south of the Visitor Center, this is a short, easy, and gradual uphill walk through the colorful badlands. Interpretive signs are scattered along the trail. Red Cathedral (once called Dripping Blood Mountain) is just half a mile up from the last numbered trail marker.

GOWER GULCH LOOP—4 MILES ROUND-TRIP

This hike is a continuation of the Golden Canyon Interpretive Trail, going beyond the last information marker (#10). This hike can end at Zabriskie Point, accessible from State Highway 190, or go down Gower Gulch to finish the loop along the base of the hills back to the Golden Canyon parking lot.

NATURAL BRIDGE CANYON—2 MILES ROUND-TRIP

Take the Badwater Road to the Natural Bridge parking area at the end of an improved dirt road. The bridge is half a mile up the canyon, a smooth but gravelly climb. The bridge is visible well before you arrive. The opening underneath Natural Bridge is about fifty feet high; the bridge itself is about thirty feet thick. Starting as a small pothole at the edge of a streambed, it grew larger as the channel near it got deeper. Eventually the bottom of the hole punched through the channel wall. Continued water flow enlarged the hole until it became the main channel. Now when a flood occurs, Natural Bridge Canyon gets deeper, whereas the bridge stands unaffected above it.

Take the time to explore farther up the canyon. Only a few hundred feet ahead, where the canyon makes a bend to the right, is Cave Fault. Named for the large cavern next to the fault trace on the north cliff of the canyon, it is a detachment fault—the block of ground on the upper side of the sloping fault slid downward relative to the under side.

BADWATER SALT FLATS—1 MILE ROUND-TRIP TO THE
SALT FLATS, 5 MILES ACROSS THE VALLEY

This walk extends across the valley floor from Badwater onto the salt flats where you can find the point of lowest elevation in North America, 282 feet below sea level (Badwater Spring itself is at elevation –279 feet). This point is not marked in any way, but for those with GPS devices, the place was surveyed by the U.S. Geological Survey as located at approximately GPS 36°14.513'N 116°49.533'W. If there has been recent rain, this hike may be impassable because of sticky, salty mud.

SALT CREEK INTERPRETIVE TRAIL—0.5 MILE ROUND-TRIP

One mile off State Highway 190 at the end of graded Salt Creek Road, this easy stroll on a boardwalk takes you into an area inhabited by the rare Salt Creek pupfish, *Cyprinodon salinus*, which lives nowhere but in this stream. The pupfish have adapted to the increasing salinity of spring-fed Salt Creek. The walk rambles along the ever-widening stream to an area where ponds have formed. Watch for the tiny waterfall. The fish can usually be seen in the spring when they are mating but are difficult to spot at most other times. Look for them in the shadows created

The scenery is unique in each of Death Valley's canyons. Golden Canyon is one of the few with an established trail, but all can be hiked.

by grasses or rocks. Please stay on the walkway. There are interpretive signs along the way.

KEANE WONDER SPRINGS AND CYTY MILL—2.5 MILES ROUND-TRIP

Take Beatty Cutoff Road to the improved dirt Keane Wonder Mine Road, and park at the end of the road 2.7 miles from the pavement. Hike north along the old pipeline that delivered water to the Keane Wonder Mill. It is less than one mile to the Keane Wonder Springs, where sulfurous water forms travertine mounds as it comes to the surface along the Keane Wonder Fault. A short way farther are the ruins of the stamp mill and cabin built by Johnny Cyty in the early 1900s. **Note**: As of 2014, this area is closed to public entry pending the mitigation of mine hazards, collapsing mill structures, and contaminated mill tailings.

THE SAND DUNES—CHOOSE YOUR OWN DISTANCE BUT ALLOW AT LEAST 1 HOUR; 2 MILES ROUND-TRIP TO THE TOP OF THE HIGHEST DUNE

Park in the new interpretive parking area (preferred) or along the shoulder of State Highway 190, east of Stovepipe Wells Village. Some of the dunes are eighty feet high. Early morning is the best time for dune wandering, as the tiny tracks of the night-feeding animals will be easy to find. Learn to read the signs. A long tail mark between tiny footprints tells you that the kangaroo rat searched for seeds. Coyote and kit fox tracks may be noted. Tiny zipper-like tracks indicate that a beetle, scorpion, or perhaps a centipede has gone by. Walk between the dunes rather than on them to preserve their aesthetic beauty. If you must climb them, try not to destroy the little desert dwellers' homes, which are usually near the base of trees and shrubs sticking out of the dunes.

TITUS CANYON NARROWS—3 MILES ROUND-TRIP

This can be reached by taking Scotty's Castle Road to the Titus Canyon sign. Drive three miles on a graded road, where you can park at the mouth of the canyon. It is an easy walk up the gravel road into the narrows. Notice the dark-green plants known as stingbush, *Eucnide urens*. Look close, but do not touch the plants, as the leaves have barbed hairs that make it impossible to remove them from your clothing. The flowers are off-white with numerous stamens. During the spring you might encounter blazing stars, *Mentzelia*, with their sun-loving bright-yellow flowers. The flower seeds were once harvested by the Indians as a food supplement.

LITTLE HEBE CRATER TRAIL—1 MILE ROUND-TRIP

Park at the Ubehebe Crater parking lot. Just south of the parking area is a trail that will take you along the rim of Ubehebe Crater and then up to Little Hebe Crater and other volcanic explosion craters. You can also walk around the rest of Ubehebe's rim, an additional 1.5 miles back to the parking lot. Take care with children.

THE CINDER CONE—3.5 MILES ROUND-TRIP

From Lower Warm Spring in Saline Valley, walk southeast toward the reddish cinder cone, sometimes called Peace Sign Mountain because of the symbol emblazoned on its side. A trail to the top of the cone provides an excellent view of the valley. To the west near the base of the cinder cone are the Seven Sisters Springs that support lush vegetation but usually are little more than damp spots in the ground.

◼ LONGER DAY HIKES

Longer hikes require equipment that will keep you safe and happy on your journey and will provide assistance if anything unexpected occurs.

What you need:

lightweight day pack	hat, securely tied
matches	pocket knife
insect repellent	sunscreen
flashlight	plastic zipper bags (to carry out trash)
identification	food
first-aid kit (Band-Aids, roll of gauze,	foil emergency blanket
elastic bandage, antiseptic cream)	bandana
windbreaker	cup
water	trash bag
camera	nature identification books
sketch pad and pencil	binoculars
during winter months, gloves and	
a warm jacket	

MOSAIC CANYON—6 MILES ROUND-TRIP

Located just west of Stovepipe Wells Village, the road climbs 2.5 miles high up the alluvial fan to the canyon entrance. The lower canyon, near the entrance, is a vast mosaic of water-polished breccia in white, black, and gray rock. As you walk a bit farther you will see how the canyon was carved by eons of rushing water. Run your hands over the wonderfully smooth walls. The first 0.5 mile is the narrowest part of the canyon, and very popular for a short walk. The canyon towers high on each side of the narrow pathway. For those who continue onward, there are spots where you must climb up, but it is quite easy. Follow the narrows for about half a mile to where the wash widens. You can go on for two or three more miles before the hike becomes fairly rough because of series of dry falls that require rock-climbing ability. The canyon head is nine miles from the entrance, far beyond day-hike status.

WILDROSE PEAK TRAIL—8.5 MILES ROUND-TRIP

Take State Highway 190 West and the Emigrant Canyon Road to Upper Wildrose Canyon Road. Drive up to the charcoal kilns and park. The trailhead is signed and starts near the first of the kilns you come to. This moderate hike offers spectacular views of both Death Valley and Panamint Valley. The summit of Wildrose Peak is at elevation 9,064 feet, so this hike is not advised during winter months.

HUNGRY BILL'S RANCH—4 MILES ROUND-TRIP

Take the West Side Road and then the 4WD road into Johnson Canyon. The hike starts at Wilson Spring at the end of the road. Within a quarter of a mile a stream appears in the gully. At about the same spot there is an old arrastre (a Spanish word meaning to "drag along")—a primitive ore-grinding device in which a burro or mule was used to pull a heavy rock around a circular pit lined with smooth stones. Gold ore would be ground to a powder, which could then be washed with water in a pan or sluice box to recover the free gold. There is a second arrastre another quarter of a mile up the canyon. Other stone remains appear to have been part of an aqueduct. These structures may be related to Shadow Mountain, a small mining camp that had an extremely brief existence in 1907.

Continuing upward, the canyon quickly narrows until the bottom is only wide enough for the stream, which is thoroughly choked with willow trees laced with the vines of grapes and morning glories. Horsetails as tall as four feet spring from shady wet spots, and myriad frogs can be heard singing in the thickets. Open places and hill-sides near the stream are populated by cliffrose and peachthorn plants up to ten feet tall. Broomlike green ephedra (also known as mountain Mormon tea) dot the slopes.

The hiker is forced to climb up and down over several sets of cliffs. After a rigorous mile and a half, you reach the site of Hungry Bill's Ranch. It was established by William Johnson during the Panamint City boom of the early 1870s. The plan was to grow vegetables and fruits to sell to the miners. All of the vegetables that could be grown were sold to the mining camp, a rugged six miles over the mountains, but Panamint City died long before the apricot, pear, apple, and fig trees bore any fruit. In later years, a Timbisha Shoshone Indian known as Hungry Bill (reportedly because of his huge girth and appetite) settled and won a homestead right to the ranch. When he died, the place was abandoned and it is slowly returning to nature. Some of the trees remain and the apple trees, especially, bear fruit.

The source of all the water is Hungry Bill's Springs, a short distance upstream from the ranch. They gush more than 100 gallons of clear cold water each minute. Unfortunately, both burros and bighorn sheep foul the spring and the water must be treated before drinking.

SIDEWINDER CANYON SLOT CANYONS—4 MILES ROUND-TRIP

Take Badwater Road/East Side Road south 14.4 miles from Badwater or 1.7 miles north of the "Mormon Point" sign. Turn east onto a short dirt road to an old gravel pit. These mountains look uninteresting from a distance, but wonders await the hiker. From the south end of the pit, walk up the alluvial fan to the south into a shallow canyon with gravel walls. About one mile in, the canyon abruptly narrows. At this point the first of several slot canyons is to the right. Scramble through the boulders and the canyon is only a few feet wide with walls nearly 100 feet high.

Hidden along the dark passageways are several natural bridges. There are other slot canyons farther up the main drainage. These canyons were carved by flash floods, so don't attempt this hike if rain is forecast.

WILLOW CANYON WATERFALL—5 MILES ROUND TRIP

This hike begins at the same old gravel pit as does the Sidewinder Canyon hike, 14.4 miles south of Badwater. From the gravel pit, hike north around the gravel hills and across several small gullies into the large wash that drains Willow Canyon. At the base of Smith Mountain you enter a narrow gorge of metamorphic rocks and soon hear the sound of water. These narrows end at a waterfall 50 feet high that flows at least a little in all but the very driest years. With a little luck, you might see some of the bighorn sheep that frequent this area.

KLARE SPRING AND PETROGLYPHS—13 MILES ROUND-TRIP

Get an early-morning start. Take Scotty's Castle Road to Titus Canyon Road. Drive the three-mile graded road to the parking area. This is a long, rigorous hike and camping is not permitted in Titus Canyon. Carry plenty of water. Hike up the canyon on the gravel road. Klare Spring only flows a gallon or two per minute but is the largest water source in a very large area; treat the water if you must use it, and do everything you can to avoid fouling the spring as it is a critical source for wildlife. Some petroglyphs are found near the spring—do not mark on or deface them in any way. You might want to carry a plant identification book so you can be introduced to the many plants along the way. Some rare plants, such as rock midget (*Mimulus rupicola*), rock lady (*Maurandya petrophila*), and Death Valley sage (*Salvia funerea*) grow in the limestone crevices of the shaded canyon walls.

FALL CANYON—6 MILES ROUND-TRIP

From the mouth of Titus Canyon, accessible from Scotty's Castle Road, hike north half a mile along an informal trail at the base of the mountains to the wash at the mouth of Fall Canyon, then proceed up the canyon. This is a spectacular slot canyon, narrow with high walls similar to Titus Canyon. About 2.5 miles up the canyon is a dry fall, which can be passed with moderate rock scrambling. Farther up the canyon are additional dry falls that can only be passed by true rock climbing.

PANAMINT DUNES—9 MILES ROUND-TRIP

Drive two miles east of the Trona Road on State Highway 190 and turn north on the Lake Hill (Big Four Mine) Road. This is best traveled in dry weather and requires a high-clearance vehicle. On the way you can park by the side of the road and explore Lake Hill to the left. Continue on a couple more miles to where the road turns right. Pull off and park. The Panamint Dunes are much larger than they look from a distance. The highest of them are about 4.5 miles to the northwest. These dunes are star-shaped and created by winds blowing from several directions with equal strength at different times of the year.

BLACK MOUNTAIN TRAIL—5.5 MILES ROUND-TRIP

Leave the Lower Warm Spring camp in Saline Valley and head north. The start of the trail is about half a mile ahead, beginning at the base of the mountain. This trail was built long ago by a few of the people who came to the springs. There is a climb up a ridge and then a sharp drop into a canyon that loops back toward the valley. In the spring watch for the charming five-spot flower along the trail. There are still a few wild burros in this area.

◼ BACKPACKING

A backpack trip into the desert is an experience that is almost indescribable. You are suddenly truly on your own—free to wander, free to explore—but no matter where you plan to go you will come face-to-face with the forces of nature. The wind is an entity to be dealt with, throwing you off balance and making headway nearly impossible. Your bed will be a cleared spot on the ground, as there are no designated campsites. The deep-cut ravines caused by water runoff from rain high up in the mountains cause the hiker to log more up-and-down miles than straight-ahead progress. Dried mud from old lake beds is crusty on top, but your boots sink through to the soft, puffy silt underneath. Sand is difficult to walk in while carrying a pack. And, of course, the ever-present rocks jar you off balance.

It sounds fairly miserable, yet more and more backpackers travel to the desert each year. Why? Because of the challenge. Because of the desert's eternal beauty, the changing colors of the mountains, the desire to go where the Indian hunters and gathers lived, to wander as did those people of the mining-boom era, and to feel truly free and independent of others. It is worth the effort. But one warning: once you have backpacked in the desert you will undoubtedly find that you want to return again and again.

A topographic map and compass or GPS unit will guide you across this country. Many places can be hiked by simply using mountain peaks as your guide. Getting lost is not a great problem; however, finding food and water is difficult and important. Because of the lack of water you must provide your own. A gallon of water weighs around eight pounds, which precludes carrying enough for more than two days at the most. This means you must cache water before starting the longer trips. You should also cache your food and keep your pack as light as possible.

How to Cache

First, plan your hike on a topographic map. Decide how many miles you will be able to hike each day, then mark that spot on your map. Think about how you will hike with your cache to the chosen spot. When the number of caches has been determined, it is time to plan the cache container and contents. You will need water bottles. Do not use plastic bottles that once contained bleach. Only food- and water-grade plastic comes from a pure source. Plastic that is not food-grade may come from many places, including recycled plastic such as detergent and oil-additive containers. Proper water containers that collapse when empty can be purchased from hiking equipment suppliers and can be used over and over. Make sure the top is secure. Caches cannot be left longer than 30 days.

For food or any small item that will need replacing, locate the smallest, toughest container that will do the job. If you want to be really lightweight, double-bag your food in zipper bags. When caching, sprinkle liberally with cayenne pepper to keep varmints away.

Plan your menu. Concentrate on carbohydrates that provide high energy. Fresh food (avoid any wilty types such as lettuce or cabbage) can be cached if you plan to eat the heavy things at the cache site. Carrots, apples, oranges, limes, and green avocados can be wrapped in paper towels and will keep for some time if the weather is cool, but never put them in plastic bags or they will rot. Take dried fruits, nuts, bulgur wheat, crackers, and anything that will keep well. Consider the packaging. If you have food in cans, you must carry out the empties.

Now you are ready to haul in your cache. Pack it, take your GPS unit or topo map, pencil, and your camera. Drive to the nearest access point, and walk in. Do not consider leaving your precious cargo near a road. Never cache in a wash. Rains could obliterate your markers and tear up the cache. If there is a large rock, set your water and food on the east side for afternoon sun protection. Pile other rocks around and over until the containers are covered. If there is no large rock, simply make your own pile. Another good spot for your cache is under a large bush. You take a chance that a mouse will chew into your plastic if you set the stuff on its door hole. Some people bury their cache. Unless you plan to carry a shovel, you will find that recovery from a hole in the ground is a hot, miserable job.

Modern GPS devices make this job much easier, as you can readily and precisely log the coordinates of the cache. Otherwise, take a compass reading and mark your map. Take at least three photos of the cache and surrounding area from the approach direction of your hike (a good idea even with GPS). Finally, walk back on your proposed route for a short distance, turn around, and return to the cache. Be very observant of the cache area, of any plants near the site, and of the overall general lay of the land. You might make a rough sketch of shrubs nearby. Caches are rather easy to miss in the desert, so care taken at this time will help save you from a night and day without food and water.

After you start your hike and locate your cache, spread the stones out in a natural manner. Cut your containers and bottles into packable pieces and take them along with you. Never leave them.

Clothing

You need cool (and warm), comfortable, protective clothing. Shorts and short-sleeved shirts may be your normal hiking gear, but such attire leads to insect bites, sunburn, scratches from the spiny shrubs, cold nights, and the possibility of skin cancer. Yellow clothing attracts bees and other insects, white reflects heat but looks scruffy almost at once, and black is miserably hot. Light tan is probably the best bet. You will not need changes of clothing, except for socks.

What you need:

hat that ties on	shirt, long-sleeved
pants, long	windbreaker with hood
rain gear, if needed	warm jacket
sunglasses	wool socks, two pairs
liner socks, two pairs	hiking boots, steel shank

Gear

What you need:

water (4 quart-sized bottles rather than one or two larger bottles reduce the slosh factor and make it easier to balance the pack)	first-aid kit—Band-Aids, tweezers, roll of gauze, elastic bandage, antiseptic cream, wet wipes, aspirin, personal medications,
topographic map	vinegar (takes the sting out of ant bites)
sleeping bag	pocket knife
cache photos	matches
sunscreen	metal cup
flashlight	windproof nylon tarp (5' × 7' size)
insect repellent	nylon cord for tying tarp
bandana	mattress
several small plastic zipper bags for "cooking" and carrying out trash	compass and/or GPS device

Food

Cooking is not required for nourishment. Take grains that are edible after soaking, fruit (both fresh and dried), and vegetables. Be creative and save weight.

A Warning

Be wary about the presence of deer mice. They tend to inhabit old cabins and are carriers of the Hanta virus. The onset of this serious lung infection is sudden and the disease is fatal without immediate medical treatment. Hanta virus has been reported near the national park, so great care should be taken when camping near old mining camps or in cabins. Ticks can also be a problem in the higher country. Tying your pant legs snuggly around each ankle will help keep them off your skin.

Note: A required backcountry registration and permit system will be instituted in 2015 as a result of the Death Valley Wilderness and Backcountry Stewardship Plan that was approved in July 2013. See the Addendum on page 455 for more information.

A group of overnight backpackers examine ruins from the borax mining days on a hike between Furnace Creek and Stovepipe Wells.

Remember—no backpack trip is recommended at low elevations during the summer months or at high elevations during the winter months. The best low-elevation months are November through early April. For the higher elevations try June, September, and October. In winter, ice axes and crampons may be required on Telescope, Wildrose, and other high mountain peaks. Check first at the Visitor Center.

TELESCOPE PEAK—14 MILES ROUND-TRIP

The trail head is next to the Mahogany Flat Campground, elevation 8,133 feet, located nine miles east of Wildrose Campground. There is no water at Mahogany Flat or along the steep trail. Some hikers leave the campground, climb to the top, sign the register, and return the same day. This requires a strong hiker, since it takes six to eight hours to reach the summit at elevation 11,049 feet. The trail can be dangerously icy from December to May. The altitude gain is 2,916 feet in a distance of seven miles. It is easier to carry a small backpack and sleep under the stars.

The views along the trail are fantastic. You should be able to see Mt. Whitney, the long stretch of the High Sierras, the White Mountains, and the Panamint Valley to the west. To the east are Death Valley and distant Charleston Peak. The trail climbs through forests of pinyon and limber pine, and ancient bristlecone pines are found near the summit.

SURPRISE CANYON—10 MILES ROUND-TRIP

This is a strenuous hike with an elevation gain of 4,000 feet in five miles. From a parking area near Chris Wicht (or Novak) Camp at the end of Surprise Canyon Road in Panamint Valley (4WD may be required), the hike follows the old, closed road up the canyon to the Panamint City ghost town in an area of abundant wildlife and gorgeous scenery. Technically, this is a "cherrystem" route, a Bureau of Land Management area that is immediately bounded by the national park, and some of the land at Panamint City is privately owned.

From Panamint City, it is possible to extend the hike an additional 7.5 miles over the mountains and down Johnson Canyon past Hungry Bill's Ranch to the end of the Johnson Canyon Road at Wilson Spring.

THROUGH CANYON—16 MILES ROUND-TRIP

Starting at the site of Confidence Mill on the Harry Wade Road, this hike crosses a narrow part of Death Valley and proceeds into Through Canyon and Death Valley's only known stand of smoke trees (*Parosela spinosa*). The standard route continues to the head of the canyon, turns a short distance north, and then drops back into the valley through Granite Canyon. It is also possible to go south across the Owl Lake basin to the area of the Black Magic Mine near Owl Hole Spring.

INDIAN PASS—6.8 MILES ONE-WAY TO/FROM END OF INDIAN PASS ROAD

The starting point for this hike is either on the floor of Death Valley at a point 6.5 miles north of the Furnace Creek Visitor Center on State Highway 190 (near GPS 36°32.939'N 116°53.457'W) or from the end of the rugged 4WD Indian Pass Road. From the valley floor, the hike follows a wash that bears to the northeast nearest a ridge. Follow this toward the obvious open pass in the mountains to the east. The route enters Indian Pass Canyon about two miles from the highway (GPS 36°35.560'N 116°51.020'W). Water is available at a spring four miles up the canyon. From there, take the small side canyon north at a spot just a few hundred feet up canyon from the spring and climb the canyon wall past a mine to the end of the Indian Pass Road (see Chapter 13, Trip Route E-7) or continue up the main canyon another two miles (there is a dry fall to negotiate) to the head of the canyon at Indian Pass itself.

TITANOTHERE CANYON TO SCOTTY'S CASTLE ROAD—12 MILES ONE-WAY

The start of this hike is about eleven miles from the entrance of the Titus Canyon Road. There are two forks into this canyon and three parking areas. This is a difficult and tiring hike, even though it is downhill all the way to Scotty's Castle Road. The problem lies in the ravines, which are deeply gouged as a result of flooding, and there is considerable brush and many boulders. The canyon is so named because the fossil bones of a Titanothere and several other extinct animals were found here.

From the Titus Canyon Road hike first to Lost Man Spring, 4.5 miles down the canyon. The spring is difficult to locate because of the profuse growth of rushes, reeds, and mesquite, but treatable water is *sometimes* available there. Soon after leaving the spring the canyon turns to the right and then back to the left before continuing fairly straight ahead. The canyon opens into a wide area, but stay on the left side, which takes you to a wide alluvial fan. Walking conditions do not improve, but there is a great view as the route drops through the Kit Fox Hills to the paved road.

LITTLE SAND SPRING TO STOVEPIPE WELLS VILLAGE— 55 MILES ONE-WAY. CACHES REQUIRED.

Plan to be dropped off at Little Sand Spring, fourteen miles north of Ubehebe Crater Road on Big Pine Road. Allow five days for this trip. Three caches should be stored before the hike, with the last of them near the mouth of Cottonwood Canyon, where you will camp on the last night out. The last day follows the road from Cottonwood to Stovepipe Wells Village. Make sure you store enough water, and take extreme care to be sure that you will be able to locate the caches.

Technically, this is a fairly easy hike. After crossing the Ubehebe Road, walk in Death Valley Wash, where flash flooding has carved deeply into the alluvium. You will walk between high sides of the wash, passing "islands" where twisted limbs and rocks have come to a momentary rest. Stay to the west side of the wash as much as possible. If you are extremely observant or use GPS, you may find the remains of the old road that trends southwest near a benchmark at GPS 36°45.448'N 117°15.420'W. If you do locate the road, follow it for smoother walking toward and around the west side of the Niter Beds. You will eventually start the arduous climb up and down the knee-high cuts in the alluvial fan that comes down from Cottonwood Canyon. There is a surprising amount of beauty on this trek, but you will probably be grateful when you arrive at Stovepipe Wells Village.

COTTONWOOD AND MARBLE CANYONS—23 MILES ROUND-TRIP

Drive from Stovepipe Wells Village on the 4WD Cottonwood Canyon Road nineteen miles to the end of the road at Cottonwood Creek. Treatable water is often available from Cottonwood Creek and at Deadhorse Canyon Spring, but it cannot be relied on. Do not attempt this hike if there is any indication of rain, as there is the strong danger of a flash flood. This hike demands the use of a topographic map as none of the route is marked. However, as this is the most popular backpacking route in Death Valley, use has developed worn paths in some areas. The Park Service also has a handout available at the Visitor Center that describes this route in detail.

The hike starts at the end of the Cottonwood Canyon Road. Follow Cottonwood Creek and then, less than a quarter-mile above the uppermost spring, turn right into a dry wash. Take this about two miles, looking for a low pass on the ridge to the right. Climb the pass and head northeast across Deadhorse Canyon, and then bear northwest into Marble Canyon. Go down Marble for 8.5 miles to its junction with Cottonwood, and then hike back up the canyon another 8.5 miles to your vehicle. You will go through narrow canyons and fairly rough wilderness country. There is an elevation gain of 3,000 feet. This is a difficult hike so do not try it if you are out of shape. Remember, no camping near water.

CHAPTER NINE

Bicycling in Death Valley

Bicycling is becoming increasingly popular in Death Valley. True, most bicyclists are seen on State Highway 190 and the other paved roads, but mountain bikes have been seen at the warm springs in Saline Valley, at the head of Johnson Canyon, in Titus Canyon, and at the Eureka Dunes. Bicycling can be done on any open road in the park, from paved state highway to rugged backcountry road. Note, however, that bicycles are considered to be vehicles and therefore are *not* allowed on any closed road, on hiking trails, or riding cross-country.

Check your bike before leaving home. Make sure it does not shimmy, squeak, shake, or tick and fix it if it does. Take anything you think you might need to keep your bike in shape because you will be a long way from a bike shop.

You should change some of your ideas about what to wear and carry in the desert, where conditions can be severe at any time of the year. Winters can bring cold wind, rain or perhaps snow. Be prepared. For traffic visibility wear brightly colored jerseys. Almost all are constructed of materials that wick water away from your skin, and now there are those that are made of a material that reflects the sun to reduce surface temperature. Wear warm-weather fingerless gloves with mesh backs. Touring shoes rather than shoes with cleats will make you more welcome in gift shops and restaurants. If you insist on wearing cleats, take along lightweight sandals for a change.

Carry water in your bottle cage. Also put a gallon in each rear rack pannier. As your small bottle empties (try using two), fill it from one of the larger ones. Drink water often; never wait until you feel thirsty.

Before starting your desert ride, look at a map and know where you will be able to find more water. Do not overestimate your riding ability. A strong desert wind hitting you head-on is comparable to trying to ride through a brick wall. And again remember—do not rely on cell phone service.

Consider carrying a nylon tarp and cord so you can create shade if you get overheated. Park off the road, put down the stand, and use the bike as a tree from which to tie your shade.

What you need:

tools: spoke wrench, two or three irons, allen wrench, open-end wrench, and screwdriver	electrolyte replacement powder
	map
	sunscreen
patch kit, complete	sunglasses or goggles
spare tube or two sew-up tires and pump	scarf for neck protection
	first-aid kit
helmet	money
2 filled quart water bottles	matches
plus 2 additional gallons	identification, medical insurance card, and
panniers with gear and extra water	name of person to contact in an emergency

Remember to practice defensive driving at all times. Be especially alert where there are deep dips and curves in the road as someone may have parked right on the roadway to take a scenic photo. Also watch for vehicles with mirrors extended far out on the sides.

Bicyclists can, of course, follow any of the main highways in Death Valley. The following are a few of the more popular bicycling routes that are recommended by the National Park Service. All of these routes are more completely described in the "Road Log" chapters of this book.

■ EASY ROADS

HARMONY BORAX BICYCLE PATH

Start: Furnace Creek Visitor Center

Distance: 1.5 miles to Harmony Borax Works; an additional 1 mile one-way through Mustard Canyon

Road type: paved and flat to the borax works; gravel through canyon

Description: This is Death Valley's only actual bicycle path. From Furnace Creek it follows the side of State Highway 190 to Harmony Borax Works. Beyond is a dirt road into Mustard Canyon, which is short but tends to have some areas of soft gravel. The return to Furnace Creek is via the highway.

SALT CREEK ROAD

Start: 13.5 miles north of Furnace Creek on State Highway 190

Distance: 1.2 miles

Road type: graded dirt road

Description: The Salt Creek Interpretive Trail starts at the end of this road. The trail is a boardwalk that follows a portion of Salt Creek, the only habitat of the Salt Creek pupfish, *Cyprinodon salinus.*

20-MULE TEAM CANYON ROAD

Start: 4.5 miles east of Furnace Creek on State Highway 190

Distance: 2.7 miles, one-way loop

Road type: graded dirt road, sandy near the start but mostly firmly packed

Description: This road passes through an area of the Furnace Creek Formation badlands of eroded lake beds. It provides the opportunity to hike up several canyons and onto Monte Blanco, where there are several small borate mines that are dangerous and should not be entered under any circumstances.

■ MODERATE ROADS

HOLE-IN-THE-WALL ROAD

Start: 6.5 miles east of Furnace Creek on State Highway 190

Distance: 5.9 miles one-way to end of road

Road type: loose gravel followed by rocky areas

Description: The first 3 miles to Hole-in-the-Wall follows a sandy wash. Beyond there is a rocky alluvial van. The road ends at the Red Amphitheater, a rich-red canyon of sandstone.

SKIDOO ROAD

Start: 9.5 miles south of State Highway 190 on Emigrant Canyon Road

Distance: 7.1 miles one-way to end of road

Road type: washboard gravel with stretches of rough bedrock

Description: Skidoo was a mining town that reached its peak from 1907 to 1909. From the end of the road, the explorer can take a short walk to the Skidoo Mill, which has been partially restored and stabilized by the Park Service.

AGUEREBERRY POINT ROAD

Start: 12 miles south of State Highway 190 on Emigrant Canyon Road

Distance: 6.3 miles one-way to end of road

Road type: washboard gravel with some rocky areas

Description: About 1.5 miles along this road is the site of Harrisburg, the mining town next to the Cashier and Eureka mines. Continuing, the road winds through hills and then up a steep grade to Aguereberry Point with its spectacular view into Death Valley.

LAKE HILL ROAD

Start: 3 miles east of Panamint Springs Resort on State Highway 190

Distance: 6 miles one-way to where the road begins a steep and extremely rough climb into the mountains

Road type: rutted gravel

Description: Lake Hill, a block of fossiliferous Tin Mountain Limestone, is about halfway along this road. The route becomes extremely rough and rocky where turns east and begins to climb into the mountains and the Big Four Mine, but this is the take-off point for a hike northwest to the Panamint Dunes.

■ DIFFICULT ROADS

ARTIST'S DRIVE

Start: 9.7 miles south of State Highway 190 on Badwater Road

Distance: 8.9 miles, one-way loop back to Badwater Road

Road type: paved with hills

Description: Although paved, this road is steep and narrow in places and also carries a lot of traffic since it is scenic and includes the Artist's Palette of colorful volcanic rocks along the way.

WEST SIDE ROAD

Start: north end 6.1 miles south of State Highway 190 on Badwater Road; south end 3.7 miles north of Ashford Junction (Jubilee Pass Road) on East Side Road

Distance: 35.6 miles one-way

Road type: level gravel but with washboard surfaces and possible sharp stream channels

Description: The West Side Road parallels the base of the Panamint Mountains. There are several important historical places along the way, and the road provides access to Trail, Hanaupah, and Johnson canyons, which lead into the mountains and are also recommended as mountain-bike routes.

WARM SPRING CANYON ROAD

Start: West Side Road

Distance: 11.0 miles to Warm Spring Camp, 22.3 miles one-way to Anvil Spring in Butte Valley

Road type: rough but firm uphill into canyon and then sandy and rocky in places until firm again in Butte Valley

Description: The series of mines below the old mine camp were Death Valley's largest talc mines. Beyond the camp is Butte Valley where there are three old cabins (possibly occupied) and several potential bicycling side trips. Beyond are Mengel Pass and the steep road down Goler Wash, which eventually connects with roads in Panamint Valley.

GREENWATER VALLEY ROAD

Start: north end 7.5 miles south of State Highway 190 on Dante's View Road; south end 5.8 miles west of State Highway 127 near Shoshone

Distance: 28.0 miles one-way

Road type: gravel road with only gentle grades but possible washboard surfaces

Description: Generally downhill toward the south, along the way are side roads to the sites of the Furnace and Greenwater ghost towns, the hike into Greenwater Canyon, and roads to Deadman Pass and Gold Valley.

TITUS CANYON ROAD

Start: 2.7 miles east of park boundary on Nevada State Highway 374

Distance: 26.8 miles

Road type: steep grades and loose gravel

Description: One of Death Valley's most famous areas, the Titus Canyon Road is tremendously scenic. Along the way are Titanothere Canyon, Red Pass, the Leadfield ghost town, Klare Spring and petroglyphs, and the Titus Canyon Narrows.

COTTONWOOD CANYON ROAD

Start: next to Stovepipe Wells Campground

Distance: 18 miles one-way to end of road

Road type: gentle grade, sometimes deep sand at start and rocky in canyon

Description: The first 8 miles of this road angle across alluvial fan areas to the mouth of the canyon and then proceeds to Cottonwood Creek at the end of the road. Not far into the canyon is a side trip to Marble Canyon.

RACETRACK ROAD

Start: Ubehebe Crater

Distance: 19.4 miles to Teakettle, 29.0 miles one-way to Homestake Dry Camp

Road type: firm washboard much of the way with occasional sandy areas

Description: This road first climbs gradually to a low pass and then gently down into Racetrack Valley where there are the famous sliding rocks on the south part of the Racetrack Dry Lake. Day use only except at Homestake Dry Camp, near where is the steep, severe Lippincott Road into Saline Valley.

HUNTER MOUNTAIN ROAD

Start: Teakettle Junction, on the Racetrack Road

Distance: about 10 miles to south end of Hidden Valley

Road type: some loose sand and gravel through Lost Burro Gap and then firm into Hidden Valley

Description: Just beyond Lost Burro Gap are the roads to the Lost Burro Mine (west) and White Top Mountain (east). The route continues through Hidden Valley to Ulida Flat and tends to get considerably rougher. It is possible to take the road onto Hunter Mountain to a connection with the Saline Valley Road, a total, rugged distance of 24.5 miles from Teakettle Junction.

SALINE VALLEY ROAD

Start: south end 13.5 miles west of Panamint Springs Resort or 4.1 miles west of Darwin Junction, on State Highway 190; north end 15.3 miles east of Big Pine, California, on Big Pine Road

Distance: 78.3 miles one-way end to end

Road Type: mostly firm gravel with possible bad washboard surfaces

Description: Obviously a long trip with elevations ranging from about 1,000 feet on the valley floor to over 7,000 feet at North Pass, this is a highly scenic area with many specific attractions.

Trip Route Road Logs

CHAPTER TEN

An Introduction to the "Trip Route" Road Logs

Part IV of this book divides Death Valley National Park into eleven geographical sections. Each of these areas is handled separately, as Chapters 11 to 21, with a map and a number of "trip route" road logs that describe each of the drives within the area. These often are accompanied by similar descriptions of "side trip" road logs. Places of interest along the way are noted with point-to-point mileages. These mileages are given to the 1/10 mile but should be taken as approximate only. For more accuracy, many of the more obscure road intersections and special features are also located with GPS coordinates (latitude-longitude, datum system NAD83) accurate to within a few tens of feet. These coordinates were obtained from a National Park Service database, and most were double-checked both in the field and against topographic maps.

Readers of the first edition of this book will notice that the names of some roads are different. They were changed by the National Park Service and, therefore, by us. This is in keeping with the same NPS database that provided the GPS coordinates.

All of the road logs have been written for travelers driving in a direction away from Furnace Creek. The location of the Death Valley National Park headquarters, Visitor Center and Museum, and major campgrounds and resorts, Furnace Creek is the center of Death Valley and perhaps the one place visited by everybody who comes to the national park. However, because most of the trip routes are two-way drives, mileages are also given for people driving toward Furnace Creek. Those drivers should start reading the descriptions from the end of a road log and use the second set of mileage numbers.

■ DEATH VALLEY ROAD CONDITIONS

We always take a conservative approach when describing Death Valley's roads. All eleven areas can be reached by paved highways, but most of the back roads are dirt routes that are seldom or never maintained. Therefore, the road conditions and vehicle recommendations given here are not guarantees. What is described as a high-clearance route might sometimes be passable in an ordinary passenger car, especially if it has been recently maintained. On the other hand, that same road might have suffered a recent flash flood washout and be all but impassable to even 4WD vehicles. Even the paved highways can be severely damaged by floods.

Always check with the National Park Service prior to attempting any of Death Valley's back roads. In case of trouble, help may be a long distance away or a long time coming—many of these roads are only infrequently patrolled by Park Service rangers, and other explorers might be days apart.

The road conditions are classified as follows:

Paved highway. These are state, county, or Park Service roads with asphalt pavement. In some cases, the paving was laid down directly on the desert floor many years ago. Although solid and suitable for any vehicle, these roads may be rough and broken, with dangerous potholes that are not marked with warnings of any kind.

High-clearance roads. These are dirt roads on which high-clearance vehicles (such as SUVs and pickup trucks) are recommended, but 4WD is not normally required. Some of these roads are graded smooth one or two times per year, and then they can be cautiously driven in any vehicle. However, they tend to develop very rough "washboard" surfaces and high centers and can also be furrowed by stream channels. They therefore may require ground clearance greater than that of a standard passenger car. Many high-clearance routes become true 4WD roads when they enter canyons or mountains.

Four-wheel-drive routes. Four-wheel-drive vehicles with high clearance are advised and may be required. This does **NOT** include all-wheel-drive passenger cars. These are unmaintained dirt roads that typically have combinations of sandy or rocky surfaces, high centers, steep grades, and/or sharply angled pitches. Tires with heavy tread (six-ply or better) and durable sidewalls (4-ply or better) are recommended. Emergency food, water, and repair supplies should be carried in the vehicle (see Chapter 7 for suggestions).

Severe or questionable routes. These are extremely rough routes that demand 4WD, high-clearance vehicles. Experienced drivers accompanied by at least one other vehicle are advised. Power winches are required in some cases. There are only a few such roads within Death Valley National Park. Although they are included in this book, attempting to drive them without current information is not recommended.

Hiking trails. Hiking is allowed in virtually all of Death Valley National Park. Only a handful of trails are maintained, but they and some other routes are especially noteworthy and are described in this book.

Death Valley Roads and Trails: Descriptions and Map Symbols

PAVED ROUTES

The main roads including state highways, paved all-weather routes suitable for any vehicle. Note that some of the park roads are narrow and may have broken asphalt and unmarked sharp curves. Obey the speed limits.

HIGH CLEARANCE ROUTES

High clearance vehicles (such as SUVs and pick-ups) are recommended, but 4-wheel-drive is not required. These are dirt roads that often can be cautiously driven in any vehicle, but which may require vehicles with ground clearance greater than that of a passenger car. Some of these roads are graded smooth one or two times per year and then can be driven by any car, but they tend to form very rough "washboard" surfaces and also may be furrowed by stream channels. Many high clearance routes become 4-wheel-drive roads when they enter canyons or mountains.

4-WHEEL-DRIVE ROUTES (4WD)

4-wheel-drive vehicles with high clearance required or advised; this does NOT include all-wheel-drive passenger cars. These are unmaintained dirt roads that typically have any combination of sandy or rocky surfaces, high centers, steep grades, and/or sharply-angled pitches. Tires with heavy tread (6-ply or better) and durable sidewalls (4-ply or better) are recommended, and emergency food, water, and repair supplies should be carried in the vehicle.

SEVERE OR QUESTIONABLE ROUTES

Short wheelbase 4-wheel-drive vehicles with high clearance and equipped with power winches may be required; experienced drivers accompanied by at least one additional vehicle strongly advised. There are only a few such roads in Death Valley National Park. They are included in this book but attempting to drive them alone is not recommended.

HIKING TRAILS

Recommended hiking routes that are described in this book. Most are cross-country routes, some follow old, now-closed roads, but only a few are along constructed, maintained trails.

■ THE ROAD LOG AREAS
Chapter 11: Southern Death Valley

This is the southernmost and least developed part of Death Valley proper. No services are available within the park area, and there are no established camp-grounds. However, all services are available in the town of Shoshone and limited services at Tecopa Hot Springs.

Trip Route S-1, Jubilee Pass Road. A paved road (in part, State Highway 178) that connects State Highway 127 near Shoshone to the East Side Road on the floor

The 4WD road in Phinney Canyon is typical of the routes in Death Valley's backcountry.

of Death Valley, and which serves as one of the major entrance/exit routes of the park.

Trip Route S-2, Harry Wade Road. A dirt road that runs from Ashford Junction to the southeast corner of the national park. Occasionally graded, this road can sometimes be driven by any high-clearance vehicle, but 4WD is recommended because of sandy areas and occasional deep washouts. The three side trips described separately are:

- *Side Trip S-2a, Owl Hole Spring Road, Black Magic Mine Road, and Microwave Road.* A high-clearance road to Owl Hole Spring, and then 4WD recommended beyond to manganese mines and/or to a microwave tower near the Epsom Salts Mine.

- *Side Trip S-2b, Denning Spring Road.* A 4WD road to Denning Spring, the site of a minor mining camp just outside the southern boundary of the national park; also provides access to Salt Basin.

- *Side Trip S-2c, Saratoga Springs Road.* A high-clearance road to a large riparian area of freshwater springs and small lakes, home to pupfish, and the site of much history.

Trip Route S-3, State Highway 127 South. The major paved highway south from the town of Shoshone to the Harry Wade Road at the southeast corner of the national park. Although entirely outside of the park, some of the route serves as the park boundary and it passes several places important to Death Valley's history.

Trip Route S-4, Ibex Valley Road. A 4WD route because of areas of deep, soft sand, this road passes the length of Ibex Valley with access to the Ibex Dunes. The one side trip described separately is:

- *Side Trip S-4a, Ibex Springs Road and Buckwheat Wash Road.* A 4WD route to the mining camp of Ibex Spring and to the remote Ibex and Rusty Pick mines in Buckwheat Wash.

Chapter 12: South-Central Death Valley

This is the lowest and narrowest portion of Death Valley proper—probably the setting most people think of when they think "Death Valley"—and the location of many of Death Valley's best-known attractions, such as Badwater, Artist's Drive, and Devil's Golf Course. It is therefore also one of the most crowded parts of the park.

Trip Route SC-1, Badwater Road. The paved road south from Furnace Creek to famous Badwater Spring, with access to Golden Canyon, Devil's Golf Course, Natural Bridge, and more. One side trip described separately is:

- *Side Trip SC-1a, Artist's Drive.* A paved, one-way road that climbs to the base of the Funeral Mountains and gives access to Artist's Palette, an area of colorful volcanic rocks.

Trip Route SC-2, East Side Road. A paved road, this is the southward continuation of Badwater Road. It includes only a few specific points of interest but serves as a connection to the Jubilee Pass Road (Trip Route S-1) and the southern end of the West Side Road (Trip Route SC-3).

Trip Route SC-3, West Side Road. A dirt road that is occasionally graded but for which high-clearance vehicles are always recommended. It includes important historic places such as Tule Spring, Eagle Borax Works, and Bennett's Well and provides access to several important canyon areas. The five side trips described separately are:

- *Side Trip SC-3a, Trail Canyon Road.* A high-clearance road to the canyon mouth, and then 4WD into the canyon to end near an old mining camp; from there, hikes in several directions lead to additional mining and riparian areas.
- *Side Trip SC-3b, Hanaupah Canyon Road.* A high-clearance road to the canyon mouth, and then 4WD into Hanaupah Canyon to end at a rocky stream only a short distance from a lush riparian area and "Shorty" Borden's old mining cabin.

- *Side Trip SC-3c, Johnson Canyon Road.* A high-clearance road to the canyon mouth, and then 4WD up the canyon to end near gushing Wilson Spring, from which a trail up the canyon leads to Hungry Bill's Ranch and over the mountains to Panamint City (ghost town).

- *Side Trip SC-3d, Galena Canyon Road.* A 4WD route of few attractions, leading to an area of old talc mines.

- *Side Trip SC-3e, Queen of Sheba Mine Road.* A very rough 4WD road that cuts straight up the alluvial fan to the Queen of Sheba Mine and the site of Carbonite (ghost town).

- *Side Trip SC-3f, Warm Spring Canyon Road and Butte Valley Road.* A high-clearance road into the canyon at Warm Spring Camp, and then 4WD beyond into Butte Valley, where there are old cabins, flowing springs, ore-processing millsites, and the ghost camp of Gold Hill. This road continues as the Goler Wash Road (Trip Route PV-3), which sometimes is only marginally passable to short-wheelbase 4WD vehicles equipped with winches.

Chapter 13: Eastern Areas and Amargosa Valley

Eastward from Furnace Creek, a great deal of this area lies outside the national park, but it includes much of Death Valley's borax, copper, and gold mining history, several of the park's most famous scenic areas, Devil's Hole (a detached unit of the park that is the only habitat of the Devil's Hole pupfish), and extensive areas of wilderness.

Trip Route E-1, State Highway 190 East. The major paved highway between Furnace Creek and Death Valley Junction, including famous Zabriskie Point and Twenty Mule Team Canyon. The three side trips described separately are:

- *Side Trip E-1a, Echo Canyon Road.* A high-clearance road to the canyon, and then 4WD through a slot canyon to Schwab (ghost town) and the Inyo Mine.

- *Side Trip E-1b, Hole-in-the-Wall Road.* A 4WD road to the short but spectacular slot canyon of Hole-in-the-Wall and to a historic quarry a short distance beyond.

- *Side Trip E-1c, Terry Mine Road and Petro Road.* Outside the national park boundary, a network of high-clearance roads (4WD recommended) that were developed because of borax prospecting. This provides access to the site of "Old" Ryan (ghost town) at the Lila C. Mine and to the east end of the Greenwater Canyon hiking route (Side Trip E-3b).

Trip Route E-2, Dante's View Road. A paved road suitable for all vehicles that leads past borax mining areas and up the side of the Black Mountains to world-famous Dante's View; also provides access to the Greenwater Valley Road.

Trip Route E-3, Greenwater Valley Road. A high-clearance road (occasionally graded and then suitable for all vehicles driven with caution) that extends the length of Greenwater Valley, from the Dante's View Road to the Jubilee Pass Road (Trip Route S-1). The three side trips described separately are:

- *Side Trip E-3a, Furnace Mine Road*. A network of 4WD roads that leads to the sites of Furnace, Kunze, and Greenwater (ghost towns) and their associated copper mines.
- *Greenwater Canyon*. A long, dry hiking route of 10.3 miles through day-use only Greenwater Canyon to Petro Road-Terry Mine Road (Side Trip E-1c) outside the national park.
- *Side Trip E-3b, Gold Valley Road*. A 4WD road into isolated Gold Valley, the location of the ghost town sites of Gold Valley and Willow Creek.

Trip Route E-4, Devil's Hole. Paved and improved dirt roads suitable for all vehicles east from Death Valley Junction to Ash Meadows National Wildlife Refuge and to Devil's Hole, an isolated unit of Death Valley National Park that is the only natural home of the Devil's Hole pupfish.

Trip Route E-5, State Highway 127. The major paved highway between Death Valley Junction and Shoshone. Although entirely outside of the national park, some of the route serves as the park boundary and it passes several places important to Death Valley's history.

Trip Route E-6, Lee Ghost Town. A drive mostly on paved roads but including a last few miles of rough 4WD road to the site of Lee (ghost town). This road continues beyond Lee to the site of the Echo (ghost camp) and Echo Pass, and then into Upper Echo Canyon (Trip Route E-1a) on a road that is passable only to short-wheelbase 4WD vehicles equipped with winches.

Trip Route E-7, Indian Pass Road. A rugged 4WD route, much of which lies in Nevada outside the national park but which provides a driving route to the east side of Death Valley's Indian Pass at the end of a recommended backpacking trip. It is likely that this road is driven less often than any other in the park.

Chapter 14: North-Central Death Valley

This encompasses the central part of Death Valley between Furnace Creek and Stovepipe Wells plus extensive mountain areas to the northeast, including Chloride Cliff, Titus Canyon, and Rhyolite (ghost town).

Trip Route NC-1, State Highway 190 Central. The major paved highway between Furnace Creek and Stovepipe Wells Village, primarily a transportation corridor but including several historical and geological points of interest. The one side trip described separately is:

- *Side Trip NC-1a, Salt Creek Road*. A graded dirt road, suitable for all vehicles, to Salt Creek, where an interpretive boardwalk trail follows a perennial stream that is the only natural habitat of the Salt Creek pupfish.

Trip Route NC-2, Beatty Cutoff Road. A paved road that serves as a shortcut between the floor of Death Valley and the Daylight Pass Road (Trip Route NC-3). The one side trip described separately is:

- *Side Trip NC-2a, Keane Wonder Road*. As of 2014, this area is closed to public entry until mine and millsite hazards have been mitigated. When reopened, this will be a high-clearance road (rough and rocky plus one sandy wash crossing, but 4WD usually not required) to the site of Keane Wonder (ghost town) at the Keane Wonder Mill, and hikes to the Keane Wonder Mine, Keane Springs, and Cyty Mill.

Trip Route NC-3, Mud Canyon Road and Daylight Pass Road. A paved road (Nevada State Highway 374 where outside the national park) that runs from the floor of Death Valley, over the mountains, and on to the town of Beatty, Nevada, where all services are available. The one side trip described separately is:

- *Side Trip NC-3a, Rhyolite Road*. A short paved road to the ghost towns of Bullfrog and Rhyolite and access to routes in the Nevada Triangle.

Trip Route NC-4, Monarch Canyon Road and Chloride Cliff Road. A 4WD route into Monarch Canyon and the site of Keane Springs (ghost town), then up the mountain to Chloride City (ghost town), and out to Nevada; the eastern part of this loop, within Nevada, is usually suitable for high-clearance vehicles.

Trip Route NC-5, Titus Canyon Road. A one-way dirt road that is occasionally maintained (high-clearance recommended, 4WD usually not required) that leads from outside the park in Nevada to and then through narrow Titus Canyon, with tremendous scenery, geologic outcrops, Leadfield (ghost town), biologically critical Klare Spring, and petroglyphs along the way.

Chapter 15: Western Areas

West from Stovepipe Wells Village, this large area encompasses numerous scenic and historic areas in the Panamint Mountains, northern Panamint Valley, and part of the Argus Range. Panamint Spring Resort is in this area. As the western entrance to Death Valley, this is one of the more heavily visited parts of the national park.

Trip Route W-1, Cottonwood Canyon Road and Marble Canyon. A high-clearance road to the canyon mouth, and then 4WD beyond to the road's end at Cottonwood Creek, a perennial stream at the start of one of Death Valley's most popular back-packing routes. A short side road leads to Marble Canyon.

Trip Route W-2, State Highway 190 West. The major paved highway west from Death Valley, across the northern portion of Panamint Valley to the Panamint Springs Resort (all services available), and then on to Owens Valley. The two side trips described separately are:

- *Side Trip W-2a, Lake Hill Road.* A high-clearance road (very rough 4WD the last one mile) past Lake Hill to the Big Four lead-silver mine in the north part of Panamint Valley, and access to a hiking route to the Panamint Dunes.

- *Side Trip W-2b, Darwin Falls Road and Zinc Hill Road.* A maintained dirt road to the perennial stream and waterfall of Darwin Falls, and then a rough road (4WD recommended) that climbs past numerous mines on Zinc Hill and to the town of Darwin (semi–ghost town).

Trip Route W-3, Emigrant Canyon Road and Wildrose Canyon Road. A paved road plus one stretch of rough but maintained dirt road in lower Wildrose Canyon suitable for all vehicles (except that vehicles and trailer combinations longer than twenty-five feet or wider than nine feet are not allowed because of narrow, twisting Rattlesnake Gulch), with numerous places of historical importance throughout the area. The four side trips described separately are:

- *Side Trip W-3a, Tucki Mountain Road.* A 4WD route that leads past Telephone Canyon and ends at the Tucki Mine, where there are old cabins and mine ruins.

- *Side Trip W-3b, Skidoo Road.* A maintained dirt road that is rough but suitable for all vehicles driven with caution that passes the Blue Bell Mine Road (hiking route) and ends at Skidoo (ghost town).

- *Side Trip W-3c, Aguereberry Point Road.* A maintained dirt road that is rough but suitable for all vehicles driven with caution and that leads past the Eureka and Cashier mines and the site of Harrisburg (ghost town) and ends at the scenic Aguereberry Point overlook into Death Valley.

- *Side Trip W-3d, Upper Wildrose Canyon Road, Charcoal Kilns Road, and Mahogany Flat Road.* A rough but paved road followed by maintained dirt to the Wildrose Charcoal Kilns. Beyond the kilns is a 4WD road (usually closed in winter) that continues past the Thorndike Campground to the Mahogany Flat Campground near the trailhead to Telescope Peak.

Chapter 16: Panamint Valley Areas

These routes lie almost entirely outside the national park boundary, and they therefore receive relatively brief descriptions in this book. However, they are included because they involve places important to Death Valley's history. Also, this area is heavily traveled as the western access route into the park.

Trip Route PV-1, Panamint Valley Road and Trona-Wildrose Road. A paved highway that extends from State Highway 190 near Panamint Springs Resort to the town of Trona.

Trip Route PV-2, Indian Ranch Road and Ballarat Road. Graded dirt roads suitable for all vehicles to Ballarat (ghost town) with access to several 4WD roads into canyons in the Panamint Mountains that are within the national park.

Trip Route PV-3, Wingate Road and Goler Wash Road. A high-clearance, then 4WD road from Ballarat into southern Panamint Valley, with access to several 4WD routes into the Panamint Mountains. This route ends as the Goler Wash Road, which usually is of severe quality but can provide access to Butte Valley (Side Trip SC-3f). The one side trip separately described is:

- *Side Trip PV-3a, Pleasant Canyon–South Park Canyon Loop*. A long 4WD loop high into the Panamint Mountains where there are numerous mines, pinyon-juniper forests, and tremendous views.

Chapter 17: Northern Death Valley

Two routes that serve primarily as transportation corridors to Scotty's Castle and Ubehebe Crater.

Trip Route N-1, Scotty's Castle Road. A paved road that extends north from State Highway 190 to Scotty's Castle. The two side trips described separately are:

- *Side Trip N-1a, Old Stovepipe Road*. A short, graded road to the site of historic Stovepipe Well and the sand dunes.
- *Side Trip N-1b, Ubehebe Crater Road*. A paved road to Ubehebe Crater, a volcanic explosion crater that is only about 300 years old.

Trip Route N-2, Bonnie Claire Road. A paved road (Nevada State Highway 267 where outside the national park) that leads northeast from Scotty's Castle past Bonnie Claire (ghost town) to U.S. Highway 95 near Scotty's Junction, Nevada.

Chapter 18: Big Pine Road and Eureka Valley

These roads give access to several historical areas in the far northern part of Death Valley National Park and adjacent Nevada and to the large Eureka Sand Dunes.

Trip Route BP-1, Big Pine Road (called the Death Valley Road where outside the national park). A dirt road occasionally maintained inside the national park (often suitable for all vehicles but high-clearance recommended) and paved between the park and the town of Big Pine, California. Primarily a transportation corridor but with access to Eureka Valley, Cucomungo Canyon, and historic sites outside the national park.

Trip Route BP-2, South Eureka Road. A maintained dirt road usually suitable for all vehicles that leads to the Eureka Sand Dunes. Past the sand dunes, this road continues as the Steel Pass Road, a 4WD route of questionable quality into Saline Valley.

Chapter 19: Racetrack Valley and Hunter Mountain

These dirt roads lead into remote areas where no services are available. Although occasionally maintained and often suitable for any vehicle driven with caution, they can deteriorate so high-clearance is recommended and 4WD may be required.

Trip Route RH-1, Racetrack Valley Road and Hunter Mountain Road. Long dirt roads that are occasionally maintained but high-clearance vehicles are always recommended. Racetrack Valley Road leads from Ubehebe Crater to Teakettle Junction and then down Racetrack Valley. From Teakettle Junction, the Hunter Mountain Road is mostly a high-clearance road but may require 4WD on the steep grade of Harris Hill and also may be closed in winter because of heavy snowfall and/or extensive muddy areas. Access to several scenic and historic areas. The three side trips described separately are:

- *Side Trip RH-1a, The Racetrack.* A high-clearance continuation of the Racetrack Valley Road leading past the Ubehebe Mine area and The Racetrack (famous for the rocks that mysteriously slide across the lakebed) to an end at the Homestake Dry Camp. Access to the Lippencott Road, a 4WD route of questionable quality into Saline Valley.

- *Side Trip RH-1b, White Top Mountain Road.* A 4WD road that climbs high into the pinyon-juniper forest of the Cottonwood Mountains, with old mining areas and spectacular scenery.

- *Side Trip RH-1c, J. O. Mine Road.* A 4WD road of that ends at an old mine; also provides access to the Spanish Spring area and what might be the oldest mine within the national park.

Chapter 20: Lee Flat and Saline Valley

Saline Valley is an isolated area with no services of any kind but heavily visited because of the spas and camping areas at Lower Warm Spring and Palm Spring.

The valley is surrounded by high mountains, and both winter snow and summer floods often close the roads for extended periods of time. There are many historical areas throughout the Saline Valley region, and Lee Flat is the location of Death Valley's most extensive forest of Joshua trees.

Trip Route SV-1, Saline Valley Road. The longest single route within Death Valley National Park, seventy-eight miles from end to end with no services of any kind. The road is occasionally maintained and usually suitable for any vehicle driven with caution, but it sometimes receives snow or rain-triggered washouts that can require 4WD and even close either end of the route. Two side trips described separately are:

- *Side Trip SV-1a, Lee Flat Road.* A high-clearance dirt road occasionally maintained across Lee Flat and the most extensive Joshua tree forest within the national park, then high-clearance (4WD sometimes required) along a branch to upper San Lucas Canyon and another branch over the Inyo Mountains to Cerro Gordo (private property ghost town) and Owens Valley.

- *Side Trip SV-1b, Lower Warm Spring Road.* An unmaintained dirt road usually suitable for any vehicle to the clothing-optional camping areas at Lower Warm Spring and Palm Spring. This route continues as the 4WD Steel Pass Road of questionable quality through Steel Pass and Dedeckera Canyon to Eureka Valley.

Chapter 21: Nevada Triangle

The Nevada Triangle is the only portion of the national park that is not within California. With the exception of Rhyolite (ghost town), it receives little visitation. No services are available in this part of the park, but all services are available in the town of Beatty, Nevada.

Trip Route NT-1, Phinney Canyon Road and Strozzi Ranch Road. A high-clearance road that deteriorates into 4WD routes after it splits into the two destination canyons.

Trip Route NT-2, McDonald Spring Road. A 4WD road to near McDonald Spring, with a branch to Hooligan Mine and Cave Rock Spring.

Trip Route NT-3, Mud Summit Road. A 4WD road that mostly follows the old Las Vegas & Tonopah Railroad grade over Mud Summit and past Currie Well to a connection with the Phinney Canyon Road.

CHAPTER ELEVEN

Southern Death Valley

Except for the paved highway of the Jubilee Pass Road (Trip Route S-1), which serves as an important access road to the national park, this part of Death Valley is remote and served only by a dirt roads. There are no services inside the national park, but all services are available at Shoshone and limited services at Tecopa Hot Springs.

Southern Death Valley, Trip Route S-1—Jubilee Pass Road (in part State Highway 178)

FROM: Ashford Junction.

TO: State Highway 127 at a point about 2 miles north of Shoshone, California.

ROAD CONDITIONS: 24.9 miles one-way, paved all-weather highway.

SIDE TRIPS: Virgin Springs Canyon Road (4WD and hike), Rhodes Spring Road (4WD), Pegma Mine (hike), Mister Mine (hike), Upper Confidence Wash Road (4WD).

GENERAL DESCRIPTION: This road serves as an alternate to State Highway 190 as a route between Death Valley and Amargosa Valley. Combined with the East Side Road (Trip Route SC-2), it is a somewhat longer and slower, but much more scenic drive as compared to State Highways 190 and 127 through Death Valley Junction. The area between Jubilee Pass and Salsberry Pass typically puts on one of the best springtime wildflower displays in years with adequate rainfall.

ROAD LOG MILEAGES	eastbound from Ashford Junction / westbound from State Highway 127.
0.0 / 24.9	**Ashford Junction**. The paved Badwater-Eastside Road through south-central Death Valley turns east at this

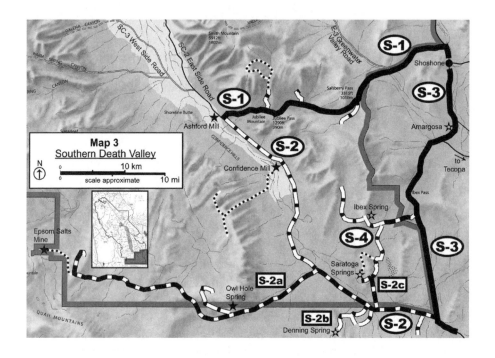

intersection and becomes the Jubilee Pass Road. The dirt road
continuing south through the rest of Death Valley to State
Highway 127 is the Harry Wade Road (Trip Route S-2), a
long, rough trip on which 4WD vehicles are recommended.

1.7 / 23.2 The small hill south of the road is composed of the Crystal
Spring and Beck Spring sedimentary rock formations of late
Precambrian age. They have been separated from the rest of
the Black Mountains by a fault that lies directly beneath the
highway.

2.5 / 22.4 The "holey" rocks on both sides of the highway are composed of a granitic breccia that could only have formed in a
huge landslide but whose source is unknown. The cavernous
holes, called *tafoni*, are an effect of weathering. They form in
places where boulders work loose and fall from the outcrop;
erosion then enlarges and smoothes the openings.

3.4 / 21.5 The outcrops of tilted sedimentary rocks south of the highway are called **Point of Rocks**. The mountains north of the
highway are composed of dark metamorphic rocks that are
as much as 1.8 billion years old. The highest peak is Ashford
Mountain. Below it is a variety of colors from younger
(though still Precambrian) sedimentary rocks that are part of

the Amargosa Chaos. See milepoint 7.2/17.7 for more information about this structure, which is widespread in this area.

4.2 / 20.7 **Virgin Springs Canyon Road** (GPS 35°54.734'N 116°35.155'W, north 1.3 miles; 4WD recommended). This road ends at a small parking area. From there it is a hike of about 0.7 mile into the entrance of Virgin Springs Canyon, where there is an excellent exposure of the Amargosa Chaos. Beyond there, the hike into the canyon reaches an old cabin 3.1 miles from the parking area. A primitive loop trail that leads to the Desert Hound Mine starts near the cabin; the trail is unimproved and the use of a map and compass or GPS device is recommended. Several buildings remain from the gold mining days. From the mine, the trail continues over a divide into another branch of Virgin Springs Canyon and back toward the road. The length of the entire loop is about 13 miles. Water is not available anywhere along this hike; Virgin Springs, where there is the remnant of a small mill, is only a damp spot.

The **Desert Hound Mine** was located by Bill Keys, a close friend and occasional "partner in crime" of Death Valley Scotty. Even though the two had been proven guilty of fraud following the debacle of the "Battle of Wingate Pass" (see Chapter 4), Keys was able to sell the Desert Hound for $25,000 to T. Coleman duPont, of the I. E. duPont de Nemours Powder Co., in 1906. DuPont spent a large amount of money building roads and a substantial camp, sinking several shafts, and drilling long tunnels, but the only ore ever shipped was worth just $12,000.

4.6 / 20.3 **Jubilee Pass** (elevation 1,290 feet). Jubilee Mountain is immediately south of the highway. A short hike to the summit provides a spectacular view of southern Death Valley.

~6 / 19 The road travels along **Rhodes Wash**, where the plants are mostly creosote bush and desert holly along with a few rounded shrubs of desert fir. During the spring wildflower season, this is often one of the most colorful places in all of Death Valley.

7.2 / 17.7 **"Exclamation Hill"** (cliff face south of the highway). This is probably the best known and most accessible exposure of the **Amargosa Chaos**. As Death Valley formed, a series of domelike (anticline) uplifts developed along the Black Mountains. In their cores were hard, erosion-resistant igneous and metamorphic rocks of Precambrian age. On top of these rocks was a series of younger, somewhat softer sedimentary rocks. These formations tended to separate themselves from the core along a series of weak zones known as detachment faults and then slowly slid downward toward Death Valley. As they moved, the rocks were broken and jumbled into a complex of huge angular blocks. This brecciated mass is the Amargosa Chaos. Farther north in the Black Mountains, the Mormon Point, Copper Canyon, and Badwater turtlebacks show where this process went to completion and the Chaos has entirely eroded away. Here, the so-called Amargosa Turtleback was not fully exposed and the Chaos is distributed over a wide area. The light, crushed rocks at the bottom of Exclamation Hill are the core metamorphics, whereas the colorful material above is the younger cover of Crystal Spring Formation, an igneous diabase, and Noonday dolomite. The contact between the two units, the Amargosa Fault detachment, is about one-quarter of the way up the cliff face.

8.2 / 16.7 **Bradbury Well** was located on the slope just across the wash south of the road. Capped and dry, it is difficult to find and not a modern source of water. Either this or nearby Rhodes Spring may have been the site of the lodging house built in 1915 by John Salsberry for the teamsters serving his Carbonate Mine on the west side of Death Valley.

8.4 / 16.6 **Rhodes Spring Road** (GPS 35°55.165'N 116°31.417'W, north 1.2 miles; 4WD recommended). This road splits within a few feet of the pavement. The left fork goes to the spring. The right fork (4WD required) ends 1.3 miles up a sandy wash; it used to lead an additional 4 miles east to small mineral prospects near the summit of Montgomery Pass but is now closed to traffic.

Rhodes Spring was named by Albert Rhodes about the same time he located the Black Metal Mine 7 miles to the south, in 1885 or 1886. After mining all the high-grade silver ore he could, Rhodes found a potential buyer in Los Angeles but died on the trip back to Death Valley to show the property. Later, Rhodes Spring served as a millsite for other mines, and in 1906 there was enough settlement in the area for the influential *Mining World* journal to refer to the place as "a lively camp." The remnants of a small mill date to the late 1930s, and a cabin, sheds, and exotic Mojave yucca plants probably date to the 1950s. The small spring is behind the trees north of the cabin.

9.6 / 15.3 **Pegma Mine** (south 0.4 mile; hike). The Pegma Mine was a small operation on a granite pegmatite dike that was mined

Rhodes Spring verged on becoming an actual town in the early 1900s and then was abandoned before the existing shacks were built decades later.

for muscovite mica during the 1950s. More than 200 tons were produced. Most of the mica was used to provide the "sparkle" in decorative concrete products.

9.8 / 15.1   **Mister Mine** (south 1.0 mile; hike). The Mister Mine worked a small deposit of specular hematite iron ore. Most of the development took place during the 1930s. There was little more than exploratory production.

~10 / 14   This open valley is called **Bradbury Park**. The prominent mountain slightly west of due north, capped by dark basalt lava flows, is Epaulet Peak. The jagged hills to the north-east are the Calico Hills, composed of Shoshone Volcanics lava flows and ash beds. Farther east are Salsberry Peak and Sheephead Mountain, with Salsberry Pass between the two. Sheephead Pass is the open summit area south of Sheephead Mountain, and the Ibex Hills are south of there.

13.0 / 11.9   **Upper Confidence Wash Road** (GPS 35°54.846'N 116°26.562'W, southwest at a sharp angle from the highway 1.7 miles, then hiking; 4WD required). About 1.3 miles down the wash is the old American Mine Road (south, closed to vehicles), which leads 3.2 miles to the **American Mine**. Worked for lead, silver, and copper as early as 1910, it was still being explored in the 1950s. The vein contained high-grade tetrahedrite ore, but it was narrow and only a little ore was shipped.

From the American Mine Road, the Upper Confidence Wash Road continues an additional 0.4 mile to a small parking area. From there a hike of 2.0 miles down the canyon reaches the **Confidence Mine**. This was a gold mine whose ore defied efficient processing. The sparse remains of the Confidence Mill are on the floor of Death Valley beside the Harry Wade Road (Trip Route S-2).

14.2 / 10.7   **Salsberry Pass** (elevation 3,315 feet) was named for John Salsberry, a promoter of the Greenwater, Ubehebe, and other mines throughout Death Valley in the early 1900s. He built this road to serve his Carbonate and Carbonite mines on the west side of Death Valley. The rocks on both sides of the road are lava flows and ash beds of the Shoshone Volcanics. The gray, prickly shrubs that are abundant just east of the pass are Death Valley Mormon tea, *Ephedra funerea*.

~16 / 8   East across Greenwater Valley are the Greenwater Range north of the highway and the Dublin Hills to the south. Both are composed of Shoshone Volcanics. The southernmost peaks in the Greenwater Range are informally called Chocolate Sundae Mountain and Gutache Mountain, names that almost certainly are related.

18.1 / 6.8   **South Greenwater Road** (southeast; 4WD recommended because of sandy areas) passes down the valley 6.9 miles to an intersection with State Highway 127 near Tecopa Hot Springs Road. It is not a recommended route as there is nothing of particular interest along the way.

19.1 / 5.8   **Greenwater Valley Road** (GPS 35°57.992'N 116°21.821'W, north; rough in places and high-clearance recommended, but normally passable by any standard vehicle driven with caution). The Greenwater Valley Road is described as Trip Route E-3. The turnoff from the Jubilee Pass Road angles sharply to the northwest and is not marked with a highway sign.

22.0 / 2.9   East across the Amargosa Valley, the **Gerstley Mine** was a small colemanite borate mine near the base of the Resting Spring Range. The Dublin Hills south of the road are composed of the Shoshone Volcanics, mostly thick rhyolite lava flows about 6.5 million years old that rest on top of late Precambrian sedimentary rocks.

24.9 / 0.0   **State Highway 127**. The town of Shoshone (all services) is less than 2 miles south of this intersection.

Southern Death Valley, Trip Route S-2—Harry Wade Road

FROM: Ashford Junction, at the south end of the East Side Road.

TO: State Highway 127 at the Harry Wade Historical Monument, 26 miles south of Shoshone or 29 miles north of Baker, California.

ROAD CONDITIONS: 31.4 miles one-way, very rough and sandy dirt road; 4WD recommended. The southernmost 12.4 miles are more frequently maintained and usually suitable for any high-clearance vehicle.

SIDE TRIPS: Confidence Mill (walk), Owl Hole Spring Road (Side Trip S-2a, high-clearance and 4WD), Denning Spring Road (Side Trip S-2b, 4WD), Salt Basin (high-clearance, then 4WD), Saratoga Springs Road (Side Trip S-2c, high-clearance), Sheep Spring Canyon Road (4WD).

GENERAL DESCRIPTION: The Harry Wade Road is the southernmost entrance into Death Valley, but it gets little use because it is usually one of the roughest routes in the national park. It is occasionally maintained with grading, but there are always long areas of rough washboard road surfaces and deeply cut stream channels, plus a sandy crossing of the Amargosa riverbed (usually dry, but impassable when flooded).

ROAD LOG MILEAGES	southbound from Ashford Junction / northbound from State Highway 127.
0.0 / 31.4	**Ashford Junction.** The Harry Wade Road heads south from where Death Valley's East Side Road (Trip Route SC-2) curves eastward into the Black Mountains and becomes the Jubilee Pass Road (Trip Route S-1). This road was named because it was once believed to have been the "escape" route out of Death Valley by the Harry Wade family of argonauts in early 1850, but they are now believed to have traveled by way of Wingate Wash a few miles northwest of Ashford Junction.
2.5 / 28.9	Jubilee Wash drains Jubilee Mountain, directly to the northeast.
~3 / 28	This part of Death Valley is known as **The Narrows**. The **Confidence Hills** to the west are the eroded scarp of the Southern Death Valley Fault Zone, which shows a combination of vertical and horizontal right-lateral movements.
4.2 / 27.2	**Rhodes Wash** drains a large area of the Black Mountains to the northeast, and this stretch of the road is cut by numerous deep gullies, the result of nearly annual flash floods.
6.6 / 24.8	**Confidence Mill** (west 0.2 mile; walk). The Confidence Mine, about 6 miles east up Confidence Wash, was located in 1895. The gold values were so high that the mine sold for $36,000

before there was any commercial production. That was probably the only money ever made off the property. To work the ores, a 20-ton crusher mill was built on the valley floor, where water was available from a shallow well. The mill was a failure, and the operation ended in July 1896. A concrete slab with an engine mount and metal debris are left at the site. Attempts to work the Confidence Mine continued into the 1930s, but none was successful.

The Confidence Mill is the starting point for a cross-country backpacking hike into **Through Canyon**, in the Owlshead Mountains to the west (the canyon mouth is at GPS 35°48.543'N 116°37.096'W). The canyon hosts the northernmost known natural stand of smoke trees (*Psorothamnus spinosus*), a plant more typical of the Mojave and Colorado deserts to the south. The canyon penetrates the mountains to the enclosed basin of Owl Dry Lake. From there it is possible to hike either north to loop back out of the mountains through Granite Canyon or south to meet the Black Magic Mine Road (Side Trip S-2a).

12.4 / 19.0	**Amargosa River**. The river rarely flows this far, and this crossing varies from smooth and firm to deep and soft sand. When there is a flood, it is impossible for any vehicle to cross.
~ 13 / 18	The low hills with smooth slopes (east) have the informal name of **Brush Stroke Hills** because of the delicate patterns of dark eroded rocks that drape down the pastel slopes.
16.8 / 14.6	An unnamed wash cuts deeply into the alluvial fan and makes one of the roughest crossings along the Harry Wade Road. The slightly low elevation compared to the surroundings means that more near-surface moisture is available, so the creosote bushes are larger and lusher than most in this part of Death Valley.
19.0 / 12.4	**Side Trip S-2a—Owl Hole Spring Road and Microwave Road** (GPS 35°41.568'N 116°29.456'W, southwest 10.0 miles to Owl Hole Spring; high-clearance to Owl Hole Spring, then 4WD recommended beyond to Black Magic Mine or to the microwave tower). This road is normally in good shape since it leads to a recently abandoned microwave relay tower and also is occasionally used by military convoys. En route, the road leads through a wide pass between the Owlshead and Avawatz mountains to Owl Hole Spring, where a side road branches northwest to the New Deal and Black Magic mines. Farther on, Microwave Road crosses the Owl Lake and Lost Lake valleys. Some of this road and Owl Hole Spring itself lie

The Confidence Mill failed to efficiently process the refractory ore of the Confidence Mine, in the canyon to the east, and had been abandoned for several years when photographed in 1909. (Photograph attributed to A. W. Scott Jr., courtesy National Park Service, Death Valley National Park)

outside of Death Valley National Park—this area likely will be added to the park lands in the future—but most of the area, including the mines and the old microwave station, is within the park.

0.0 Turnoff from Harry Wade Road. The 10 miles to Owl Hole Spring climb a gentle alluvial fan with no points of particular interest. Much of the road is wide and solid with only one short stretch of soft gravel.

10.0 **Owl Hole Spring** (GPS 35°38.322'N 116°38.860'W) was a rest and water stop for the 20-mule teams that hauled borax from the Amargosa Borax Works during the 1880s. Starting around 1910, it was the mine camp and millsite for the New Deal and Black Magic manganese mines farther up the road. Outside of the national park, the old camp is a messy area littered with trash, a trailer, a shed, mining and milling equipment, a large bulldozer, and stockpiles of manganese ore. The place was occupied as recently as 1991. The spring is a stagnant pool surrounded by tamarisk trees, one fan palm, and reeds. It comes to the surface at a scarp that marks one of the northernmost segments of the Garlock Fault Zone.

The road forks at Owl Hole Spring. The main **Microwave Road** angles to the southwest, and the **Black Magic Mine Road** continues straight ahead. On this road:

1.0   **New Deal Mine** is less than 0.5 mile up a small canyon to the north; the road leading to it is completely washed out. The geology and mineralogy are identical to that of the Black Magic Mine at the end of the road. This was the larger of the manganese mines in this area and produced about 15,000 tons of ore during the 1910s, 1940s, and 1950s, when warfare demanded large amounts of manganese for military hardware.

2.8   Looking southward, the view is into Leach Lake Valley, which is within the U.S. Army's Fort Irwin National Training Center, where troops can often be seen training with tanks, armored vehicles, and live ammunition. Leach Lake Valley is elongated east-west along the Garlock Fault, a major left-lateral strike-slip fault along which the opposite sides have been offset by as much as 40 miles. The fault serves as the geological boundary between the Basin and Range Province and the Mojave Desert Province to the south.

3.2   A stockpile of high-grade ore from the Black Magic Mine is beside the road. 4WD vehicles are recommended beyond this point, as some of the road is badly rutted and rocky.

3.9   Just beyond a wooden ore chute is a fabulous view north over Owl Dry Lake and the northern Owlshead Mountains. Death Valley and Smith Mountain are beyond.

4.8   The **Black Magic Mine** was worked by a series of open cuts. The quarry faces expose high-grade manganese ore (primarily pyrolusite [manganese oxide] and psilomelane [manganese oxide-hydroxide] mixed with considerable powdery red-brown hematite [iron oxide]). Manganese is an important industrial metal, almost never used in pure form but vital to the production of steel; also, the alkali of ordinary alkaline batteries is manganese hydroxide. In spite of the extensive workings, this mine only produced a few hundred tons of ore. Like the New Deal Mine, the Black Magic was worked only during the war years. Note that these mines are within the national park where mineral collecting is prohibited. The Black Magic Mine Road ends at the mine.

The road log continues on Microwave Road from Owl Hole Spring.

11.2	After continuing southwest from Owl Hole Spring, bear right at this junction. According to some maps, this portion of the road is actually within the Fort Irwin National Training Center of the U.S. Army. There is a gate and signs admonish you to keep out of the military area to the south, where "war game" training exercises with live ammunition are often visible. Unexploded shells were reportedly found along the public road during the 1980s. Once upon a time this road was paved, but the old surface is now broken and very rough where traces of it remain.
12.4	The road curves back north, away from Fort Irwin and back into the national park. It crosses miles of creosote bush scrubland that is more typical of the high desert than of Death Valley.
29.1	Just where Microwave Road turns north and begins to climb up the mountain ridge, a hiking route leads about 3 miles to **Crystal Camp** at the historic Epsom Salts Mine and the remains of its **Epsom Salts Monorail** (see Appendix B). This is mostly a cross-country route. Hike west from the road until you reach a fence that marks the boundary of Naval Air Weapons Station–China Lake Range B, and then north and west along the fence to a road north to Crystal Camp (GPS 35°43.384'N, 116°56.207'W). Some wooden debris, including remnants of the monorail, is scattered about the area.
31.3	The road ends at an abandoned microwave repeater. There are wonderful views west into the restricted lands of the Naval Air Weapons Station–China Lake Range B, south into For. Irwin, and northeast over the Owlshead Mountains.

End of Owl Hole Spring Road–Microwave Road side trip.

~ 20 / 11	On the flat valley floor to the northeast, the **Amargosa River** flows as a permanent stream of bitter (*amargosa* in Spanish) salt water. It is not a likely looking habitat for fish, but the Amargosa River pupfish, *Cyprinodon nevadensis amargosae*, makes its home here and in the Amargosa River Gorge near Tecopa. The thick stands of green plants in the valley bottom near the river are arrowweed, and somewhat sparser and paler desert spinach saltbushes grow on the slopes near the road. The sandy hummocks are "locked dunes" held in place by mesquite trees.
	The wide valley extending northeast into the Ibex Hills is Buckwheat Wash, the location of the Ibex, Orient, Rusty Pick, and other silver mines that were active during the 1880s

and later as satellites of the Greenwater mining boom of 1906–1908. See Trip Route S-4.

24.1 / 7.3   **Side Trip S-2b—Denning Spring Road** (GPS 35°39.056'N 116°24.932'W, south 6.2 miles one-way; high-clearance recommended to Salt Basin, 4WD required in canyon to Denning Spring). This road is entirely outside of Death Valley National Park and ends for public travel at the boundary of the Fort Irwin National Training Center, just a short distance beyond Denning Spring. This area was included in the original national park bill but was deleted from the final legislation at the request of the military. This BLM area between the national park and military lands is expected to be added to the park in the future.

After climbing an alluvial fan, the road enters a shallow canyon in the Noble Hills. The **Salt Basin Road** forks left (GPS 35°38.574'N 116°26.210'W) 1.4 miles from the Harry Wade Road and ends in **Salt Basin**, a strange little valley completely enclosed by colorful, salt-rich rocks. Solid rock salt is exposed in the bottom of the basin. This was the destination of the proposed Amargosa Valley Railroad in the early 1900s (see Appendix C).

The Denning Spring Road continues up the canyon through the hills. The rocks are tiled and folded because this area is the intersection between the Garlock and Southern Death Valley fault zones. The rocks were deposited in a restricted desert lake about 11 million years ago and locally contain considerable rock salt, gypsum, and celestite (strontium sulfate). There are small mine prospects throughout the hills.

Above the canyon, the road angles southwest across a rocky alluvial fan and becomes rougher as it climbs. Denning Spring Canyon is a short, wide gully through faulted and broken granite where some of the shear zones were mineralized with gold-bearing quartz veins. These small mines supported the small "town" of Denning Springs in the early part of the twentieth century. The sparse remains are 6.2 miles from the Harry Wade Road. The spring is little more than a seep that supports a few small trees.

End of Denning Spring Road side trip.

24.9 / 6.5   **Salt Basin Road** (south; high-clearance recommended to a camping area, 4WD required beyond into Salt Basin). There is a wonderful flat camping area 1.2 miles from the Harry Wade Road. Vehicles with 4WD may be able to continue from there, but the road becomes very rough at best where it crosses a wash to drop into Salt Basin itself; reaching Salt Basin via the Denning Spring Road is much easier.

25.6 / 5.8   **Side Trip S-2c—Saratoga Springs Road** (north 3.9 miles one-way plus short walks to the springs and pools; improved road normally suitable for all vehicles). This road leaves the Harry Wade Road to lead north across the valley and then west to a parking area. This is a strongly recommended trip. The large pools at Saratoga Springs are one of the most important riparian habitats in the entire Death Valley region and are critical for local wildlife and migrating birds.

0.0   Turnoff from the Harry Wade Road. Each of the washes crossed by this road is a part of the Amargosa River. The smooth mud surfaces can be dangerously slick when wet.

2.4   **Amargosa River** (main channel). The riverbed is usually dry here, but there is abundant salt water within a few inches of the surface, and a permanent surface flow that supports a population of Amargosa River pupfish is just 2 miles downstream to the west.

2.7   **Ibex Junction**. Ibex Valley Road (north; 4WD required) is described as Trip Route S-4. The Saratoga Springs are to the left. If there has been recent rainfall, it may be impossible to drive beyond this intersection.

3.3   The colorful rocks up the canyon to the north are siltstone and sandstone of the Johnnie Formation of Precambrian age. Just around the next bend in the road, where there is no good parking, is thinly bedded siltstone. Some of the smooth surfaces of the slabs have markings that look like animal tracks. However, this is unlikely since the rocks date to millions of years before the first known animals were around to leave trackways. Just what caused these marks is uncertain, but they may be raindrop impressions.

3.9   **Saratoga Springs** parking area.

The **Saratoga Springs**, pools, and marshes are the largest water source and riparian environment in the southern one-third of Death Valley. They are the only home of the Saratoga Springs pupfish, *Cyprinodon nevadensis nevadensis*, which apparently breed only in the source springs but populate the open pools with numbers into the millions. These were the first of the Death Valley region pupfish to have been described, in 1889 (from specimens collected in 1881).

Saratoga Springs also have hosted at least 150 species of birds (a flamingo was seen here years ago), 15 species of reptiles and amphibians, and 18 species of mammals.

The springs were named by the Wheeler Survey in 1871, when Lt. David A. Lyle wrote: "Saratoga Springs—a fictitious name for a damnable spring, whose only merit is that of size, being actually 10 feet across at its southern end." That is an interesting comment, since there are four springs that yield about 50 gallons of water per minute. Later, between 1883 and 1888, the springs served as an important watering hole for the 20-mule team wagons hauling borax from the works at Amargosa, and a small community was developed to serve the teamsters. Even then, though, there was never a discussion about large, open pools of water.

The large pools that now cover 15 acres are partially artificial and did not exist until the early 1900s. Nitrate minerals can exist only in the driest deserts. We can now synthesize all the nitrates we need using atmospheric nitrogen, but natural deposits used to be critical for fertilizers, explosives, and chemicals. In 1909 the Pacific Nitrate Company began to explore some deposits in southern Death Valley and by 1910 there was a substantial camp of wood, stone, and tent buildings. Additional development took place in 1914 under the name of the California Nitrate Development Company. It obtained water rights to the Saratoga Springs and dug out and enlarged the small original pools to serve the processing plant—a plant that was never built because the nitrate deposits turned out to be low grade and unmineable. Additional modifications to the pools were probably done during the 1930s when the Saratoga Water Company bottled the water as a cure-all, built a health resort, and used the pools for swimming.

End of Saratoga Springs side trip.

~27 / 5   The view north takes in the Ibex Valley and the Ibex Dunes. The white scars on the mountains at the head of the valley are the Moorehouse, Pleasanton, and Monarch talc mines. These areas are described in Trip Route S-4.

29.6 / 1.8   **Sheep Creek Spring Road** (south; 4WD required) extends 4.8 miles to the Sheep Canyon talc mine near Sheep Creek Spring. The spring produces a flow of good water, which of course should be treated before drinking.

~30 / 1   To the south are the **Avawatz Mountains**. The name has had several suggested origins. The most likely source is the Indian

The stone ruins of two buildings constructed around 1884 lie next to the old road at Saratoga Springs.

From the air, the unnaturally straight sides and angled corners of the pools at Saratoga Springs are obvious. The original, smaller pools were altered during nitrate mine activities around 1909. The springs are to the right of the pools, and the access road is at the bottom of this 1972 picture.

(Photograph by Peter G. Sanchez, courtesy National Park Service, Death Valley National Park)

The Saratoga Water Company tourist camp in 1930. Guest cabins are visible at the upper right and a shed covering one of the Saratoga Springs is at the left. This was a successful enterprise until gasoline rationing during World War II eliminated tourism. (Unknown photographer, courtesy National Park Service, Death Valley National Park)

avi-ahwat, which has been translated both as Chemehuevi for "red rock" and as Shoshone for "white sheep." Another story, popular but no doubt incorrect, is that "Avawatz" is a corruption of "Eva Watts," supposedly the wife of an early storekeeper or miner.

31.4 / 0.0   **Harry Wade Monument**, junction with State Highway 127. Drivers on the highway should note that the turnoff is not signed but is next to the historical monument that is marked. Via State Highway 127 South (Trip Route S-3), this is 26.2 miles south of Shoshone and 29.4 miles north of Baker at Interstate 15. The state of California erected the historical plaque here to commemorate the trials of the 49er Harry Wade family, once believed to have escaped Death Valley at this point. Most historians are now convinced that the Wades found their escape by way of Wingate Wash, 40 miles northwest of here.

The Old Spanish Trail came out of the Amargosa River Gorge to the north and passed the west side of the **Salt Spring Hills** (the hills east of the highway) before swinging around the east end of the Avawatz Mountains en route to San Bernardino. At about the same time some of the 49ers were finally reaching the floor of Death Valley (see Chapter 3), the argonauts who stayed on the Spanish Trail with Captain Hunt found gold in the Salt Spring Hills. The actual discovery was made by James Brown and Addison Pratt, Mormon missionaries on their way to Tahiti. Although the mine was worked intermittently into the 1930s and yielded a lot of gold—only three other gold mining areas in Death Valley (Rhyolite, Skidoo, and Keane Wonder) produced more—not a single miner ever made a profit because of the remoteness of the site and extremely hard nature of the ore. Foundations, crumbling walls, and mine dumps mark the mine and camp near a small canyon where there is a permanent but brackish stream of water.

Southern Death Valley, Trip Route S-3—State Highway 127 South

FROM: Shoshone, California.

TO: Harry Wade Monument and Road.

ROAD CONDITIONS: paved all-weather highway, 26.2 miles one-way.

SIDE TRIPS: South Greenwater Valley Road (4WD), Tecopa Hot Springs and town (all vehicles), Paddy's Pride Mine (4WD), Giant Mine (4WD), Ibex Valley Road (4WD, Trip Route S-4), Dumont Dunes Road (all vehicles), Salt Spring Mine (4WD).

GENERAL DESCRIPTION: State Highway 127 lies entirely outside of Death Valley National Park, but its southernmost 10 miles serve as the park boundary. It provides direct access to the Saratoga Springs, Owlshead Mountains, and Ibex Valley areas, and a number of places along the highway are important in Death Valley's history. Just east of the highway is the spa resort area of Tecopa Hot Springs.

ROAD LOG MILEAGES	southbound from Shoshone, California / northbound from Harry Wade Monument.
0.0 / 26.2	**Shoshone, California**. This small town (permanent population about 200) offers all basic services: gas, grocery, motel,

RV park, restaurants, post office, art gallery, and museum. National Park information is available at the museum (hours of operation vary; phone 760-852-4414).

0.1 / 26.1   State Highway 178 (east) to Pahrump, Nevada (27 miles, all services), and Las Vegas (84 miles).

~4 / 22.5   The grade of the Tonopah & Tidewater Railroad is visible east of the highway for much of the distance between Shoshone and Tecopa Hot Springs Road.

5.1 / 21.1   **South Greenwater Road** (west; 4WD) connects to State Highway 178 (Trip Route S-1) but affords no particular attractions along the way.

    The horizontal layers of clay sediment in this area are called the Tecopa Lakebeds. Laid down in one of the many Ice Age lakes of the region, they contain gem-quality opals that formed as warm water related to the nearby Tecopa Hot Springs percolated through the clay.

5.3 / 20.9   **Tecopa Hot Springs (Zabriskie) Road** (east; paved all-weather road). The Tecopa Hot Springs, about 2.7 miles east of State Highway 127, support spa motels and RV parks. The Tecopa Hot Springs Campground and Pools at the springs is operated by California Land Management as a concession for Inyo County. It offers thermal baths, a campground with RV hookups, and a small convenience store and gift shop.

    The town of **Tecopa** is 1.7 miles beyond the hot springs. Although it has a population of about 100, essentially no services are available. The road through town is called the **Old Spanish Trail Highway**. The Spanish Trail came across Nevada, passed through the Pahrump Valley and over the Nopah Mountains toward Tecopa. Resting Spring (private property) a few miles northeast of Tecopa was an important layover for the pioneers, the last place where they and their animals could rest and find good feed and water before tackling the dry Mojave Desert to the south. In those days, present Tecopa was a small Southern Paiute village. It became an important mining town with the development of the Gunsight, Noonday, and other silver-lead mines to the east starting around 1906. The road west from the town leads back to State Highway 127 at milepoint 8.2/18.0.

5.5 / 20.7   **Amargosa Borax Works**. The adobe block walls on both sides of the highway are the remains of the residential community of **Amargosa**. From June to October in 1884–1888, when the summer heat made it too hot to operate the

Harmony Borax Works on the floor of Death Valley, production was shifted to this area. It was actually here that the famous 20-mule teams were devised, and they were used to haul borax following the route of the modern highway between here and the Ibex Valley Road (southbound milepoint 16.4).

8.2 / 18.0   **Old Spanish Trail Highway** (east; paved all-weather road) leads 3.8 miles to Tecopa.

9.2 / 17.0   An unmarked road (west; 4WD) leads to small mines on the east face of the Ibex Hills. The national park boundary follows the crest of the ridge.

14.1 / 12.1   **Giant Mine Road** (west; 4WD) cuts through a small part of national park land and ends at a moderate-sized talc operation 4.1 miles from the highway.

14.5 / 11.7   **Ibex Pass** (elevation 2,090 feet). By a chance of geography, the summit of Ibex Pass lies precisely at the Inyo–San Bernardino county line.

16.4 / 9.8   **Ibex Valley Road** (west, 4WD required in Ibex Valley) is separately described as Trip Route S-4. It leads to the site of the Ibex Spring mining camp and Buckwheat Wash, and via Ibex Valley, the Ibex Dunes and Saratoga Springs. From this point south to the Harry Wade Road, all land west of the highway is within Death Valley National Park.

22.1 / 4.1   **Dumont Dunes Road** (east; all vehicles). The Dumont Dunes are among the most extensive sand dunes in the California desert and are administered by the Bureau of Land Management as an authorized off-road-vehicle area. Northbound travelers begin the climb up the steep Ibex Grade. It is a long pull, and in hot weather drivers should turn off the car's air conditioning until over the summit of Ibex Pass.

22.3 / 3.9   A closed road (west) provides an easy hike 3.8 miles to a low pass through the Saddle Peak Hills and the small field of the Ibex Dunes.

24.0 / 2.2   **Amargosa River**. There is often a trickle of salty water in this part of the Amargosa River. Geologists referred in literature to the single tamarisk tree here as the "Amargosa National Forest," but it has disappeared.

25.8 / 0.4   **Salt Spring Mine Road** (east; 4WD recommended because of soft sand) passes through the Little Dumont Dunes just east of the highway and then into the Salt Spring Hills, where it ends at the Salt Spring Mine. The history of the mine is given at the end of Trip Route S-2.

Only small adobe walls remain of the borax processing camp of Amargosa.

26.2 / 0.0   **Harry Wade Monument** (west side of highway). This brass plaque commemorates the trials of the 49ers in Death Valley, noting that the Harry Wade family escaped Death Valley and rejoined the Spanish Trail at this spot. This story is now believed to be incorrect, as there is evidence that the Wade's route from Bennett's Well was southwest through Wingate Wash and Pass instead.

Unmarked but leading west from the monument is the **Harry Wade Road**. Described as Trip Route S-2, it leads into Death Valley and is the main access route to the Saratoga Springs.

South from here, State Highway 127 crosses the length of Silurian Valley and a slight divide into Silver Lake Valley before it ends at the town of Baker, California (all services), at Interstate Highway 15, 29.4 miles from the Harry Wade Monument.

Southern Death Valley, Trip Route S-4—Ibex Valley Road

FROM: State Highway 127 at a point 16.4 miles south of Shoshone, California, or 9.8 miles north of the Harry Wade Monument.

TO: Harry Wade Road at Saratoga Springs Junction.

ROAD CONDITIONS: 11.5 miles one-way, rough 4WD dirt road with areas of deep, soft sand.

SIDE TRIPS: Ibex Spring Road and Buckwheat Wash Road (Side Trip S-4a, 4WD), Superior Mine (hike), Ibex Dunes (hike), and Saratoga Springs Road (Side Trip S-2c, high-clearance).

GENERAL DESCRIPTION: Although this appears to be an excellent road at each end, within Ibex Valley there is one stretch of deep drift sand within a wash where there are also large boulders, making 4WD necessary. The side trip to Ibex Spring and Buckwheat Wash also requires 4WD. It used to be paved with concrete to the spring, but the paving is now severely broken and washed away in places, and the road in Buckwheat Wash crosses many sandy stream channels.

ROAD LOG MILEAGES	southbound from State Highway 127 / northbound from the Harry Wade Road at Saratoga Springs Junction.
0.0 / 11.5	The junction at State Highway 127 is not marked (GPS 35°46.345'N 116°19.535'W), but it leads past the obvious microwave tower near the highway. This is 1.9 miles south of the summit of Ibex Pass or 9.8 miles north of the Harry Wade Monument.
1.6 / 9.9	The gray rocks eroded into badlands on both sides of the road are rhyolite ash beds of the Ibex Pass Volcanics, a localized bit of explosive volcanism that took place about 12.5 million years ago. The rocks in the Saddle Peak Hills farther south are metamorphosed sedimentary rocks of the late Precambrian Pahrump Group.
	Most of the plants in the wash are cheesebush (*Hymenoclea salsola*), named because of the pungent cheeselike smell of its foliage. In the spring the shrubs are covered with tiny flowers surrounded by creamy-white bracts.
2.8 / 8.7	**Side Trip S-4a—Ibex Spring Road** (GPS 35°45.628'N 116°22.193'W, west 2.5 miles; 4WD required) leads to the townsite of Ibex Springs at Ibex Spring and to the start of the **Buckwheat Wash Road.**
0.0	Turnoff from the Ibex Valley Road. During talc mining days, this road was paved with concrete, but the remnants of that

are now badly broken and even washed away where the road crosses a series of deep, sandy washes.

2.5   **Ibex Spring** was first used as a millsite for the Ibex Mine in 1882, and between then and 1889 the mill is said to have produced an average of $6,000 in silver every month—it was supposed to produce much more than that, but the ore was "rebellious." The stone ruins at the base of the hill north of the spring date to that time, or to 1907 when Ibex Springs was described as "a fine camp with bunkhouses, a boarding house, etc." The existing buildings were constructed between the late 1930s and 1968 when talc mining took place at the Moorehouse, Pleasanton, and Monarch mines in the hills to the north.

    The **Ibex Springs** townsite has been adopted by the Mojave River Valley Museum of Barstow, California, which has done a photographic documentation of how fast a townsite decays when "preserved in benign neglect." Please look, but do not alter any of the remains.

    From a point just below the Ibex Springs townsite (at GPS 35°46.285'N 116°24.725'W), the **Buckwheat Wash Road** heads southwest. After winding along a sandy canyon through the Ibex Hills, it crosses Buckwheat Wash and follows that drainage north to the Ibex Mine.

7.9   The **Ibex Mine** (GPS 35°48.505'N 116°27.225'W) is 5.4 miles from Ibex Springs. The mine was located in 1881 by Frank Denning (for whom Denning Spring was named) and Stanley Miller, and after a change in ownership, it steadily produced silver until 1889. Additional mining took place around 1907, and the mine had 20 employees from 1915 to 1917. The property consists of several dangerous open cuts and collapsing tunnels that should not be entered.

8.3   The Buckwheat Wash Road ends at some small silver prospects a short distance north of the Ibex Mine, so hiking is required to reach the **Rusty Pick** (GPS 35°50.061'N 116°27.037'W) and **Evening Star** mines about 1 mile farther up the wash. The Rusty Pick was discovered in June 1906. It contained pockets of high-grade gold-copper-silver ore. Mining there continued at least into 1910.

    End of Ibex Spring Road–Buckwheat Wash Road side trip.

4.6 / 6.9   The Ibex Valley Road follows a stream channel that is filled with soft windblown sand studded with large boulders and several sharp dropoffs. 4WD vehicles are generally required.

Ibex Spring has been occupied as a townsite on three occasions: in the 1880s and again in the early 1900s when there was silver mining in the area, and then starting in the 1950s during talc mining, which is when the existing buildings were constructed.

Drive at a steady speed, do not turn sharply, and keep at least one tire on firm ground whenever possible.

6.2 / 5.3 The road crosses the bottom of Ibex Wash, another place where there is soft sand.

7.0 / 4.5 **Superior Mine** (west 1.2 miles; hike). This hike leads to the Superior and Whitecaps mines, the largest of several talc mines in the Saratoga Hills. Most of the production took place between 1941 and 1959, but some mining occurred as recently as the 1970s. The Superior Mine alone yielded 141,000 tons of high-grade steatite (the purest form of talc). The mines are now worked out, and the claims have been deeded to the National Park Service. Note that there are numerous dangerous quarry faces and mine tunnels in this area.

7.8 / 3.7 **Ibex Dunes** (east). The Ibex Dunes cover only about 2 square miles, making them the smallest dune field in the Death Valley region. They are impressive in height, however, with the sand peaks rising fully 160 feet above the valley floor. It is a 3-mile round-trip walk to the tallest of the dunes.

8.8 / 2.7 **Ibex Junction** at Saratoga Springs Road. The quarry just north of the road yielded gravel that was used to build up the road above the moist, salty ground of the Amargosa riverbed to the south. The road west leads 1.2 miles to Saratoga Springs; it and the springs are described as Side Trip S-2c.

9.1 / 2.4 **Amargosa River**. The roadbed, built up with gravel to limit flooding and avoid salty soil, crosses one of the major drainages of the Amargosa River. Although normally dry in this area, about 2 miles downstream (west) there is a perennial flow. The Amargosa River pupfish (*Cyprinodon nevadensis amargosae*) lives only there and in the permanent water of the Amargosa River Gorge near Tecopa.

11.5 / 0.0 **Saratoga Springs Junction** at the Harry Wade Road (Trip Route S-2). State Highway 127 is 5.2 miles east, and the paved East Side Road–Jubilee Pass Road intersection at Ashford junction is 25.6 miles north.

CHAPTER TWELVE

South-Central Death Valley

This is one of the most heavily visited parts of Death Valley National Park. Paved Badwater Road includes the famous attractions of Badwater, Artists Drive, the Devil's Golf Course, and Natural Bridge. The West Side Road passes numerous important historic sites with access to several canyons in the Panamint Mountains.

South-Central Death Valley, Trip Route SC-1—Badwater Road

FROM: Furnace Creek Visitor Center.

TO: Badwater.

ROAD CONDITIONS: 17.6 miles one-way, all-weather paved road.

SIDE TRIPS: Breakfast Canyon, Golden Canyon, Desolation Canyon, Artists Drive (Side Trip SC-1a), Devil's Golf Course, and Natural Bridge (all accessible to standard vehicles).

GENERAL DESCRIPTION: Because it leads to Badwater, perhaps the single most famous place in Death Valley, this is one of the major driving routes of the park. Along the way are numerous scenic, geological, and archaeological sites.

ROAD LOG MILEAGES	southbound from Furnace Creek Visitor Center / north-bound from Badwater.
0.0 / 17.6	Entrance to **Furnace Creek Visitor Center** on State Highway 190.
0.3 / 17.3	**Furnace Creek Ranch** has had a long and intriguing history. In 1874 and 1875 it was a hay farm owned by Andrew Jackson "Bellerin' Teck" Laswell, who sold the hay to teamsters at

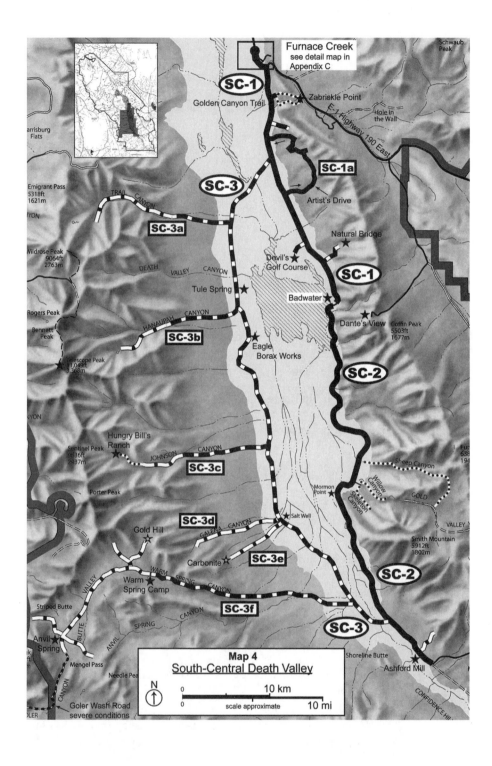

Map 4
South-Central Death Valley

N
0   10 km
0   10 mi
scale approximate

The chicken yard at "Furness Creek Ranch" in 1921. The yard was located near the highway where the date palm grove, planted that same year, stands today. (Unknown photographer, courtesy National Park Service, Death Valley National Park)

Panamint City. Then in the 1880s it became Greenland Ranch, where vegetables, fruits, and alfalfa were grown and stock was raised for the borate mining operations. When Death Valley was declared a national monument in 1933, low-cost lodging was needed. Pacific Coast Borax moved a few buildings from the town of Ryan, purchased 18 tent cabins from the construction camp at the just-completed Boulder Dam, and opened the resort in 1934. The borax company continued the operation of the resort until it was leased to the Fred Harvey Corporation in 1955. Harvey later purchased the Furnace Creek Ranch outright, and it in turn was absorbed into the modern Xanterra Parks and Resorts.

0.5 / 17.1 Road to Sunset and Texas Spring campgrounds (east). The road (west) leads into the private lands of the Timbisha Shoshone Indian Village. Please respect the privacy of the Indian residents and stay out unless they advertise a public event.

1.2 / 16.4 **Badwater Road** junction with State Highway 190 (turn south). The Furnace Creek Inn is on the hill to the north.

Built by Pacific Coast Borax, the Inn opened for business in February 1927.

1.8 / 15.8 **Breakfast Canyon** was named because of organized breakfast picnics that were conducted for early guests of the Furnace Creek Inn. This small canyon is threaded by a road about 0.3 mile long. Usually blocked to traffic by a closed gate, Breakfast Canyon provides a convenient and private walk through the yellow lake beds of the Furnace Creek Formation.

2.0 / 15.6 A fault scarp just a few feet east of the road was produced by a prehistoric earthquake. Based on the scarp's height of up to 6 feet, some have estimated that the quake's Richter magnitude might have been at least 7.0. Judging by the relative lack of erosion in places where the scarp has not been covered by recent flood debris and by the age of archaeological sites built on top of it, the quake probably took place less than 500 years ago.

2.6 / 15.0 Notice the extensive mesquite groves at the base of the alluvial fan west of the road. These trees are supported by the water that flows from Travertine Springs, located about 1 mile up State Highway 190 along Furnace Creek Wash above the Furnace Creek Inn. The water percolates down through the porous sands and gravels of the fan and then flows horizontally between the bottom of the fan and the impermeable valley fill beneath. The trees grow where the water finally nears the surface. This semicircle of vegetation provided abundant crops of mesquite beans and is one reason why the Timbisha Shoshone Village at Furnace Creek was one of the largest, though seasonal, Indian communities within the Death Valley region. Unfortunately, the trees are slowly dying and seedlings cannot take root since the water has been diverted to the resorts and campgrounds.

3.2 / 14.4 **Golden Canyon Interpretive Trail** parking area. A hiking trail offers three options: up and back within the canyon, on to the Zabriskie Point viewpoint, or looping through Gower Gulch. The Golden Canyon Trail network is described in Chapter 8.

3.9 / 13.7 **Gower Gulch** alluvial fan and arroyo. The deep, sheer-sided arroyo cutting through this alluvial fan is a result of human activity. In 1942 and 1943 the drainage through Furnace Creek Wash was artificially diverted just above Zabriskie Point into Gower Gulch in order to prevent flooding at the Furnace Creek Inn. Gower Gulch had been a small canyon with only a tiny drainage area of its own. Now, it carries the runoff from most of Furnace Creek's 200 square miles of headwaters. As a result, the canyon has been severely altered and its alluvial fan deeply cut.

4.9 / 12.7   **Desolation Canyon Road** (east 0.5 mile; dirt road, easy for any vehicle). This road is unmarked except for a sign with a "no camping" symbol. The large open area near the head of this road was the site of the first Death Valley '49er Encampment held in 1949. The road into the canyon was washed out by a flash flood in 2004 and it now ends at a small parking area. Hike another 0.5 mile east to the base of the mountains, and then south along the main drainage wash where there are several small slot canyons on the face of the Black Mountains.

5.6 / 12.0   **Borax Trenches** (west of road). About 100 feet onto the salt flat are some trenches and mounds of low-grade borax that were dug during mining claim assessment work around 1905.

6.0 / 11.6   Exit of Artists Drive, which is a one-way road. The modern entrance is 3.7 miles south (at milepoint 9.7/7.9). Historically, what is now the exit used to be the entrance of Volcano Road.

7.1 / 10.5   **West Side Road** (west; high-clearance recommended) crosses the valley and follows the eastern base of the Panamint Mountains past several historical sites. It is also the access to several mountain canyons. West Side Road is described as Trip Route SC-3.

7.8 / 9.8   Looking east, you can see some of the colors that have made the Artists Drive Formation famous.

9.7 / 7.9   **Side Trip SC-1a—Artists Drive** (east, one-way 8.9 miles to end of loop; steep and narrow paved road suitable for all standard automobiles; vehicles longer than 25 feet or wider than 9 feet not allowed because of the grades and sharp turns).

0.0   Turnoff from Badwater Road.

0.8   From the entrance, the road climbs up an alluvial fan. Stop someplace to take a close look at the surface of the fan. Later on this drive you will see cross-sections of this same kind of "fanglomerate." The rocks are dark in color because of desert varnish, a thin surface coating of iron and manganese minerals that gradually accumulates during weathering.

1.5   A trail up the hillside (right) leads to a view of an active alluvial fan, pale in color, unlike the varnished older fan surface examined at the last stop. Growing among the rocks on the hill are specimens of rigid spiny-herb, *Chorizanthe rigida*, a member of the buckwheat family. An annual, it is lush green in the spring but quickly dries to a spiny remnant that is sometimes mistaken for a cactus.

2.8 The road drops into the first of several deep washes, where it is easy to see the erosive force of desert floods. Notice the dark lava flows interbedded with lighter ash layers in the hills to the west.

3.0 The rounded, dark-green shrubs among the white-leaved desert holly are called desert fir or spruce bush (*Peucephyllum schottii*) because of the thin, needle-like leaves. It is a member of the composite (sunflower) family and in the spring has fuzzy yellow flowers at the end of every stem.

4.3 This short spur ends at **Kaleidoscope View** (a largely forgotten name), the overlook at **Artists Palette**. The rich blue, violet, and green colors of the Artists Palette are something of a mystery. Chemical analyses of these rocks, which are volcanic ashes and lavas of the Artists Drive Formation, always give nearly identical results. So how can the range of colors be explained? Apparently it is caused by slight variations in the original chemistry and degree of weathering of mica minerals within the ash. Under the right lighting conditions, especially just after a rain, the colors are intense.

4.6 Return to Artists Drive.

5.2 All along the road are exposures of fanglomerate—coarse blocks of rock contained within finer sand and gravel. Sometimes called the Funeral Formation, it represents old alluvial fans, deposits from an earlier cycle of mountain erosion. Now they are being eroded in their own turn.

5.9 SLOW DOWN! Sharp 180° curve.

6.9 Summit. In this area is a miscellany of colorful views of the Artists Drive Formation.

8.9 End of Artists Drive at Badwater Road.
End of Artists Drive side trip.

~11 / 6 Continuing south from the entrance to Artists Drive, the Badwater Road crosses a wide alluvial fan. Desert pavement—a ground surface composed of flat, compacted gravel-size stones covered with desert varnish—limits soil development and plant growth. Desert holly is virtually the only perennial growing here.

12.1 / 5.5 **Devil's Golf Course Road** (southwest 1.2 miles one-way; improved dirt road suitable for any vehicle). The Devil's Golf Course is the lowest salt flat of Death Valley but in turn is

The Devil's Golf Course is composed of salt that has weathered into exceptionally jagged forms because of both rain and wind.

only the top of a sequence of mixed clay and salt beds at least 1,500 feet thick. Groundwater is constantly seeping into the beds. As it rises to the surface, bringing dissolved salt with it, the forces of evaporation and crystallization buckle the crust upward along fractures and extrude pinnacles. Aided by rain and wind erosion, the formations develop razor-sharp edges and points, between which are fresh, pure-white pans of new salt.

When moisture, temperature, and seepage conditions are all just right, weird worm-like growths of salt develop upward and outward from the more massive formations. These grow in exactly the same way as do helictites in underground caverns. Water carries a bit of dissolved salt to the end of a mineral tube and then deposits a new ring of salt at the end of the tube as it evaporates. Please do not touch these growths; they are extremely fragile.

The **Pluto Salt Pools**, open pools of saturated salt water lined with exquisite salt crystals, are scattered around this area. Old pools constantly fill themselves in, but new ones always develop to replace the old. Although a 1938 guidebook stated: "The salt forms so rapidly that the pools must be blasted each year," that unnecessary practice was discontinued long ago. Long-term drought lowers the water table and the pools dry up; wetter seasons bring more water and new pools form, as happened extensively following the extraordinarily wet year of 2005.

14.1 / 3.5 **Natural Bridge Road** (1.5 miles one-way; steep and rough in places, but accessible to all standard vehicles; large motor homes and vehicles with trailers not recommended). Next to the parking area at the end of the road is a kiosk with information about Natural Bridge and its canyon. The opening beneath the bridge, which is 0.5 mile up the canyon, is 50 feet wide and 30 feet high; the rock arch is about 30 feet thick. It is possible to hike beyond the bridge about 1 mile up the canyon to where a dry waterfall blocks the way.

15.2 / 2.4 The smoothly curving mountainside visible to the east is the Badwater turtleback. The exposed rocks are Precambrian metamorphic gneiss and schist about 1.8 billion years old. At one time younger sedimentary rocks lay on top of these. As Death Valley and its mountains were formed, tension caused the younger, softer rocks on top of the metamorphics to physically slide downward toward the valley. Shattered by the movement, they quickly eroded away, leaving the harder, erosion-resistant metamorphic rocks exposed. The slip surface separating the different rock units is a detachment fault. There are two other turtlebacks farther south in the Black Mountains, beyond Badwater. Another area, known as the Amargosa Chaos, in which the rocks have been severely broken into a "megabreccia," represents another place where the detachment process was not completed. These places are described in Trip Routes SC-2 and S-1.

16.2 / 1.4 Traces of a fault scarp can be seen just east of the road. This scarp probably resulted from the same earthquake that produced the scarp 2 miles south of the Furnace Creek Inn.

17.6 / 0.0 **Badwater** (parking lot, interpretive signs, and chemical toilets). Although a sign here has claimed this to be the lowest point in North America, that is not quite the case. The honor goes to two spots out on the salt flats, both of which are officially listed as lying 282 feet below sea level. Badwater is "only" 279 feet below sea level. Notice the "sea level" sign high on the cliffs across the road. The famous vista of Dante's View is more than a mile up those same cliffs (see Trip Route E-2).

The water in Badwater Spring is not poisonous, as some early tourist brochures claimed. It is actually very similar to

Badwater is probably the most famous single place in Death Valley. The pool of salty water lies 279 feet below sea level whereas the summit of Telescope Peak in the Panamint Mountains beyond is 11,049 feet above sea level.

seawater, except that it contains more calcium and carbonate and is slightly more saline as a result. Accordingly, plants and animals live here. Along the shore of the pond are pickleweed (*Salicornia rubra*). In the water are numerous insects, other arthropods, and the Badwater snail (it is about the size of this capital letter "O"), which is known to live only in this one small pool. Please stay on the boardwalk.

Badwater is the hottest known place in the world. Death Valley's record high temperature of 134°F (56°C) was registered at Furnace Creek Ranch on July 10, 1913. (The World Meteorological Association has stripped Azizia, Libya, of its reported higher temperature.) However, for one year a weather-recording station was maintained at Badwater. Its temperatures were consistently hotter than those at Furnace Creek. Some authorities believe that when it was 134°F at Furnace Creek, it probably was several degrees hotter at Badwater.

A hiking route extends from Badwater out onto the salt flats. How far you want to walk is your decision. It is rough in places, but eventually you can reach those lowest spots in all of North America, one of which was surveyed by the U.S. Geological Survey as being at GPS 36°14.513'N 116°49.533'W.

South-Central Death Valley, Trip Route SC-2—East Side Road

FROM: Badwater.

TO: Ashford Junction at the east end of Jubilee Pass Road (Trip Route S-1).

ROAD CONDITIONS: 28.9 miles one-way, paved all-weather road.

SIDE TRIPS: Ashford Mill (all vehicles) and Ashford Canyon (4WD).

GENERAL DESCRIPTION: This route, which is also known as South Badwater Road, boasts relatively few specific points of interest, but when combined with Jubilee Pass Road it is a good alternative to State Highways 190 and 127 between Death Valley and Shoshone. It is somewhat longer and slower, but it is a much more scenic drive.

ROAD LOG MILEAGES	southbound from Badwater / northbound from Ashford Junction.
0.0 / 28.9	**Badwater**. The East Side Road is the southward continuation of the Badwater Road.
1.3 / 27.6	The pure-white salt pan of Death Valley's floor is immediately next to the road, more accessible here than in any other

part of the valley. Although the deposit is composed mostly of common table salt, it tastes bitter because of the presence of small amounts of other salt minerals such as calcium chloride, sodium sulfate, and alum.

2.9 / 26.0 A prominent fault scarp is visible up the alluvial fan at the base of the cliffs east of the road. This same scarp lies near the road at many places both north and south of here.

3.9 / 25.0 A series of salt pools similar to Badwater lie at the base of the alluvial fan just west of the road.

6.8 / 22.1 **Coffin Canyon** (east) cuts into the Black Mountains and eventually leads up near Dante's View. Although the name is undoubtedly related to "Death" Valley and "Funeral" Range, a popular story holds that the canyon, a mountain, and a mine were named after a Mr. Coffin who was associated with the Greenwater copper boom around 1906. This is unlikely, however, as there is no other record of such a person, and the Coffin Mine was opened for gold, not copper, in the 1920s.

8.5 / 20.4 **Copper Canyon** (east) slices into the Black Mountains at the top of a large alluvial fan. The mountain immediately to the south is the Copper Mountain turtleback. Composed of hard, erosion-resistant metamorphic rocks, its uplift caused softer, younger rocks on top to slide down along a detachment fault into Death Valley, where they were eroded away. The Badwater turtleback to the north and Mormon Point turtleback to the south are similar in the way they were formed.

9.5 / 19.4 The Mormon Point (or Smith Mountain) turtleback is directly south of this point. **Willow Creek Canyon** just east of the mountain leads to Gold Valley, the site of two early mining camps. The bright white spots on the mountains across Death Valley are the talc mines of **Galena Canyon**.

12.8 / 16.1 **Sheep Canyon** (east) slices far into the Black Mountains. Overnight backpackers can follow the canyon past Sheep Spring, through a pass into Gold Valley, then down Willow Creek, and back to Death Valley. Moderate rock-climbing skills are needed for parts of this hike, which is a strenuous round-trip loop of 22 miles.

16.1 / 12.8 **Mormon Point**. Nobody knows how or why this spot got its name, only that it first appeared on a map published in 1891.

18.1 / 10.8 A large pool of salt water is just west of the road.

19.9 / 9.0 **Coyote Hole** is a pool of brackish water surrounded by a thick growth of rushes on the west side of the road.

Across the valley, the low pass between the Owlshead Mountains (south) and Panamint Mountains (north) is

Wingate Pass, at the west end of Long Valley. The valley is drained by Wingate Wash. It was the route out of Death Valley for some of the emigrants in 1850 and later was used by the 20-mule team borax wagons.

21.3 / 7.6   The low, red hill a short distance southwest across the valley is **Cinder Hill**, a cinder cone that was split in two by horizontal movements on the Southern Death Valley Fault Zone. See Trip Route SC-3, milepoint 33.9 / 1.7, for more about this curious volcano.

24.3 / 4.6   Just east of the road, a fault scarp more than 50 feet high exposes basalt lava flows. A series of "locked dunes" held in place by large mesquite trees lines the bottom of the valley to the west.

25.2 / 3.7   **West Side Road** (west; high-clearance recommended) is a dirt route that follows the west side of Death Valley's salt flats, passing several important historical sites and roads into Panamint Mountain canyons. It joins the paved Badwater Road between Badwater and Furnace Creek. It is described as Trip Route SC-3.

25.6 / 3.3   An interpretive sign describes Lake Manly and **Shoreline Butte** across the valley. As Lake Manly slowly evaporated away at the end of the last Ice Age, erosion left wave-cut beaches and terraces all around Death Valley. Shoreline Butte has some of the best examples.

26.9 / 2.0   **Ashford Mill** (west 0.2 mile) was built in 1914 to process the gold ore from the Golden Treasure Mine in Ashford Canyon to the east. Although it operated for several years, the mill was never a truly profitable concern. The walls are thick because the owners received twice as much concrete as they ordered, so they used it all.

The **Ashford Canyon Road** (east 3.0 miles; 4WD) leads east toward the mountains opposite the Ashford Mill Road and ends at the canyon mouth. From there it is a hike of about 1.5 miles to the Golden Treasure Mine, which supplied gold ore to the Ashford Mill. You will find the remains of a few buildings and lots of mining debris. The mine was discovered in 1907. The value of its early production is unknown but was substantial enough that the property was sold for $150,000 in 1914. It was following this that the Ashford Mill was built to process the ore. Unfortunately, the mill was not very efficient, and it ultimately yielded only $125,000 worth of gold.

Scotty's Canyon is the first canyon north of Ashford Canyon. It can be reached by an easy 1-mile hike from the

The Ashford Mill was still a substantial building in 1942, but only massive concrete foundations and walls remain today. (Photograph by W. H. Alexander, courtesy National Park Service, Death Valley National Park)

end of the Ashford Canyon Road. There are several erosional caves in the canyon walls, one of which was Death Valley Scotty's "Camp Holdout" when he was courting the financial support of wealthy eastern grubstakers years before the construction of Scotty's Castle.

28.9 / 0.0 **Ashford Junction**. The paved highway continuing east from this intersection is the Jubilee Pass Road, described as Trip Route S-1. The dirt road continuing south through the rest of Death Valley to State Highway 127 is the Harry Wade Road, Trip Route S-2, a long, rough trip on which 4WD vehicles may be required.

South-Central Death Valley, Trip Route SC-3—West Side Road

FROM: Badwater Road 7.1 miles south of State Highway 190.

TO: East Side Road 3.7 miles north of Ashford Junction.

ROAD CONDITIONS: 35.6 miles one-way, rough dirt road often open to all vehicles but with high-clearance recommended.

SIDE TRIPS: Trail Canyon Road (Side Trip SC-3a, 4WD), Hanaupah Canyon Road (Side Trip SC-3b, 4WD), Johnson Canyon Road (Side Trip SC-3c, 4WD), Galena Canyon Road (Side Trip SC-3d, 4WD). Queen of Sheba Mine Road (Side Trip SC-3e, 4WD), and Warm Spring Canyon–Butte Valley Roads (Side Trip SC-3f, high-clearance, then 4WD); plus short spurs to Tule Spring, Shorty's Well, and Eagle Borax Works.

GENERAL DESCRIPTION: The West Side Road parallels the base of the Panamint Mountains along the western side of Death Valley. It follows the route taken by the Bennett-Arcan party of 49ers and later by the 20-mule-team wagons. There are several important historic sites along the way, and the West Side Road also provides access to scenic canyons in the Panamint Mountains.

ROAD LOG MILEAGES	southbound from Badwater Road / northbound from East Side Road.
0.0 / 35.6	Junction with the Badwater Road (Trip Route SC-1) at a point 7.1 miles south of State Highway 190.
1.8 / 33.8	**Salt Creek** is the drainage from northern Death Valley to the salt flats near Badwater. Only when there has been substantial rainfall is there an actual stream at this crossing, but there are usually a few small pools of saturated salt water in the area. The puddles are often covered with thin layers of salt crystals formed by the rapid evaporation of the water. These pure-white formations are mostly common table salt (sodium chloride) but taste bitter because of the presence of other compounds, including potassium chloride, calcium chloride, sodium sulfate, and alum.
	The rugged areas surrounding Salt Creek are part of the **Devil's Golf Course**, where salty water seeps upward, fracturing and buckling the ground into jagged pinnacles. Imagine, if you can, having to build a wagon road across these formations, which is what the Bennett-Arcan party of 49ers did in December 1849 and January 1850. Their route was later followed by the Chloride Cliff Road of the 1870s and the 20-mule-team wagon road in the 1880s. Traces of the old route are barely visible about 0.25 mile north of the modern road.
3.7 / 31.9	**Devil's Speedway**. Compared to the nearby Devil's Golf Course, this damp mud flat is deceptively smooth. But do not drive too fast—large holes, swales, and jarring drainage chan-

Alluvial fans are covered with a layer of desert pavement, pieces of gravel efficiently fitted together in a mosaic that prevents the growth of most plants.

nels scar the road. This area is covered by lakes several feet deep during wet winters, such as those of 1983 and 2005.

4.2 / 31.4 The plants along the road are pickleweed (*Salicornia rubra*), a halophyte that can grow with its roots in saturated salt water.

5.2 / 30.4 **Side Trip SC-3a—Trail Canyon Road** (GPS 36°18.187'N 116°53.430'W, west 9.5 miles one-way; high-clearance to canyon mouth, then 4WD required). This road climbs the Trail Canyon alluvial fan, and then follows the floor of Trail Canyon to its three forks. The first 4.5 miles can cautiously be driven by standard vehicles, although there are some high centers and one very rough wash crossing. High-clearance 4WD is required within the canyon because of high centers, large rocks, sharply canted roadbeds, and sharp curves in the soft gravel of the wash.

0.0 Turnoff from the West Side Road. The first part of the road to the canyon crosses nearly barren desert pavement—rocks and pebbles fitted together with a jigsaw puzzle–like fit that prevents plant roots from penetrating into the soil beneath.

4.5 The road enters Trail Canyon by dropping steeply into the wash. The most common plant in the canyon is desert broom; stingbush and brittlebush are also found. On high-standing "islands" are scattered shrubs of creosote and desert fir.

7.0 The road passes next to the cliff face. This rock is Paleozoic limestone, as is most of the rock in Trail Canyon.

9.3 The old road to Aguereberry Point branches to the right into the North Fork of Trail Canyon. It is barely visible on the canyon floor but can be seen switchbacking up the mountainside far above. The road climbed more than 2,500 feet in just 4 miles. It was a dangerous route and when some of it washed in the 1980s, it was permanently closed to vehicles. About 0.5 mile along this road is the **Tarantula Mine**, a profitable tungsten producer during the 1950s. The mine's owners built the road up the mountain and the Broken Pick millsite camp at the nearby forks of the canyon.

9.4 The road branches into the Middle Fork (straight ahead) and South Fork (left) of Trail Canyon. The south fork road used to extend about 1.5 miles to the **Old Dependable Mine**, which produced antimony, and some springs that support a small stream and lush riparian habitat. Beyond the springs are the remains of a tramline that served small lead-silver mines still farther up the mountain. This road is in extremely poor condition and only marginally drivable in vehicles that have exceptionally high clearance.

9.5 Just up the Middle Fork is the mining camp at the **Broken Pick Millsite** (GPS 36°19.036'N 117°02.702'W), established during the heyday of the Tarantula Mine and other tungsten operations in the early 1950s. The Tarantula might have been Death Valley's only truly profitable metal mine during that entire decade. It led to a considerable prospecting rush into Trail Canyon and vicinity. Hundreds of mining claims were filed in the area by dozens of prospectors, and Broken Pick, intended as a company-owned milling and residential camp, became a sort of community center. People obviously intended to return here because the remaining buildings and trailer were left with beds, chairs, a dresser, water heaters, and stoves; much trash and two junk cars also litter the site.

The middle fork road ends at Broken Pick, but hikers can continue another 1 mile to the **Ronald A. Millsite** near the Victory Tungsten Mine. The Victory was originally located in the early 1900s, but no significant mining took place there until World War II, when there was a large demand for tung-

The Lucky Find Millsite is in the South Fork of Trail Canyon, a hike of about 1.5 miles from the Trail Canyon Road. (Photo by Park Ranger Hill, courtesy National Park Service, Death Valley National Park)

sten. High-grade ore was shipped in 1943, and there was additional activity in the 1950s. There is a small spring just beyond the mine.

End of Trail Canyon Road side trip.

5.9 / 29.7   East of the West Side Road is an area of small sand hummocks anchored in place by mesquite trees and arrowweed.

9.4 / 26.2   **Tule Spring** (east 0.2 mile to parking area). Within the dense stand of arrowweed right next to the parking area is a small pool of marginally drinkable water. (As with any natural water source, it should be treated before use.) It is interesting that no tules grow here, although they do at the Eagle Borax Works, about 3 miles to the south.

10.6 / 25.0   **Shorty's Well** (east 0.1 mile to turnaround). Although there was no natural spring here, there is freshwater only about 6 feet below the surface. Shorty's Well tapped this supply with a hand pump mounted on a concrete base right next to the car turnaround. The pump is now gone and the well hole is filled with rocks, so water is not available here. The well was named for Alexander "Shorty" Borden, who also built the Hanaupah Canyon Road to serve his mines.

Side Trip SC-3b—Hanaupah Canyon Road (GPS 36°13.536'N 116°52.883'W, west 8.3 miles one-way; 4WD required). Like all the other canyon routes leading west from the West Side Road, the Hanaupah Canyon Road begins by climbing up a sloping alluvial fan that supports little vegetation other than a scattering of creosote bushes and desert holly. Some of the first part of the road is very rough and rocky, and 4WD vehicles are definitely needed to navigate through the gravel of the canyon floor.

The name "Hanaupah" was probably derived from the Indian *hunup'i*, the root for "canyon," plus *pah*, which means "water." Thus, the name might be translated as "Water Canyon." This interpretation is supported by the modern Timbisha; alternate published translations that refer to bears are clearly incorrect.

0.0	Turnoff from West Side Road.
0.8	**Hanaupah Fault Scarp**. Up to 25 feet high and one of the largest in Death Valley, this scarp exists only on the Hanaupah Canyon alluvial fan. Its curving form and limited extent imply that this is a low-angle detachment fault.
4.8	The road drops into Hanaupah Wash and the canyon.
5.5	The outcrop right next to the road is Precambrian age sandstone metamorphosed into quartzite. Many of the boulders in the wash are studded with large, rectangular crystals (phenocrysts) of potassium feldspar. This is the Little Chief granite porphyry that composes much of Telescope Peak.
6.8	High on the cliffs to the north is an angular unconformity—the rocks below it were uplifted, tilted, and eroded before the rocks on top were deposited.
8.3	The road gradually becomes the bed of Hanaupah Creek, which flows from a series of springs about 0.5 mile farther up the canyon. It is possible to drive a short distance beyond the first water only if your vehicle has exceptionally high clearance; otherwise, it is an easy walk. The springs discharge more than 250 gallons per minute and support an extensive riparian habitat with abundant wildlife. The small mines and cabin of "Shorty" Borden are on the hillside above the springs.

End of Hanaupah Canyon Road side trip.

12.1 / 23.5	**Dayton-Harris Graves** (historical monument at east side of road). In July 1898, Jim Dayton, the caretaker of the Furnace Creek Ranch, began a trip to Daggett to get supplies. Ill at

Snowclad Telescope Peak is reflected in one of the pools at Eagle Borax Works. This was probably the location of Bennett's Long Camp in 1850.

the time, he managed to cover barely 20 miles in the mid-summer heat. He was buried where he was found, along with his wagon mules. Years later, Frank "Shorty" Harris, who had discovered Rhyolite's Original Bullfrog and many other mines, was laid to rest here at his request. The monument reads: "Bury me beside Jim Dayton in the Valley we loved. Above me write 'Here lies Shorty Harris, a single blanket jackass prospector.'—Epitaph requested by Shorty (Frank) Harris, 1856–1934. Here lies Jas. Dayton, perished, 1898.—To these trailmakers whose courage matched the dangers of the land, this bit of earth is dedicated forever."

12.6 / 23.0   **Eagle Borax Works** (east 0.1 mile to parking area). Isadore Daunet found borax on the floor of Death Valley in 1875, but not until the later discovery of more borax by Aaron Winters in 1881 and the pending development of those deposits into the Harmony Borax Works near Furnace Creek did he decide to work his own property. Daunet constructed the Eagle Borax Works and began production in 1882, but the output was limited and impure. Daunet went bankrupt, lost his home and wife as well as the mine, and committed suicide in 1884.

The large mound next to the interpretive sign is partially processed borax that was never shipped to market. Beyond the rush-filled pools are scattered mounds of unprocessed ore.

"Bennett's Long Camp," where the Bennett, Arcan, and other families camped in January and February 1850, was probably here rather than at Bennett's Well, 3 miles south.

A few years ago Eagle Borax was marked by huge tamarisk trees. A National Park Service eradication program begun in the 1970s largely succeeded in removing the invasive, nonnative plants. Natural pools of water choked by bulrush and Cooper rush have returned, and the surrounding acres are covered with yerba mansa, alkali sacaton, and salt grass.

15.8 / 19.8 **Bennett's Well** (GPS 36°09.969'N 116°51.728'W at the well, east 0.3 mile walk among groves of large mesquite trees). A California state historical marker next to the road tells the story about "Bennett's Long Camp," the long stay by the Bennett, Arcan, and other 49er families in early 1850 while awaiting the return of Manly and Rogers with supplies. According to the sign, the camp was located here, but it more likely was at the later site of the Eagle Borax Works—the 49ers camped where there was no shade, but there are large mesquite trees around Bennett's Well. The name seems to have been given by Asa Bennett, after himself, during a prospecting trip in 1860. In one of those curious duplications of names, Bennett's Well was improved by Charles Bennett, a freighter during the Harmony Borax days, and in its time it had a wind pump, barns, and feed storage bins. Now those structures and the well have disappeared.

17.2 / 18.4 Note the huge boulders on the alluvial fan below **Starvation Canyon** to the west. Some of them are 10 feet high with at least as much hidden below ground. These rocks were carried out of the canyon by the kind of flash flood called a debris flow—more mud and rock than water. Imagine how much force would be needed to even budge such a boulder, yet alone carry hundreds of them as far as several miles.

21.7 / 13.9 **Side Trip SC-3c—Johnson Canyon Road** (GPS 36°05.889'N 116°50.723'W, west 9.8 miles one-way; high-clearance vehicles can negotiate the first 5 miles, 4WD vehicles are required in the canyon). Johnson Canyon is named after William Johnson, who established a truck farm and sold vegetables to the miners at Panamint City in the mid-1870s. After the end of the mining, Johnson's farm was taken over by Hungry Bill, a Timbisha Shoshone, and he raised squash, melons, corn, wheat, beans, alfalfa, grapes, peaches, and figs. Hungry Bill's Ranch is the best known attraction in Johnson Canyon. It is a rigorous hike from the end of the road, but along the way there are gushing springs, dense vegetation along a year-round stream, several small mines and primitive milling works (these might relate to the brief 1907 mining camp of **Shadow Mountain**), many interesting geological structures, and tremendous scenery. Johnson Canyon is one place within Death Valley that you should make every effort to see.

0.0 Turnoff from the West Side Road. Like all of these side roads, the first several miles are a gradual climb up the alluvial fan. The road is fairly rough, but there are no dangerously high centers.

6.1 The remains of a burro loading pen, apparently used during the roundups in the 1980s, is next to the road just before the drop into the canyon.

6.4 The road pitches down a steep grade into Johnson Canyon. The drive from here is entirely within the wash, with many areas of loose gravel and large rocks in the roadbed where 4WD is required.

8.8 Angling left is the South Fork of Johnson Canyon where a closed road provides a hiking route up the canyon. After about 1 mile, the canyon splits and an additional 0.5 mile up each fork leads to several gushing springs: the Dog Springs in the north branch and Feather Spring and Greenleaf Spring in the south branch, all flowing several tens of gallons of water per minute. There are small mining prospects in both canyons.

9.8 **Wilson Spring** is just beyond the end of the road. This is a beautiful spot, shaded by large cottonwood trees among willows and grass. The spring discharges about 6 gallons per minute, enough to form a short but considerable stream. Remember, camping within 100 feet of any water source is illegal in Death Valley, and here the Park Service requests that you park where the stream reaches the road below the oasis.

The hike to Hungry Bill's Ranch begins at Wilson Spring. The old trail was recently improved but can still be difficult to find in places. Look for it cutting the hillsides, sometimes north and sometimes south of the canyon bottom, much of which is choked by dense willow groves along a dashing mountain stream. The ranch (GPS 36°05.668'N

Low stone walls and fruit trees remain at Hungry Bill's Ranch in upper Johnson Canyon.

117°02.114'W) is a strenuous round trip of about 4 miles. See Chapter 8 for details.

End of Johnson Canyon Road side trip.

22.4 / 13.2 The scars on the mountain above Galena Canyon (south-west) are open-cut talc mines that stopped operating in 1981. Somewhere in this area was **Gravel Well**, once said to have "the sweetest water in Death Valley." The well went dry many years ago and was capped.

24.1 / 11.5 **Mesquite Well**, within the mesquite groves about 200 feet east of the road, was a poor but vital water source to the 20-mule teams of the 1880s. The well was abandoned years ago, and the site is now only an area of damp ground among mesquite trees, arrowweed bushes, and debris. This general area must also have been the location of a "sulfurous water hole" that was briefly used by the emigrants in January 1850 before they moved back north to better water at Bennett's Long Camp.

25.4 / 10.2 **Side Trip SC-3d—Galena Canyon Road** (west 5.4 miles one-way; 4WD recommended). Although Galena Canyon has some interesting attributes—most authorities believe that it was the "escape route" for the Bennetts, the Arcans, Manly, and Rogers in 1850—it does not match the scenic qualities of

Johnson, Hanaupah, or Trail canyons to the north. Talc mining was the entire reason for this road's existence.

0.0   Turnoff from the West Side Road. The alluvial fan is covered with a typical barren desert pavement surface.

4.4   The road (south) to the Bonney Talc Mine, the lowest of the Galena Canyon mines, has been blocked and scarified to prevent vehicle access. Although these were open-cut mines, they are nearly as dangerous as underground mines. The steep faces of such cuts can give way, especially when the mineral is soft like talc.

4.6   The Mammoth Mine workings are high on the south face of the canyon. Of the two big tanks, one once held diesel fuel and the other ammonium nitrate, the ingredients of an explosive used in mining.

4.7   The road (south) to the Mammoth Mine is extremely steep and badly washed in places. If you must go up to the mine, then please walk and stay well away from the open-cut mine faces.

5.1   The Galena Canyon Road splits in two directions. The north branch continues up the main channel of Galena Canyon but ends in only another 0.4 mile at a deep washout.

5.4   The south branch of the road ends in a side canyon at the large ore-loading chute of the White Eagle Talc Mine. Some of the specimens of talc are a beautiful silky, translucent, pastel green. This talc is 100 percent pure steatite, the highest quality talc—but remember that mineral collecting is not allowed. A hike of about 0.5 mile up the canyon from the end of this road leads to Talc Springs, two seeps that support small areas of vegetation a bit more lush than the surroundings.

End of Galena Canyon Road side trip.

25.5 / 10.1   **Salt Well** (east, among mesquite trees near two water tanks). As the name implies, this well (actually 2 deep holes) yielded brackish water unsuitable for drinking. It disappeared years ago. Most of the smaller shrubs in this area are inkweed (*Sueda moquinii*) and honey sweet, plants that can tolerate the alkaline soil conditions just above the salt flats. A new primitive campground is planned for this site.

Side Trip SC-3e—Queen of Sheba Mine Road (GPS 36°01.802'N 116°49.768'W, west 3.8 miles one-way; 4WD required). This road was graded arrow-straight up the alluvial fan. It completely ignores anything in its path and cuts

Miscellaneous wood and stone ruins remain at the Queen of Sheba Mine.

directly across numerous active washes, making this a slow, rough trip. There is no point of specific interest along the way, but the mines were among Death Valley's most profitable and boast extensive ruins. Through their history, these mines yielded more than 5 million pounds of lead along with small amounts of copper, silver, and gold.

The site of the mining camp at the Queen of Sheba Mine consists of two wooden buildings, an outhouse, ore-loading bins, and the remains of processing works. These date to the 1940s, when the Queen of Sheba was extensively worked. It had enough potential to merit the construction of a new mill in 1947, but actual production was minimal.

On the ridge north of the Queen of Sheba are the Carbonite and Carbonate mines, named because their ore contained large amounts of lead carbonate (the mineral cerussite). These properties were mined by Jack Salsberry between 1908 and the end of World War I. The town of **Carbonite** (a name supported by archival documents) boasted several stores in its time, but little remains at its site in the wash north of the Queen of Sheba camp (see Appendix A).

All of these mine workings are unstable. For safety's sake, keep out.

End of Queen of Sheba Mine Road side trip.

32.7 / 2.9   **Side Trip SC-3f—Warm Springs Canyon Road and Butte Valley Road** (GPS 35°57.248'N 116°44.799'W, west 11.0 miles to Warm Spring Camp and 22.3 miles to Anvil Spring Junction; high-clearance vehicles first 11 miles, then 4WD required to Butte Valley). Butte Valley, named after Striped Butte in the middle of the valley, is one of Death Valley's best known and most heavily visited backcountry areas. The miners who built the cabins in the valley were contemporaries of "Shorty" Harris, Pete Aguereberry, and other famous prospectors, but rather than wandering throughout the region, they stayed near Butte Valley and were more profitable as miners. Warm Spring Canyon, the eastern entry road, was the site of the largest-scale talc mining in Death Valley. Goler Wash, the route from the west, is famous as a rugged "road with serious character."

0.0   Turnoff from the West Side Road. This road was maintained by frequent grading while the talc mines were in operation, but now the road is deteriorating.

The Wingate Wash Road once led southwest from near here, snaking up Long Valley, over Wingate Pass, and down into Panamint Valley. This route was used by the Wade and Earhart families in 1850, silver miners in the 1870s, borax wagons in the 1880s, manganese miners in the 1910s and 1940s, and another silver producer in the 1970s. Part of it was even followed by the Epsom Salts Monorail in the 1920s. But the road was closed when it washed out in 1993, and today the route provides a true wilderness hike.

4.0   **Anvil Spring Canyon Wash** drains Butte Valley through Anvil Spring Canyon.

7.2   The road (south) leads 1.2 miles to the Panamint Mine, the easternmost of many talc mines in and about Warm Spring Canyon. The massive black cliffs near the canyon entrance are made of an iron-rich igneous rock called diabase, and the bedded rocks are dolomitic limestone of the Precambrian age Crystal Springs Formation. The white streaks and blotches near the contacts between these two kinds of rock are talc, produced by hydrometamorphism (recrystallization accompanied by the addition of water) of the dolomite by the diabase intrusions. There are hundreds of talc deposits in this part of Death Valley, but only those that were large and pure were mined.

8.6   The large mine dumps on the south side of the road are from the Grantham, or Big Talc, Mine, a series of pits and underground tunnels between here and Warm Spring. This was the single largest and longest-lived of all the talc mines in the Death Valley region. The operation was permanently shut down in 1988 and the property is now owned by the National Park Service.

10.7 The **Pink Elephant Mine** (north), high on the north wall of the side canyon, was developed for fluorite (calcium fluoride), a vital industrial mineral used as a flux in the steel and other metallurgical industries, for processing aluminum ore, and in the production of hydrofluoric acid and fluorine gas. However, large volumes are necessary before a fluorite mine will pay. The veinlets at the Pink Elephant Mine contain as much as 65 percent fluorite by volume but are much too small to have supported a bona fide mine.

11.0 **Warm Spring Camp** (GPS 35°58.097'N 116°55.798'W). At first glance, the buildings look new, but they have actually been abandoned since the 1980s. Among them are houses and a large bunkhouse, a garage, a repair shop, and milling equipment. The springs within the trees flow more than 15 gallons of lukewarm water each minute, providing a considerable stream and keeping a swimming pool filled. Camping is allowed in the old house and on the grounds.

Nearer the road are the rusty remains of the **Gold Hill Mill**. It was apparently built in 1939 and was rather innovative. Much of the grinding of gold ore was done by a mechanized arrastre that was powered by a diesel engine rather than animals, so it is much larger than is usual. The equipment also includes a complex set of flywheels; a serpentine belt-and-pulley system; a set of jaw, cone, and ball crushers; an ore bin and chute; and conveyor belts. Most of the ore came from the Panamint Treasure Mine high in the mountains to the northwest.

Beyond Warm Spring, the road to Butte Valley is very rough in places. It is especially bad next to the Gold Hill Mill, but there is no bypass through the camp.

12.7 Panamint-Montgomery Mine Road (north) has all but washed away. It used to lead up the mountain to another large open-pit talc mine.

13.3 The **Contact Mine** is the small quarry on the north side of the road. It was worked for wollastonite, a calcium silicate mineral used in ceramics. Specimens show bladed crystals as much as 3 inches long and half as wide. Please remember that mineral collecting is illegal within the park.

The Gold Hill Mill, next to the road in Warm Spring Canyon, was built in 1939 and crushed gold ore from several nearby mines into the 1950s.

15.4   **Arrastre Spring–Gold Hill Road** (GPS 35°59.132'N 117°00.025'W, north; 4WD required). These roads separate about 0.2 mile from the Warm Springs Canyon Road.

Arrastre Spring (2.2 miles along the northwest fork, then 0.5 mile hike) is little more than a seep, and most of the flow is lost in a boggy area. Arrastre Spring is believed to have been the first campsite used by Manly and Rogers when they left Death Valley in search of supplies and help in January 1850. The remains of two old arrastres (crude stone ore-grinding devices) are hidden in a clump of willow trees 100 feet upslope northwest of the spring. Who built them is lost to history—they apparently already existed in 1889 when the first mining took place at nearby Gold Hill. The property was later patented as the Taylor Millsite.

Gold Hill (3.2 miles to the end of the northeast fork). The Gold Hill mines were initially located in May 1875, but little activity took place until 1889, when the Death Valley Mining Company was established. The company considered building a mill but decided to simply sell out instead. Later successors did build a mill—the Gold Hill Mill at Warm

Spring—but although it was fairly sophisticated it was never much of a success. Most of the mine workings on Gold Hill are little more than scrapings in the soil. Remains of the short-lived community of **Gold Hill** are sparse, if there are any at all (see Appendix A); stone walls in the area probably date to the 1920s or later.

17.8   The road crosses a gentle summit and immediately begins to drop into Butte Valley. **Striped Butte** (elevation 4,773 feet), which gave the valley its name, is straight ahead. Manly Peak (elevation 7,196 feet), the southernmost high peak of the Panamint Range, is beyond the butte.

20.3   A road northwest serves as both an access to Striped Butte and a cutoff toward Redlands Canyon. A hike to the top of Striped Butte (originally called Curious Butte) is a relatively gentle climb; it is easiest from the toe at the west end of the butte. Look for fossils in the Paleozoic limestones.

22.3   **Anvil Spring Junction** (GPS 35°55.412'N 117°04.951'W) offers four choices. The road right leads up to nearby Anvil Spring and the Stone Cabin. From near there, another road goes back north to the upper part of Redlands Canyon. Turning left takes one down the valley to Willow Spring in the upper part of Anvil Spring Canyon. Straight ahead leads to Greater View Spring, Russell's Camp, Mengel Pass, and Goler Wash.

The cabins—if not occupied by Park Service rangers, interpretive volunteers, or other users—are available to visitors on a first-come, first-serve basis with a 3-day camping limit. You are asked to respect the historic sanctity and cleanliness of the buildings. Fires are not allowed inside any backcountry cabin; they are allowed in outside fire rings where provided. Under no circumstances can a cabin be locked. Permits for cabin use may be required in 2015. Check with the Park Service for current information.

Anvil Spring, next to a single large cottonwood tree just above the junction, flows about 1.5 gallons of water per minute through a pipe. The spring was named in 1867 when a blacksmith's anvil was recovered from the small pool. It had been thrown in seven years earlier by prospectors who, disgusted at not finding the rich gold ore of Charles Alvord's lost gold mine, were unwilling to haul it back to San Bernardino. This sounds like a tall tale, but it is true. The rock cabin above the spring, known as the Stone, or Geologist's, Cabin, was probably built about 1935.

Anvil Spring, next to the major road junction in Butte Valley, is a reliable water source.

A short distance northwest, around the hillside 0.5 mile from the spring, is a series of mine workings. Although they were located for silver, their ore mostly produced lead. The settlement of **Striped Butte** briefly existed here in 1899. Beyond the mines are the ruins of the **Butte Valley Stamp Mill**, which has an uncertain history. Some reports claim that it was built in 1889, but it was not mentioned in mine promotions in 1899 and 1900. Another source says that it was erected in 1904, and still another gives 1913. Later construction added concrete, with the date "1937" scratched into the foundation.

Up the valley west of the mill are Robber's Roost, Outlaw Cave (an old Wells Fargo strongbox was once found inside), and several more mines.

The road to **Redlands Canyon** runs northwest from Anvil Spring, wraps around the mountain, and drops onto the west side of the Panamint Mountains about 3.4 miles from Anvil Spring. This road ends at a mine in Wood Canyon, a tributary of Redlands Canyon.

Turning east at Anvil Spring Junction leads down across Butte Valley 1.9 miles to **Willow Spring** (GPS 35°54.647'N 117°03.565'W), an extensive area of springs and seeps that have a total flow of about 5 gallons per minute. The thickets are one of the best wildlife habitats around. Stone foundations on the slopes about 0.25 mile below Willow Spring are the remains of a mill. This might be Pages' Mill, which was built in 1889. However, Pages' might have been somewhere in Goler Wash. Alternately, this could be Mysic (Mystic?) Mill, whose millsite claim east of Anvil Spring was also filed in 1889.

The road is closed beyond the millsite but can be hiked down the canyon, and then back southwest up the mountain 8 miles one-way to **Squaw Springs**, where there are the ramshackle remains of an old cabin. The springs produce water at a combined rate of about 4 gallons per minute.

The road south from Anvil Spring Junction continues 0.5 mile to **Greater View Spring**, where water flows at a rate of 4 gallons per minute. Carl Mengel, once the prospecting partner of Frank "Shorty" Harris and Pete Aguereberry, settled here in 1912 while working claims in Goler Wash, over the mountain to the southwest. His opinion was that the view from here was better than that from his friend's Aguereberry Point, hence the name. The old stone cabin at Greater View was probably built by Mormon prospectors in 1869, making it the oldest structure within Death Valley National Park; Mengel rebuilt and added to it in 1912.

Just around the hill farther southwest is **Russell Camp** at Jubilee Spring. It was established by Asa Russell in the early 1930s, after he retired from the Los Angeles Department of Water and Power and became a prospector.

Beyond Greater View Spring, the road continues southward. Definitely for 4WD vehicles only, it leads over **Mengel Pass** (GPS 35°53.996'N 117°04.941'W, elevation 4,328 feet) and down Goler Wash, to Panamint Valley. This route has been described as "a road with character." It certainly is that. For details, see Trip Route PV-3.

End of Warm Springs Canyon Road–Butte Valley Road side trip.

33.5 / 2.1   The open area to the west of West Side Road and south of Warm Springs Canyon Road is Wingate Wash. Leading through Long Valley to Wingate Pass, it had historic importance as the route out of Death Valley for some of the 49ers and the 20-mule teams, the site of Death Valley Scotty's "Battle of Wingate Pass," and more recent freighting endeavors. In spite of its long history, it was officially closed after flood washouts in 1993.

33.9 / 1.7   **Cinder Hill** (reddish hill west of road). Cinder Hill is a small, volcanic cinder cone that lies directly on top of the Southern Death Valley Fault Zone, a strike-slip fault with horizontal, right-lateral motion. The two halves of Cinder Hill are just that—it was split by the fault and the western part moved several hundred feet to the north. It is clear that the fault served as the conduit for the magma that built the cone. Although Cinder Hill might be as much as 400,000 years old, seismic studies indicate that there might be magma (molten rock) at a depth of about 9 miles below this area.

34.8 / 0.8   **Shoreline Butte** (southwest). The prominent horizontal lines on this mountain are beaches and terraces cut by wave action in Ice Age Lake Manly. Once as deep as 640 feet, the lake was 90 miles long and up to 8 miles wide when full. These beach lines were formed as Lake Manly slowly evaporated away at the end of the last glacial episode of the Ice Age, beginning around 130,000 years ago.

35.0 / 0.6   **Amargosa River**. The Amargosa River is the drainage into Death Valley from the southeast. The river's headwaters are in the mountains north of Beatty, Nevada. It then "flows" southward through the Amargosa Desert, past Shoshone and Tecopa, and finally back northward through the far south end of Death Valley. Only rarely does surface water actually run the entire distance. Although people in kayaks were seen here in early 2006, this crossing is almost always dusty.

35.6 / 0.0   Junction with the East Side Road (Trip Route SC-2).

CHAPTER THIRTEEN

Eastern Areas and Amargosa Valley

This is a diverse and fascinating part of the Death Valley region, boasting several of the park's best known viewpoints and canyons, numerous ghost town sites, major borax mining areas, and the most endangered of all pupfish. Nicely, most of the roads are paved or improved dirt accessible to most vehicles.

Eastern Areas and Amargosa Valley, Trip Route E-1—State Highway 190 East, between Furnace Creek and Death Valley Junction

FROM: Furnace Creek Visitor Center.

TO: Death Valley Junction.

ROAD CONDITIONS: 29.9 miles, paved, all-weather highway.

SIDE TRIPS: Echo Canyon Road (Side Trip E-1a, 4WD), Zabriskie Point (all vehicles and short walk), Twenty Mule Team Canyon (all vehicles), Hole-in the-Wall Road (Side Trip E-1b, 4WD), Naval Spring (all vehicles plus hike), and Terry Mine Road and Petro Road (Side Trip E-1c, 4WD); access to Dante's View Road (Trip Route E-2) and Greenwater Valley Road (Trip Route E-3).

GENERAL DESCRIPTION: This major highway passes through some of Death Valley's spectacular scenery and geology, including the Furnace Creek Badlands and borate mining areas, and provides access to several popular side trips.

ROAD LOG MILEAGES	eastbound from Furnace Creek Visitor Center / westbound from Death Valley Junction.
0.0 / 29.9	**Furnace Creek Visitor Center**.
0.3 / 29.6	**Furnace Creek Ranch**.

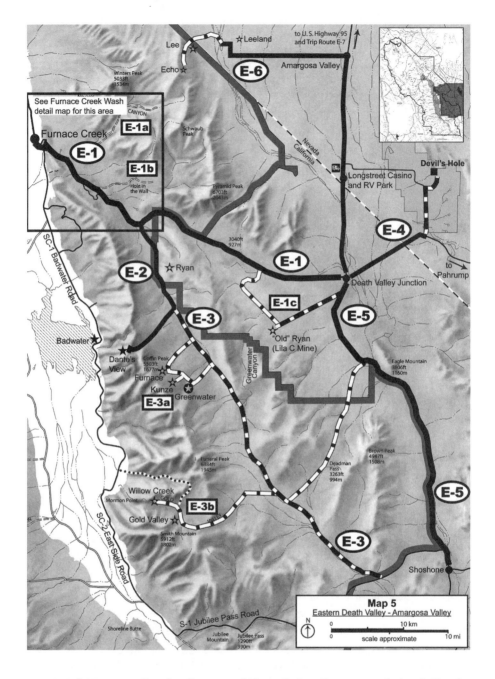

Map 5
Eastern Death Valley - Amargosa Valley

0   10 km
0   10 mi
scale approximate

0.5 / 29.4   Road to Sunset and Texas Spring Campgrounds (east). Road to Indian Village (west; please respect the private property rights of Death Valley's native Timbisha Shoshone people).

1.2 / 28.7   **Badwater Road** (south) is described as Trip Route SC-1.

1.4 / 28.5	The **Furnace Creek Inn** is located on the bluff north of the road.
2.5 / 27.4	**Travertine Springs.** These springs discharge more than 3 million gallons of fresh warm water per day (more than 2,000 gallons per minute). Many of the 1849 argonauts rested here for several days before tackling the floor of Death Valley. A few years later, surveyors with the boundary commission of 1861 found Furnace Creek to be "a bold torrent, which dashes noisily down its descent . . . lined by a fringe of grass and willows." The springs now provide most of the domestic and agricultural water for the Furnace Creek developments and Indian village—more than 85 percent of the flow is consumed by the facilities, and the stream was little more than a trickle. However, introduced date and fan palms, and tamarisk trees have now been removed. Groves of native mesquite and arrowweed grow among the springs, which extend a considerable distance north of the highway, and Furnace Creek again reaches its alluvial fan.
3.3 / 26.6	**Side Trip E-1a—Echo Canyon Road** (GPS 36°26.257'N 116°49.447'W, north 10.8 miles one-way to the road's end in Lower Echo Canyon; 4WD required). There is a rough bedrock cascade 3 miles from the highway and deep gravel within the canyon narrows. No camping first 2 miles or at the Inyo Mine.
	Echo Canyon is a classic example of a desert hourglass canyon: the canyon's lower alluvial fan and upper drainage areas are separated by abrupt narrows carved into Paleozoic sedimentary rocks. Along the way are a natural arch and an extensive area of old mines, and there are petroglyphs a short hike from the end of the road.
0.0	Turnoff from State Highway 190.
3.3	Entrance to the lower Echo Canyon narrows.
4.1	Entrance to the upper Echo Canyon narrows. This is the most spectacular part of Echo Canyon, where the walls tower several hundred feet above a canyon floor only a few tens of feet wide.
4.9	**Eye of the Needle** is a natural arch best seen looking down the canyon from the upper side of a narrow fin of rock that the canyon and road wind around. The opening formed when chunks of rock fell from the cliffs, creating a hole through the fin.
5.4	Leave the Echo Canyon narrows. Beyond here the canyon gradually widens, and the hills become gentler.

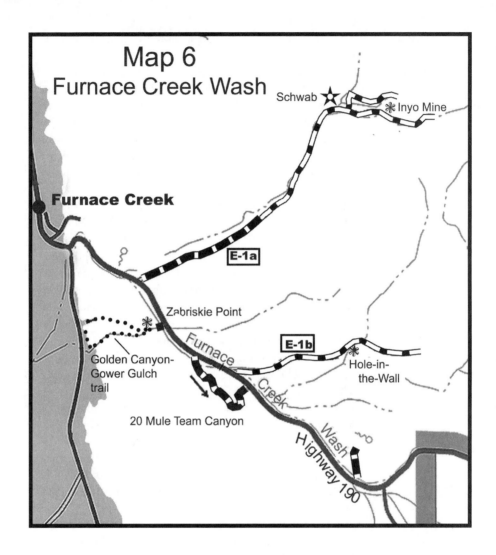

Map 6
Furnace Creek Wash

Schwab

Inyo Mine

Furnace Creek

E-1a

Zabriskie Point

Furnace

Golden Canyon-
Gower Gulch
trail

E-1b

Hole-in-
the-Wall

Creek

20 Mule Team Canyon

Wash

Highway 190

8.0 Small mines show up on both sides of the road. These were all located for gold during the Rhyolite gold rush, mostly from 1905 to 1907, and led to the founding of Schwab. The small sizes of the mine dumps indicate that these properties had free gold only in the upper few feet of ore.

9.0 **"Saddle Cabin Junction"** (GPS 36°29.771'N 116°42.619'W). The so-called cabin, actually once a well-built house, was still standing in the early 1970s, but now only the concrete foundation slab and debris are left. Little is known about the cabin's history except that it had to do with the Inyo Mine, a short way farther up Echo Canyon.

Eye of the Needle is a natural arch in Echo Canyon.

Most old guidebooks misplaced the ghost town of **Schwab** (Appendix A). It is neither Saddle Cabin nor the Inyo Mine farther up the road. To find the townsite, take the side road (north) that leads past the cabin's foundation and over a low pass (the "saddle") into the adjacent Upper Echo Canyon. In the canyon bottom, hike left down the canyon about 0.5 mile. The site of Schwab is marked by a few leveled tent sites, rusty cans, and broken bottles. It is not much, but then Schwab did not last long enough for even a single wood-frame structure to be built.

The **Upper Echo Canyon Road** leads up the canyon past several mines, across a summit at Echo Pass (the location of Echo, a town even less successful than Schwab), down the east side of the Funeral Mountains to the townsite of Lee, and finally into Amargosa Valley, Nevada. Maps show two 4WD routes between the canyon and the pass. The one to the south is now totally impassible. The other is as bad as a road can be. It is negotiable only by short-wheelbase 4WD vehicles, and then at least two cars with winches should travel together. Check for information at the Furnace Creek Visitor Center before attempting this route.

9.4 **Inyo Mine** (GPS 36°29.599'N 116°42.251'W). Continuing east past Saddle Cabin Junction, the Inyo Mine was the most important in the Echo Canyon Mining District. Discovered in January 1905, the operation had enough employees during 1906 and 1907 to support its own blacksmith shop, boarding-house, and store. The nationwide financial panic that shut down most mines throughout the country also closed the Inyo, and there was almost no mining from 1907 until 1928. It was then worked on and off into 1940. The buildings, mill, cyanide tank, and diesel engine date to this later episode of activity. These buildings have sometimes been incorrectly identified as Schwab. The mine itself is next to the large wooden ore bin high on the mountainside to the north.

10.8 End of the Echo Canyon Road. Walking at least the first 0.5 mile on up the canyon is recommended. The canyon walls are composed of metamorphic quartzite—sedimentary sand-stone that was recrystallized by high temperature and pres-sure. The original sediment was deposited in shallow water, as shown by the ripple marks that decorate some of the bed-ding surfaces.

Just before this little canyon opens out into rolling hills is a small gorge. A single mesquite tree shows that water lies near the surface, possibly close enough to be reached by shal-low digging. Look for petroglyphs along the route, especially on some of the smooth rock faces within the gorge. Several have already been damaged by vandals, who also added some "modern art." Remember that these drawings were made as long as 2,000 years ago and are irreplaceable. Please do not disfigure them.

End of Echo Canyon Road side trip.

4.7 / 25.2 **Zabriskie Point** (spur to parking area, then a short walking trail up a low hill to the viewpoint). Named for Christian B. Zabriskie, the general manager of Pacific Coast Borax, this is one of Death Valley's most famous viewpoints, overlooking the Furnace Creek Badlands with Death Valley beyond. Most of the rock is barren yellow siltstone and claystone; dark lay-ers are basalt lava flows, and white streaks and veinlets are borate minerals. The prominent sharp peak toward the valley is **Manly Beacon**.

Just downslope on the west side of Zabriskie Point is the trailhead for the Golden Canyon–Gower Gulch trail system. This network of scenic trails is described in Chapter

Petroglyphs can be found in many parts of Death Valley's backcountry. All are protected by law against any form of vandalism.

The Furnace Creek Badlands, composed of soft, infertile clay and silt, are most easily viewed from Zabriskie Point.

8. Explorers can also hike a mile or more along the dark red-brown ridge extending west from Zabriskie Point.

Notice how Furnace Creek has carved a deep, sheer-sided arroyo into the bed of the wash upstream from Zabriskie Point but that there is no similar arroyo downstream from the parking area. Following a serious flood on August 2, 1942, the Park Service and highway department created an artificial cut in order to divert the flow from Furnace Creek into Gower Gulch. The cut is immediately upstream from Zabriskie Point. The purpose was to prevent flood damage at the Furnace Creek Inn. The effort was successful, but Gower Gulch was geologically unprepared for such runoff. Its natural drainage area was just 2 square miles, but today it covers more than 200 square miles. The canyon has been deepened and widened by erosion, and a deep arroyo has been carved into the alluvial fan at the mouth of Gower Gulch, where Badwater Road has been washed out a number of times.

5.8 / 24.1   Beds of the Furnace Creek Formation on the north side of the highway have been steeply tilted. Some of the original bedding surfaces are now exposed along the base of the cliff. Several of these exhibit ripple marks, mud cracks, and other secondary sedimentary features. Straight lines of bumps are probably animal tracks, but they are too poorly preserved for identification. (Note: what you are seeing here are the bottom sides of beds that were laid down on top of an existing surface, so these secondary features are inverted casts of the originals. The tracks show up as bumps, for example.)

5.9 / 24.0   **Twenty Mule Team Canyon Drive** (southeast 2.7 miles; maintained dirt road normally suitable for standard vehicles; motor homes and trailers not permitted because of tight turns, narrow clearance, and steep grades). Twenty Mule Team Canyon is incomparably the best place to experience the Furnace Creek Formation and its deposits of borate minerals. Small-scale mining took place here during the 1910s and 1920s. Note that 20-mule teams never passed through this canyon.

0.0   Entrance from State Highway 190. If the road has been badly washed by floods or when severe storms threaten, the road will be closed with a locked gate.

0.3   Very small borate prospect mine (left). As with all mines, no matter how small, KEEP OUT. The weathered ceiling of soft rock could easily collapse.

0.4   The black lava flow (right) is typical of those in the Furnace Creek Formation. The white veinlets and nodules within the lava are mostly priceite and bakerite, calcium borate minerals. Although similar to colemanite, they are harder and more difficult to process and have never been mined as borate ore.

0.9   The view straight ahead is toward **Monte Blanco** ("White Mountain"). White streaks of borate minerals gave the hill its name. During part of Death Valley's earliest tourism era, Monte Blanco was promoted as another of Death Valley's mysteries—here, they said, is a mountain perpetually covered with snow.

1.8   Summit at sharp left curve. This is an excellent place to park (wide spots let you pull out of the line of traffic) in order to explore the area and its rock formations. This open wash was once the site of a small mining camp. The building that houses the **Borax Museum** at the Furnace Creek Ranch was moved from here. The hole in the ground a few feet east of the road was the building's cellar. The hiker is free to walk in any direction, but perhaps the best route is to cross the low ridge into the next wash to the south (to the right when looking up toward Monte Blanco). Upstream, this quickly becomes a canyon, along which are numerous small borate mines. Although the specimens are often covered with beautiful crystals, please remember that Death Valley is a unique resource where mineral collecting is not allowed. Studies of these deposits have shown that they contain at least 26 distinct borate minerals, many of which have been found nowhere else in the world. Most specimens contain several minerals intimately mixed together and are only a soft, white powder. Few plants grow here, even in a prime wildflower season; the clay-rich lakebeds form almost no soil. The exception is on the weathered lava flows, which form rich soil and can be covered with annual wildflowers.

2.7   End of Twenty Mule Team Canyon Drive at State Highway 190 milepoint 7.5/22.4.

6.6 / 23.3   **Side Trip E-1b—Hole-in-the-Wall Road** (GPS 36°24.296'N 116°46.945'W, northeast 5.9 miles one-way; high-clearance to Hole-in-the-Wall, 4WD required beyond). This route is within an active wash of loose sand and gravel. Standard vehicles driven with care can make it to Hole-in-the-Wall, 3.6 miles from the highway. No camping is allowed in the first 2 miles.

0.0	Turnoff from State Highway 190. Many of the plants growing in the wash are rounded, dark-green desert fir, a member of the composite (sunflower) family. These are among the largest specimens found anywhere. The rock outcrops all along the road are lake bed sediments of the Furnace Creek Formation. This is the top part of the formation, and there are no borate deposits.
3.6	**Hole-in-the-Wall** is a water gap, cut by an existing stream flowing over ground being gradually uplifted; the stream stayed in place by carving a canyon through the rising rocks. This is the Furnace Creek Fault Zone, one of the most important fault systems of the Death Valley region. The rocks are hard sandstone and conglomerate of the upper Furnace Creek Formation. As the rocks were thrust upward by movements on the fault, the softer clay lake beds above and below the sandstone were rapidly eroded away, leaving this rock standing as a thin erosional fin.

Beyond Hole-in-the-Wall, the road turns east and develops a very rough surface of loose rock.

5.9	**Red Amphitheater** is just north of the end of the road. Walking the last 100 yards is advised because the rough, narrow, sharply tilted road reaches a dead end at an awkward place to turn around. A small travertine quarry near the road and another in the red sandstone of the amphitheater-like canyon over the ridge produced building stones that were used in the construction of both the Furnace Creek Inn and the Pacific Coast Borax headquarters in Oakland, California.

Maps label an open area about 2 miles farther up the valley from here as the "Red Amphitheater." We and Park Service interpreters are convinced that the maps are wrong and that the Red Amphitheater is the little canyon instead. It is a small enclosed valley in which the sandstone is rich red in color. By contrast, there is nothing either red or amphitheater-like about the area identified on the maps. It is simply a wide valley that has no outstanding attributes.

End of Hole-in-the-Wall Road side trip.

7.5 / 22.4	Exit of one-way Twenty Mule Team Canyon Drive. The entrance is 1.7 miles west, down Furnace Creek Wash at milepoint 5.9/24.0.
8.6 / 21.3	Corkscrew Canyon. The road into Corkscrew Canyon is blocked by a locked and posted gate. The Corkscrew, White Monster, and deBely mines, about 1 mile up the canyon,

EASTERN AREAS AND AMARGOSA VALLEY

underwent significant mining for colemanite during the 1920s, and again during the 1960s when much of the production was used to make the zinc borate fire retardant slurry used in fighting wildfires. These properties have been quitclaimed to the National Park Service, but the canyon is closed to public entry because of significant mine hazards.

10.6 / 19.3   **Navel Spring Road** (GPS 36°22.145'N 116°43.776'W, northwest 0.5 mile to water tank; dirt road easy for any vehicle). Date palm trees visible from State Highway 190 are at **Salty Navel Spring**. It supports a tiny flow of poor water in the small gorge below it, but contrary to some maps, it is not Navel Spring.

Navel Spring might be a spring described by Lewis Manly in December 1849. It is located in a small canyon in the bluff to the northeast, at the end of a closed, gated road leading away from the water tank. Although the road provides the easiest walking route, the explorer should cut directly up the alluvial fan. There is a concentration of beavertail cactus plus a few golden cholla and cottontop barrel cacti among the creosote and desert holly bushes. The spring has been developed by a tunnel sealed with a locked door. The water was piped to the water tank and used at the borate mining operations near Ryan.

The open area south of the highway has only a thin surface cover of sand and gravel on top of the Furnace Creek Formation. Exploratory drilling in the 1960s revealed a number of high-grade but small borate deposits at shallow depths. The mining companies have now relinquished the rights to these deposits to the National Park Service.

11.5 / 18.4   **Boraxo Mine** (south). The medium gray, smoothly contoured slopes on the alluvial fan south of the highway are the waste dumps from the Boraxo Mine. This large, pure deposit of colemanite was mined by the Tenneco Corporation and the American Borate Company between 1971 and 1978. If any one mining operation resulted in the Mining in Parks Act of 1976, it was this. The Boraxo was an open pit mine, about 1,100 feet long, 700 feet wide, and more than 400 feet deep. Lawsuits against the mining were jointly filed by several environmental organizations. The Boraxo was closed, in part because of the legal pressures and because most of the accessible ore was worked out (more than 10 million tons of colemanite had been removed), but more significantly because the nearby Billie deposit—larger and richer but deep below the surface—was ready for production. The company contoured the dumps to resemble natural slopes, but since even weathered claystone from the Furnace Creek Formation is infertile, these dumps are nearly barren. (The Billie Mine is discussed under Trip Route E-2.)

11.9 / 18.0 **Dante's View Road** is a scenic side trip past the largest borate mines in Death Valley, across the north end of Greenwater Valley, and up a steep grade to the famous Dante's View. It is described as Trip Route E-2.

12.3 / 17.6 An information kiosk (north) includes a park entry fee machine and interpretive displays plus a telephone, chemical toilet, and trash can.

~14 / 16 **Dead Horse Canyon** was one of the main supply routes between the Tonopah & Tidewater Railroad and Greenwater, and later was followed by part of the Death Valley Railroad. The name may have originally applied to today's Greenwater Canyon. If that is correct, then this canyon actually has no official name. The national park boundary is in the lower part of the canyon.

The high mountain to the east is well-named Pyramid Peak. Like all of the southern end of the Funeral Mountains, it is composed of early to middle Paleozoic Era sedimentary rocks.

14.7 / 15.2 **Travertine Point**. In the cliffs south of the highway, the Furnace Creek Formation contains considerable limestone, some of which may be travertine deposited by the volcanic hot springs associated with the borate minerals. Down the canyon, the light-colored ridges eroding out of the cliffs are gypsum.

15.9 / 14.0 Ragged cuts in the side of **Mesa Negra** south of the highway mark the location of a trestle on the Death Valley Railroad. When the railroad was dismantled in 1931, the timbers were used in a number of buildings owned by the borax company, including the bar at the Furnace Creek Inn.

17.5 / 12.4 The grade of the Death Valley Railroad is visible gently cutting across the hillside south of the wash. Westbound travelers are entering Dead Horse Canyon.

19.1 / 10.8 **Pyramid Pass**, elevation 3,042 feet, is the divide between the Death Valley drainage of Dead Horse Canyon (west) and the Amargosa River drainage (east).

South of the highway just west of the summit are the cement slab remains of **Tidewater**, a modern "ghost town." It was a trailer park community for the borate miners and their families between 1975 and 1986. The population was as great as 150 people.

23.2 / 6.7 **Side Trip E-1c—Terry Mine Road–Petro Road** (GPS 36°18.705'N 116°32.036'W, south 13.2 miles via Lila C. Mine to State Highway 127; 4WD recommended) serves as a convenient connection to the east end of Greenwater Canyon (see Side Trip E-3b). The original town of Ryan and the Lila C. Mine are 6.9 miles south, beyond Greenwater Canyon. This road was not intended to be a public route. Entirely outside of the national park, much of it crosses patented mining claims owned by Rio Tinto Borax, and access to this area could change in the future.

0.0 Turnoff from State Highway 190.

0.2 Just after climbing out of the wash, the road crosses the grade of the Death Valley Railroad.

1.8 The **Terry Mine** is an open pit initially developed by the American Borate Company on a small deposit of colemanite. It was mined in 1974 and 1975 but contains only 2,000 tons of reserves.

2.2 The route continues southeast from a T-junction in the road. The west branch leads to a low-grade deposit of zeolite minerals, used experimentally as water-filtering agents.

2.6 The **Cone Hill Mine** is owned by Rio Tinto Borax, the modern descendant of Francis "Borax" Smith's Pacific Coast Borax. Exploratory drilling proved the mine to be the tip of a very large deposit of colemanite ore at depth—this is the only property in the Death Valley region that Rio Tinto Borax will not relinquish. Although it has never yet been a commercial producer, it probably will be in the future.

4.7 Greenwater Canyon (west) provides a 10.3-mile hike through the mountains to the Greenwater Valley Road. South of here, the Terry Mine Road becomes **Petro Road**.

6.7 The road crosses the grade of the Lila C. branch of the Death Valley Railroad.

6.9 The road west leads about 0.5 mile to the **Lila C. Mine** at the site of "Old" Ryan. To the northeast, Petro Road follows the old Death Valley–Lila C. railroad grade, ending at State Highway 127. It crosses several washes where it is subject to washouts.

13.2 **State Highway 127** at a point 1.3 miles south of Death Valley Junction.

End of Terry Mine Road–Petro Road side trip.

29.9 / 0.0	**Death Valley Junction** is immediately south of the intersection of State Highways 190 and 127. The town and the driving route to Devil's Hole, a detached parcel of Death Valley National Park, are described in Trip Routes E-4 and E-5.

South-Central Death Valley, Trip Route E-2—Dante's View Road

FROM: State Highway 190 at a point 11.9 miles east of Furnace Creek Visitor Center.

TO: Dante's View, at the end of the road.

ROAD CONDITIONS: 13.2 miles; paved, all-weather road.

Special Note: Motor vehicles and trailer combinations more than 25 feet long and 9 feet wide are not allowed beyond a parking area near the Greenwater Valley Road turnoff (milepoint 7.4).

SIDE TRIPS: None; access to Greenwater Valley Road (Trip Route E-3).

GENERAL DESCRIPTION: The Dante's View Road starts by crossing gentle terrain, but it is narrow and steep on its final climb to the best-known viewpoint in Death Valley, a place you must see.

ROAD LOG MILEAGE	southbound from State Highway 190.
0.0	Turnoff (south) from State Highway 190. The elevation here is just under 2,000 feet.
0.5	The dumps of the **Boraxo Mine** are south of the road. After the mine stopped operating in 1978, the pit was used as a repository for waste rock from the nearby Billie Mine. The dumps below the pit were contoured to resemble natural slopes, but the claystone is barren and supports little vegetation.
1.4	Boraxo Mine Road (south) is closed to the public.
1.7	The grade of the **Death Valley Railroad** is visible up the draw to the east, beyond the ridge fronted by the large headframe of the Billie Mine.
1.9	The **Billie Mine's** headframe and waste dumps across Furnace Creek Wash are outside of the national park, but the ore deposit itself is within the park, as much as 700 feet beneath the surface between the shaft and Dante's View Road. The Billie deposit is much larger than the one that was mined at the nearby Boraxo Mine, but although it was expected to be producing ore well into the twenty-first century, the mine was permanently closed in 2005. The property has been donated to the National Park Service, which may

use it for the interpretation of the park's mining history in conjunction with the proposed education center at Ryan.

2.4   **Ryan Road** (east) leads to a locked gate below the townsite of Ryan and the restricted access entry to the Billie Mine. The borax companies maintained the town for possible future use as a mine camp, but now Rio Tinto Borax has donated the town property to the Death Valley Conservancy for possible future use as an education center.

Sigma Mine Road (west) is also closed to public use. The Sigma Mine was a small open-pit ulexite mine.

3.6   The road enters **Furnace Creek Canyon**. The middle of the canyon serves as the boundary between the national park and the Bureau of Land Management lands to the east.

4.9   The mine workings on the mountainsides (east) are the Biddy McCarty and Widow mines. They were connected to Ryan by the "Baby Gauge Railroad" (see Appendix B). It was referred to in promotional literature as a toy train, but in reality it was a workhorse, carrying millions of tons of borate ore from the mines to the Death Valley Railroad. After the mines closed, the Baby Gauge carried visitors between the town and the mines until an expensive lawsuit shut it down in 1950.

A better view of these mines and of the Baby Gauge grade switchbacking on the hillside is available from mile-point 8.5.

7.4   **Greenwater Valley Road** (south, high-clearance recommended but normally accessible to all vehicles driven with care; see Trip Route E-3). The trailer parking area (north side of road) must be used if you are pulling a trailer; vehicle combinations longer than 25 feet are not allowed beyond this point.

8.5   The mountain to the north is Mt. Perry; its bright colors are because of volcanic rocks in the Artists Drive Formation. Much farther north, beyond Furnace Creek Wash, are Schwaub Peak (misspelled but named after financier Charles Schwab) and Pyramid Peak.

10.4   The road enters **Dante's Canyon**, which extends nearly to Dante's View. The low, spindly gray-green plants are Death Valley joint fir (*Ephedra funerea*), one of the several types of Mormon tea. It is a gymnosperm, related to the pines and firs.

12.5   This parking lot also serves a picnic area with tables and a chemical toilet (there is neither at the viewpoint).

13.2   **Dante's View**. This viewpoint, 5,475 feet above sea level, is almost directly above Badwater, which is 279 feet below sea

The famous overlook at Dante's View is directly above Badwater, more than a mile below.

level. Because of the elevation difference, Dante's View is usually 25°F cooler than the valley floor.

Dante's View boasts one of the most wonderful scenic vistas anywhere, spanning almost a full circle. To the south are the Avawatz and Owlshead mountains. To the right of the Owlsheads, the obvious gap west through the mountains is Long Valley where Wingate Wash leads to Wingate Pass, the route of some of the 49er argonauts and the 20-mule team wagons. Continuing to the right are the Panamint Mountains, with Telescope Peak (11,049 feet) and Hanaupah Canyon almost due west. In the distance to the northwest it is usually possible to see some of the higher peaks of the Sierra Nevada, including Mt. Williamson (Mt. Whitney is not quite visible). Thus, in one quick shift of the eyes you can scan from nearly the highest to the lowest elevations in the lower forty-eight states. Farther north are the Cottonwood Mountains on the west side and the Grapevine Mountains on the east side of Death Valley. The highest range east is the Spring Mountains, with Charleston Peak (11,916 feet) their tallest point. In the distance northeast (left) of the Spring's foothills is the Nevada Test Site and the route of the argonauts who chanced onto Death Valley in 1849, and now the location of the cancelled Yucca Mountain nuclear waste site.

Eastern Areas and Amargosa Valley, Trip Route E-3—Greenwater Valley Road

FROM: Dante's View Road at a point 7.4 miles south of State Highway 190.

TO: State Highway 178 (Jubilee Pass Road, Trip Route S-1) at a point about 8 miles west of Shoshone, California.

ROAD CONDITIONS: 28.0 miles one way; rough dirt road with high-clearance recommended but usually suitable for standard vehicles driven with caution.

SIDE TRIPS: Furnace Mine Road (Side Trip E-3a, 4WD recommended), Green-water Canyon (Side Trip E-3b, hike), Gold Valley Road (Side Trip E-3c, 4WD), and Deadman Pass (4WD).

GENERAL DESCRIPTION: Greenwater Valley is a wide valley that extends from the upper reaches of Furnace Creek south almost to Tecopa, a distance of about 40 miles. There are few specific attractions along the road itself, but it is the access to several of the national park's most important archaeological and historical sites.

ROAD LOG MILEAGES	southbound from Dante's View Road / northbound from State Highway 178
0.0 / 28.0	The turnoff from the Dante's View Road (Trip Route E-2) is well marked.
2.8 / 25.2	**Side Trip E-3a—Furnace Mine Road** (GPS 36°14.118'N 116°38.230'W, southwest 3.4 miles to the townsite; 4WD recommended because of steep rocky grades near the townsite). This road cuts southwest up the slope to the townsite of Furnace, then loops southward to Kunze and Greenwater before returning to the main road. The history of the Greenwater copper boom and these ghost towns is discussed in more detail in Appendix A.
0.0	Turnoff from the Greenwater Valley Road.
2.0	The low, rounded, and exceedingly spiny plants between the creosote bushes are spiny menodora (*Menodora spinescens*), a member of the olive family. Although common throughout the higher elevations of the California and Nevada deserts, it may be more abundant in this part of Greenwater Valley than anywhere else. Many of the shrubs among the menodora and creosote will look dead unless you are here in spring or early summer. One is blackbrush (*Coleogyne ramosissima*), a member of the rose family that is naked of foliage most of the year but bears yellow springtime flowers.
3.4	**Furnace** (GPS 36°11.469'N 116°39.888'W). By late 1906 the town of Furnace had a population reported as 500 served

Furnace in early 1907. (From *Desert Magazine,* November 1938)

by a post office, a store, a boardinghouse, and a restaurant-saloon, but it lasted only a few months. Although located close to some of the largest mines of the Greenwater copper boom, the town's position on this windswept ridge exposed it to horrendous weather. In early 1907, all the residents moved to Greenwater. See Appendix A for more about the town.

The dumps of the Furnace Creek Copper Company mine reveal the true nature of the Greenwater District's copper ore—some specimens are quite pretty, with colorful chrysocolla, malachite, azurite, and other copper minerals, but most of the rock is barren. The high-grade primary ore that everybody expected to find at depth did not exist.

A poor 4WD road heads north from Furnace. It ends at the Coffin Mine, which has a mysterious history but apparently was opened for gold during the 1920s.

4.6   From Furnace, the 4WD road heads south along the base of the mountains. The first of the side roads leads west 1.6 miles to the townsite of Kunze; a second road to Kunze is another 0.5 mile farther from Furnace.

Kunze (GPS 36°10.955'N 116°38.735'W) is scattered along a shallow canyon just below the Greenwater Copper Company mine. The first of two towns known as Greenwater, it is the original location of the post office and newspaper offices. Starting in late November 1906, the entire town moved to the platted townsite of Ramsey, in part because there was more room for growth there and in part

Kunze was photographed by H. C. Cloudman after a snowfall in December 1906, when it was still an active town but was soon to be abandoned in favor of nearby Greenwater. (County of Inyo, Eastern California Museum)

because of promotion. Ramsey was renamed Greenwater and the old site, which reverted to the name of its founder, Arthur Kunze, faded away. However, there are more remains of Kunze than of any of the other Greenwater District ghost towns—stone walls, terraced building sites, and debris of soldered cans, broken bottles, and wood.

6.9   **Greenwater** (GPS 36°10.754'N 116°37.073'W). A return to the Furnace-Greenwater Road leads another 2.3 miles to the site of Greenwater. Virtually nothing is left of the "Greatest Copper Camp on Earth"—wooden structures were moved to other places, tent buildings left only faint flattened pads, and much of the original trash was removed by collectors years ago.

A hike to **Greenwater Spring** (southwest 1.1 miles), the namesake of the mining district, heads up the slope from the Greenwater signpost; the old, closed road more directly west ends among some small copper mines. Along the way, the trail passes a copper mine, its waste dump of bright-red rock sparsely stained with copper minerals. The shaft has been screened over for safety. East of this mine, and immediately south of a small hill, is the **Greenwater Cemetery** (GPS 36°09.919'N 116°36.693'W). Beyond the mine is **Greenwater Spring** (GPS 36°09.084'N 116°37.448'W). Once a small pool of stagnant, greenish water, it was unsuccessfully "developed" by a short tunnel in an attempt to provide water for the city below. It was never a good source, the tunnel has collapsed, and the spring is only a shallow, moist depression.

Eastward from "downtown" Greenwater, the road splits; one branch returns to the main Greenwater Valley Road at milepoint 5.8/22.2, the other at milepoint 8.3/19.7.

End of Furnace Mine Road side trip.

4.8 / 23.2	Continuing on the main Greenwater Valley Road, the plants in this part of the Greenwater Valley are mostly creosote bushes surrounded by spiny menodora, blackbrush, and Death Valley joint fir.
5.8 / 22.2	**Greenwater Road** (west 1.7 miles; usually accessible to 2WD). This road winds up a gentle alluvial fan directly to the site of **Greenwater**. Downtown Greenwater was located where a metal post topped by a diamond-shaped sign (now unreadable) was erected years ago by the Automobile Club of Southern California. Because of its remote location and the high price of lumber, few substantial buildings were ever built. Most businesses and homes were in tents or tent cabins, and when their owners left, so did the structures. Although this ultimately was the largest of the Greenwater District boomtowns, with a population of about 2,000 people in early 1907, virtually all that remains to mark the city is a sparse litter of tin cans and broken bottles surrounding the level tent sites. See Appendix A for more about Greenwater's history.
7.7 / 20.3	A short hike (east, 0.7 mile one-way) follows a closed road up a hill to an outstanding view into Greenwater Canyon.
8.3 / 19.7	A road into the ghost town of Greenwater angles to the northwest. For northbound travelers with high-clearance vehicles, this is a convenient 2.4-mile shortcut to the site.
8.4 / 19.6	Greenwater Canyon (GPS 36°10.166'N 116°34.574'W at old north access road, east 10.3 miles one-way to Terry Mine Road–Petro Road intersection outside the national park (see Side Trip E-1c; hike on closed road). This trail drops gradually eastward through Greenwater Canyon. A former road that never got much use, it required careful 4WD driving because of one sharply angled hillside, several steep bedrock cascades,

and extensive areas of deep sand and gravel. The Greenwater Canyon Trail now gets far less use than the road ever did. It is a long, hot, and bone-dry route through complete wilderness. Camping is not allowed.

When included within Death Valley National Park, the Greenwater Canyon Road was closed to vehicles is because the canyon and its surroundings make up Death Valley's richest archaeological zone. There are panels of petroglyphs and pictographs, stone circles, rock walls, and more—features whose locations are intentionally left unspecified in the following description of the canyon hike. The campsites of some of these early people must have been occupied for long spans of time. The soil around them is black with fire soot, and the ground is littered with lithic scatter chips of jasper and quartz left over from tool making.

The first mile of the hike crosses a smooth flat with rather lush vegetation. Most of the larger plants, with small gray leaves and large seed bracts, are hopsage (*Grayia spinosa*), a member of the goosefoot family that includes the saltbushes.

The old road can be seen climbing the hill near the head of Petroglyph Canyon. The basalt lava flows of the canyon walls are the first and only readily accessible of several petroglyph localities in Greenwater Canyon. Based on the types of abstract figures on the panels, it is believed that the art was carved between 3,000 and 6,000 years ago during the Mesquite Flat (Death Valley II) cultural period. Most of the rock art is near the entrance to the canyon and safely high near the canyon rim. Lower down are some modern "petroglyphs," such as dollar signs and initials—deplorable acts that detract from an irreplaceable archaeological heritage.

Petroglyph Canyon is nearly a mile long. The hike continuing down Greenwater Canyon proper is rather uninspiring, consisting of the gravel floor of the wash and a few stretches of bedrock cascades. About halfway down the canyon is an area with nice exposures of volcanic agglomerate; that is, a coarse tuff breccia that contains a miscellany of jagged rock fragments within explosive ash. This is part of the Greenwater Volcanics, about 5 million years old.

In this remote area is the surprise of square wooden poles. No longer standing, most measure about 6 by 6 inches and are as long as 20 feet. These carried the telephone wires from Death Valley Junction to Greenwater, which is actually quite close by over the ridge to the west. An explorer might find the boulder that is inscribed with "W. B. Reed 1907," perhaps related to the construction of the telephone line. No further information about this person is known.

Among the archeological sites deep within Greenwater Canyon are campsites that can be dated on the basis of the Silver Lake type of spearpoints they left behind. These people were not of the same culture that produced the petroglyphs. They were here between 8,000 and 10,000 years ago, as much as 3,000 years before the Egyptians began building their pyramids!

All these archaeological sites imply that Greenwater Canyon—and for that matter, all of Death Valley—was a much more hospitable place 5,000 and more years ago than it is now (see Chapter 2). Although there probably was no permanent stream of consequence in the area, there must have been good sources of spring water where now there are none at all.

The eastern, downstream end of Greenwater Canyon is at the national park boundary. From there the old road is still in existence and leads 3.8 miles to **Terry Mine Road–Petro Road**. Access to that area is described in Side Trip E-1c.
End of Greenwater Canyon hiking route.

9.6 / 18.4	The old southern entrance road to Greenwater Canyon. See the description at milepoint 8.4/19.6, above.
10.2 / 17.8	The hills to the east are dotted with dozens of small mine prospects, all of which were explored for copper during the Greenwater boom of 1906–1907. Someplace in this area—nobody seems to know just where—is the site of **East Greenwater**, a short-lived tent camp during the Greenwater boom. The most likely spots are short distances east of the Greenwater Valley Road where networks of now-closed roads have common intersections. One of these is at GPS 36°08.501'N 116°33.380'W; the other is about 1.5 miles farther south at GPS 36°07.452'N 116°32.811'W.
11.7 / 16.3	The top of this gentle rise is the highest elevation on the floor of Greenwater Valley (elevation about 4,050 feet). To the west, the mountain with the smooth face is Funeral Peak (elevation 6,382 feet), an easy and popular hiking destination.
17.5 / 10.5	**Side Trip E-3b, Gold Valley Road** (GPS 36°03.348'N 116°30.447'W, west 12.1 miles one-way; 4WD required). Although the first part of this road can probably be handled

by 2WD vehicles, the road climbing the pass and down into Gold Valley is definitely a 4WD route. It includes sharp curves, very steep grades, canted roadbeds, bedrock climbs, and loose gravel as it crosses the summit.

0.0 Turnoff from Greenwater Valley Road.

3.0 A faint trail along a closed road leads 2.7 miles to Hidden Spring, a critical water source for wildlife. Nearby is the Hidden Spring Mine, one of the hundreds of copper prospects that were explored during the Greenwater rush.

6.7 This is a very bad road. Drive slowly through this small canyon. The greatest hazard is the sharp sideways angle necessary to negotiate a badly washed portion of the roadbed.

6.9 **Gold Valley Pass** (elevation approximately 4,450 feet). The road proceeds into the valley by way of several short but very steep grades. The road north from the summit is a short dead end.

7.1 The ghost of **Gold Valley** (GPS 36°01.340'N 116°38.644'W) is on a side road (west 0.5 mile). The townsite is marked only by a few leveled tent cabin sites, rock walls, and debris. The town was established in 1908. It had 96 surveyed city blocks and businesses to serve a population that apparently reached 200 people. A post office was approved but Gold Valley was abandoned before it was actually established (Appendix A). The mines are about 0.5 mile up the canyon to the south. From the townsite, this road leads down into the valley, where it rejoins the main road at milepoint 10.3.

8.9 The **Upper Sheep Creek Spur Road** (GPS 36°02.356'N 116°37.985'W, northeast 2.3 miles) is a faint track that leads to the start of a hiking route that crosses a low divide into Sheep Canyon. The informal trail can be followed down Sheep Canyon past some springs to the floor of Death Valley. The total distance is about 9 miles; some rock scrambling is required.

10.3 The ghost town road rejoins the main Gold Valley Road.

12.1 End of the road at the site of **Willow Creek** (GPS 36°02.942'N 116°41.310'W). The last 0.5 mile is extremely rough, and this part of the road may be closed to vehicles. Just before its end are a few stone foundations that mark the site of Willow Creek, a town that survived as an offshoot of the Greenwater boom for about a year from late 1906 until the establishment of nearby Gold Valley. The substantial rock foundation north of the road probably was the site of Willow Creek's first, and last, general store. A scar on the slope to the south has been identified as the remains of the Willow Creek Mill, except that facility was never more than a proposal. See Appendix A.

Just beyond the road's end in a thicket of willow trees are the **Willow Springs**, which yield several gallons per minute and support a stream that flows down the canyon for about a mile.

End of Gold Valley Road side trip.

17.8 / 10.2   A trail (northeast 2.6 miles one-way) leads to a small unnamed mine that was prospected for both copper and barite (barium sulfate). Some of the barite occurs as well-formed crystals. There are similar deposits in the hills farther to the northeast.

18.0 / 10.0   **Deadman Pass Road** (GPS 36°03.057'N 116°30.028'W, east 13.8 miles one-way to State Highway 127; 4WD required). This route, named because an unidentified person was found dead of dehydration beside the road during the Greenwater boom, served as the heavy freight road for the Greenwater mines. It crosses Deadman Pass (at elevation 3,263 feet) and then drops into the Amargosa Valley. Four wheel-drive vehicles are needed because of several sandy wash crossings east of the pass. Aside from being a transportation route, there are no particular attractions along this road.

19.5 / 8.5   **Miller Spring** (east, northern route; short hike). Miller Spring (GPS 36°02.144'N 116°26.664'W) is little more than a seep, but during the Greenwater boom it supplied small amounts of water to freight teams. It was named after George Miller, who settled in Pahrump Valley, Nevada, in 1869. Just up the slope from the spring is the Miller Spring Mine, a small copper prospect with no recorded production.

20.5 / 7.5   A few feet west of the road is a pile of rocks, neatly filled and flat-topped with soil. Next to it is a shallow pit amid a lot of rusty cans. This was a small-scale loading platform for some nearby mining operation (possibly the Miller Spring Mine).

20.8 / 7.2   **Miller Spring** (east, southern route; short hike). See the description at milepoint 19.5/8.5.

24.7 / 3.3   The road drops into Greenwater Wash. The plants here are a desert broom that has been identified as *Baccharis sergiloides*, a species different from that found in most of the Death Valley region. This broom has also been called Indian water and seep willow because dense stands such as this often indicate that fresh water is within a few feet of the surface.

| 28.0 / 0.0 | **Junction with State Highway 178** (GPS 35°57.992'N 116°21.821'W). No signs mark the Greenwater Road turnoff on the highway, but it is 5.8 miles west of State Highway 127 near Shoshone and 4.9 miles east of the summit of Salsberry Pass. |

Eastern Areas and Amargosa Valley, Trip Route E-4— Death Valley Junction to Devil's Hole

FROM: Death Valley Junction.

TO: Devil's Hole.

ROAD CONDITIONS: 12.2 miles one-way, paved all-weather highway, then graded gravel roads accessible to all vehicles.

SIDE TRIPS: None.

GENERAL DESCRIPTION: Devil's Hole, a detached unit of Death Valley National Park within the Ash Meadows National Wildlife Refuge, is the only habitat of the Devil's Hole pupfish, the most endangered of pupfish species.

ROAD LOG MILEAGES   eastbound from Death Valley Junction.

0.0	**State Line Road** (east, paved highway) begins opposite the Amargosa Opera House and Hotel in Death Valley Junction. See Trip Route E-5 for more information about this facility.
0.1	The State Line Road crosses the old Tonopah & Tidewater Railroad grade.
5.2	California-Nevada state line.
6.8	The road to Devil's Hole turns sharply north near where the highway curves south. The turnoff is marked for the wildlife refuge.
7.4	**Ash Meadows National Wildlife Refuge**, administered by the U.S. Fish & Wildlife Service, was established in 1984. Covering 12,736 acres of wetlands and alkaline desert uplands, it is the habitat for at least 24 plants and animals that are found nowhere else in the world. These Class I endemics include 4 fishes. This is the greatest concentration of endemic species of any area of similar size in the United States. Brochures about the refuge are available in leaflet boxes at the entry signs and at the refuge headquarters where there is a self-guided interpretive trail.
10.8	Turn east on a graded dirt road. The road to the west passes the refuge headquarters and reaches Nevada State Highway 373 (the continuation of California State Highway 127) in 7.3 miles.

Devil's Hole is a narrow slit into a limestone cavern, where the water above a shallow shelf is the only habitat of the Devil's Hole pupfish.

12.2 **Devil's Hole** is the surface opening of an extensive underground cavern that is mostly filled with water. Almost 50 feet below the outside ground surface, the pool is not accessible but is visible through the chain-link fence. A limestone shelf with an area of only about 80 square feet and under water less than 3 feet deep is the *only* habitat of the Devil's Hole pupfish (*Cyprinodon diabolis*). This is incomparably the most restricted habitat of any vertebrate animal in the world, and at times, the total fish population is less than 100.

The continued existence of the Devil's Hole pupfish depends entirely on limits to the amount of water that can be pumped by agricultural pursuits in Ash Meadows. After these limits were confirmed by a U.S. Supreme Court ruling, much of the surrounding area was purchased by the nonprofit Nature Conservancy. The land was later donated to the U.S. Fish & Wildlife Service for the Ash Meadows National Wildlife Refuge. The situation remains critical for the fish. Because of its status, Devil's Hole itself cannot be entered by casual visitors, but it is possible to peer through the fence and into the cavern.

Eastern Areas and Amargosa Valley, Trip Route E-5—State Highway 127, Death Valley Junction to Shoshone

FROM: Death Valley Junction at State Line Road.

TO: State Highway 178 near Shoshone, California.

ROAD CONDITIONS: 24.9 miles one-way, paved all-weather highway.

SIDE TRIPS: None.

GENERAL DESCRIPTION: Although this highway is entirely outside of Death Valley National Park, a few historic sites important to Death Valley's past lie along the route. Also, about 17 miles of the road serve as the national park boundary.

ROAD LOG MILEAGES southbound from Death Valley Junction / northbound from State Highway 178.

0.0 / 24.9 **Death Valley Junction** claims a population of 20. The town consists of several buildings on both sides of State Highway 127. In 1923 well-known author Zane Grey publicly decried the dilapidated state of Death Valley Junction. These fancy arcaded buildings were constructed by the borax company as a result. The two public facilities are the Amargosa Opera House and the Amargosa Hotel and Gift Shop (which sells soda, ice cream, and snacks); there is no restaurant. Operating seasons and hours are subject to change.

The Amargosa Hotel operates year-around. Each of the 14 rooms has air conditioning but no telephone or television. Telephone (760) 852-4441 for information and reservations.

The Amargosa Opera House, Inc., is a non profit corporation operated by Marta Becket, who purchased the opera house in 1968. The entire building had to be renovated before it could be used. She then painted wall murals to provide a "permanent audience" and the ceiling dome in which 16 ladies with antique musical instruments are the "orchestra." For the 2008–2009 season, shows were presented only on Saturday evenings at 8:15 PM (doors open at 7:45 PM); tickets are $15 for adults, $12 for children ages 5 through 12. Reservations are required by telephone at (760) 852-4441, or by Internet at reservations@amargosa-opera-house.com. (Note: Becket's partner, Tom Willett, passed away, and the future operation of the opera house is uncertain.)

There are no other services in Death Valley Junction. The Longstreet Inn and Casino, at the Nevada state line 7 miles north of Death Valley Junction, has a store, gas station, hotel, RV park, restaurant, and casino.

0.1 / 24.8 The remains of the old Pacific Coast Borax processing mill are marked by ruins and large waste piles east of the highway. This was at the intersection between the Tonopah & Tidewater Railroad and the Death Valley Railroad.

0.3 / 24.6 The grade of the Death Valley Railroad crosses the highway and can be seen extending in a straight line for several miles to the west. Its history is described in Appendix B.

1.3 / 23.6 **Petro Road** (west). This road extends across the gentle alluvial fan 5.5 miles to the Lila C. Mine and the site of (Old) Ryan, and then northwest past Greenwater Canyon. There it becomes the Terry Mine Road and continues to State Highway 190. This route is described as Side Trip E-1c.

7.2 / 17.7 **Deadman Pass Road** (GPS 36°12.647'N 116°23.745'W, west 13.8 miles to Greenwater Valley Road; 4WD required) is a poor road that cuts through the Greenwater Range to Greenwater Valley (see Trip Route E-3). There are no particular attractions along the route.

8.2 / 16.7 The peak east of the highway is **Eagle Mountain** (elevation 3,806 feet). It is composed of Paleozoic sedimentary rocks tilted almost vertically on end.

10.3 / 14.6	The grade of the **Tonopah & Tidewater Railroad** parallels State Highway 127, usually to the west but cutting back and forth across the road several times. The power line generally is right next to the grade; a few square-cut wood poles that date to the early 1900s are still standing. A large tamarisk tree marks the site of Evelyn (named after "Borax" Smith's daughter), a siding station and water stop for the T&T trains. Remnants of the original wooden drainage culverts under the railroad grade and concrete abutments where there were trestles are visible at several places. A short history of the T&T is given in Appendix B.
21.1 / 3.8	The grade of the Tonopah & Tidewater Railroad crosses the highway for the last (southbound) or first (northbound) time.
24.9 / 0.0	**State Highway 178** (west) is Death Valley's Jubilee Pass Road, described as Trip Route S-1. It extends into Death Valley where it becomes the East Side Road (Trip Route SC-2) and Badwater Road (Trip Route SC-1). The town of Shoshone, 1.6 miles south, offers all basic services: gas, grocery, motel, restaurants, post office, and museum–art gallery.

Eastern Areas and Amargosa Valley, Trip Route E-6—Lee Ghost Town

FROM: Amargosa Valley, Nevada (town) via Amargosa Farm Road.

TO: Lee ghost town and Echo Pass.

ROAD CONDITIONS: 15.9 miles one-way, paved and improved dirt roads except 4WD required on the last 3.9 miles.

SIDE TRIPS: None.

GENERAL DESCRIPTION: The ghost town of Lee, California, with its associated sites of Lee Annex and Lee, Nevada, was one of the longest-lasting boom towns of the Rhyolite rush. Lee is within Death Valley National Park, and this route is the only practical access to the site. The community of Amargosa Valley, Nevada, is scattered over a wide area and offers most basic services. There are many roads in the valley, and the route described here is the most direct among several possibilities. Explorers with short-wheelbase 4WD vehicles equipped with winches can continue beyond Lee, over the Funeral Mountains at Echo Summit, and into Death Valley by way of Echo Canyon.

ROAD LOG MILEAGES	westbound from Nevada State Highway 373 at Amargosa Valley (town).
0.0	**Amargosa Farm Road** is well marked on the highway 3.0 miles north of the Amargosa Valley post office. This point is

17.3 miles north of California State Highway 190 at Death Valley Junction, or 4.9 miles south of Lathrop Wells at U.S. Highway 95.

2.7   The road passes the elementary school, health clinic, fire station, and community building.

7.2   **Valley View Road**. Turn north 1 mile to Frontier Road. Valley View Road is paved north an additional 6.8 miles to U.S. Highway 95.

8.2   **Frontier Road** (graded dirt). Turn west on Frontier Road. The site of **Leeland** (GPS 36°35.155'N 116°35.235'W), a station on the Tonopah & Tidewater Railroad, is north of the road about 0.2 mile west of the Valley View–Frontier intersection. (Although not posted, this might be private property.)

11.9   **Saddleback Court**. Continue west on Frontier Road an additional 0.1 mile beyond Saddleback Court.

12.0   The route to Lee is the dirt road that bears northwest about 0.1 mile west of the intersection of Saddleback Court and Frontier Road, at GPS 36°34.998'N 116°36.763'W. As it begins its climb up the alluvial fan, it quickly deteriorates into a rocky track with high centers and sharp washouts that require 4WD vehicles.

14.6   The California-Nevada state line, which is also the national park boundary, is marked by a series of metal posts.

14.9   **Lee Annex** was a suburb of Lee. Straddling the state line, its founder intended it to replace the two towns of Lee, California, and Lee, Nevada (in the hills to the northeast), with a single community more accessible to the Tonopah & Tidewater Railroad. Although the railroad never built the anticipated spur into town, a number of substantial buildings were built. Several rock walls and tin can dumps are scattered north of the road.

15.9   **Lee, California** (GPS 36°34.890'N 116°40.123'W). The Hayseed Mine just south of town was the big discovery here. Its surface ore was laced with free gold and led to a rush starting in 1906. Lee became a substantial city of 500 people by the end of 1907 but was abandoned by 1912. Rows of building sites, extensive rock walls, and large piles of tin can and broken bottle debris remain. The longest of the walls probably marks the site of the two-story Lee Hotel. See Appendix A for more of this history.

Beyond Lee, the road continues into a small canyon, with numerous small mines along the way. It is about 4 miles from the ghost town to the summit of Echo Pass, the site of the brief 1907 tent town of Echo that left behind no remains whatsoever. From there, the road continues into Upper Echo Canyon. It is a tortuous drive. One of the two branches shown on some maps is completely washed away. The other demands short-wheelbase 4WD vehicles with winches and is recommended only to drivers with considerable experience and accompanied by others.

Eastern Areas and Amargosa Valley, Trip Route E-7—Indian Pass Road

FROM: U.S. Highway 95 in Nevada.

TO: Summit near Indian Pass.

ROAD CONDITIONS: 13.9 miles one-way, unmaintained dirt road, high-clearance first 2.1 miles to Ashton Station, then 4WD.

SIDE TRIPS: None.

GENERAL DESCRIPTION: Note: the Indian Pass Road is well-removed from other Death Valley routes, so it is shown on a separate map. When viewed from the east, Indian Pass appears to be an obvious route through the Funeral Mountains. Because of the deep canyon on its west side, however, it has seldom been used. It is quite certain that Indian Pass was used by the Georgian party of the 49ers, but not by any of the other argonauts. Now this road provides access to a rarely visited part of Death Valley National Park and serves as a potential pick-up point for backpackers. This road, which is probably driven less often than any other in the national park, ends on a flat, mesa-like area, across a canyon fully 1 mile from Indian Pass itself.

ROAD LOG MILEAGES	westbound from U.S. Highway 95.

0.0	**Indian Pass Road** (GPS 36°44.510'N 116°38.760'W, southwest; 4WD required) leaves U.S. Highway 95 at a point 15.3 miles northwest of Lathrop Wells, Nevada, or 13.9 miles southeast of Beatty, Nevada. When last seen, the turnoff to this road was not marked.
2.1	**Ashton Station**. Ashton was a minor station along the Tonopah & Tidewater Railroad. At this point the road turns more to the south to continue across flat Amargosa Valley where there are several deep, sandy wash crossings.
7.3	The old road between the mining towns of Lee and Rhyolite comes in from the north.
7.4	At this three-way junction (GPS 36°38.996'N 116°42.440'W), the road to Indian Pass is the fork to the right. If not before, then 4WD vehicles are required beyond this point.

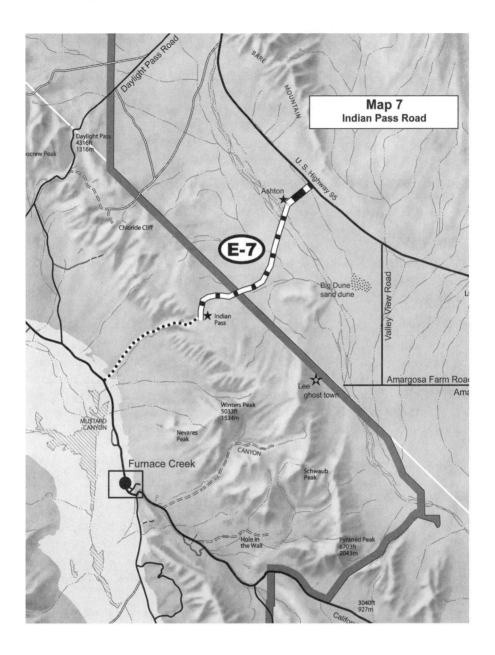

Map 7
Indian Pass Road

E-7

Daylight Pass Road

B.A.R.E MOUNTAIN

Daylight Pass
4316ft
1316m

screw Peak

Chloride Cliff

U. S. Highway 95

Ashton

Big Dune
sand dune

Indian
Pass

Valley View Road

Amargosa Farm Road

Ama

Lee
ghost town

Winters Peak
5033ft
1534m

MUSTARD
CANYON

Nevares
Peak

CANYON

Furnace Creek

Schwaub
Peak

Hole in
the Wall

Pyramid Peak
6703ft
2043m

3040ft
927m

Califor

The road straight ahead ends at the national park boundary at the state line; beyond there, hikers can continue about
1.5 miles on a closed road to a few mining prospects of no
importance. The branch to the left is the continuation of
the Rhyolite-Lee road; it reportedly is washed out in several
places and not recommended.

9.0   **Death Valley National Park** boundary at the Nevada-California state line (GPS 36°38.596'N 116°43.797'W). This stretch of road climbs an alluvial fan where there are numerous rough, sandy washes, and then passes through a small canyon, across an open valley, and into another canyon.

12.0   The road to the right where there is a "mine hazard" sign (GPS 36°37.992'N 116°46.803'W) leads to several small mines that evidently were prospected for gold during the Bullfrog rush circa 1906. None of them had significant production.

The Indian Pass Road turns south down the canyon.

12.6   The road climbs out of the main wash to cross a gentle slope that is cut by numerous small gullies. There are several mine prospects on the far side of the ridge to the west.

13.9   The Indian Pass Road effectively ends at this point (GPS 36°36.750'N 116°47.420'W). A two-track route does continue a short distance farther south, but hikers will probably prefer to take the faint road to the west. It ends at the rim of Indian Pass Canyon above a mine, from which an informal trail drops to the bottom of the canyon. Once there, reliable water is available at a spring only a few hundred feet down the canyon. From the spring, it is a hike of about 6 miles to State Highway 190, on the floor of Death Valley at a point 6.5 miles north of Furnace Creek.

CHAPTER FOURTEEN

North-Central Death Valley

This is a heavily visited portion of Death Valley. State Highway 190 is a major transportation corridor connecting the developed areas at Furnace Creek and Stovepipe Wells. This part of the park also includes the popular attractions of Harmony Borax Works, Salt Creek, the Mesquite Flat Sand Dunes, Chloride Cliff, Rhyolite ghost town, and Titus Canyon. **Special note:** the Keane Wonder mine, mill, and springs are also in this part of Death Valley, but as of September 2008 that area was closed to public entry because of the hazards of unstable structures and millsite contamination. No date for reopening has been set, so check at the Furnace Creek Visitor Center for current information.

North-Central Death Valley, Trip Route NC-1—State Highway 190 Central, Furnace Creek to Stovepipe Wells Village

FROM: Furnace Creek Visitor Center.

TO: Stovepipe Wells Village.

ROAD CONDITIONS: 24.1 miles one-way, all-weather paved highway.

SIDE TRIPS: Harmony Borax Works and Mustard Canyon (all vehicles), Salt Creek Road (Side Trip NC-1a, all vehicles), and Grotto Canyon Road (4WD); access to Beatty Cutoff Road (Trip Route NC-2) and Scotty's Castle Road (Trip Route N-1).

GENERAL DESCRIPTION: Although State Highway 190 is primarily a through route, the drive between Furnace Creek and Stovepipe Wells will take you through diverse scenery and some of Death Valley's scenic side trips.

ROAD LOG MILEAGES   northbound from Furnace Creek Visitor Center / southbound from Stovepipe Wells Village.

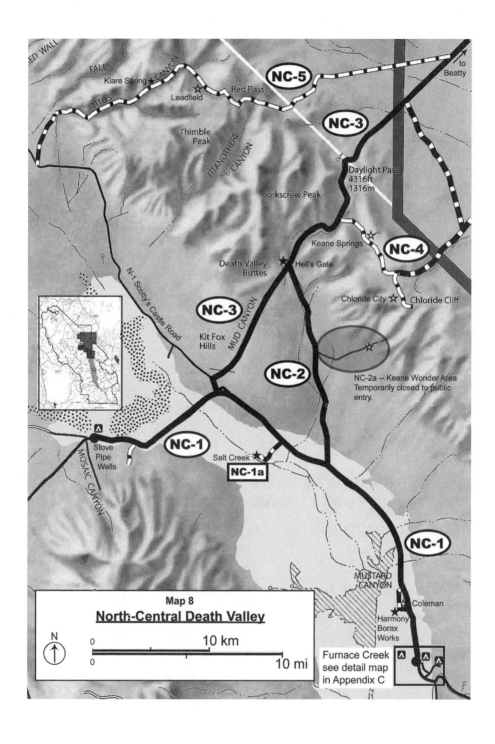

to Beatty

RED WALL

FALL
Klare Spring ★
Leadfield ☆
Red Pass

TITUS CANYON

NC-5

NC-3

Thimble Peak

TITANOTHERE CANYON

Daylight Pass
4316ft
1316m

Corkscrew Peak

N-1 Scotty's Castle Road

Keane Springs ☆

NC-4

Death Valley Buttes ★ Hell's Gate

Chloride City ☆ ┤ Chloride Cliff

NC-3

MUD CANYON

Kit Fox Hills

☆

NC-2

NC-2a -- Keane Wonder Area Temporarily closed to public entry.

MOSAIC CANYON

NC-1

Stove Pipe Wells ⛺

Salt Creek ★

NC-1a

NC-1

MUSTARD CANYON

Coleman

Harmony Borax Works ★

Furnace Creek see detail map in Appendix C ⛺ ◮ ◮

Map 8
North-Central Death Valley

N ↑

0   10 km

0   10 mi

0.0 / 24.1	**Furnace Creek Visitor Center**.
0.4 / 23.7	Furnace Creek Campground entrance.
1.0 / 23.1	To the east are the Funeral Mountains, dominated by Nevares Peak and higher Winters Peak beyond. The rocks in this part of the range are Paleozoic sedimentary formations, mostly Cambrian Period limestones. To the north the rocks are older and more extensively recrystallized by metamorphism.
	Near the west side of the highway, the light-colored ground is clay-rich sediment that was deposited about 2,000 years ago in the most recent extensive lake in Death Valley. Reflecting the ongoing geologic development of Death Valley, these beds have been tilted so that they are higher in elevation here than are the equivalent beds on the west side of the valley.
1.3 / 22.8	**Harmony Borax Works** and **Mustard Canyon Road** (west; paved to parking lot, then graded dirt passable by any vehicle). This short side trip is a great way to see several aspects of the history and geology of borax mining.
0.0	Turnoff from Highway 190 at a California historic monument.
0.2	**Harmony Borax Works** parking lot. From here, a loop trail circles the remains of the borax processing plant that was constructed in 1883 and operated during October to June of each year through 1888. Display panels explain the various parts of the plant. A foot trail at the far side of the works leads west 2.5 miles onto the salt flats, where piles of salt-encrusted mud called haystacks were scraped up during mineral claim assessment work in the early 1900s.
0.3	**Coleman**. Coleman was the location of the office, storage sheds, and blacksmith plus the residential area for the 30 Chinese miners at the Harmony Borax Works (the non-Chinese operators of the borax plant apparently lived at Greenland Ranch). The adobe walls beside the Mustard Canyon Road are the remains of a warehouse and the company office. All the other structures were tents that left no evidence of having been there.
0.8	The road makes a sharp right turn into **Mustard Canyon**, which cuts completely through the **West Coleman Hills**. The rich-yellow rocks are lakebed sediments of the Furnace Creek Formation. Throughout the canyon are white veinlets and patches of borate minerals, primarily powdery masses of ulexite (sodium-calcium borate) and a little crystalline

The Harmony Borax Works operated from 1883 to 1888.

colemanite (calcium borate). The mineralization exists only in trace amounts, so there has never been any mining here.

1.2   Exit from the Mustard Canyon narrows.

1.5   Junction with State Highway 190.

End of Harmony Borax–Mustard Canyon side trip.

2.0 / 22.1   Mustard Canyon Road exit.

2.2 / 21.9   **Gnomes' Workshop** is an area of strange salt formations along a small perennial stream of concentrated salt water. See Chapter 8 for details about the short hike into this fascinating area.

3.0 / 21.1   Cow Creek Road (east). This is the housing, office, and maintenance area for the National Park Service, Caltrans, Inyo County, and other government agency employees, and the location of Death Valley Elementary School. There are no commercial facilities.

4.0 / 20.1   The dominant shrubs on this alluvial fan are creosote bushes along with a few specimens of desert holly saltbushes. Looking west from the road, notice how the creosotes abruptly thin out and the desert holly grows thickly just at the point where the slope begins to merge with the salt pan of the valley floor. Although the creosote is the most ubiquitous of desert plants, it cannot tolerate strongly alkaline soil conditions, whereas the well-named saltbushes, such as desert holly, can.

A series of low fault scarps cut horizontally across the slope to the east. These mark the northernmost trace of the Furnace Creek Fault Zone. Especially visible in low morning sunlight, they have often been incorrectly described as wave-cut shorelines of ancient Lake Manly.

5.2 / 18.9 **Salt Springs Fault Scarp** (GPS 36°32.154'N 116°53.032'W). Just south of Salt Springs is a prominent fault scarp as high as 10 feet. It climbs out of the salt pan, crosses the highway, and disappears about a mile to the northeast. This is the northernmost trace of the Black Mountain (or Central) Death Valley Fault Zone. Based on the morphology of this scarp, it may have formed as little as 600 years ago.

7.1 / 17.0 Large mounds of "cottonball" ulexite borax ore are visible at the edge of the salt flat below the highway. This is the site of the **East Side Borax Camp**, a semi-permanent community of miners during the days of the Harmony Borax Works. There was a similar camp called **Shoveltown** on the far side of the valley. It is possible that these camps actually mined sodium carbonate, which was necessary for the ore processing at Harmony Borax Works, rather than borax itself.

To the east are the "**Three Bare Hills**" where the U.S. Geological Survey has conducted wind-erosion studies.

7.5 / 16.6 Downslope next to the dirt track of the original highway is a grave that sometimes is marked with a crude cross (GPS 36°33.532'N 116°54.214'W). This victim of Death Valley's extremes was found beside the old road in 1933. He was never identified.

10.5 / 13.6 **Beatty Cutoff Road** (northeast; see Trip Route NC-2). Directly east of here, the Funeral Mountains are composed of late Precambrian and early Paleozoic sedimentary rocks that have been extensively recrystallized by metamorphism. The high peak marked by two white stripes of Beck Spring Formation dolomite is Chloride Cliff (the stripes tend to disappear into afternoon shadows). The western base of the mountains is defined by the Keane Wonder Fault. White patches of travertine mark places where sulfurous warm springs reach the surface along the fault.

11.2 / 12.9 A series of ridges extending northerly at an angle to the road are aligned along the trace of the **Northern Death Valley Fault Zone**.

An interpretive boardwalk parallels Salt Creek, the only habitat of the Salt Creek pupfish.

11.9 / 12.2 The groves of dark-colored plants on the flats west of the highway are honey mesquite trees, watered by the subsurface flow from Salt Creek just to the north. The grave of famous miner Jean Lemoigne, for whom Lemoigne Canyon is named (see Trip Route W-2), is at the edge of one of the groves.

12.9 / 11.2 **Side Trip NC-1a—Salt Creek Road** (west 1.2 miles one-way; graded dirt road suitable for all vehicles). This road ends at a parking area where there are picnic tables, trash cans, and chemical toilets at the **Salt Creek Interpretive Trail**.

Salt Creek rises from a series of springs about 2 miles upstream from the parking area; the largest is **McLean Spring**. During the winter the stream sometimes reaches beyond the parking area to open valley floor, but often during the summer it does not even reach the upper end of the boardwalk.

Despite the extreme conditions, Salt Creek is inhabited by the Salt Creek pupfish (*Cyprinodon salinus*), which lives nowhere else. During the winter months it is sometimes impossible to see a single fish—the cold water causes them to migrate into deeper pools near the headwaters of the stream. Apparently they do not enter a completely inactive state, as has been reported. Spawning takes place as the water temperature increases in late winter, and usually peaks in March and April. The male fish flash brilliant blue as they defend their tiny territories. The springtime population may be as great as 1 million fish, yet most die as the creek dries up in the heat of summer. By September the population is only a few thousand with the survivors restricted to the deep upstream pools. The average Salt Creek pupfish lives only 4 to 6 months.

A great variety of insects and their larvae live in the water, and they attract many birds. Killdeer, common snipe, and spotted sandpiper are especially common.

Almost all of the plants along Salt Creek are pickleweed and saltgrass. In places slightly elevated above the stream are a few iodine bushes, four-winged saltbush, and desert holly.

The rocks of the Salt Creek Hills bordering the stream are lake bed sediments of the Furnace Creek Formation. Unlike the exposures along Furnace Creek Wash to the south, there are no deposits of borate minerals. Fossil footprints are common, though. Camel, horse, antelope, and bird tracks have been positively identified by paleontologists, and their abundance indicates that 12 million years ago the area around the lake was a lush grassland.

End Salt Creek Road side trip.

13.8 / 10.3   About 0.25 mile east of the highway, the trace of the Northern Death Valley Fault Zone is marked not only by a fault scarp but also by stream channels that show a right-lateral offset from their original positions by as much as 35 feet.

~15 / 9   View south. The Funeral Mountains are to the east, with famous Chloride Cliff near the highest crest. Straight ahead across the salt flats are the Black Mountains. The Panamint Mountains form the west side of Death Valley, ending at Tucki Mountain directly to the west. The low Salt Creek Hills are below the highway. Mesquite groves mark the area of **McLean Spring**, the main source of Salt Creek, where a "trading post" apparently existed in 1906–1907 and then again in 1932–1933 when Bill and Edna Price sold 49er relics to tourists. Near the spring is **Burned Wagons Point**, where some of the 49ers burned their wagons in order to cook and dry the meat of their slaughtered oxen. The resultant jerky was nearly all they had to eat until they reached civilization.

~16 / 8   View north. The **Kit Fox Hills**, composed of a miscellany of lake, stream, and alluvial fan deposits, are straight ahead. Although it is not clearly visible from the ground, the west edge of the hills lies along a razor-sharp line marking the trace of the Northern Death Valley Fault Zone, a major right-lateral fault with horizontal movement totaling as much as 50 miles. Farther ahead across the valley is the Last Chance Range; the highest summit is Tin Mountain (elevation 8,951 feet).

16.9 / 7.2   **Sand Dune Junction** at **Scotty's Castle Road**. This road is the access to Scotty's Castle, Ubehebe Crater, and other points in northern Death Valley. It is described as Trip Route N-1.

17.8 / 6.3   **Sand Dunes Hike** (north). This popular side road has been closed to vehicles but can be used as a hiking route. The northern extension of the road, leading from Scotty's Castle Road to the site of historic Stovepipe Well, remains open (see Trip Route N-1, Side Trip N-1a). The hiking distance from State Highway 190 to the historic Stovepipe Well is 2.6 miles one-way.

The entire route extends along the contact between the sand dunes and a smooth alluvial fan, features that are geologically related yet present sharply different visual appearances.

West of the road are large hummocks of sand held in place by mesquite trees. These are called locked dunes. The trees keep the sand in place, and a constant addition of more sand forces the tree to grow ever larger. The result is gigantism—although little of the mesquite is visible, the whole plant is huge, and the distance from the tip of its growth to the bottom of its roots can be as great as 100 feet.

The alluvial fan east of the road has formed a surface of well-developed "desert pavement." Mechanical weathering breaks down an original rock into an assortment of silt, sand, and pebbles. Erosion by wind then strips away the silt as wind-blown dust and carries the sand across the surface into the dunes. Only the pebbles are left behind. Sifted together like the pieces of a jigsaw puzzle, the result is a water- and erosion-resistant surface. It is almost impossible for plants to take root in such an area, explaining why the ground is so barren.

Both the sand dunes and desert pavement have formed since Ice Age Lake Manly dried up less than 10,000 years ago. Each windstorm makes the dunes a little bit larger, but curled and cracked mud flats of the old lake bed are exposed between some of the dunes.

Early morning is the best time to visit sand dunes, here or anywhere. This is just after the nighttime activity of the dune animals and before daytime wind has a chance to erase the tracks. Although the dunes look barren, they are home to or are visited by numerous insects, birds, lizards, snakes, and mammals. As you explore, try to stay back from the mesquite trees to avoid collapsing animal burrows.

At the end of the sand dunes hike, the route meets Old Stovepipe Road at the site of Stovepipe Well. The original well, now long gone, was a shallow hole dug through the sand to brackish but drinkable water. A lifesaver to many prospectors traveling between Rhyolite and Skidoo, it was the only water hole along the cross-valley route. Here, too, was the short-lived settlement of Stovepipe Well (see Appendix A).

End of Sand Dunes Hike.

19.3 / 4.8   **Devil's Cornfield** (both sides of the highway). The plants that look like shocks of corn are arrowweed (*Pluchea sericea*). It is a common plant in low-elevation desert areas where there is abundant water, which lies only a few feet below the surface here. Gradual erosion has lowered the ground surface as the plants grew. What were the roots are now exposed as hard, woody tissue below the leafy crowns. Drifting sand sometimes forms coppice dunes around the base of each plant. Arrowweed is a member of the composite (sunflower) family. It bears abundant purple flowers in the spring. The long, straight stems were, indeed, used by Indians for making arrow shafts, as well as for basketry, traps, cages, and storage bins.

20.3 / 3.8   The remnants of a clay playa (dry lake bed surface) lie along both sides of the highway. This was Lake Manly, the Ice Age lake whose evaporation at the end of the last glacial episode some 10,000 years ago deposited the salts on the floor of Death Valley around places like Badwater and the Devil's Golf Course (see Trip Route SC-1). This clay surface can be seen at many places among the sand dunes and proves that the dunes have grown from nothing to their present size in less than 10,000 years.

20.5 / 3.6   **Little Bridge Canyon** (south 3 miles one-way; hike). The large wash that reaches the road here comes out of Little Bridge Canyon. It is a steep 2 miles from the highway to the mouth of the canyon. Within the canyon are both a natural bridge and a natural arch. The arch, which is reached first, is a small span on the right about 0.5 mile into the canyon. The bridge is 20 feet high and spans part of the left side of the canyon another 0.5 mile in. Neither the bridge nor the arch is as big as Natural Bridge near Badwater (see Trip Route SC-1). Those wanting to explore Little Bridge Canyon encounter narrow side canyons of polished white quartzite above the natural bridge.

20.8 / 3.3   North of the highway is a series of locked dunes. Each has formed around a large plant, usually mesquite but sometimes creosote, whose roots helped keep the sand in place while the unanchored sand of the surrounding ground was blown away.

21.7 / 2.4   **Grotto Canyon Road** (south 1.1 miles one-way; 4WD required). This road leads up the alluvial fan to the mouth of Grotto Canyon, which some people feel is more spectacular than nearby Mosaic Canyon (see Chapter 8). You can to walk about 2 miles up the canyon through numerous water-worn grottos and narrows of polished rock. Further progress is blocked by a high, dry waterfall.

22.4 / 1.7   **Sand Dunes parking area** (north side of highway). You can walk to the sand dunes anywhere you like, but this large parking lot has interpretive displays about the dunes and their ecology. Often called the Death Valley Dunes but officially named the **Mesquite Flat Sand Dunes**, these cover about 14 square miles and are surrounded on the north and west by another 15 to 20 square miles of lower dunes. The tallest crest reaches 60 to 80 feet above its base (the exact height can change in any windstorm). The dunes are well worth exploring. They are especially fine in the morning of a calm day, when countless stories are told by the tracks of the many animals who roamed the sand overnight. Sand dunes may look barren, but they really are not. Obviously, though, they are unstable, and this is an extremely fragile habitat for life. Please do all you can to avoid collapsing any burrows you find under the bushes.

24.1 / 0.0   **Stovepipe Wells Village.** Stovepipe Wells Hotel was founded by Bob Eichbaum in 1926. A veteran of the Rhyolite and Skidoo mining booms, he saw tourism as Death Valley's real gold. He was granted a franchise to build a scenic toll road into Death Valley. The 38-mile route from Darwin Wash over Towne Pass to the sand dunes was completed in May 1926. The fee was $2 per car plus 50¢ per person. The hotel (initially known as "Bungalow City") opened for business the

The Mesquite Flat (or Death Valley) Sand Dunes from the air.

following November 1 and was Death Valley's first tourist facility.

Stovepipe Wells Village is operated by the Death Valley Lodging Company. Services include a store, gas station, gift shop, restaurant, saloon, RV park, and motel. (See Appendix C.) Adjacent to the village is the Park Service's Stovepipe Wells Campground. The Park Service also operates an information and ranger station just east of the village. (Note that although the Park Service uses a one-word version of the name "Stovepipe," the original name used by Eichbaum and sometimes still today by the resort is two words, "Stove Pipe.")

North-Central Death Valley, Trip NC-2—Beatty Cutoff Road

FROM: Beatty Junction on State Highway 190.

TO: Hell's Gate on Mud Canyon–Daylight Pass Road.

ROAD CONDITIONS: 9.9 miles one-way, all-weather paved road.

SIDE TRIP: Side Trip NC-2a, Keane Wonder Mine Road and vicinity (all vehicles); see below.

GENERAL DESCRIPTION: As the name implies, the Beatty Cutoff Road was developed in order to reduce the driving distance between Furnace Creek and Beatty, Nevada. Few features of interest lie along the road itself. **Note:** the Beatty Cutoff Road also provides access to the Keane Wonder Mine, one of Death Valley's most important historic areas. However, the Keane Wonder area was closed to public entry in September 2008 because of the dangers of collapsing mine and mill structures, and soil contamination with heavy metals and cyanide in the millsite area. No date for reopening has been set, so check at the Furnace Creek Visitor Center for current information.

ROAD LOG MILEAGES	northbound from State Highway 190 / southbound from Hell's Gate.

0.0 / 9.9	**Beatty Junction** at the turnoff (northeast) from State Highway 190, 10.5 miles north of the Furnace Creek Visitor Center. All of this route is across alluvial fans, a steady climb of more than 2,000 feet in 9.9 miles. The high point in the Funeral Mountains to the east, marked by two white stripes of the Beck Spring Formation, is Chloride Cliff; it can be reached by 4WD vehicles (Trip Route NC-4).
~2 / 7	These hills are composed of the old fanglomerate of the Funeral Formation; that is, alluvial fan sediment compacted into a solid rock of sand and angular boulders. It has been uplifted by movements along the Northern Death Valley Fault Zone and is now being eroded.
1.9 / 8.0	The road cuts through a low, rounded gravel bar that was formed by wave action along the shore of Lake Manly. That much is certain, but just when this bar actually formed is very uncertain—various geological studies have produced ages as young as 9,000 years and as old as 130,000 years.
5.6 / 4.3	**Keane Wonder Area**. As of September 2008, this road, the Keane Wonder Mine and Millsite at its end, and the nearby Keane Wonder Springs and Cyty Mill were closed to public entry pending work to stabilize the historic structures and mitigate toxic contamination in the area. The following description is included in this book in the event that the area is re-opened; check at the Furnace Creek Visitor Center for current information.

The Keane Wonder Mine Road (GPS 36°39.974'N 116°57.256'W, east 2.7 miles one-way; all vehicles) is rough and rocky, especially near its end at the Keane Wonder Mill, but there are no high centers and any standard vehicle driven with care can make this highly recommended trip. The first mile is a gradual descent to the bottom of a wide wash; the road then climbs steadily up to a parking lot below the Keane Wonder Mill. |

Keane Wonder Mill and townsite. Immediately north of the parking area are remnants of the milling operation that worked the rich gold ore of the Keane Wonder Mine high up the mountain. The remains of the mill itself are a short walk up the old road from the end of the parking lot. An interpretive display describes the area's history and includes a photograph that shows the mill when it was operating.

The Keane Wonder Mine was discovered by Jack Keane in January 1904. The ore was so rich that the property sold for $10,000 cash against a $150,000 option only five weeks after its discovery. By that time an estimated 500 prospectors were swarming the nearby hills. That first financial arrangement fell through, however, and the property was sold, and re-sold, three additional times in the next three years.

The mill and tramway were finally built in 1907, and the mining operation got underway that October. The tramway was itself a wonder. With an upper and a lower station plus 13 towers in between, its construction required more than 75,000 board feet of lumber. The total length was slightly more than 1 mile, with a vertical fall of almost 1,500 feet. The tram operated using gravity alone, without any kind of motor. The weight of loaded ore buckets at the mine was enough to lower them to the mill while raising empty buckets back to the mine, and there was enough excess energy to operate equipment in the mine. Mine workers sometimes rode the buckets from the mill up to the mine.

The Keane Wonder Mine and Mill operated continuously into 1911, and then intermittently until 1916. There was enough activity with other mining in the area that the town of **Keane Wonder**, with a post office, school, boardinghouse, store, and other businesses, survived until the mine closed. Additional operations took place during the 1920s and 1930s, bringing the total gold production to more than $1 million. The Keane Wonder Mine closed for good in 1942.

Hike to Keane Wonder Mine (2 miles round-trip). From the mill, a trail winds its way up the mountain, roughly following the route of the tramway line. This is a very strenuous hike—although the distance is only 1 mile, the climb to the lowermost mine workings is more than 1,500 feet. About halfway up there is a spectacular view of the tramway cables still strung between towers across the canyon. Upon reaching the mine area, remember the hazards. The shafts and tunnels

Extensive ruins remain at the Keane Wonder Mill.

are within deeply weathered metamorphic rocks and are very unstable. KEEP OUT!

Hike to Keane Wonder Springs and Cyty Mill (2 miles round-trip to the springs, 3 miles round-trip to the mill). The sharp base of Funeral Mountain marks the Keane Wonder Fault Zone, a dip-slip fault with vertical movement that has uplifted the range with respect to the valley. The water supply for the Keane Wonder operation came from some springs that rise along the fault zone north of the mill. The Keane Wonder Springs flow about 60 gallons per minute. Most comes from a single source above the old road. The water is warm and sulfurous and has deposited extensive terraces of travertine (calcium carbonate).

Many other mineral claims were filed at about the same time as that of the Keane Wonder Mine. One of them was the Big Bell Mine, discovered by Johnny Cyty and Mike Sullivan. The property was sold to mining promoter E. Burdon Gaylord in 1905. Gaylord financed Death Valley Scotty's record-breaking "Death Valley Coyote" train run from Los Angeles to Chicago in a failed effort to promote this mine by making Death Valley famous. The mill was purchased and moved by Cyty from the fading town of Lee. Unfortunately, it was very inefficient and apparently made only one or two ore runs. Its wooden ruins and the remains of Cyty's cabin lie near more springs around a hill about 0.5 mile beyond the main springs (GPS 36°40.569'N 116°55.620'W).

End of Keane Wonder Mine Road side trip.

~9 / 1	View north. Straight ahead is **Corkscrew Peak** (elevation 5,804 feet). It is composed of Cambrian age sedimentary rocks. The cliffs are Wood Canyon Formation, and the summit is Carrara Limestone.
9.9 / 0.0	**Hell's Gate** is at the junction where the Beatty Cutoff Road meets the Daylight Pass Road (east)—Mud Canyon Road (west). The elevation is 2,262 feet. There is an information kiosk next to picnic tables, trash cans, and a chemical toilet.

North-Central Death Valley, Trip Route NC-3—Mud Canyon Road and Daylight Pass Road (State Highway 374 outside the park in Nevada)

FROM: Scotty's Castle Road near State Highway 190.

TO: Beatty, Nevada.

ROAD CONDITIONS: 25.8 miles one-way, all-weather paved road.

SIDE TRIPS: Hole-in-the-Rock Spring (hike), Daylight Spring (hike), and Rhyolite, Nevada (Side Trip NC-3a, all vehicles); access to Monarch Canyon Road–Chloride Cliff Road (Trip Route NC-4) and Titus Canyon Road (Trip Route NC-5).

GENERAL DESCRIPTION: The Daylight Pass Road is narrow and steep in places, but it is suitable for all vehicles as a major connecting route between western Nevada and eastern California. There are spectacular vistas. The famous ghost towns of Rhyolite and Bullfrog, although outside of the national park, are on a side road near Beatty.

ROAD LOG MILEAGES	eastbound from Scotty's Castle Road / westbound from Beatty, Nevada.

0.0 / 25.8	The **Mud Canyon Road** climbs up an alluvial fan nearly barren of plants because of well-developed desert pavement.
0.5 / 25.3	**Northern Death Valley Fault Zone** at the entrance to Mud Canyon. This fault is one of the most important structural features of Death Valley. It is a right-lateral strike-slip fault—whichever direction you look across it, the opposite side appears to have moved horizontally to your right, in this case possibly by as much as 50 miles. Only a little vertical movement takes place on this fault, but the Kit Fox Hills are a result. Mud Canyon cuts completely through the hills, which are composed of old fanglomerates and stream sands of the Funeral Formation.
3.5 / 22.3	**Death Valley Buttes** to the north-northeast are somewhat detached from the rest of Grapevine Mountains, but like them, are composed of Cambrian age sedimentary rocks.
6.6 / 19.2	**Hell's Gate** is located at the junction with the Beatty Cutoff Road (Trip Route NC-2), elevation 2,262 feet. There is an information kiosk next to picnic tables, trash cans, and a chemical toilet. East from here, the road is called the Daylight Pass Road; west from here it is the Mud Canyon Road.
7.6 / 18.2	The deep-red rocks visible about 0.25 mile north of the road mark the trace of the Keane Wonder Fault. This fault runs parallel to the Northern Death Valley Fault Zone (see milepoint 25.3 if driving westbound) but is different in that it is a dip-slip fault with vertical rather than horizontal movements. The Keane Wonder Fault is responsible for uplifting the Funeral Mountains south of the Daylight Pass Road, but it suddenly disappears only a short distance north of these red outcrops.
7.8 / 18.0	**Hole-in-the-Rock Spring** (GPS 36°44.418'N 116°58.014'W, north 0.3 mile up a small canyon just east of the highway

sign marking Corkscrew Peak; hike). Hole-in-the-Rock Spring produces little water, but it was an important resource along the road between Rhyolite and Skidoo. The spring maintains a small pool within a travertine cavern partially hidden by shrubbery. Enough people take this walk that you will probably be able to see the informal trail to the spring.

Corkscrew Peak is straight north of the road. Its prominent cliffs are exposures of the Wood Canyon Formation, whereas the summit is Carrara Formation limestone. Both rock units date to the Cambrian Period.

Eastbound drivers enter **Boundary Canyon**, probably named because the California-Nevada state boundary line was once thought to cross through the canyon.

8.8 / 17.0   The **Boundary Canyon Fault** crosses the road. It is most visible to the south, where it separates light-colored sedimentary rocks on the west side from dark metamorphic rocks on the east. This is a major thrust fault. Studies show that the rocks on the upper (east) side have been moved northwestward as far as 25 miles over the underlying rocks—in essence, the Grapevine Mountains to the north used to lie above the Funeral Mountains to the south.

10.0 / 15.8   **Monarch Canyon Road** (south). This road is passable to high-clearance 2WD vehicles for the first 2.2 miles, to the bottom of Monarch Canyon. It is a rough 4WD road beyond there but provides the shortest and most scenic route to Chloride City and Chloride Cliff. Explorers can exit the mountains by the gentler Chloride Cliff Road. This loop is described as Trip Route NC-4.

11.5 / 14.3   The abundant low, gray shrubs on the hillsides are the Death Valley joint fir, *Ephedra funerea*. This plant is difficult to distinguish from the closely related Nevada joint fir, *E. nevadensis*, but it tends to branch from main stems at a 60° rather than a 45° angle. Both plants are probably present in this area.

The view south is toward Chloride Mountain. Some of the tortuous Monarch Canyon Road that leads to Chloride City is visible winding up the distant mountain.

12.8 / 13.0   **Daylight Pass** (elevation 4,317 feet); **Daylight Spring** (hike 0.3 mile north). It has been said that this name is a corruption of Delightful Spring, which was shortened to Delight and then somehow became Daylight. However, it is likely that that is an untrue story, as the name first appeared as "Day Light Cañon" on a map published in 1865. Little more than a seep, the spring is visible as a pocket of vegetation on the slope north of the pass. It was a water source for travelers between the boomtowns of Rhyolite and Skidoo in the early 1900s. Westbound travelers begin the drop into **Boundary Canyon**.

13.1 / 12.7 California-Nevada state line. The hills in this area are composed of red volcanic agglomerate; that is, miscellaneous rocks enclosed within ash. They are the result of large-scale explosive eruptions that took place about 28 million years ago in the mountains within the Nevada Test Site.

17.1 / 8.7 **Death Valley National Park boundary; Chloride Cliff Road** (south, high-clearance first 10.8 miles to Chloride Junction, 4WD required beyond). If you want to visit Chloride City without traversing a long 4WD road, this is the route to take. It is rough in places, but there are no high road crowns or steep grades until the final climb up Chloride Mountain to the ghost town. See Trip Route NC-4 for details.

19.7 / 6.1 **Titus Canyon Road** (angling west; see Trip Route NC-5).

21.5 / 4.3 The unmarked dirt road (north) leads directly to the ghost town of Bullfrog. A much easier, paved route to Bullfrog and Rhyolite leaves the highway at milepoint 21.9 eastbound.

21.9 / 3.9 **Side Trip NC-3a—Rhyolite Road** (north 1.8 miles; paved, all-weather road).

0.0 Turnoff on paved road from Nevada State Highway 374. Between the highway and Bullfrog Road, traces of the old grade of the **Bullfrog Goldfield Railroad** are visible at the base of Ladd Mountain just east of the road.

0.8 Bullfrog Road goes west to **Bullfrog** (0.4 mile, paved to the townsite, high-clearance dirt beyond; see Trip Routes NT-2 and NT-3). The only significant ruin in this town, which once had a population of more than 2,000 people, is the Bullfrog Ice House, across the street from the more modern Bullfrog Coffee Shop (closed). The Original Bullfrog Mine that started the Rhyolite boom is about 3 miles farther west, just inside the national park boundary.

1.6 **Rhyolite**—"the tattered remains of a golden dream"—Bullfrog, and several other towns were once home for more than 10,000 people. Frank "Shorty" Harris and Ed Cross discovered rich gold in a knobby green rock a few miles west of here in 1904. Named the Original Bullfrog Mine, its announcement led to the last great gold rush in U.S. history. The peak came in late 1907, when three railroads—the Las Vegas & Tonopah, the Bullfrog Goldfield, and the Tonopah & Tidewater—served the city. But the end came soon. A financial panic swept the nation in October 1907. Rhyolite hung on for a while, but most of its mines had closed before the end of 1908.

Major ruins in Rhyolite include the bottle house (partially reconstructed for a movie in 1926), a jail, a schoolhouse, Porter Brothers Store, Overbury Block office building, and the three-story J. S. Cook Bank. There are a many lesser ruins and foundations along the numerous streets, most of which are still clearly delineated.

1.8 The **Las Vegas & Tonopah Railroad Depot** stands at the upper end of town. It is fenced and closed to the public. Of the three railroads, only the LV&T had a fancy station. The small wooden Bullfrog Goldfield Railroad station down the hill near the jail was sometimes used by the Tonopah & Tidewater Railroad; that building has completely disappeared.

End of Rhyolite Road side trip.

22.1 / 3.7 Portions of the huge LAC/Bullfrog mining operation are on both sides of the highway. In the boom days of Rhyolite, gold ore had to be rich in order to cover the costs of mining, milling, and freight shipping over long distances. Today it is another story. The rock on Ladd Mountain, between Rhyolite and the highway, contained about $5 of gold per ton. Whereas it was not remotely ore-grade material a century ago, now such rock is ore that can be mined by the millions of tons and efficiently leached of its metal content using cyanide solutions. That is what the LAC/Bullfrog Mine did until it closed in 1998; final "cleanup" work ended in 2001.

23.4 / 2.4 The grade cut for the Las Vegas & Tonopah Railroad crosses the hillside just north of the highway.

24.2 / 1.6 The dirt road (north) at **Doris Montgomery Summit** is a secondary route into Rhyolite, but it is sometimes blocked where it crosses private property. Doris Montgomery was the wife of E. A. "Bob" Montgomery, owner of the Montgomery-Shoshone Mine at Rhyolite and the Skidoo Mine in Death Valley.

24.4 / 1.4 The built-up dirt railroad grade of the Las Vegas & Tonopah Railroad is visible in the canyon north of the highway.

25.8 / 0.0 **National Park Service Information Station**, Beatty, Nevada. This office has all the general information, brochures, maps, and books that are available at the Furnace Creek Visitor

Center in Death Valley, but there are no other services. Phone (775) 553-2200.

Beatty is the only survivor of the Rhyolite gold rush. Named after prospector Montillion Murray Beatty, it is an important supply point and the only true town between Tonopah and Las Vegas. All services are found, including motels, restaurants, casinos, service stations, and a grocery store.

North-Central Death Valley, Trip Route NC-4—Monarch Canyon Road and Chloride Cliff Road

FROM: Daylight Pass Road, in Boundary Canyon 3.4 miles east of Hell's Gate.

TO: Daylight Pass Road at the Death Valley National Park boundary sign 8.7 miles west of Beatty, Nevada.

ROAD CONDITIONS: 16.1 miles one-way; rough, dirt road mostly accessible to high-clearance vehicles but with 4WD required between Monarch Canyon and Chloride Junction, and from Chloride Junction to Chloride City and Chloride Cliff.

SIDE TRIPS: Keane Spring (hike), Monarch Canyon (4WD plus hike), and Chloride City and Chloride Cliff (4WD).

GENERAL DESCRIPTION: The road is the shortest and most scenic route to the Chloride City ghost town and Chloride Cliff, but 4WD vehicles are required for the steep, narrow climb out of Monarch Canyon. High-clearance vehicles can negotiate only the first 2.2 miles in from Boundary Canyon, but they can drive from the state line entrance all the way to Chloride Junction, leaving a relatively short hike to Chloride City.

ROAD LOG MILEAGES	eastbound from Boundary Canyon / westbound from national park boundary.
0.0 / 16.1	The **Monarch Canyon Road** turnoff from the Daylight Pass Road is not marked except by a small sign that recommends 4WD vehicles (GPS 36°45.031'N 116°56.200'W).
0.5 / 15.6	Most of the vegetation within the wash is desert broom, whereas the hillsides support a mixture of creosote, princes' plume, blackbrush, and Death Valley ephedra.
2.0 / 14.1	**Keane Springs** (east 0.75 mile; hike). The road that led to Keane Spring itself and the ghost town site is barricaded and is the easiest hiking route to the ghost town and spring. About 0.25 mile from the road are low stone walls of unknown origin (apparently they were not part of the town). An additional 0.5 mile along the alluvial fan and then down

into the wash reaches the site of **Keane Springs** (approximate GPS 36°44.689'N 116°54.158'W), which extends a few hundred feet down the drainage below the spring. For a brief time in 1906, Keane Springs became a commercial center because of its water supply. It never had a substantial residential population but did boast several businesses (see Appendix A).

The spring above town is surrounded by dense reeds and willow trees that make it difficult to get to the water, which is surrounded by old concrete work and now yields less than 1 gallon per minute.

2.2 / 13.9   **Monarch Canyon Mine Road** (west; 4WD plus hike). This road leads a short distance down the canyon to a washout. Beyond is a hike of 1.2 miles to the Monarch Canyon Mine. Discovered in 1905, the mine was worked regularly for about a year until it lost its financial support because of the San Francisco earthquake in April 1906. On-and-off operations followed, and a one-stamp mill was erected in 1910. The mill still stands and is in excellent condition.

The road continuing toward Chloride City begins a steep, rough climb immediately beyond the bottom of Monarch Canyon. High-clearance 4WD vehicles are absolutely required for the next 2.3 miles. Caution is advised, as there are very high centers, climbs over jagged bedrock outcrops, and sharply tilted roadbeds.

2.5 / 13.6   The water tank (east) was installed in 1935 by the Coen Corporation, which was reopening Johnny Cyty's old Big Bell Mine between Chloride City and Keane Wonder. Keane Spring, through the use of a pipeline and this tank, was the water supply. The remains of a powerful diesel engine that pumped the water all the way over Chloride Mountain to the mine are in the ruins behind the tank.

4.5 / 11.6   The top of the steep grade is where the road reaches the lower end of a smooth gravel wash.

4.6 / 11.5   The road (west, 4WD) leads to some small mines that were outliers of the Chloride City district.

5.3 / 10.8   **Chloride Junction** (GPS 36°43.059'N 116°53.099'W). The road to Chloride City and Chloride Cliff is west, immediately beginning a steep climb up Chloride Mountain; 4WD vehicles are recommended if not actually required.

0.0   Turnoff (west).

0.9   Overlook above Chloride City. The center of town, such as it was, lay in the bottom of the shallow valley. Chloride Cliff

One freestanding building remained at Chloride City in 1968. It collapsed long ago, but numerous "Cousin Jack" cabins of stone are scattered around the area amid considerable trash.

and the original Franklin Mines of the 1870s are over the ridge beyond the town. Nearby to the west are the ruins of the Crowell Mercury Mill. Chloride City's last commercial mining enterprise, the Crowell Mining and Milling Company, began to produce quicksilver, but the mill burned in 1941 before most of its 500 tons of ore had been processed.

1.3   "Downtown" **Chloride City**. None of the original wooden buildings from 1905 and 1906 remain standing at Chloride City—the biggest pile of fallen lumber was a boarding-house—but there are several stone shacks and "Cousin Jack" shelters scattered throughout the area. Near one of these, whose back door leads directly into a mine tunnel, is the grave of James McKay. No one knows who he was and when or why he died, but his is the only grave at Chloride City. In the canyon to the west are more ruins, including the foundations of the Lane Mill, erected in 1916.

2.0   The road switchbacks up the ridge and into another small canyon with numerous stone and wood ruins, then to the top of the mountain at Chloride Cliff (GPS 36°41.807'N 116°52.736'W, elevation 5,279 feet). The Franklin Mines, initially opened in 1871, were along and below the cliffs to

The grave of James McKay is located near a cabin at one of the Chloride City mines.

the east. There are several spectacular viewpoints into Death Valley, more than a mile below.

End of Chloride Cliff side trip.

7.8 / 8.3   The signed California-Nevada state line is also the national park boundary.

9.3 / 6.8   This road log turns north at this intersection (GPS 36°44.825'N 116°49.876'W). This is the most direct route to Death Valley, but it is a slow drive across alluvial fans and numerous washes and gullies. The route directly northeast is easier but longer, ending at U.S. Highway 95 about 7.2 miles south of Beatty, Nevada.

16.1 / 0.0   **Daylight Pass Road** (Trip Route NC-3) at a spot 8.7 miles west of Beatty, Nevada, and adjacent to the well-signed Death Valley National Park boundary.

North-Central Death Valley, Trip Route NC-5—Titus Canyon Road

FROM: Daylight Pass Road (Nevada State Highway 374) 7.1 miles west of Beatty, Nevada.

TO: Scotty's Castle Road in Death Valley.

ROAD CONDITIONS: 26.4 miles of one-way dirt road, high-clearance recommended but 4WD usually not required.

SIDE TRIPS: None.

GENERAL DESCRIPTION: The Titus Canyon Road is variously narrow, steep, rocky, and gravelly, and it is therefore recommended for high-clearance vehicles, but 4WD is not usually required. If there has been recent rain the road is likely to be closed. This area is a scenic geological wonder that includes important historical and archaeological sites. Titus Canyon is a day-use-only area where camping is not allowed. The Titus Canyon Road is currently open all year, but in the past it was closed in summer and that policy might be reinstituted at any time.

ROAD LOG MILEAGE	westbound from Nevada State Highway 374.
0.0	The **Titus Canyon Road** turnoff (north) from Nevada State Highway 374 is clearly marked. The first 1.8 miles are outside of Death Valley National Park; once inside the park, the road to the canyon is one-way westbound.
0.9	The dirt road cutting sharply east is the original Rhyolite-Skidoo road, built in 1906. In early 1907, a steam-traction engine called Old Dinah used this road to haul ore between the Keane Wonder Mine and a mill at Rhyolite. "Old Dinah" is now on display at the Furnace Creek Ranch.
1.8	Death Valley National Park boundary.
2.0	The road gradually climbs up an alluvial fan where creosote bush, blackbrush, burrobush, rabbitbrush, and saltbushes are thicker and lusher than in lower, drier Death Valley.
6.1	The road drops into a wash. With more moisture available there than on the open alluvial fan, there is a still greater diversity of plants. The most common are princes' plume, Great Basin sagebrush, and two kinds of joint fir.
6.5	The rounded hill south is composed of basalt lava flows 4 to 6 million years old. This is the youngest of several volcanic rock units in the area. The large shrub-like trees, up to 12 feet high, are Utah juniper (*Juniperus osteosperma*).
7.4	The jagged outcrop of rocks to the north is an erosional remnant of a thick layer of volcanic ash that blanketed the countryside during a tremendous eruption 11 million years ago. The eruption took place near Yucca Flat, within the Nevada Test Site.
8.0	The road crosses from Nevada into California. The rocks throughout this area go by the general name of "Grapevine Volcanics," but they really represent several separate epi-

sodes of volcanism with different source areas. The rugged outcrops south of the road at this point are layers of chert (microcrystalline silica) enclosed by thick beds of explosive ashfall rocks. These were blasted from huge volcanoes in the Nevada Test Site; in this case the eruption occurred near Timber Mountain roughly 28 million years ago. The miscellaneous red and yellow colors are caused by mixtures of iron oxide minerals.

9.7 **White Pass** (elevation about 5,130 feet) is an open area without a distinct summit. Directly ahead are the headwaters of Titanothere Canyon. The ragged ridges farther northwest are basalt lava flows believed to have erupted from a volcano near Red Pass (see milepoint 12.9). Note the abundance of two kinds of Mormon tea: bright-green mountain ephedra (*Ephedra viridis*) and gray Death Valley ephedra (*E. funerea*).

Although Titus Canyon Road is one-way from east to west, should you get caught in a rainstorm you are advised to turn around at this point—portions of the road ahead are very steep and underlain by claystone that becomes extremely slippery when wet.

10.2 If you look closely down the east fork of Titanothere Canyon, across Death Valley, and into the Panamint Range beyond, you can see State Highway 190 winding up the alluvial fan toward Towne Pass, the low point in the Panamint Range.

10.7 The white layer of rock in the cliffs above the road is volcanic ash. This and some of the other volcanic rock in the Titus Canyon area bear witness to a geological mystery: they represent a very large-scale, explosive sequence of volcanic eruptions that took place somewhere *west* of Death Valley, where no trace of the volcanoes themselves can be found.

11.0 **Titanothere Canyon** received its name when fossils were found near here in 1933. In addition to the titanothere (a copy of the skull is on display at the Furnace Creek Visitor Center), various oreodont, tapir, squirrel, dog, camel, and horse fossils were recovered. The fossils are within the lower portion of the **Titus Canyon Formation**, which is composed of conglomerate, sandstone, and shale that was deposited in river and lake environments about 31 million years ago.

11.1 The beautiful conglomerate exposed in the roadcut is part of the Titus Canyon Formation.

12.3 Note the cliffs on the mountain to the north. The prominent rock layers, from bottom to top, are a white volcanic ash (the same as that seen at milepoint 10.7); greenish, stream-deposited siltstone; a pale layer of sandstone; and a rough mountaintop of volcanic ash erupted from Monotony Valley, Nevada.

12.6 The rocks at **Red Pass** (GPS 36°49.721'N 117°01.950'W, elevation 5,250 feet) are stream and lakeshore sandstones, another fossil-bearing part of the Titus Canyon Formation.

 A hike of about 2 miles up the ridge to the south leads to **Thimble Peak**, at elevation 6,375 feet the highest summit in this part of the Grapevine Mountains.

12.9 After winding around a sharp turn to the right, a dark, jagged outcrop of basalt is directly ahead. This is a volcanic neck, the conduit that fed magma to a volcano that has been completely eroded away. The lava flows near White Pass are believed to have come from this volcano. Nearby is a small natural arch.

13.9 Small mines are visible south of the road.

15.7 **Leadfield** (GPS 36°50.977'N 117°03.624'W) was a town based on ore that averaged a decent 7 percent lead plus 5 ounces of silver per ton, but also on much speculation. Unlike as is usually reported, however, there was no fraud in the promotions. At its peak in mid-1926, the town had a population of 300. Unfortunately, as was so often the case, the ore that held high promise at the surface was not found when the vein was reached at depth. Leadfield was completely abandoned in early 1927. (See Appendix A.) Although the remaining buildings and foundations are along the canyon bottom west of today's road, most of the community occupied structures along and upslope east of the road where there are few remains.

16.3 The road enters a little gorge where there is a spectacular exposure of tilted sedimentary rocks. The layers appear to have been sharply folded, but they actually are not folded at all. The bent appearance is an illusion caused by the curving shape of the cliffs. These rocks are part of the Bonanza King Formation, dating to the Cambrian Period around 500 million years ago.

16.4 **Titus Canyon** proper joins the road from the north. For the next several miles the commonest plant in the wash is the desert broom, *Baccharis serothroides*, and large specimens of cottontop cactus (*Echinocactus polycephalus*) decorate the canyon walls.

18.1 **Klare Spring** (GPS 36°50.443'N 117°05.468'W) is the only reliable source of water in all of the Titus Canyon drainage

The post office at Leadfield operated for less than seven months, but it outlived the rest of the town that existed largely because of promotions based on low-grade lead ore.

system and so is critical for wildlife. It flows about 2.5 gallons per minute. The water rises to the surface along the Titus Canyon Fault. Although it may not seem so as you drive, most of Titus Canyon follows a remarkably straight line defined by this fault.

Where there is water, there are often petroglyphs. On the rock faces just up the canyon from Klare Spring are some good examples, unfortunately marred by modern scratches.

Immediately down the canyon from Klare Spring, the deformed rocks in the cliffs are Wood Canyon Formation, which dates to the very earliest part of the Cambrian Period, when complex animals made their first abundant appearance.

19.6 A small mine prospect of unknown origin is to the right.

22.0 The **Titus Canyon Narrows** are barely wide enough for a vehicle in some places, yet the vertical cliffs tower several hundred feet high. The Cambrian age limestones have been twisted, folded, and broken by mountain building. Mosaics of shattered blocks healed by recrystallized white calcite make up many of the cliff walls. Ripple marks and mud cracks can be found on some of the original bedding surfaces.

24.1 The slot canyon ends suddenly at a wide vista of northern Death Valley. The road up the alluvial fan from Scotty's

Castle Road is open to two-way traffic, so there is a parking area at the canyon mouth.

26.3   The smooth slope of the alluvial fan is interrupted here by an eroded fault scarp of the Northern Death Valley Fault Zone. Its rounded form indicates that the last earthquake of large size on this portion of the fault probably took place well over 2,000 years ago.

26.4   Scotty's Castle Road (Trip Route N-1). State Highway 190 is about 14.8 miles to the south and Scotty's Castle is 21.2 miles north.

Western Areas, including the "Wildrose Country"

State Highway 190 West (Trip Route W-2) is primarily a transportation corridor (it is the second-most heavily traveled entrance into Death Valley), but it includes several places important to Death Valley's history as well as the privately operated Panamint Springs Resort. The other areas covered here offer aspects of the park that are far different from those of the valley floor, and the high-elevation Wildrose area is a popular year-round destination.

Western Areas, Trip Route W-1—Cottonwood Canyon Road

FROM: State Highway 190 at the entrance to Stovepipe Wells Campground.

TO: Cottonwood Creek at the end of the road.

ROAD CONDITIONS: 19.2 miles one-way, dirt road with high-clearance recommended to canyon mouth; 4WD may be required within the canyon.

SIDE TRIP: Marble Canyon (4WD).

GENERAL DESCRIPTION: The Cottonwood Canyon Road starts by crossing the flat floor of Death Valley toward the mountains, and then gently climbs across the alluvial fan to the mouth of Cottonwood Canyon. On the canyon floor it is packed gravel. Vehicles with 4WD are not usually required unless the road has been freshly washed by major floods. Camping is not allowed along the first 8 miles to the mouth of the canyon.

ROAD LOG MILEAGES   westbound from Stovepipe Wells Village.

....

0.0   Junction with State Highway 190. The **Cottonwood Canyon Road** bears to the left at the entrance to the Stovepipe Wells Campground.

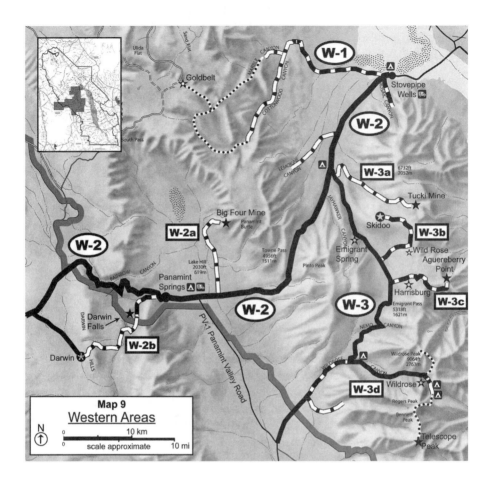

4.0   Note the flatirons—smooth, steeply tilted rock faces—on the mountain ahead. Flatirons develop where a relatively hard sedimentary rock is tilted to a high angle and then exposed by erosion as a surface resistant to further weathering. In this case the rock unit is the Tin Mountain Limestone of Carboniferous age.

8.4   The road drops into **Cottonwood Wash** and turns toward the canyon mouth. The route is gravelly, with occasional high centers beyond this point.

9.3   A pass through the mountains to the north is composed of soft red-and-white siltstone of the Carboniferous Perdido Formation.

9.5   The road passes through the short lower narrows of Cottonwood Canyon. The rocks are limestone; fossils are present in some of the beds, but most are incomplete and poorly preserved. A few petroglyphs can be seen at the north side of the canyon entrance.

10.7   **Marble Canyon** (GPS 36°37.908'N 117°17.709'W, north 2.6 miles one-way; 4WD required). It is hard to imagine how two canyons side by side like these can be so different. Whereas Cottonwood is mostly open with a wide, flat bottom, Marble is rocky and narrow. This road is rough, with high rocky centers in several places.

0.0   The Marble Canyon Road is marked with a small sign; there are some dead-end turnoffs in the same direction before the actual road is reached. This road simply follows the rocky alluvial fan of Marble Wash up to the canyon itself.

2.3   Enter Marble Canyon proper. It is recommended that people park here, at the mouth of the canyon, if they plan to hike farther up the gorge.

2.6   The road officially ends at a spot where the canyon walls are only 7 feet apart and where most vehicles cannot turn around. Beyond the end of the road, Marble Canyon winds many miles into the Cottonwood Mountains. Much of the route is within a deep, narrow gorge with sheer cliffs. This is a great backpacking region, and hikers have several options. The most popular is a 23-mile loop that includes part of Cottonwood Canyon (see Chapter 8).

End of Marble Canyon side trip.

11.3   With increased elevation and water supply, the vegetation on the canyon floor includes desert fir, brittlebush, stingbush, and desert broom in addition to creosote.

13.3   Massive sedimentary conglomerate of the Pleistocene age is exposed in the canyon walls.

13.8   Specimens of cottontop and calico cacti can be seen on the hillsides and growing out of cracks in canyon-wall bedrock.

14.5   A large erosional cave is on the south. Popular as a campsite, it formed as floodwaters came sweeping around the bend of the canyon and washed against the cliff face. The **Devil's Slide** is across the canyon to the north. Its bright-orange slopes rimmed by harder beds of limestone are part of the Perdido Formation of Carboniferous age.

14.7   The road passes through the short upper narrows of Cottonwood Canyon.

15.4   Looking at the cliff down the canyon there is an obvious angular unconformity between old Paleozoic limestones and younger Quaternary conglomerates.

17.0	The last 2 miles of the road are frequently washed out and usually require high-clearance 4WD vehicles. Willow and cottonwood trees show that water is always near the surface and sometimes the stream reaches this far down the canyon.
19.2	**Cottonwood Creek**, at the end of the road, is a permanent stream with a flow of about 100 gallons per minute. This is one of Death Valley's most extensive riparian environments, and a great concentration of wildlife lives in this area. Remember that camping is not permitted within 100 feet of open water and that as inviting as it may seem, the water of Cottonwood Creek should be treated before drinking.

Western Areas, Trip Route W-2—State Highway 190 West between Stovepipe Wells Village and Darwin Road

FROM: Stovepipe Wells Village.

TO: Darwin Junction, on State Highway 190 at a point about 26 miles east of Olancha or Lone Pine.

ROAD CONDITIONS: 47.8 miles, paved all-weather highway.

SIDE TRIPS: Mosaic Canyon (all standard vehicles), Lemoigne Canyon (4WD), Emigrant Canyon Road (Trip Route W-3), Jayhawker Canyon (hike), Lake Hill Road (Side Trip W-2a, rough, high-clearance plus hike), Darwin Falls Road (all vehicles) and Zinc Hill Road (4WD), and Saline Valley Road (Trip Route SV-1).

GENERAL DESCRIPTION: This part of State Highway 190, also known as the Towne Pass Road, is the main access into Death Valley from the west via connections with the Panamint Valley Road from Trona to the south and from U.S. Highway 395 at Olancha or Lone Pine to the west.

ROAD LOG MILEAGES	westbound from Stovepipe Wells Village / eastbound from Darwin Junction.
0.0 / 47.8	**Stovepipe Wells Village**.
0.1 / 47.7	**Mosaic Canyon Road** (south 2.1 miles one-way; improved dirt road suitable for all standard vehicles; motor homes and vehicles with trailers not recommended). Near its lower end Mosaic Canyon is a spectacular slot canyon of colorful stream-polished marble breccia. About 0.5 mile up, the canyon opens out and then narrows again into steeper terrain. If you have the rock-climbing skills to negotiate dry waterfalls, you can hike far up Tucki Mountain (see Chapter 8).
6.0 / 41.8	**Lemoigne Canyon Road** (GPS 36°32.313'N 117°12.844'W, west 4.4 miles one-way; 4WD required). The turnoff from

the highway is marked with a small sign but is difficult to spot. This road is extremely rough, as it crosses a long series of deep, sandy washes en route to Lemoigne Canyon.

The canyon was named for Jean Lemoigne, a highly educated mining engineer from France. Some historians say that he came to the United States to serve as the supervisor at fellow Frenchman Isadore Daunet's Eagle Borax Works in 1881, but mining claims were filed in his name in Butte Valley as early as 1878 and at Panamint City in 1880. After the failure of Eagle Borax in 1884, Lemoigne remained in the Death Valley region as a prospector and he located the Lemoigne Mine (originally called the Bullet Mine) in 1887 (possibly 1882). This mine was actually one of the better properties in the region, but Lemoigne never had the resources to work it properly. During the Rhyolite boom he was offered $80,000 to sell, but he refused to accept any payment other than cash in full. He died in 1919 at the age of 77 and was buried near Salt Creek. In later years, the mine yielded over 370,000 pounds of lead and 52,000 pounds of zinc plus significant amounts of gold and silver.

Vehicle travel is not allowed beyond the mouth of the canyon, where a careful search will reveal leveled tent sites of mysterious origin. Jean Lemoigne's cabin and mine are about 1.5 miles farther up the canyon. Unfortunately, the cabin was vandalized by persons unknown in late 2007.

~7 / 41 The bold basalt lava outcrops of **Black Point** south of the highway mark Towne Pass Fault Zone. The scarp's freshness where it cuts alluvial fans farther southwest indicates that significant earthquakes have taken place here within the last 500 years.

8.9 / 38.9 **Emigrant Junction**. A rest area with restrooms, picnic tables, and drinking water is on the north side of the road. The **Emigrant Campground** is open all year (tents only). The buildings are historic structures constructed by the Civilian Conservation Corps during the 1930s.

9.1 / 38.7 **Emigrant Canyon Road** (south) crosses some of the most scenic parts of the national park and includes many important historic sites. It is described as Trip Route W-3.

11.0 / 36.8 **Jayhawker Canyon** (southwest about 1.5 miles one-way from near the 3,000-foot elevation sign along the highway; hike). Jayhawker Canyon was the route followed by some of the Death Valley argonauts in 1850—exactly which of the argonauts is uncertain, but Jayhawkers and Georgians were among them. An often-repeated story has it that Jim Martin carved his famous gunsight at a camp in this canyon. William B. Rood, one of the 49ers, left his initials and the date— "W.B.R. 49"—scratched into a rock in 1861, when he and others returned to the area in search of the Lost Gunsight Lode.

16.6 / 31.2 **Towne Pass** (elevation 4,956 feet). This pass was named after Paschal H. Townes, one of the members of the Mississippian party of 49ers. Townes was one of the 49ers who did not find success in California, so he quickly returned to Mississippi, where he died in 1852. Note that the "s" in Townes's name was dropped in naming the pass.

20.4 / 27.4 A scenic viewpoint looks out over the northern part of Panamint Valley to the southern end of the Inyo Range and the highest peaks of the Sierra Nevada Mountains. The rocks along the road between here and Towne Pass are basalt lava flows 5 to 6 million years old that lie on top of Paleozoic sedimentary rocks.

23.6 / 24.2 The road crosses the **Panamint Valley Fault Zone**. Although there is geological evidence that this fault system experiences earthquakes more frequently than does the fault zone in Death Valley, only small, eroded scarps are visible in this area.

25.8 / 22.0 **Side Trip W-2a—Lake Hill Road** (GPS 36°20.519'N 117°23.325'W, north 7.2 miles one-way; 4WD recommended). Also known as the Big Four Mine Road, this route is rough and rocky but can be negotiated by high-clearance vehicles as far as the turn into the mountains; deep gravel leading up to the canyon and the Big Four Mine requires 4WD. This road is the closest access to the Panamint Dunes, a small area of tall sand dunes that hosts several endemic plants.

0.0 Turnoff from State Highway 190.

3.0 **Lake Hill** (summit elevation 2,030 feet) is a block of Ely Spring Formation, a dolomite of Ordovician age believed to have slid from the face of Panamint Butte by gravitational detachment faulting. Parts of it are fossiliferous, mostly with brachiopods that are not well preserved. This is within the national park, so look but please do not collect.

6.1 A walk northwest from where the road turns sharply east up the alluvial fan is the shortest route to the Panamint Dunes, 4 miles across the valley.

7.2 The small mine prospects on the canyon wall north of the road are part of the Big Four Mine developments. They were explored because of the existence of the primary ore minerals galena (lead sulfide) and sphalerite (zinc sulfide), which are not present in the Big Four itself, but the ore minerals proved to be sparse. The rocks in the canyon are thin-bedded limestone of the Keeler Canyon Formation of early Permian age.

The road effectively ends near the mouth of the canyon. The **Big Four Mine**, another 0.5 mile up the canyon, was discovered in 1907, but there was little mining until after it was relocated in 1940. Major production occurred between 1944 and 1952, when rich pockets of supergene lead (cerussite) and zinc (hemimorphite) minerals were mined; silver was a secondary by-product.

End of Lake Hill Road side trip.

26.7 / 21.1	The bed of **Upper Panamint Lake** is a clay playa. **Lake Hill** rises above the east side of the lake bed. It is a mass of rock (mostly Ely Spring dolomite) that slid from the face of Panamint Butte by gravitational detachment faulting. The Panamint Valley is topographically divided into two parts. This upper valley floor has an elevation of 1,542 feet. Southward, a range of low hills separates the lower valley, whose floor is 500 feet lower at 1,038 feet.
27.7 / 20.1	**Panamint Valley Road** (south, paved all-weather county road). This route runs south through Panamint Valley and over Slate Range Pass to the town of Trona. It is briefly described in Chapter 16 as Trip Route PV-1.
30.2 / 17.6	**Panamint Springs Resort**. This small, independent resort is open year-around with a bar, restaurant, motel, small store, gas station, campground with hookups, and an improved dirt landing strip. (See Appendix C.)
31.2 / 16.6	**Side Trip W-2b—Darwin Falls Road** (west 2.4 miles one-way to Darwin Falls parking area, graded dirt road suitable for all vehicles; **Zinc Hill Road** continues an additional 10.4 miles with 4WD recommended to Darwin). Darwin Canyon, the path followed by the Mississippian and Georgian parties of 49ers and much later by the Stovepipe Well Toll Road, was named by Dr. Darwin French after himself while searching for the Lost Gunsight Lode in either 1859 or 1860. In 1849, he was at Rancho San Francisco and sold stock animals to Manly and Rogers so that they could carry provisions back to Death Valley to rescue the Bennett and Arcan families.
0.0	Turnoff from State Highway 190.
2.4	Parking area for **Darwin Falls**. The waterfall is about 1 mile up the wash; it is easy walking on a gentle grade. The water-

fall is 25 feet high within an oasis of willow and cottonwood trees. It is fed by a permanent stream that flows from China Garden Spring a short distance above.

From near the parking lot, the **Zinc Hill Road** follows the steep, winding grade up Zinc Hill where 4WD vehicles are recommended.

4.5   Death Valley National Park boundary (GPS 36°18.495'N 117°30.709'W). There are numerous mines on Zinc Hill. As always, they are dangerous and should never be entered. However, if not otherwise posted, mineral collecting is permitted on mine dumps that are outside of the national park.

5.2   Top of Zinc Hill.

6.3   The Zinc Hill Road turns sharply to the west. **China Garden Spring** is about 1 mile down this side road where there is a meadow with pools of water amid large cottonwood trees. During the early days of mining around Darwin, some Chinese people developed a vegetable garden to serve the miners, and so the name. Near the spring are the ruins of an old mill.

8.6   **Miller Spring**, the site of another ore mill, is on private property.

12.8   **Darwin**. From near Miller Spring, the road continuing to the near-ghost of Darwin is paved with broken asphalt. There are no commercial services in Darwin, which is still occupied by about 50 people (see Appendix A). On a paved county road, Darwin Junction at State Highway 190 is 5.5 miles north of the town.

End Darwin Falls Road–Zinc Hill Road side trip.

31.3 / 16.5   Westbound, State Highway 190 begins a steep climb through an assemblage of lavas called the Darwin Hills Volcanics that are as little as 2 million years old.

33.3 / 14.5   The road cuts directly through a cinder cone volcano. It is difficult to see from the road while driving, and eastbound travelers have the better view. A "valley" in the side of the cone is the remnant of the volcano's crater.

34.3 / 13.5   The road cuts through the remains of a small, red cinder cone volcano. Other roadcuts in this area expose silicified and metamorphosed rocks of Paleozoic age. The recrystallization does not allow them to be identified as to exact formation or age.

38.0 / 9.8   **Father Crowley Point** (east; parking area with view into Rainbow Canyon). Father John J. Crowley (1891–1940), for whom Crowley Lake north of Bishop was also named, was a missionary to the Paiute Indians of Owens Valley. The brass plaque near the viewpoint was dedicated in his honor by the Death Valley '49ers, Inc., during the 1963 encampment.

Rainbow Canyon has been carved into the basalt lava flows and lapilli beds of the Darwin Hills Volcanics. These volcanoes last erupted between 2 and 4 million years ago. Hunter Mountain Granite and several formations of metamorphosed Paleozoic limestones are exposed beneath the lavas in the deeper parts of the canyon.

From the viewpoint at the end of the spur road, the northern part of Panamint Valley and its sand dunes are visible. The large mountain almost directly east is Panamint Butte, and the flat-topped, forested summit to the northeast is Hunter Mountain.

42.1 / 5.7   Eastbound drivers begin a descent down the steep grade of the Rainbow Canyon drainage. The elevation at the summit is 4,865 feet above sea level.

42.7 / 5.1   Death Valley National Park boundary.

43.7 / 4.1   **Saline Valley Road** (north) is the access to a large portion of the national park. It ends at the Big Pine Road beyond the north end of Saline Valley, 78 miles from this turnoff. The nearest services of any kind via that route are in Big Pine nearly 100 miles away. The Saline Valley Road is described in Chapter 20 as Trip Route SV-1.

46.1 / 1.7   The **Lead Hope Mine**, an outlier of the Darwin district, is visible at the base of the hill south of the highway. All old mines are dangerous, and you should not enter the tunnel. It was dug into the Keeler Canyon Formation, a limestone of Permian age that contains well-preserved, disk-shaped fossils called fusulinids.

47.8 / 0.0   **Darwin Junction**. Darwin, which is almost a ghost town, is 5.5 miles south of the junction. Its success as a mining town was based on rich lead-silver-zinc ore that was discovered in 1873 by prospectors searching for the Lost Gunsight Lode. After a short-lived boom, mining was spotty until the 1930s. Large-scale production then took place into the 1950s. The town has never been completely abandoned, and most of the buildings are privately owned. There are no services.

Western Areas, Trip Route W-3—Emigrant Canyon Road and Wildrose Roads

FROM: State Highway 190 at Emigrant Junction.

TO: Trona-Wildrose Road in Panamint Valley.

ROAD CONDITIONS: 30.5 miles one-way; mostly paved but steep, narrow, and winding in places; rough dirt portions in Lower Wildrose Canyon near Panamint Valley.

SPECIAL NOTES: Motor vehicles and trailer combinations more than 25 feet long and 9 feet wide are not allowed on these roads because of steep, narrow, and sharp curves in Rattlesnake Gulch and extremely rough conditions in lower Wildrose Canyon. Also, with the exception of Wildrose, Thorndike, and Mahogany Flat campgrounds, this entire area is designated day-use only.

SIDE TRIPS: Tucki Mountain Road (Side Trip W-3a; 4WD), Journigan's Mill (short walk), Skidoo Road (Side Trip W-3b; high-clearance), Aguereberry Point Road (Side Trip W-3c; high-clearance), Argenta Mine (4WD), Christmas Mine (4WD and hike), Upper Wildrose Canyon Road and Mahogany Flat Road (Side Trip W-3d; standard vehicles to Charcoal Kilns, then 4WD), and Tuber Canyon Road (4WD).

GENERAL DESCRIPTION: Often called the Wildrose Road, this is a major access route into Death Valley from the southwest via Trona and Panamint Valley. It crosses one of the most scenic parts of Death Valley, covering a number of biological habitats and numerous historic sites.

ROAD LOG MILEAGES	southbound from Emigrant Junction / northbound from Trona-Wildrose Road.

0.0 / 30.5	**Emigrant Junction** at State Highway 190, just uphill from the rest area.
1.5 / 29.0	**Side Trip W-3a—Tucki Mountain Road** (GPS 36°28.605'N 117°12.901'W, east 9.9 miles one-way; 4WD required) negotiates some alluvial fans before climbing into Telephone Canyon and across an open alluvial area to the Tucki Mine, just over a pass through the mountains. It is mostly a gentle grade, but some sandy areas and a few rough bedrock cascades make 4WD vehicles necessary.
0.0	The turnoff is barely visible at its junction with the Emigrant Canyon Road just below the mouth of the canyon, but the roadcut up the arroyo wall across the wash is obvious.
1.6	The road drops down an old alluvial fan surface until it abruptly turns to climb a smaller fan into Telephone Canyon.
2.0	The road passes underneath wide overhangs of coarse conglomerate and sandstone of the Nova Formation.
2.5	**Telephone Canyon** proper bears to the right (GPS 36°29.211'N 117°11.953'W). There is a natural arch in the rocks about 0.25 mile from the Tucki Mountain Road. **Telephone Spring**, another 0.25 mile beyond the arch, is usually dry. During Skidoo's boom days, the Rhyolite-Skidoo road and telephone line passed up this canyon, the spring was

Old cabins and mine equipment remain at the Tucki Mine.

maintained as a water stop, and a short-lived stage station was located nearby.

5.0 A series of rough bedrock cascades requires 4WD vehicles, although the worst of them has been partially improved with loose stones to smooth the jagged grade.

9.4 The road reaches a summit elevation of about 4,890 feet. A branch (north) winds up and over the steep hill to small mine prospects about 1 mile away.

9.9 The **Tucki Mine** was located in 1909, but there was little gold production until 1927. Miscellaneous operators worked the mine from then until 1951. Most of the output was unrecorded, but at least $18,000 worth of gold was produced in 1941 alone. In 1974 and 1975 the owners constructed a sophisticated processing plant that was designed to recover every trace of gold down to submicroscopic particles using activated carbon filtration and cyanide. The system worked, but the mine was shut down as a result of the Mining in Parks Act of 1976. The mine shafts and tunnels on the mountainside have not been stabilized. Any old mine is a dangerous place, so keep out.

There are three buildings at the Tucki Mine, one of which recently collapsed. The middle one is maintained by the Park Service for emergency use, a policy that may change at any time.

End of Tucki Mountain Road side trip.

1.9 / 28.6 A fault cuts through the small ridge on the west side of the road, offsetting a basalt lava flow and underlying coarse sedimentary rocks by several feet. The series of cavernous openings separated by rock pillars just north of the fault is known as **The Palisades**. These rocks are part of the Nova Formation that was deposited within a long, narrow basin about 6 million years ago, before modern Death Valley and Panamint Valley had formed. It is exposed throughout Emigrant Canyon, near Nemo Summit, in lower Wildrose Canyon, and along the western base of the Panamint Mountains.

2.3 / 28.2 Above the road, the Nova Formation has eroded into a series of odd cliffs and pinnacles, sometimes referred to as "hoodoos."

4.7 / 25.8 **Emigrant Spring** is within a small canyon on the west side of the road, where there is a dense growth of rushes. The spring flows 2.5 gallons of water per minute and is part of the water supply for the rest area and buildings at Emigrant Junction.

5.1 / 25.4 The road passes through a short canyon cut into the **Skidoo Granite**, a porphyry that contains pinkish-gray crystals of orthoclase feldspar as much as 2 inches long. This is the only spot on any of the park's paved roads where intrusive igneous rock is exposed.

5.5 / 25.0 **Upper Emigrant Spring** is in the small canyon west of the road. A metal pipe sticking through a low concrete dam produces about 1 gallon of water per minute in the winter and spring but tends to go dry by midsummer.

The town of **Emigrant Springs** was probably in the wash just above Upper Emigrant Spring rather than at Emigrant Spring. Founded in May 1906, the settlement lasted into 1907 and consisted of at least one grocery store, one combined restaurant-saloon, a lodging tent, and several residential tents on the canyon floor. One report claimed that the town had a population of 200, but clearly that is only the number of people who did business there. The remains of the community have long since washed away.

Just down the road is the site of **Starr's Mill**, a cyanide mill associated with gold mining in Nemo Canyon several

As poor as its quality may be, this is the only known photo to show the community of Emigrant Springs. Although published in the April 19, 1907, issue of the Rhyolite Herald *newspaper, the photograph was probably taken about a year earlier.*

miles to the south during the 1930s. A series of settling tanks lined with concrete were built directly into the bedrock outcrop. The tanks are fairly large, but the remains are difficult to see as only low, rock walls are visible from the road.

6.6 / 23.9   **Journigan's Mill** (west side of road), also known as the Gold Bottom Mill, was a large cyanide mill that worked gold ore from the nearby Gold King Mine and did custom milling for other miners. It was built in 1937 by Roy Journigan. He sold the mill in 1939, and it continued operating under a series of owners until 1967. Large concrete cyanide leach tanks, foundations, and trash remain. There was another mill here as early as 1909, and the temporary team of Frank "Shorty" Harris and Alexander "Shorty" Borden used the site in 1924. Water came from a series of springs up the small side canyon on Pinto Mountain.

Journigan's Mill was an active place in 1935. (Photograph by George Grant, courtesy National Park Service, Death Valley National Park)

6.8 / 23.7   The **Gold King Mine**, which supplied ore to Journigan's Mill, is located up the canyon to the east. It consists of shallow cuts in the hillside 0.5 mile from the road.

9.4 / 21.1   **Side Trip W-3b—Skidoo Road** (east 7.1 miles one-way; improved dirt road suitable for all vehicles) is periodically graded. It tends to develop rough washboard surfaces and there are some short, steep grades with exposed bedrock, but it is generally suitable for any standard vehicle. This is a day-use-only area where camping is not allowed.

0.0   The turnoff from Emigrant Canyon Road is well marked.

0.3   Someplace on Harrisburg Flat south of here is the site of **Wild Rose** (not to be confused with Wildrose; see Appendix A), which hardly existed as a town. Prospecting triggered by the gold discovery of the Eureka and Cashier mines at Harrisburg 2 miles south brought hundreds of miners and a few business owners into the area in late 1905. The competing settlements of Harrisburg and Emigrant Springs were developed. With the discovery of the gold at Skidoo, centrally located Wild Rose was intended to replace the other communities. The town was surveyed in mid-1906 and a few lots were sold, but the growth of Skidoo drew everybody away, and it is unlikely that Wild Rose ever amounted to more than a handful of tents.

1.4 To the north is the **Tiny Mine**, a relatively small gold property discovered during the Skidoo excitement.

2.0 The route of the famous "23-skidoo" waterline that served Skidoo is barely visible cutting along the base of the hills southeast of the road. The scar is most visible in low morning sun. Nothing remains of the pipeline itself—it was removed by the Civilian Conservation Corps in the 1930s—but a few rock supports and abutments still exist.

2.7 The rocks in this small canyon are Skidoo granite porphyry.

2.9 A number of small mines near the road just east and south of the canyon were located for silver during the Panamint City rush in the 1870s, 30 years before the Skidoo gold rush. Their total production was minimal.

4.5 A spectacular view into Death Valley takes in the square patch of green at the Furnace Creek Ranch.

4.8 **Blue Bell Mine Road** (GPS 36°26.386'N 117°09.302'W, east 0.8 mile; hike). This trail along an old road drops down a steep slope into the wash, and then follows the canyon down to a ramshackle cabin at the Blue Bell Mine's millsite. Beyond the cabin, the trail climbs steeply back up the hillside. On the flat area above, walking past some leveled building sites and wooden roofing trusses takes the hiker to a metal tramway tower. The cable still stretches between the tower and the **Hanging Cliff Mine** across the precipitous canyon.

Explorers game for a very strenuous hike can continue along the trail to the **Garibaldi Mine**, several hundred feet down the east face of the mountains. Little remains at the mine—a wooden ore wagon is about all—but it is an intriguing historic site. The Garibaldi silver was located in 1874 and was worked on a small scale continuously into the 1900s. Some historians believe this was the true source of the "Lost Gunsight" ore. More interesting are claims that the mine was first worked by Spaniards (or Mexicans) long before the "discovery" of Death Valley. Early mine reports stated that rock ruins and shallow workings were already present when the property was opened in 1874. No written record exists of Spaniards having explored the Death Valley area, but Indian pictographs in Greenwater Canyon east of Death Valley predate American settlement and appear to show horseback riders. A National Park Service study could not prove a Spanish connection, but neither did it discard the idea.

7.1 **Skidoo**. Interpretive and hazard warning signs are located at the center of the town, which had a population as great as 500 from 1907 to 1909 and then persisted with a declining population into the 1920s. Only sparse debris and leveled building sites remain; the last structure disappeared around 1960.

Exactly how Skidoo got its name is uncertain. The most popular, but clearly incorrect, story is that it resulted from the pipeline, supposedly 23 miles long, that brought water to the town and mill. However, Skidoo was named before the pipeline was built, and the pipeline was only 22 miles long in any case. Other ideas consider that the initial mining claim was located on January 23, 1906; that the mining district was established when 23 claims had been filed; or that a group of 23 men incorporated to create the city. Perhaps the name came about simply because "23 skidoo" was a popular phrase at the time.

Several roads extend beyond the townsite, but they might all be closed to vehicles. The one that leads up the hill to the south ends at the Skidoo Mine. The road that goes down the canyon ends near the **Skidoo Mill**, an impressive wood and metal structure that is listed in the National Register of Historic Places. The National Park Service has stabilized part of the building, but it still is not safe to enter. The mill was built by E. A. "Bob" Montgomery in 1908. The pipeline was constructed as part of the same project. Its water was used to run Pelton wheel generators to power the mill's electric motors. The total cost was $300,000, but the eventual profit was $1.5 million, making the Skidoo Mine one of the few in Death Valley to have actually made money for its owner. The original mill burned in 1913; it was immediately replaced by the present one.

Across the canyon from the mill and northwest of the townsite is the Del Norte Mine. It was active in the early 1970s when the owners proposed a large strip-mining and cyanide-leaching operation on low-grade gold ore. The project was not successful and ended in 1975.

End of Skidoo Road side trip.

10 / 20   This open valley is called **Harrisburg Flat**. **Eureka Hill**—called Providence Ridge during the mining boom—stands out

Skidoo was still growing when this picture was taken in 1907. Note the patches of snow along the street. (Courtesy National Park Service, Death Valley National Park)

from Harrisburg Flat to the southeast. It is the location of the two gold mines that started the Harrisburg and Skidoo gold rushes beginning in July 1905. The high mountain beyond is Wildrose Peak.

11.8 / 18.7 **Side Trip W-3c—Aguereberry Point Road** (east 6.3 miles one-way to Aguereberry Point; improved dirt road). Like the Skidoo Road to the south, this route is well marked and occasionally graded so that it is suitable for any standard vehicle. There are rough areas within canyons and steep grades on the final climb to the viewpoint. This is a day-use-only area where camping is not allowed.

0.0 The turnoff from Emigrant Canyon Road is marked by a small sign.

0.6 The **Napoleon Mine** (south; hike on a closed road) was a small gold producer opened by Pete Aguereberry several years after the Harrisburg excitement.

1.3 The scar of the Skidoo water pipeline forms a straight line running across the valley to the north.

1.4 **Aguereberry Camp** (south; short walk) is a cluster of dilapidated buildings at the base of Eureka Hill. Pete Aguereberry lived here and worked the Eureka Mine until 1938. The camp was occasionally occupied as a vacation home by his children into the 1970s, but it is now national park property.

1.5   Litter and traces of leveled tent pads mark the site of **Harrisburg** on the low knoll just south of the road. The town was founded within days of the discovery of the Cashier and Eureka mines and had a population of 300 people by November 1905. It was virtually abandoned with the better discoveries at Skidoo in January 1906, and since most of the buildings were wood-frame tents, there have never been substantial ruins.

1.7   A short side road leads to a parking area where walks lead to the **Eureka Mine**, **Cashier Mine**, and **Cashier Mill**. Both Frank "Shorty" Harris and Jean Pierre "Pete" Aguereberry claimed to have made the original discovery of gold here on July 1, 1905. They were traveling together to participate in the Fourth of July celebration at Ballarat. Harris ran the Cashier Mine and Aguereberry worked the Eureka Mine.

The Eureka Mine has been stabilized by the National Park Service to allow visitors to explore it (rare is the old mine that can be safely entered). Still, from October 1 through April 15 the mine entrance is closed with a locked gate because it serves as the winter home to colonies of big-eared brown bats and California myotis bats, both of which are rare and require undisturbed winter hibernation.

The Cashier Mill is a short distance around the south side of the hill. The mill's history is a bit of a mystery. It apparently operated from 1909 into 1914, yet already appeared dilapidated when photographed in 1916.

2.4   The rock exposed in the bottom of the small canyon is the Skidoo granite porphyry. Metamorphosed Paleozoic sedimentary rocks are present higher up on the hillsides.

2.9   The jagged peak on the skyline almost straight ahead is Aguereberry Point, where the road ends.

4.8   The side road (GPS 36°21.138'N 117°04.071'W, south) ends at the top of the ridge. It used to follow a tortuously steep, dangerous grade to the bottom of Trail Canyon, but the Park Service decided to not allow repairs when the road washed out in the 1980s. It is now a strenuous hiking route that meets the Trail Canyon Road near the Broken Pick millsite. See Chapter 12, Side Trip SC-3a, for more about that area.

6.3   **Aguereberry Point** (elevation 6,433 feet according to the sign but 6,279 feet per a GPS unit). The road to this famous overlook was built by Pete Aguereberry because he thought the view so spectacular that others ought to see it too. The scene is east over Death Valley. The green square of vegetation on the far valley floor is the Furnace Creek Ranch. Closer at hand is the deep north fork of Trail Canyon. Its rocks are all early Paleozoic sedimentary formations. Aguereberry Point itself is composed of Eureka Quartzite, which is the prominent white band of rock in the canyon.

End of Aguereberry Point side trip.

13.5 / 17.0   **Emigrant Pass** is a short canyon that connects Harrisburg Flat with the upper part of White Sage Flat.

Wood Canyon Road (east 1.5 miles one-way; 4WD recommended) begins where the road curves sharply at the north (bottom) end of Emigrant Pass. Less than 0.2 mile from the highway is a paved road maintenance yard. The road to the mine jogs north from the start of this area, and then continues east along the base of the ridge. Take the left fork 0.8 mile from the highway, and the **Argenta Mine** is another 0.5 mile (the right branch of the road gradually disappears in the wash).

There was an Argenta Mine discovered in 1875, but it may have been different from this one. The major developments here were begun in 1924 by George C. Crist, who 50 years earlier had been the so-called sheriff of Panamint City. Foundations left from a row of 20 mine employee cabins, the cookhouse, a boardinghouse, an assay office, a power plant, and a deep cistern remain amid a great amount of debris—substantial work for a property that apparently never produced a profit. The mine above the large dump is extremely dangerous and shows signs of caving at its entrance.

~14 / 16   **White Sage Flat** is the gentle open valley west of the road. The "white sage" is actually Great Basin sagebrush, *Artemisia tridentata*, which is present with numerous other high-elevation plants such as burrobrush, spiny menodora, shadscale, and a few Joshua trees.

15.0 / 15.5   **Nemo Crest** (elevation 5,547 feet) is the nondescript high point of Emigrant Canyon Road. The origin of the name is not known, but it was in use before 1880.

15.5 / 15.0   A dirt viewpoint beside the road looks south into **Nemo Canyon**. The rocks in this area include a stretched-pebble metaconglomerate, part of the Surprise Formation of the Precambrian age. The metaconglomerate is best seen in roadcuts where there is no parking, down the hill south of the viewpoint. The summit above the canyon is Wildrose Peak, with Rogers Peak, Bennett Peak, and Telescope Peak farther south along the crest of the Panamint Range. Building ruins and scars of the Christmas Mine are visible on the far side of the canyon. To the southwest beyond Nemo Canyon is the Panamint Valley; Maturango Peak is the high point in the Argus Range on the far side of the valley.

17.4 / 13.1   The **Christmas Mine** (east 2.1 miles; hike along a closed road), originally called the Nemo Mine, is on the hillside up Nemo Canyon, about 0.4 mile beyond some cabin ruins. There is historical confusion between this mine, which worked for silver sometime during the 1800s, and the Christmas Gift Mine in upper Wildrose Canyon, which was located in 1860 for silver but mostly mined for antimony during World Wars I and II. Little else is known about this Nemo-Christmas Mine. Its last minor production took place in the early 1970s.

18.2 / 12.3   The dirt road (east) into **A Canyon**, where there are a few small mining claims, was closed to vehicles long ago and has almost disappeared. The name apparently dates to an early mining survey—this first main canyon north of Wildrose Canyon was simply identified as "A" on the map.

20.5 / 10   **Rattlesnake Gulch** is a steep, narrow, and winding canyon. Drive cautiously, and watch your downhill speed. Vehicles longer than 25 feet and wider than 9 feet are not allowed.

20.9 / 9.6   **Side Trip W-3d—Upper Wildrose Canyon Road** and **Charcoal Kilns Road** (east 8.7 miles one-way; narrow pavement and improved dirt to the Wildrose Charcoal Kilns, 4WD required beyond) starts at well-signed Wildrose Junction. Also known as Charcoal Kilns Road, it passes the Wildrose Campground and Ranger Station before heading up Wildrose Canyon to the Wildrose Charcoal Kilns. Beyond the kilns, high-clearance 4WD vehicles are required for the final steep, rocky climb on **Mahogany Flat Road** to the Thorndike and Mahogany Flat campgrounds and the trailhead to Telescope Peak. This last portion of the road is closed during the winter. This is a day-use-only area where camping is not allowed except in the established campgrounds.

0.0   Turnoff from the Emigrant Canyon Road.

0.1   **Wildrose Campground** (left; see Appendix C).

0.3   **Wildrose Ranger Station**. The old Wildrose Ranger Station is no longer staffed and park information is not available.

1.0   The summit nearly straight ahead with radio towers on top is Rogers Peak, named for John Rogers of the 49ers. The transmitters serve various county, state, and federal government agencies.

2.0   The **Christmas Gift Mine** (GPS 36°15.651'N 117°10.344'W, southeast 1.2 miles; hike along a closed road) was discovered on Christmas Day 1860 by Dr. S. G. George while looking for the Lost Gunsight Lode. So far as is definitely known, this is the earliest mine location within Death Valley National Park. It was developed for silver, but most of the metal values were in antimony. Major mining took place during both world wars.

3.6   **Skidoo Pipeline**. An interpretive sign and a section of the original metal pipe are next to the road, and the scar of the pipeline is visible both north and south. The pipe carried water from Birch Spring in Jail Canyon 22 miles to Skidoo, primarily to run Pelton wheel electric generators at the Skidoo Mill. The pipe was removed by the Civilian Conservation Corps in the 1930s.

4.0   **Pinyon Mesa Road** (GPS 36°14.910'N 117°07.638'W, south; 4WD recommended) winds into a small valley in a pinyon-juniper forest. Camping and fires are not allowed. Beyond the road a 0.7-mile hike on an unimproved trail leads to some seeps at **Hummingbird Spring**.

5.0   The asphalt pavement ends next to a weather-recording station.

7.1   The **Wildrose Charcoal Kilns** were built in 1876 to supply pinyon pine charcoal to the silver smelter at the Modoc Mine across Panamint Valley. Cordwood was gathered and stacked in the area where the parking lot is now. When the wood was burned, the large opening into a kiln was blocked off so that air could enter only through the small ducts around the base of the kiln. The wood would smolder for several days as it turned into charcoal. There was enough activity here to support the small town of **Wildrose** (distinct from the later Wild Rose on Harrisburg Flat; see Appendix A). The kilns were last used in 1878.

The **Wildrose Peak Trail** begins just west of the kilns. The one-way distance to the summit is 4.1 miles (see Chapter 8).

The road continues as a 4WD route beyond the charcoal kilns to the Thorndike and Mahogany Flat campgrounds. It is closed in the winter, from about November 1 to May 15.

7.8   **Thorndike Campground**. At an elevation of about 7,500 feet, this is a popular campground during the summer heat. Long-time Panamint Mountains prospector John Thorndike

The Wildrose Charcoal Kilns produced the fuel for the silver smelter at the Modoc Mine in Panamint Valley from 1876 into 1878.

saw the potential of Death Valley tourism and dreamed of building a hotel actually on top of Telescope Peak. Another gentleman actually talked of developing a ski resort on the mountain and proposed Thorndike's place as the lodge. Both dreams were obviously impractical, and Thorndike settled on this canyon instead. The 160-acre homestead served primarily as Thorndike's personal residence from the early 1930s to 1954, but several small cabins of "Thorndike Camp" were sometimes available for rent. Concrete stairs and foundations remain within the campground.

8.7   At an elevation of 8,133 feet, **Mahogany Flat Campground** is the highest campground in Death Valley National Park. There is a beautiful view into Death Valley. The curl-leaf mountain mahogany, *Cercocarpus ledifolius*, is abundant. It is a tough little tree with stout branches. Note the slightly barbed, twisted tails of the seeds.

The **Telescope Peak Trail** begins at the south end of the campground. Ending at the summit of Death Valley's highest point (11,049 feet), the hike is described in Chapter 8.

End of Upper Wildrose Canyon Road, Charcoal Kilns Road, and Mahogany Flat Road.

20.9 / 9.6   The continuation of the Emigrant Canyon Road, now called the Lower Wildrose Canyon Road, continues around the sharp curve at Poplar Spring and Roadside Spring, where the large trees are willow and cottonwood. Southbound travelers note that the road down the canyon is steep, with areas of broken pavement and rough dirt.

22.6 / 7.9   **Wildrose Station Picnic Area.** This place down canyon from the abundant water of Poplar, Roadside, Wildrose, and Wildrose Station springs was the meeting location for the miners when they formed the Rose Springs Mining District in 1873 and then the Wild Rose Mining District in 1888. Later, it served as a stage station on the line between Skidoo and Ballarat. In time developments known as Wildrose Station eventually included a small motel, restaurant, gift shop, and gas station. Among the last operators were the Barkers, the owners of Barker Ranch in Goler Wash and the grandparents of one of the girls of Charles Manson's notorious "family." Wildrose Station closed and the buildings were removed in 1971.

23.1 / 7.4   The small, unnamed canyon (north) is one of only four places where the endangered Class II endemic Panamint daisy (*Enceliopsis covillei*) is known to grow. In the spring it has large woolly leaves and sunflower-like blooms up to 6 inches across. Remember: look but do not collect specimens.

23.9 / 6.6 On the north side of the road is a prominent angular unconformity in sedimentary rocks. The older rocks on the underside are coarse sandstone and conglomerate of the **Nova
Formation**, which was deposited in a long, narrow sedimentary basin about 6 million years ago, before Death Valley and
Panamint Valley existed. The rocks above the unconformity
are comparatively recent alluvial fan deposits, equivalent to
Death Valley's Funeral Formation.

25.5 / 5.0 **Wildrose Graben** is crossed by the highway. A graben is a
block of ground that has been dropped down between faults.
This famous but small example is very young, as shown by
the bounding scarps that are only slightly eroded. This is part
of the Panamint Valley Fault Zone.

26.0 / 4.5 **Tuber Canyon Road** (GPS 36°13.346'N 117°15.429'W, southeast 3.1 miles one-way; 4WD required) is in very poor condition but leads to the mouth of the canyon. The name is a
corruption of the Timbisha word *tuba*, meaning pinyon pine.
From the end of the road, one can hike as far as 8 miles, to an
elevation of about 8,000 feet near the crest of the Panamint
Mountains. There is a lush riparian environment along a permanent stream in much of the canyon. Along the way is the
O. B. Joyful Mine. Named after a popular brand of whiskey,
the mine was discovered in 1897 and proved to be one of the
better gold properties in the Panamint Mountains. After a
mill was built in 1900, it yielded over $250,000 worth of gold
in less than 3 years.

30.5 / 0.0 **Middle Panamint Junction**. Four roads come together at
this junction. The paved Trona-Wildrose Road (south) and
the Panamint Valley Road (north) are described together in
Chapter 16 as Trip Route PV-1, and the nearby Indian Ranch
Road is Trip Route PV-2.

Panamint Valley Areas

The Panamint Valley lies mostly outside of Death Valley National Park. However, the Trona-Wildrose Road is the second busiest corridor route to the park and includes many places important to Death Valley's history. It also provides access to several canyons in the Panamint Mountains that are within the national park.

Panamint Valley Areas, Trip Route PV-1—Panamint Valley Road and Trona-Wildrose Road

FROM: State Highway 190 near Panamint Springs Resort in northern Panamint Valley.

TO: Inyo–San Bernardino county line near Trona, California.

ROAD CONDITIONS: 42.1 miles of paved all-weather county road.

SIDE TRIPS: Minnietta and Modoc Mines (high-clearance plus 4WD), Snow Canyon Road (4WD), Slate Range Road and Nadeau Road (all vehicles); access to Wildrose Canyon Road (Trip Route W-3), Indian Ranch Road (Trip Route PV-2), and Wingate Road–Goler Wash Road (Trip Route PV-3).

GENERAL DESCRIPTION: This highway is one of the three major access routes to Death Valley from southern California and therefore carries a lot of traffic. Although the road is almost entirely outside of the national park, a number of points along it bear strongly on Death Valley's history. The name "Panamint" sounds like it might refer to the mining industry, but that is not the case. "Panümünt" (no known translation) was a Southern Paiute name for the Kawaiisu people, Indians that ranged the western Mojave Desert into southern Panamint Valley; the Kawaiisu were also known as the Mugunüwü, apparently in reference to Telescope Peak ("Mugudoya").

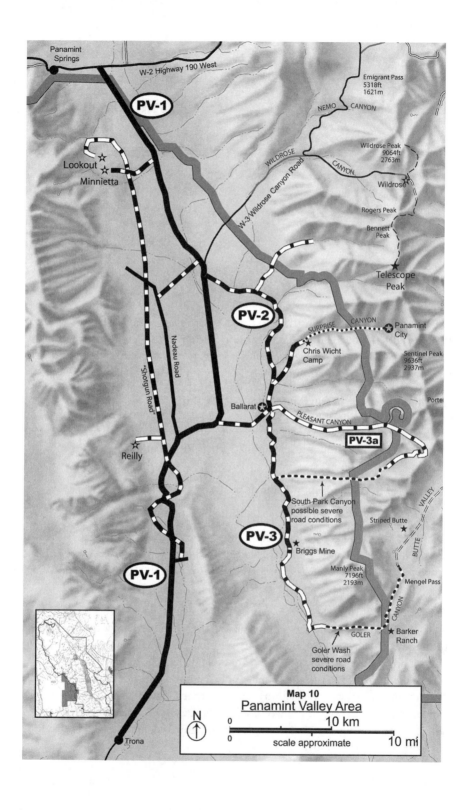

Panamint Springs

W-2 Highway 190 West

PV-1

Emigrant Pass
5318ft
1621m

NEMO   CANYON

Lookout

Minnietta

WILDROSE

W-3 Wildrose Canyon Road

Wildrose Peak
9064ft
2763m

CANYON

Wildrose

Rogers Peak

Bennett
Peak

Telescope
Peak

PV-2

Nadeau Road

SURPRISE   CANYON

Panamint
City

Chris Wicht
Camp

Sentinel Peak
9636ft
2937m

"Shotgun Road"

Ballarat

PLEASANT CANYON

Porte

PV-3a

Reilly

South Park Canyon
possible severe
road conditions

VALLEY

Striped Butte

BUTTE

PV-3

Briggs Mine

Manly Peak
7196ft
2193m

Mengel Pass

CANYON

PV-1

GOLER

Barker
Ranch

Goler Wash
severe road
conditions

Trona

Map 10
<u>Panamint Valley Area</u>

N

0   10 km

0

scale approximate   10 mi

southbound from State Highway 190 / northbound from the county line near Trona.

0.0 / 42.1	Junction with State Highway 190 near Panamint Springs Resort.
7.4 / 34.7	**Minnietta Mine Road** (west 3.9 miles one-way; high-clearance recommended). Access to the Minnietta and Modoc mines and the associated townsite of Lookout is always changing. Some of the mines remain as active claims, and small-scale silver mining took place as recently as 1991. From below the Minnietta, a 4WD road continues north and then west to climb the mountain to Lookout.

The first discovery here was at the **Modoc Mine**, in 1875. The ore was very high grade and contained large masses of the rare mineral coronadite (a lead manganate, $PbMn_8O_{16}$) that contained considerable silver. Some authorities feel that the Modoc, rather than some location within Death Valley, is the site of the Lost Gunsight Lode. The mining led to the establishment of **Lookout** on top of the mountain, where foundations, rock walls, and collapsed buildings remain just west of the Modoc tunnels (Appendix A). A large amount of charcoal was required to process the ore in smelters. The closest source of wood was in the Panamint Mountains, and the charcoal kilns in Wildrose Canyon were built to supply the smelter (see Chapter 15, Side Trip W-3d). The Modoc Mine shut down in 1878 after producing an estimated $1.9 million worth of silver, plus gold, copper, lead, and zinc.

The **Minnietta Mine**, low on the mountain south of the Modoc, was most active from 1895 into the 1920s. The remains of the mine's camp remain on the slopes below the mine. An old house was partially restored by volunteers who worked in cooperation with the Bureau of Land Management; most of the other structures were destroyed by vandals. Rock walls in the bottom of the wash are all that is left of the commercial town of **Minnietta**, which briefly boasted a store and a saloon.

10.6 / 31.5	**Snow Canyon Road** (west 7.3 miles; 4WD recommended into the canyon) leads to the Golden Lady Mine in Snow Canyon. During many of the early mining years within Death Valley, the Snow Canyon Mill was available for custom work.
13.4 / 28.7	**Slate Range Road** (southwest 5 miles to Nadeau Road; all vehicles) is simply a connecting route across the valley. It is

A 1976 snowstorm was clearing the Panamint Mountains as seen from the Minnietta Mine in 1976. Unfortunately, this cabin was burned by vandals a few years later.

dirt but is periodically graded by Inyo County. Paved Nadeau Road then continues south 8.1 miles to the Trona-Wildrose Road.

13.8 / 28.3 **Middle Panamint Junction.** Lower Wildrose Canyon Road (northeast) leads into the national park via Wildrose Canyon and Emigrant Canyon; it is described as Chapter 15, Trip Route W-3. Southbound travelers turn right at the junction to continue along the Trona-Wildrose Road; northbound travelers turn left to continue on the Panamint Valley Road.

14.2 / 27.9 **Indian Ranch Road** (east) parallels the Trona-Wildrose Road along the base of the Panamint Mountains. It is described as Trip Route PV-2.

~ 18 / 24 The highest point in the Panamint Mountains (east) is Telescope Peak (elevation 11,049 feet). The large canyon draining directly west from the peak is Hall Canyon. The next major canyon to the south is Surprise Canyon, the location of the famous ghost town of Panamint City. To the west are the Argus Mountains where the highest summit is Maturango Peak (elevation 8,839 feet).

23.2 / 18.9 **Ballarat Road** (east 3.6 miles; graded dirt county road suitable for all vehicles). Although Ballarat's days as a mining camp ended around 1917, the town has seldom been completely abandoned. Much of the town is private property, and as of late 2008 one small store selling snacks and souvenirs (no gas) was in business.

26.9 / 15.2   **Nadeau Road** (north; paved, light-duty county road). About 3.6 miles from the highway, a side road west ends at an onyx mine that produced decorative stone from 1925 until commercial operations ended in the 1990s. Nadeau Road continues north past the Slate Range Road and ends about 13.6 miles from the highway at a limestone quarry operated by the North American Chemical Corporation to supply carbonate for its mineral processing plants at Trona.

27.3 / 14.8   Remi Nadeau's **Shotgun Road** (north; high-clearance vehicles) was constructed by freighter Remi Nadeau in the 1870s to serve the Modoc Mine. Much of the route is arrow-straight up the valley. About 1.1 miles from the Trona-Wildrose Road, a side road leads west 1.6 miles to the site of **Reilly**, a mining camp that boasted rich but strictly surficial silver ore and only lasted from 1882 into 1884 (see Appendix A). Although Shotgun Road is near and parallel to the paved Nadeau Road, the road to Reilly does not connect the two, so Shotgun Road must be used for access.

28.4 / 13.7   **Iron Caps Mine** is the large cut on the hillside (west). It was first opened in 1876 as a source of flux for the Modoc Smelter in northern Panamint Valley. Additional production occurred during World War II, when small amounts of iron ore were mined.

28.8 / 13.3   **Water Canyon** (west) climbs into the Argus Range and quickly narrows into a slot canyon. Some authorities believe that a few of the 49er argonauts took this canyon in order to leave Panamint Valley.

30.5 / 11.6   **Slate Range Crossing**. A pullout at the summit gives an outstanding view north through Panamint Valley with its salty lake bed floor bounded by the Panamint Mountains (east) and the Argus Mountains (west). Cutting down the slopes east of the highway is the original Nadeau Road, constructed by Chinese laborers around 1875 to serve the Modoc and other silver mines. Notice the extensive rock work that shores up the road in several places, still durable after more than 130 years. Once off the mountain, the road followed an arrow-straight "Shotgun Road" line north.

35.7 / 6.4   Homewood Canyon Road (west) leads to an area of private homes.

~38 / 4	**Manly Pass** (east) is the low gap through the Slate Range. Some of the Death Valley argonauts crossed Manly Pass (and definitely not Slate Range Crossing) in early 1850 en route from Death Valley and Panamint Valley to the San Fernando Valley.
39.9 / 2.2	**Wilson Canyon Road** (west, improved dirt road, 2.9 miles one-way). After crossing the Slate Range and finding only salt water in Searles Lake, the 49ers apparently went up this canyon, where they found salvation in the water of "Providence Spring," probably today's Indian Joe Spring. From there they climbed west into what is now the Naval Air Weapons Station–China Lake, areas off limits to explorers.
42.1 / 0.0	**Inyo–San Bernardino county line**. The residential community of Pioneer Point is named after the 49ers because some of them camped at the base of the large rock outcrops next to the road at the south end of the town. Few services operate at Pioneer Point. The industrial town of Trona about 2 miles farther south has small stores and gas stations.

Panamint Valley Areas, Trip Route PV-2—Indian Ranch Road

FROM: Trona-Wildrose Road just south of Middle Panamint Junction.

TO: Ballarat.

ROAD CONDITIONS: 11.7 miles one-way; graded dirt road, suitable for any vehicle.

SIDE TRIPS: Jail Canyon (4WD), Surprise Canyon (4WD), and Happy Canyon (4WD).

GENERAL DESCRIPTION: This road is maintained by Inyo County but often develops areas of rough washboard and may be muddy near Warm Sulphur Springs. Although it lies outside the national park, it provides the only access to several canyons in the Panamint Mountains that are within the park.

ROAD LOG MILEAGES	southbound from Trona-Wildrose Road / northbound from Ballarat.
0.0 / 11.7	The north end of Indian Ranch Road is marked by a small road sign, about 0.4 mile south of Middle Panamint Junction where the Panamint Valley, Trona-Wildrose, and Lower Wildrose Canyon roads meet.
4.0 / 7.7	**Jail Canyon Road** (GPS 36°08.690'N 117°14.026'W, northeast 6.2 miles one-way; 4WD required) wanders up the alluvial fan into the lower reaches of Jail Canyon. The road enters the national park 2.7 miles from Indian Ranch Road. The

canyon reportedly was named because the only way in or out is through the narrow canyon mouth. The **Corona Mine** is at the end of the road, about 3 miles into the canyon. It consists of numerous tunnels driven into a complex system of quartz veins that contain free gold in association with several silver, lead, and copper sulfide minerals.

A hike from the Corona Mine up Jail Canyon leads to the **Gem Mine**, where there are the remains of 2 or 3 cabins and scattered trash.

Just before the end of the Jail Canyon Road at the Corona Mine, a closed side road (south) provides a spectacular hike to **Hall Canyon**. The route slices across the steep face of the Panamint Mountains before dropping into Hall Canyon itself. The trail ends at a small gold prospect near a perennial stream in a pinyon pine forest. Nearby are the remains of a cabin.

Another trail along a closed road in this area branches from the Jail Canyon Road on the alluvial fan just inside the national park boundary. It curves northeast about 2 miles to the mouth of **Tuber Canyon**, which can also be reached via a rough 4WD road from the Lower Wildrose Canyon Road (see near the end of Trip Route W-3). Up the canyon is the O. B. Joyful Mine. Named after a popular brand of whiskey, the mine was discovered in 1897 and proved to be one of the better gold properties in the Panamint Mountains. After a mill was built in 1900, it yielded more than $250,000 worth of gold in less than 3 years.

4.6 / 7.1   **Indian Ranch** is an Indian reservation once populated by just one person, "Indian George Hanson," a Timbisha Shoshone. As a child he is said to have observed the 49ers at Burned Wagons Point, and he guided prospecting parties in the 1860s and 1870s, including those headed by Dr. Samuel G. George in search of the Lost Gunsight Lode. (This is the origin of his name, "George"; the government added the "Hanson" because "he had to have a last name.") In later years he settled at what became Indian George's Ranch. He passed away sometime after 1938 when he was over 100 years old. At times the Indians have granted leases to Indian Ranch for commercial operations by others—in the mid-1970s there was a small store, restaurant, and bar with live dance music— but it is presently closed private property.

6.3 / 5.4   **Warm Sulphur Springs** has enough flow to support small permanent ponds. Most of the trees are screwbean mesquites, but there are also honey mesquites and willows. Some of the Death Valley argonauts rested at the springs in early 1850. They called it "Horse Bone Camp" because of the litter of skeletons around an abandoned Indian settlement.

9.8 / 1.9 **Surprise Canyon Road** (GPS 36°04.481'N 117°13.264'W, east 4.1 miles one-way; high-clearance recommended) climbs a steep alluvial fan to enter the canyon. Although the canyon includes the famous ghost town of Panamint City, a flash flood destroyed the road in 1984, and it has not been repaired beyond the remains of **Chris Wicht Camp**, which now marks the end of the road.

Chris Wicht was a saloonkeeper and one-time "mayor" at Ballarat. Following that boom he single-handedly built this complex of buildings, first based on mining but later to serve as a tourist camp. Cabins cost $1 per night in 1938. Stream water powered a Pelton wheel generator on the way to a swimming pool 75 feet long. The site was more recently called Novak Camp, but the building burned in 2006 and the place is now abandoned.

Beyond Chris Wicht Camp, the road used to continue up the canyon to **Panamint City**, one of the most famous of Death Valley's ghost towns (Appendix A). It now requires a hike to reach the townsite. This route is a "cherrystem" of Bureau of Land Management ground that is immediately bounded by the national park. After a flash flood in 1984, 4WD vehicles with winches were required to climb over the series of long, steep, dry cascades on the canyon floor. Even doing that was difficult and now is impossible, as the road was closed to all traffic in 2001.

Hikers will find the route fairly strenuous since it is rocky and climbs more than 4,000 feet in elevation in the 6 miles to the upper end of the townsite. Along the way are Limekiln Spring (2 miles from Chris Wicht Camp) and Brewery Spring (3.5 miles), which are large enough to produce a stream that sometimes reaches all the way to the mouth of the canyon. The city was spread out for more than a mile along the canyon, and litter is encountered well before the townsite is reached. The ruins of the famous Surprise Valley Mill smelter, complete with brick smokestack, are located at the upper end of town.

10.1 / 1.6 An unmarked road (west 0.2 mile) ends at the sparse remains of **Shermantown** (GPS 36°04.234'N 117°13.572'W), where adobe walls have nearly disappeared into the ground. They

Miscellaneous adobe walls are still standing at Ballarat.

are the only remnants of a stage station at what was planned to be the shipping center for Panamint City at the terminus of the Los Angeles & Independence Railroad (see Appendix B). The community lasted less than 2 years.

10.6 / 1.1   **Happy Canyon Road** (east 2.5 miles one-way; 4WD required) winds up the alluvial fan into Happy Canyon. The road deteriorates as it passes through groves of mesquite and willow trees, and then disappears at a permanent stream. Hikers can follow the canyon floor an additional 4 miles to the ruins of a large mill.

11.7 / 0.0   **Ballarat** ghost town (see Appendix A). From Ballarat, where a small store (no gas) is usually open for business, there is a good road west across Panamint Valley to the Trona-Wildrose Road (3.6 miles). South is the Wingate Road (Trip Route PV-3), and east is the Pleasant Canyon Road (also described in Trip Route PV-3).

Panamint Valley, Trip Route PV-3—Wingate Road and Goler Wash Road

FROM: Ballarat, in Panamint Valley.

TO: Anvil Spring Junction in Butte Valley.

ROAD CONDITIONS: 26.5 miles one-way; graded dirt first 3.9 miles, then high-clearance vehicles farther south through Panamint Valley to lower Goler Wash; 4WD only through Goler Wash into Butte Valley.

SIDE TRIPS: Pleasant Canyon (Side Trip PV-3a, 4WD), South Park Canyon (4WD), lower Redlands Canyon (high-clearance), Coyote Canyon (4WD), and Barker Ranch and Myer's Ranch (4WD).

GENERAL DESCRIPTION: Wingate Road on the floor of Panamint Valley is normally passable to any high-clearance vehicle. The continuation through Goler Wash (also called Goler Canyon and Goler Gulch) has frequently been described as "a road with serious character." The climb on both sides of Mengel Pass, between Goler Wash and Butte Valley, is one of the roughest within the national park, with long series of bedrock cascades on very steep grades. It absolutely demands 4WD vehicles driven with care and patience. The lower reaches of Goler Wash often flood and wash out the road. However, it receives occasional informal road maintenance by area miners, so it varies from being easily passable by high-clearance vehicles to almost impassable even in short-wheelbase 4WD.

ROAD LOG MILEAGES	southbound from Ballarat / northbound from Anvil Spring Junction (Butte Valley). People driving the Wingate Road south from Ballarat should use the road log following Side Trip PV-3a.

Side Trip PV-3a—Pleasant Canyon–South Park Canyon Loop (east, 4WD required) begins in "downtown" Ballarat. It climbs to near the top of Pleasant Canyon, turns south over the crest of the Panamint Mountains at Rogers Pass (elevation 7,160 feet), drops into the highest reaches of Middle Park Canyon, and finally winds down South Park Canyon. In general, the road up Pleasant Canyon is relatively easy, but 4WD vehicles are required because of a number of rough bedrock stairs and wet areas in the lower part of the canyon. Also, beyond Rogers Pass the road is of questionable quality. In early 1994 the old road through South Park Canyon was reopened when a mining group rebuilt a washed-out bridge. This made a long loop trip connecting Pleasant Canyon with South Park Canyon possible, but Inyo County inspectors found the bridge to not meet safety specifications and posted it for a maximum vehicle weight of 6,000 pounds. As a result, the status of this road could change at any time. Also, there are many active mines in the area, and the privacy at some is guarded by the owners.

Briefly, the route up Pleasant Canyon is as follows:

0.0   Ballarat.

0.5   A side road (north) leads into **Jackpot Canyon**. Just up the canyon from there, the Pleasant Canyon Road reaches a stream and for the next 1 mile or so is rough and overgrown with desert willow trees, cattails, and grasses. A cable stretching across the canyon above the road leads to the Anthony Mine, one of the many gold producers in this area. A short distance farther another cable stretches above the road.

6.0   The most substantial ruins in the canyon are at **Clair Camp** (GPS 36°01.989'N 117°08.004'W), which was the site of short-lived **Pleasant City** in 1897–1898 following the discovery of the adjacent Ratcliff and numerous other area mines. The **Ratcliff Mine** produced over $1,000,000 in gold plus smaller amounts of silver, lead, and tungsten. Clair Camp has been abandoned for many years and the structures are collapsing.

As the road continues up the canyon, it passes below the **World Beater Mine**.

8.1   **Stone Corral** (GPS 36°02.020'N 117°05.812'W) is just inside the Death Valley National Park boundary. A steep side road to the north ends at the **Porter Mine** (also called the Mountain Girl Mine), a gold mine that was deleted from the national park as it is still active as gated, guarded private property.

9.8   **Mormon Gulch Cabin.** Still farther up the canyon, the road passes the remains of the small **Cooper Mill** before coming to a three-way road junction (GPS 36°01.548'N 117°04.411'W). Nearby is the Mormon Gulch Cabin, which is maintained by the park service and available for overnight use if not occupied by others. The road to the left is the Mormon Gulch Road, where there is nothing in particular. The road to the right leads directly to Middle Park but is in poor condition, and the center road continues toward Rogers Pass.

11.8   **Rogers Pass** (GPS 36°00.744'N 117°03.286'W). From the cabin, the center road gradually climbs up and out of the canyon to reach Rogers Pass. There is a historical monument at the pass. After their return to Death Valley with supplies, it is likely that Manly and Rogers led the Bennett and Arcan families over this pass in early February 1850—and so it *might* have been here that the famous words "Goodbye, Death Valley" were spoken. From this point, it is only 1.4 miles east to Arrastre Spring, accessible from the Warm Spring Canyon Road (Chapter 12, Side Trip SC-3f).

From the pass, the road continues into **Middle Park** and then down **South Park Canyon**—remember, though, that this part of the route might be closed. If open, then it is about 13 miles from Rogers Pass to Wingate Road, on the floor of Panamint Valley at a point 3.9 miles south of Ballarat, making the complete Pleasant Canyon–South Park Canyon Loop a trip of about 29 miles.

End of Pleasant Canyon–South Park Canyon Loop.

0.0 / 26.5 **Ballarat** is a semi–ghost town. Founded in 1897 when rich gold mines were located in the nearby mountains, Ballarat grew into a small city of several hundred people, with all the usual services and a post office, until 1917 (Appendix A). Since then, it has never been completely abandoned. There is now one small store (no gas) amid numerous adobe ruins and some modern structures. The townsite is private property, and although you are generally free to explore, you should probably ask for permission at the store.

0.6 / 25.9 **Post Office Spring** (west side of road) has been a Panamint Valley meeting place since the earliest records. After following various routes over the mountains, many of the Death Valley 49ers rested here before tackling the Slate Range and other mountains to the west. Later, it was a place where messages were left in a can near the spring, hence the name, and there was a small settlement here during the Panamint City silver rush in the 1870s.

1.3 / 25.2 **Gold Bug Road** (east) is a private road that climbs toward Middle Park Canyon and the Gold Bug Mine, one of the many properties first located by Frank "Shorty" Harris.

~2.5 / 24 A series of saltwater springs lies along the west edge of the road, and small pools similar to Badwater are located at their south end.

3.7 / 22.8 **South Park Canyon Road** (east; high-clearance to Suitcase Mine, then 4WD to head of canyon if open). Gold and lead-silver mines are scattered the length of South Park Canyon. The road is in good condition the first 4.1 miles up to the Suitcase Mine, but questionable beyond there. See Side Trip PV-3a (above) for more information about this area.

6.3 / 20.2 A double ring of rocks just east of the road—one small circle inside a larger about 6 feet in diameter—is the remains of an arrastre, a primitive ore-grinding device. Although crude, arrastres took the place of more sophisticated but expensive stamp mills. The crushed rock was further treated with simple pans, sluice boxes, or dry washers to recover the free gold. The history of this example is unknown.

7.9 / 18.6   **Redlands Canyon Road** (east; high-clearance). This road leads toward the huge mining scars on the mountains that make up the Briggs Mine, a large-volume, low-grade gold mine that operated into the 2000s. The road leads to Brigg's Camp, a private mining settlement built by long-time miner-prospector Harry Briggs at the mouth of the canyon, but that area and nearby **Manly Fall** have been severely altered by the mining.

It is quite certain that Lewis Manly and John Rogers passed down this canyon after they left the Bennett and Arcan families in Death Valley. The waterfall they described was probably Ox Jump Fall, farther up the canyon, rather than Manly Fall, but it was because of these falls that they chose to return to Death Valley and then lead the others out by way of Rogers Pass and South Park Canyon.

~8 / 18.5   The salt pan west of the road is the lowest place in Panamint Valley (elevation about 1,038 feet). It is much like Death Valley only narrower. Most of the plants growing along the edge of the salt pan are pickleweed.

~11 / 15.5   **Manly Pass** is the low spot through the Slate Range to the west. Although they followed several different routes out of Death Valley, most of the argonauts ended up crossing the Slate Range through this pass in early 1850. Two men died of exhaustion during the trek. The final resting place of "Old Man" Fisch is somewhere in Fish Canyon on the near (east) side of the pass, and that of William Isham is near the mouth of Isham Canyon on the west side.

13.2 / 13.3   **Coyote Canyon Road** (southeast; 4WD) is a poor road that goes to mining claims a short distance into Coyote Canyon.

14.9 / 11.6   **Wingate Junction** (GPS 35°51.537'N 117°10.789'W) is where the Goler Wash Road branches east from the Wingate Road on the valley floor. Wingate Road continues south but is closed to public travel at the boundary of the Naval Air Weapons Station–China Lake Range B, 5.5 miles from Wingate Junction. There is little point to driving it unless one is seeking an isolated camping spot. It used to connect with the road through Wingate Pass, Long Valley, and Wingate Wash into Death Valley, but that route was closed many years ago.

16.1 / 10.4   There are some substantial stone ruins related to mining in Goler Wash about 100 feet north of the road. They probably date to around 1900.

16.4 / 10.1   The lower reaches of the wash are a narrow slot canyon often called Goler Gulch. It is at this point that the road often deteriorates so that 4WD is required.

    The canyon was named after John Goller (note the change in spelling), who prospected a wide region as early as 1860. Someplace around Death Valley he supposedly found placer gold in a rugged canyon. It was so rich that he could fill a pack with pure gold nuggets in a matter of minutes. Of course, Goller never found the location again, either alone or with well-equipped parties. The "Lost Goller Mine" remains lost. Nobody has ever found placer gold nuggets to match his anywhere in the Mojave Desert.

17.0 / 9.5   Just above the narrowest part of the canyon are several small mine prospects and a good spring. Mojave fire-barrel cactus, *Ferocactus acanthodes*, grows on the rocky cliffs. These are different from most fire-barrels because their spines are yellow rather than red. Just above the spring is a dry bedrock cascade that sometimes blocks almost all traffic. On the other hand, if it has recently been improved, then it may be passable in any high-clearance vehicle.

17.9 / 8.6   The wooden ore tipple south of the road is at the bottom of a cable tram that stretches overhead to the Lestro Mountain Mine, a rather small gold mine high on the mountain to the north. There are some stone ruins just up the canyon.

18.3 / 8.2   A cable tramline extends northward from the canyon floor.

18.7 / 7.8   **Lower Lotus Spring** is a reliable enough water source that this part of Goler Wash supports a short stream and boasts one of the best spring wildflower displays anywhere. Especially prominent are evening primrose, mallow, prickly poppy, brittlebush, stingbush, and Indian paintbrush.

19.4 / 7.1   The **Keystone Mine** (originally called the Lotus Mine) is far up the mountain to the south, where there are a number of tunnels served by a rail tramway 2,800 feet long and two overhead cable trams. Some of the gold ore is worth $1,500 per ton at modern prices. The complex of buildings on the canyon floor is occupied private property.

19.9 / 6.6   Concrete ruins next to the road are the site of a gold mill that was built in the 1920s.

20.5 / 6.0   Boundary of Death Valley National Park.

20.6 / 5.9   **Sourdough Spring** is the water supply for the Keystone Mine camp. It flows about 2 gallons per minute from within a dense grove of willow trees tangled with wild grapevines.

20.9 / 5.6 **Myers Ranch/Barker Ranch Road** (GPS 35°51.642'N 117°05.799'W, south). **Barker Ranch** and **Myers Ranch**, a bit farther up the side canyon, became notorious in 1969 when Charles Manson and his "family" took refuge at the ranches following their murder spree in Los Angeles. The family members were arrested at Barker Ranch. Interestingly, they had not been connected with the murders at the time of arrest but instead were wanted by Inyo County authorities on various drug charges and for the arson burning of National Park Service road equipment in Racetrack Valley.

The house at Barker Ranch, which is National Park Service property, burned in early May 2009. Myer's Ranch is still private property; its building burned in 1999. The road beyond Myer's Ranch used to reach Wingate Pass, but it enters military land is closed to travel.

21.9 / 4.6 For those driving up Goler Wash, the Barker Ranch Road is always the limit for vehicles without 4WD. The road continues through a steep, narrow canyon to a divide between branches of the canyon, and then travels along a gravel wash toward the roughest part of the trip.

Travelers driving down Goler Wash should turn sharply left into the canyon, rather than taking the obvious road up the ridge—it simply ends on the far side of an extremely steep hill.

23.6 / 2.9 **"Hubcap Rock"** sticks out into the road at a narrow bedrock cascade. It has a healthy appetite for tires and hubcaps. The rock is marked by a pipe sticking up from the boulders beside the road. **"Oilpan Rock"** a few feet farther up the canyon has a similar appetite.

24.3 / 2.2 **Mengel Pass** (GPS 35°53.996'N 117°04.941'W, elevation 4,328 feet) is the divide between Goler Wash and Butte Valley. The mile or so of road on either side of the pass is the "road with serious character," so called because of the exceptional number of bedrock cascades and outcrops in the roadbed.

The cairn of rocks at the summit is the Mengel Monument atop the grave of Carl Mengel. An acquaintance of "Shorty" Harris and Pete Aguereberry, he favored the southern part of the Panamint Mountains and found numerous gold and lead-silver deposits of above-average quality. Among them was the Lotus Mine (now the Keystone Mine) in Goler Wash. Mengel settled at Greater View Spring in Butte Valley in 1912 and lived out his life there. By his request, his ashes were interned on the pass after his death in 1944.

25.9 / 0.6	**Russell Camp Road** (west) leads to the camp built by Asa "Panamint Russ" Russell around 1930. He lived here as a full-time prospector after he retired from the Los Angeles Department of Water and Power. The buildings are now available for camping on a first-come, first-serve basis with a 3-day stay limit.
26.1 / 0.4	**Greater View Spring** (west) is the location of Carl Mengel's home. The buildings are now available for camping on a first-come, first-serve basis with a 3-day stay limit.
26.5 / 0.0	**Anvil Spring Junction.** The Stone Cabin, just above Anvil Spring and a single large cottonwood tree, was probably built in 1935, although Asa Russell claimed to have done so in 1930. Anvil Spring is the central place in Butte Valley, where roads radiate in five directions. These destinations, including the eastern access road into Butte Valley by way of Warm Springs Canyon, are described in Chapter 12, Side Trip SC-3f.

■ ■ ■ ■ ■ ■CHAPTER SEVENTEEN
Northern Death Valley

These two routes are transportation corridors with relatively few specific points of interest along them, except for the two primary attractions of northern Death Valley: Scotty's Castle and Ubehebe Crater.

Northern Death Valley, Trip Route N-1—Scotty's Castle Road

FROM: State Highway 190 at Sand Dunes Junction.

TO: Scotty's Castle.

ROAD CONDITIONS: 36.0 miles one-way, all-weather paved road.

SIDE TRIPS: Old Stovepipe Road (Side Trip N-1a, all vehicles), Palm Spring (hike), Triangle Spring (hike), Midway Well (hike), mouth of Titus Canyon (all standard vehicles), and Ubehebe Crater (Side Trip N-1b, all vehicles); access to Bonnie Claire Road (Trip Route N-2), Big Pine Road (Chapter 18, Trip Route BP-1), and Racetrack Valley Road and Hunter Mountain Road (Chapter 19, Trip Route RH-1).

GENERAL DESCRIPTION: This route is the access from the central part of Death Valley to the two prime attractions in northern Death Valley, Scotty's Castle and Ubehebe Crater, plus several hiking routes and historic sites.

ROAD LOG MILEAGES	northbound from Sand Dunes Junction / southbound from Scotty's Castle.
0.0 / 36.0	**Sand Dunes Junction** at State Highway 190, 16.9 miles north of Furnace Creek and 7.2 miles east of Stovepipe Wells Village.
0.5 / 35.5	**Mud Canyon Road** (east) ends at Beatty, Nevada. It is described as Trip Route NC-3 in Chapter 14.

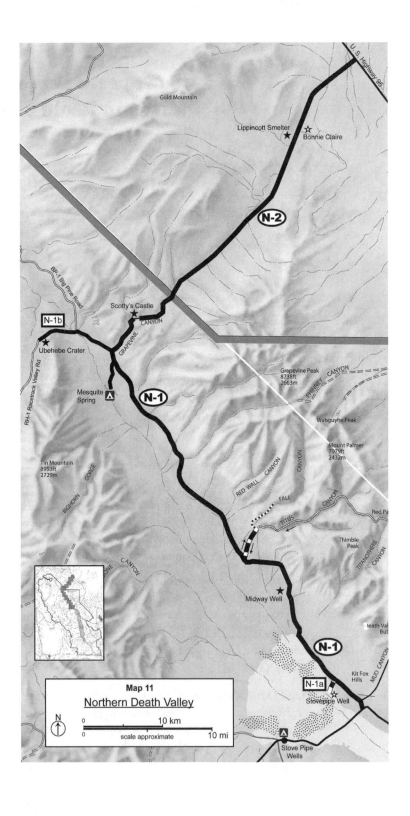

Map 11

Northern Death Valley

0   10 km

N

0   scale approximate   10 mi

0.7 / 35.3	An information kiosk on the east side of the road is next to picnic tables, trash cans, and a chemical toilet.
2.5 / 33.5	**"Wagon Wheel History"** interpretive sign (west side of road). The road between the boom towns of Rhyolite and Skidoo came down the canyon to the east, crossed the modern highway here, and continued down the alluvial fan toward Stovepipe Well. The old road is barely visible, especially in the downslope direction.
2.9 / 33.1	**Side Trip N-1a—Old Stovepipe Road** (west, graded dirt suitable for all vehicles) runs straight down the alluvial fan to the site of the original Stovepipe Well.
0.0	Turnoff from Scotty's Castle Road.
0.4	**Val Nolan Grave.** Val Nolan may have been an automobile prospector who died of dehydration after his car broke down in the summer of 1931. He is said to have been in Beatty on July 4, 1931. His body was found in early August by a Hollywood film crew but was not buried until November 6, 1931. However, he has also been reported to be a completely fictional victim of the elements during early tourism promotions. Other stories have been told as well, so nobody really knows who—if anyone—is buried in the grave.
0.8	**Stovepipe Well** was a shallow hole dug through the sand to slightly salty but drinkable water. Because of drifting sand, the location was marked with a section of old stovepipe. The well was the only water hole on the floor of Death Valley along the Rhyolite-Skidoo road and was a true lifesaver on many occasions. When the well was improved to provide abundant fresh water, it became the site of the Stovepipe Well Road House that in February 1908 included a boardinghouse, grocery, restaurant, saloon, feedstore, and bathhouse. Its telephone was the first in Death Valley. Nothing remains of the settlement and the well is capped.

From Stovepipe Well, one can hike 2.6 miles south along a closed road to State Highway 190 or explore the sand dunes to the west.

End of Old Stovepipe Road side trip.

| 5.0 / 31.0 | The abrupt face of the **Kit Fox Hills** just east of the road marks the trace of the Northern Death Valley Fault Zone. It is a right-lateral strike-slip fault on which the Death Valley side has crept northward perhaps as much as 50 miles with respect to the Grapevine Mountains to the east. |

The Stovepipe Well Road House was a cluster of tent buildings and corrals along the Rhyolite-Skidoo road. It boasted a solar water heater and the first telephone in Death Valley. (Unknown photographer, courtesy National Park Service, Death Valley National Park)

7.1 / 28.9	**Palm Spring** at the base of the fault scarp can be glimpsed to the north from where the road begins to climb up onto the scarp. The spring supports a small pool. The namesake, non-native palm trees have been removed. Water from the Grapevine Mountains to the east percolates through the sub-surface of the alluvial fan but is forced to the surface by the crushed rock of the fault zone, which acts as a dam.
7.9 / 28.1	The **Triangle Springs** (GPS 36°43.639'N 117°08.156'W, west 0.5 mile on a long-closed road onto the flat floor of Death Valley; hike) are spread along a zone several hundred feet long. They once had reliable water and were named because of a triangular concrete catch basin that was built at one of the springs near the turn of the twentieth century. Now they are little more than seeps. Closer to the road along the scarp of the Northern Death Valley Fault Zone are numerous other seeps where small stands of reeds grow in moist, salty ground. There is no open water.
9.4 / 26.6	**Midway Well** (GPS 36°44.767'N 117°08.187'W, west 0.25 mile; hike). The Midway Well Campground had only 10

campsites. Because each was isolated from the others by the mesquite-locked sand dunes, it was a popular place that suffered from overuse. A flash flood in 1971 clinched a decision to close the campsites. Some of the wooden tables and fire rings remain in place. The standpipe of the well is visible from the highway. It sometimes leaks enough water to maintain a small pool at its base.

Surveyors Well (GPS 36°44.788'N 117°09.124'W, west 0.9 mile from Midway Well; hike) was a natural source of water reliable enough that the Timbisha called it Ohyu ("Mesquite") and Indian families lived there much of the time. The well also served as a descriptive location on the boundaries of early mining districts.

11.7 / 24.3   "When Flood Waters Churn" interpretive sign (east side of road) describes the alluvial fan below an unnamed canyon. The relative ages of different parts of the fan can be told by the amount of desert varnish that has formed on the rock's surfaces—the older the rocks, the darker their color.

14.8 / 21.2   Titus Canyon Road (east 2.7 miles one-way; graded dirt road accessible to all standard vehicles). The road through Titus Canyon (Chapter 14, Trip Route NC-5) is one-way from the east (the entrance is on Daylight Pass Road, Trip Route NC-3), but this two-way stretch allows you to reach the mouth of the canyon for a hike into the spectacular narrows. Try to figure out the location of the canyon as you drive—on approach, nowhere else is the mouth of a major canyon as invisible as this one.

16.5 / 19.5   Fall Canyon (east, hike directly from the road or more easily along a primitive trail north from the mouth of Titus Canyon) is a slot canyon named for a series of dry waterfalls. It is possible to hike about 2.5 miles into the canyon to a fall that blocks further walking. A long roundabout back track or good climbing skills are needed to continue farther, but then Fall Canyon can be followed almost to the crest of the Grapevine Mountains.

18.6 / 17.4   Red Wall Canyon (east; 2 miles to canyon mouth at GPS 36°51.732'N 117°12.453'W, marked by bright-red and black rocks; hike) is a narrow canyon of brilliant colors. A dry waterfall about 1 mile into the canyon requires climbing skills for those who wish to go higher into the Grapevine Mountains.

25.5 / 10.5   From near the top of the grade, the view south takes in Tucki Mountain above the sand dunes and Stovepipe Wells

Village. The barren, white lake beds to the front right of the dunes are called the Nitre Beds. Nitrate minerals are soluble in water, so they occur only in the very driest of deserts. Although the Nitre Beds were once explored for mining, only trace amounts of the minerals are present and no mining took place.

27.0 / 9.0 The high peak in the Cottonwood Mountains (west) is Tin Mountain (elevation 8,953 feet), and the major drainage down its face is Bighorn Gorge. This general area, especially in the disturbed soil right along the road, is host to several species of annual buckwheat plants. Most common is inflated stem buckwheat (*Erigonum inflatum*), but the Rixford pagoda buckwheat (*E. rixfordii*), a Class II Death Valley endemic, forms some thick stands. Golden cholla, beavertail, and cottontop cacti are common on the rocky alluvial fans.

32.5 / 3.5 **Mesquite Springs Campground Road** (west 1.9 miles). This is the only established campground in the northern one-third of the national park. It is especially popular because of its small size, proximity to Scotty's Castle and higher, and somewhat cooler temperatures, at an elevation of 1,800 feet above sea level.

32.8 / 3.2 **Grapevine Entrance Station and Ranger Station**. The Northern Death Valley Fault Zone crosses the highway at this point, running almost underneath the ranger station building. Across the road is a Park Service housing area, also constructed essentially on top of the fault.

33.1 / 2.9 **Side Trip N-1b—Ubehebe Crater Road** (northwest 5.7 miles one-way; all-weather paved road). Ubehebe Crater is the largest and youngest of a series of volcanic explosion craters that formed as little as 300 years ago.

0.0 **Grapevine Junction** at the Scotty's Castle Road.

1.8 The gated road (northeast) leads to the Grapevine Springs and Lower Vine Ranch, an area closed to public entry. The springs support a very sensitive riparian habitat that includes several Class I endemic springsnails and other invertebrate animals. The ranch was occupied by Death Valley Scotty and Albert Johnson during some of the time that Scotty's Castle was being built, and then it served as Scotty's private residence. The National Park Service occasionally leads walking tours from Scotty's Castle to Lower Vine Ranch; check at the visitor centers for availability.

2.8 **Big Pine Road** (also called Death Valley Road and North Entrance Highway) leads north into Death Valley Wash, through the Last Chance Range, and across Eureka Valley and the Inyo Mountains and ends at the town of Big Pine, California. It is described as Trip Route BP–1 in Chapter 18.

3.8   The road winds through some low hills composed of ash and lapilli beds erupted from the Ubehebe Crater complex.

5.5   **Racetrack Valley Road** (unimproved dirt; high-clearance required, 4WD recommended) heads south. Its major destination is The Racetrack, with its moving rocks, but it also leads to important mining districts and Hunter Mountain. The road is described as Trip Route RH-1 in Chapter 19.

5.7   **Ubehebe Crater** is a young phreatic maar (or cryptovolcanic) explosion crater. Based on charcoal that was found underneath the eruption deposits and can be dated using Carbon-14, Ubehebe Crater formed only about 300 years ago. Imagine the amount of force needed to instantly create this great hole, 2,000 feet across and 700 feet deep. Ubehebe is the largest and youngest in a field of at least 16 craters. They all formed when magma rose close to the surface and caused groundwater to flash into steam. Only two of them erupted actual lava, but the successive explosions blanketed the surrounding countryside with as much as 150 feet of ash and cinders. The colorful rocks inside the crater are sedimentary deposits that were altered by the hot volcanic fluids. They are blanketed by many layers of pulverized volcanic rock spewed out by Ubehebe's predecessors.

The other craters, all smaller than Ubehebe, are short distances to the south along the **Little Hebe Trail** and to the west.

The road south from Ubehebe Crater is a long route up Ubehebe Valley, into Racetrack Valley, and on to Hunter Mountain. It is described in Chapter 19, Trip Route RH-1.
End of Ubehebe Crater Road side trip.

34.2 / 1.8   The conglomerate rock outcrops a short distance into **Grapevine Canyon** are studded with cavernous holes called *tafoni*. They formed when cobbles fell from the conglomerate and the remaining hole eroded faster than its surroundings.

34.6 / 1.4   Concrete fence posts decorated with a "J S" logo mark the boundary of Death Valley Ranch, the property that includes Scotty's Castle. The initials represent Albert Johnson, the millionaire who built the castle, and Walter "Death Valley Scotty" Scott.

"Scotty's Castle," the house at Death Valley Ranch.

35.5 / 0.5   Colorful beds of gray and green volcanic ash appear in the roadcuts. Part of what is sometimes called the Grapevine Volcanics, they were erupted about 28 million years ago from volcanoes within what is now the Nevada Test Site.

36.0 / 0.0   **Scotty's Castle** is the common name for the house built at the **Death Valley Ranch**. The construction began in 1922. Construction supplies reached the area via Bonnie Claire on the Bullfrog Goldfield Railroad about 20 miles east (Trip Route N-2). Although the house was completed, other planned facilities, including the swimming pool, remain unfinished.

Scotty's Castle is owned and operated by the National Park Service. Entry onto the grounds, the picnic area, museum, and book-sales area is free, but there are fees for tours through the castle. (See Appendix C for details.)

A gift shop and snack bar is operated by the Death Valley Natural History Association; gasoline is no longer available. The nearest camping is at Mesquite Springs Campground. There is no lodging at Scotty's Castle.

Northern Death Valley, Trip Route N-2—Bonnie Claire Road (including Nevada State Highway 267)

FROM: Scotty's Castle.

TO: U.S. Highway 95 near Scotty's Junction, Nevada.

ROAD CONDITIONS: 25.9 miles one-way; all-weather paved road.

SIDE TRIPS: Bonnie Claire Playa (walk) and Lippincott Smelter (all vehicles to viewpoint).

GENERAL DESCRIPTION: The Bonnie Claire Road between Scotty's Castle and Scotty's Junction, Nevada, is the primary access route into Death Valley from northern Nevada and Utah.

ROAD LOG MILEAGES	eastbound from Scotty's Castle / westbound from U.S. Highway 95.
0.0 / 25.9	**Death Valley Ranch** (Scotty's Castle). The National Park Service operations and commercial facilities at Scotty's Castle are described in Appendix C.
1.1 / 24.8	**Steininger's Springs** is the main water source for the Death Valley Ranch complex. The flow is nearly 250 gallons per minute. The cottonwood and willow trees support a tangle of wild grapevines (the native desert grape, *Vitis girardiana*). In 1881, years before Albert Johnson decided on this canyon as the site of his Death Valley Ranch, Jacob Steininger settled this same area. He harvested the grapes to make a wine described as "potent" but popular in nearby Nevada mining camps.
2.3 / 23.6	An exceptionally coarse sedimentary breccia (like conglomerate except that the boulders are angular) is exposed on both sides of the road. This old fanglomerate is equivalent to the Funeral Formation of central Death Valley.
2.4 / 23.5	The **Grapevine Canyon Narrows** are eroded into the Zabriskie Quartzite, a hard metamorphosed sandstone of Cambrian age. Grapevine Canyon is one of two in the park with that name. The other is at the south end of Saline Valley (Chapter 20, Trip Route SV-1).
4.5 / 21.4	The California-Nevada state line is also the national park boundary.
~6 / 19	Most of the plants growing in the open valley of upper Grapevine Wash—desert holly, shadscale, hopsage, and true greasewood—are members of the saltbush family; creosote bush and Mormon tea are also found. To the south is Batus

Mountain, the northernmost high summit of the Grapevine Mountains (elevation 6,508 feet).

14.0 / 11.5   **Bonnie Claire Playa** is the dry lake bed along the north side of the road. It occupies a shallow depression along the Grapevine Wash drainage and at its deepest fills with only about a foot of water.

17.6 / 8.3   The road crosses an indistinct summit (elevation 4,035 feet) that separates west-flowing Grapevine Wash from the Sarcobatus Flat drainage on the east. The road north (4WD) leads to the Gold Mountain, Oriental Wash, and Hornsilver mining districts.

19.5 / 6.4   The **Lippincott Smelter** at the base of the mountain (north) is where the lead ore from the Lippincott Mine was smelted from 1935 to 1953. The mine is located at the south end of Racetrack Valley (see Chapter 19, Side Trip RH-1a). This was the third mill built here. The first was constructed in 1880 to serve mines on Gold Mountain a few miles to the northwest. A new, larger mill was built by the Bonnie Claire Bullfrog Mining Company in 1904 at the start of the Rhyolite boom. The modern ruins are on private property posted against trespassing.

The town of **Bonnie Claire** was located about where the highway crosses the faint traces of the old railroad grades (GPS 37°13.650'N 117°07.467'W). Starting in 1906, first the Bullfrog Goldfield Railroad and then the Las Vegas & Tonopah Railroad passed through the town, which was an important water stop for the trains and a freight transfer point to the mining districts west and north. Its final glory was during the construction of Scotty's Castle. The last Bullfrog Goldfield train ran in 1928, and the post office was abandoned in 1931. For more about the town and railroads, see Appendixes A and B.

~23 / 3   **Sarcobatus Flat** is the long, open valley to the south. It is an enclosed valley without external drainage. In places there are unusual dunes made of alkaline clay whose odd soil supports dense, pure stands of *Sarcobatus vermiformis*, the true greasewood.

25.9 / 0.0   U.S. Highway 95. The Scotty's Junction store and gas station that used to operate about 1 mile south of the highway intersection burned, so there are no services here. All services are available in Beatty 36 miles south; minimal services are available at Goldfield 31 miles north, and full services in Tonopah 56 miles north.

CHAPTER EIGHTEEN

Big Pine Road and Eureka Valley

The Big Pine Road extends through Death Valley Wash, the northernmost part of Death Valley, and then crosses the Last Chance Range and Eureka Valley, the location of the second-tallest set of sand dunes in North America. Of the park's seven entrance roads, this is the least used. No services are available between Scotty's Castle and the town of Big Pine, California.

Big Pine Road and Eureka Valley, Trip Route BP-1—Big Pine Road

FROM: Ubehebe Crater Road.

TO: U.S. Highway 395 at Big Pine, California.

ROAD CONDITIONS: 72.4 miles one-way, combinations of dirt roads with rough washboard surfaces and good asphalt pavement, normally suitable for any vehicle driven with care.

SIDE TRIPS: Skookum (long hike), Sand Spring (standard vehicles), Last Chance Canyon and Spring (4WD), and Eureka Valley Road (high-clearance) and Cucomungo Canyon (4WD); also, access to Oriental Wash, Nevada (4WD); Tule Canyon, Nevada (high-clearance); Crater mining area (4WD, if open); Eureka Valley and Sand Dunes (Trip Route BP-2; all vehicles); and Saline Valley (Chapter 20, Trip Route SV-1; usually all vehicles but check current road conditions).

GENERAL DESCRIPTION: The Big Pine Road is the only route into the northern end of Death Valley National Park, where there are the Eureka Dunes and the northern access to Saline Valley. This is an area of diverse scenery, with an altitude range from under 3,000 feet to over 7,000 feet. Much of this road is paved; however, the dirt portion in Death Valley Wash is only occasionally maintained and can be very rough because of washboard surfaces and rocky centers.

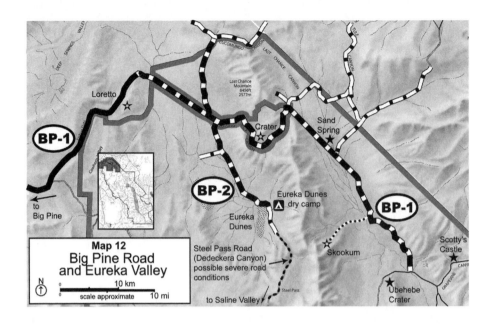

Map 12
**Big Pine Road
and Eureka Valley**

N ↑

0 _____ 10 km
0 _____ 10 mi
scale approximate

ROAD LOG MILEAGES   northbound from Ubehebe Crater Road / southbound from Big Pine, California.

0.0 / 72.4   The turnoff (north) from the paved Ubehebe Crater Road is signed at a point 2.8 miles north of Grapevine Junction.

2.7 / 69.7   A stand of cottontop, beavertail, and golden cholla cacti grows on the hills around this summit, which provides a good view southwest through Ubehebe Valley to Tin Pass on the road to Racetrack Valley. Tin Mountain (elevation 8,953 feet) is the peak to the south, and Marble Peak (elevation 7,759 feet) is the highest summit in the Last Chance Range to the west.

3.8 / 68.6   Badlands with cathedral-like cliffs have been eroded into the soft sediments in the bottom of the valley. Although referred to as Lake Rogers, this was probably never more than a marshy area rather than a true lake.

9.9 / 62.5   **Chuckawalla Canyon** (GPS 37°05.927'N 117°29.255'W at the old road, southwest about 7 miles one-way; hike) leads to **Skookum** on Chuckawalla Hill, where small gold prospects were briefly active during the late 1920s. Although the surface ore was rich, the community existed more on speculation than it did on ore, given that there was only one significant deposit (see Appendix A). The old road can be followed for much of the route, but it is thoroughly washed out in Death Valley Wash and at places along Chuckawalla Canyon, and it is not open to vehicles. Other than mine dumps and a bit of trash, there is little to see at Skookum.

~10 / 55 **Death Valley Wash** is the name applied to both the drainage in the valley bottom and this far northern part of Death Valley as a whole. The Last Chance Mountains (west) are composed of early Paleozoic sedimentary rocks capped in places by young basalt lava flows. The Eureka Sand Dunes are directly over the mountains, just southwest of Sand Mountain Peak (elevation 7,062 feet).

13.6 / 58.8 **Oriental Wash Road** (GPS 37°10.058'N 117°32.121'W, east; 4WD recommended) leads out of the national park into Nevada where there are several ghost towns in the Slate Ridge area. Most of the roads (of which there are many) are in good condition but there are places with deep sand in the lower end of the wash just across the state line. It is about 18 miles to the paved road at the near–ghost town of Gold Point, Nevada, and about 7 miles more from there to Nevada State Highway 266.

Several of the mining camps in this area bear strongly on Death Valley's history. Most important was **Gold Point** (originally called Lime Point, then Hornsilver), which boomed in the 1880s, from 1903 to 1909 when it included at least 225 buildings and tents, and from 1915 until the mines closed in 1942. Never completely abandoned and with minimal services available, Gold Point had a population of 7 in 2008. A second important place was at the Stateline Mine, where the town of **Gold Mountain** included several saloons, stores, a hotel, along with a post office that operated from 1881 to 1891. A few miles away was **Oriental**, whose mine's jewelry-rock ore was spectacular enough to be exhibited at the Centennial Exposition in Philadelphia in 1876; the post office there was open from 1887 to 1900. And the mine at **Tokop** was once owned by Christian Zabriskie, who later was the general manager of the Pacific Coast Borax operations in Death Valley and the namesake of Zabriskie Point.

14.0 / 58.4 **Little Sand Spring** (GPS 37°10.334'N 117°32.308'W, east side of road) produces enough near-surface moisture to support mesquite trees and arrowweed, but it is not a reliable source of water. Per modern geologic mapping, Little Sand Spring serves as the dividing point between the Northern Death Valley (south) and Fish Lake Valley (north) fault zones.

Sand Spring, in Death Valley Wash, is believed to be the place described by John C. Frémont in 1854 as "a very poor camping place."

15.4 / 57.0   **Sand Spring** (GPS 37°11.295'N 117°33.225'W, east 0.1 mile) is one of the first specific places in all of Death Valley to have been described. John C. Frémont was in this area in March 1854 during his nearly forgotten, privately financed Fifth Expedition. In his never-published report he described a place in this area as "a very poor camping place . . . with very little unwholesome grass. The water is entirely too salty to drink." It is probable that this was Sand Spring, as poor as it is, still the best source of water in Death Valley Wash. During the 1920s, when the Skookum mines were being developed 10 miles south, Sand Spring served as the water supply and was the location of a gas station and store known as **Desert Gold**.

Sand Spring, like Little Sand Spring to the south and Last Chance Springs to the north, rises to the surface along the trace of the Fish Lake Valley Fault Zone. The hills here are an eroded fault scarp. This is the section of the fault zone that has enjoyed the longest time period without experiencing significant earthquake activity. No young scarps are visible anywhere along Death Valley Wash, implying that it has been perhaps several thousand years since the last significant earthquake here. Perhaps this is a warning for the future.

| 21.8 / 50.6 | **Crankshaft Junction** (GPS 37°14.604'N 117°37.983'W). The road sign at this junction is decorated with several old engine crankshafts. Presumably, somebody once had serious engine trouble here and started a tradition. The Big Pine Road turns sharply south at Crankshaft Junction. From this point west the road itself lies outside the national park whereas most of the land immediately to the south and some to the north is within the park—because of the extensive sulfur and mercury mining at and near Crater, that area and the road leading to it from the west were deleted from the national park. |

Tule Canyon Road heads north from Crankshaft Junction, and then east into Nevada via Tule Canyon.

From a junction on Tule Canyon Road 0.9 mile north of the Big Pine Road, the **Last Chance Spring Road** leads 2.8 miles northwest toward Last Chance Springs. The springs (of which there are several) yield about 25 gallons of water per minute but are polluted by cattle and wild burros. There are two stories about Last Chance Springs. In the fall of 1853, a survey party of 17 people led by "Major" John Ebbetts and financed by the proposed Pacific & Atlantic Railroad, passed through this area. Desperate for water, they found it at the spring and camped there for two days before heading north via Last Chance Canyon on November 11, 1853. In 1871, a U.S. Army expedition that was part of the Wheeler Survey was assigned the task of finding a route between Owens Valley and the booming mining district at Pioche, Nevada. It was midsummer in very rugged terrain. The party found itself short of water, and only after some wandering did they finally find the spring at their "last chance." That is the origin of the name.

In Nevada, Tule Canyon is about 15 miles long. It was the site of placer gold mining throughout its length, starting as early as 1848 by Mexicans and then by Americans well into the 1900s. There was enough population in the area to support a post office called **Senner** in the early 1890s and then three small towns from 1904 into 1906. The largest of these was **Roosevelt**, which left scattered ruins and a mill on the hillside about 9 miles from Crankshaft Junction. **Summerville** and **Fairbanks** farther up the canyon left few remains.

| ~23 / 49 | **Breakneck Canyon** was named by the same 1871 expedition that named Last Chance Spring. Dropping down this canyon from the west, the group encountered a series of dry waterfalls |

and had to use ropes to lower their pack animals. The name was given not because of an accident but because of the difficult ("breakneck") effort that was involved.

A number of early Paleozoic sedimentary rocks crop out in this part of the Last Chance Range. In upper Breakneck Canyon, they are capped by basaltic lava flows and cinder beds. Just south of the road is the eroded remnant of one of the actual volcanoes. This member of the Saline Range Volcanics is about 2.5 million years old.

24.7 / 47.7   The elevation at the gentle pass is slightly over 5,000 feet.

~28 / 44   The sedimentary rock tilted to a high angle in these canyons is the Bonanza King Formation, a dolomite limestone of Cambrian age.

29.0 / 43.4   **Crater**. This is the largest deposit of sulfur west of the Mississippi River. The entire Crater–El Capitan mining district was omitted from the national park because the mines are on patented (private) property. However, mining there has ended, some reclamation of the property has been performed, and the area will likely be added to the park lands in the future.

Although the deposits had been discovered in 1917, little mining took place until 1929. The company town of Crater had its heyday from then to 1931 (see Appendix A). Additional mining continued intermittently into 1953, when a sulfur-dust explosion destroyed the mill and temporarily ended the mining. Small-scale operations between 1957 and 1986 yielded sulfur for use as a soil additive, and a few building ruins from the early eras remained until then. They are now gone, removed by much larger developments during the 1990s. It is estimated that the mine's total production amounted to 50,000 tons (100 million pounds) of sulfur.

Crater Road (north 3.2 miles; 4WD) passes through the main mining area and ends at the El Capitan mercury mine. Another road branches east just 0.5 mile from the Big Pine Road and ends at the top of the mountains where there is an excellent view southeast into Death Valley Wash.

The sulfur was formed by a hot spring system that also deposited mercury at the **El Capitan Mine** 2 miles north of Crater and at several properties in the Last Chance Range to the south. The El Capitan was discovered by accident during sulfur explorations, and from 1968 to 1971 produced about 3,400 flasks of mercury (a flask contains 76 pounds of liquid quicksilver, so this total was about 260,000 pounds).

~ 31 / 41	**Hanging Rock Canyon**. A series of low-angle thrust faults has produced thin slabs of Carboniferous age Perdido and Rest Spring formations, bounded by Cambrian age Zabriskie quartzite and Carrara limestone in a complex arrangement. Much of the brilliant coloration is because of rock alteration and oxidation related to the Crater hydrothermal system.
31.2 / 41.2	Just north of the road is the tunnel and small dump of the **Lucky Strike Mine**, which was located for uranium. Although not a rich deposit, the ore contains both autunite, a pale-yellow calcium-uranium phosphate, and torbernite, an emerald-green copper-uranium phosphate.
34.0 / 38.4	**South Eureka Road** (south 9.6 miles one-way to picnic area; graded dirt with some washboard, suitable for any vehicle) is also called the Eureka Dunes Road. It is described as Trip Route BP-2.
34.7 / 37.7	**Eureka Valley Road** (north 7.8 miles to Cucomungo Canyon; high-clearance recommended first 7.8 miles to Cucomungo Canyon at the national park boundary, and then 4WD recommended either east into Cucomungo Canyon or north to State Highway 168). Upon leaving the Big Pine Road, this route immediately enters national park land. After traveling across northern Eureka Valley toward the **Horse Thief Hills**, the road enters Willow Wash to reach Cucomungo Canyon. There the main road leaves the national park and bears northwest via Horse Thief Canyon and Piper Summit an additional 12.9 miles to a junction with California State Highway 168; 4WD may be required at Willow Wash and near the pass between the Piper (west) and Sylvania (east) mountains.

The **Cucomungo Canyon Road** (GPS 37°20.120'N 117°45.951'W, east; 4WD recommended) serves as the national park boundary (the road is outside the national park but the land immediately to the south is within it). It passes a verdant oasis at **Willow Spring**, reaches Nevada after 6 miles, and continues to paved Nevada State Highway 266 an additional 6.9 miles from the state line.

The canyon has developed along the **Fish Lake Valley Fault Zone** and separates Paleozoic sedimentary rocks in the Last Chance Range on the south from granitic rocks in the Sylvania Mountains to the north. The fault zone goes through a gentle S-bend in the canyon, and the rocks have been severely crushed as a result. In the mountains just to the north is a huge porphyry deposit of molybdenum; that is, a granitic rock body containing disseminated molybdenite (molybdenum sulfide). Molybdenum is vital to the production of specialty steel alloys, but although exploration showed this deposit to contain at least 2 *billion* pounds of the metal, it was judged too low in overall grade to justify mining.

End of Eureka Valley Road.

~ 37 / 35   The numerous piles of dirt scattered about many square miles of the floor of Eureka Valley are the result of placer mine claims filed in a search for gold, but no production resulted. On May 17, 1993, a moderate, magnitude 6.2 earthquake occurred with the epicenter about 6 miles south of the road, near a prominent straight-line ridge along the west side of the valley. The tremor caused the warm spring in Saline Valley to nearly stop flowing for several weeks.

41.0 / 31.4   Westbound from this point, where dirt roads extend in several directions, all land north and much of the land south of the road is outside of the national park. Eastbound, although the road is a cherry-stem route not part of the park, the land immediately on both sides of the road is within the park.

41.5 / 30.9   Rock walls on the south side of the road probably date to 1909, when the **Victor Consolidated Mine** (visible on the mountain to the south) was developed on high-grade, near-surface copper ore as a follow-up to the nearby Loretto rush. During World War II, the same property produced some steatite talc.

45.3 / 27.1   **Loretto** was a copper-mining town with a brief existence in 1906 and 1907, during the same time as the Greenwater and Ubehebe copper booms in Death Valley. The town consisted of several businesses, some housed in durable stone buildings whose collapsed walls remain.

The Loretto and other mines in the mountains to the south were located before 1888, but no development took place until the regional copper excitement. The biggest developer was financier and steel magnate Charles Schwab, who was also involved in mining at Greenwater. The ore was exceptionally rich near the surface—rich enough to merit building a $2 million smelter—but did not continue at depth. The mining company spent 8 years digging a shaft 1,800 feet deep in search of primary ore. Although a large tonnage of low-grade rock was found, it could not support the smelter, and ultimately the Loretto Mine had total commercial production of zero.

In the 1970s, the Bristlecone Copper Company smelted a few hundred tons of sorted copper ore that contained 1 percent to 2 percent metal, most of which was recovered from the old mine dumps and a small open pit. They built a mill on the north side of the Big Pine Road but removed all equipment when they quit operating in 1977.

~ 46 / 26 There are several roads in this area, all leading south to talc mines. Most of the mines had little production, but the **Nikolaus-Eureka Mine** yielded 75,000 tons of high-quality steatite talc between 1945 and 1970. Smaller mines are visible high on the mountainside to the southwest.

49.4 / 23.0 **Lime Hill Summit** (elevation about 6,060 feet). The same metamorphism that produced talc deposits nearby to the east also formed some low-grade tungsten deposits. The **Scheelite Mine**, the largest and only one to have had commercial production, is just over the hill to the north.

~ 50 / 22 **Joshua Flat** is named after its dense stand of Joshua trees. The specimens here and in other parts of the Joshuas' northern range tend to send up new shoots from the roots without growing branched crowns. This may be because of the greater soil moisture available at this altitude, but some researchers feel that these plants merit a separate subspecies designation, *Yucca brevifolia herbertii*.

~ 54 / 18 The road passes through a small forest of pinyon pines and juniper trees and then over a low summit into Little Cowhorn Valley.

55.5 / 16.9 **Cowhorn Pass** (elevation 7,350 feet). There is a wide variety of late Precambrian and Paleozoic sedimentary rocks in this area, but those most commonly exposed along the road are the Campito, Poleta, and Harkless sandstone formations of Cambrian age.

57.1 / 15.3 **Saline Valley Road** (marked as "Saline Waucoba Road") leads south through Saline Valley to State Highway 190. There are no services along the 78-mile route, which is described as Trip Route SV-1. Westbound the road drops into **Deadman Canyon**.

66.2 / 6.2 **Devil's Gate** is a narrow slot carved into an outcrop of Precambrian metamorphic rock much harder than the young gravels that line the rest of Deadman Canyon.

70.2 / 2.2 State Highway 168. Eastbound explorers turn south.

72.4 / 0.0 Junction with U.S. Highway 395 at the north end of **Big Pine, California**. Most services such as groceries, gas, and motels are available in Big Pine, and an even wider assortment of services exists in Bishop, 12 miles north.

Big Pine Road and Eureka Valley, Trip Route BP-2— South Eureka Road (Eureka Dunes Road)

FROM: Big Pine Road.

TO: Eureka Sand Dunes.

ROAD CONDITIONS: 9.6 miles, maintained dirt road normally suitable for all vehicles.

SIDE TRIPS: None.

GENERAL DESCRIPTION: This road leads to the Eureka Dunes, which are among the highest in the Western Hemisphere, perhaps exceeded only by the Great Sand Dunes of Colorado. Their high points reach almost 700 feet above the dry lake bed on the valley floor. Because of their size and a number Class I endemic plants and animals, the dunes have a special designation as a National Natural Landmark.

ROAD LOG MILEAGE	southbound from Big Pine Road.
0.0	The turnoff from the Big Pine Road is well marked. The road immediately enters the national park.
3.4	The **Eureka Valley Well Road** (GPS 37°10.910'N 117°44.907'W, 4WD required) leads west-southwest across the valley to the old Eureka Valley Well (water not available). From there it is possible to hike about 3.5 miles southwest into the hills, beyond which are little-known sand dunes (called the **Hidden Dunes** by some) that host endemic plants otherwise known only on the Eureka Dunes.
4.9	The **Up & Down Mine** (east 2 miles; hike on closed road) worked a mercury deposit related to the mineralization at Crater, which is only about 3 miles distant over the ridge. In 1995 the site included a cabin, ore crusher, ore chute and hopper, a roasting furnace, and a mercury recovery retort. The mine appears to have had considerable commercial production but there is no known record of the amount.
	Several other closed roads farther south also led to small mercury deposits. They are all mineralized by bright-red cinnabar and black metacinnabar (both mercury sulfide) within shear zones along the Last Chance Thrust, a complex fault system that served as the conduit for the ore-forming fluids. The deposits are low grade and are no longer valid claims. Remember: no mineral collecting is allowed within the national park.
9.6	**Eureka Dunes Dry Camp and Picnic Area** (picnic tables, trash cans, chemical toilet, interpretive sign, and visitor reg-

The Eureka Dunes are the second tallest sand dunes in North America, exceeded only by the Great Sand Dunes in Colorado.

ister). Camping is allowed in the picnic area, near but not on the sand dunes, and fires are allowed within the established fire pits. Camping is also permitted on the short, dead-end spur roads about 0.5 mile farther southeast, but fires are not permitted in those places.

The Eureka Dunes are one large sand mountain plus a series of somewhat lower sand hills that extend south about 3 miles. They are static in that they do not physically move, but in time they do grow larger and cover a wider area as more sand is added by each windstorm. Most of the sand comes from the north end of Eureka Valley, but some may blow in from Saline Valley via Steel Pass. In either case, the shape of the valley forces the wind to swirl and rise above the dunes, dropping the sand. The highest point on the Eureka Dunes is more than 680 feet above the valley floor, making these the second-tallest dunes in North America (only the Great Sand Dunes of Colorado are taller).

At least three plants are Class I endemics unique to the sand dunes of Eureka Valley. Common near the picnic area are the shining locoweed (*Astralagus lentiginosis micans*) with beautiful white and pale-purple flower heads, and the Eureka

Dunes evening primrose (*Oenothera avita eurekensis*) with large white flowers, both of which bloom in the spring. The Eureka Valley dune grass (*Swallenia alexandre*), a perennial grass that is the only member of its genus, binds the sandy slopes on even the highest dune crests. Also, five beetles found nowhere else have been identified on these dunes. As you explore the dunes, please do everything you can to avoid stepping on any plant or insect.

There are several other sets of sand dunes in Eureka Valley, such as those southwest of the Eureka Valley Well. At least some of the endemic plants and animals of the Eureka Dunes apparently also exist on these other dunes.

The Last Chance Mountains just east of the dunes are a geological showcase. They expose a series of early Paleozoic sedimentary rocks. The obvious layer, which is bounded top and bottom by white beds, is part of the Bonanza King Formation. The hilly mountains to the southwest are the Saline Range. Composed of basaltic lava flows and cinder (lapilli) beds mostly between 2 and 4 million years old, the remains of at least two dozen eroded volcano cones have been mapped along the divide between Eureka and Saline valleys.

12.0 From the picnic area, the road heads east and then south around the sand dunes. A short side road (east) leads to a good camping area.

12.4 The road continues south along the east side of the sand dunes. After passing through some stretches of soft sand it climbs toward the hills and becomes a rough 4WD route. This is the start of the Steel Pass Road, a route of questionable quality through Dedeckera Canyon and Steel Pass to Saline Valley (see Chapter 20, Side Trip SV-1b).

CHAPTER NINETEEN

Racetrack Valley and Hunter Mountain

Racetrack Valley and Hunter Mountain, Trip Route RH-1—
Racetrack Valley Road and Hunter Mountain Road

These two roads combine as a single long trip into one of the most amazing parts of Death Valley National Park. The area boasts numerous important mines, rocks that slide across a lakebed, pine-clad mountains, abundant wildlife, and solitude. In the winter, the road over Hunter Mountain is often closed because of snow and ice, and 4WD vehicles are always recommended. There are no services of any kind along these roads.

FROM: Ubehebe Crater.

TO: State Highway 190 at a point 13.5 miles east of Panamint Springs Resort.

ROAD CONDITIONS: 59.4 miles one-way; dirt road, occasionally maintained and often suitable for high-clearance vehicles; 4WD required on some side trips and possibly on Hunter Mountain.

SIDE TRIPS: The Racetrack (Side Trip RH-1a; high-clearance), Ubehebe Mine (4WD), Lost Burro Mine (high-clearance), White Top Mountain Road (Side Trip RH-1b; 4WD), Ulida Mine (hike), Ubehebe Talc Mine (4WD), Quackenbush Talc Mine (4WD), Goldbelt Spring (high-clearance), J. O. Mine Road (Side Trip RH-1c; 4WD), and Hunter Cabin (high-clearance).

GENERAL DESCRIPTION: If any trip covers the entire variety of scenery, geology, biology, and history that Death Valley National Park has to offer, then this is it; only the below-sea-level salt flats are missing. It is a long trip on dirt roads that are occasionally maintained. It is recommended for 4WD vehicles, which might be required because of flood washouts, muddy areas, and very steep grades on Hunter Mountain.

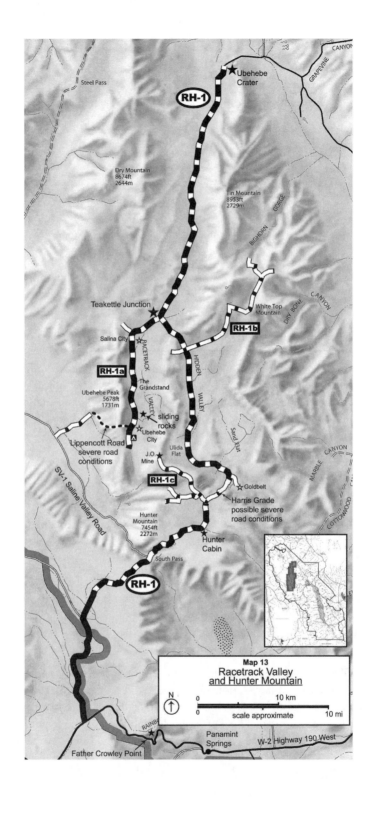

RH-1

Ubehebe
Crater

GRAPEVINE CANYON

Steel Pass

Dry Mountain
8674ft
2644m

Tin Mountain
8953ft
2729m

BIGHORN GORGE

DRY BONE CANYON

Teakettle Junction

White Top
Mountain

RH-1b

Salina City

RACETRACK

HIDDEN VALLEY

RH-1a

The Grandstand

Ubehebe Peak
5678ft
1731m

VALLEY

sliding
rocks

Sand Flat

MARBLE CANYON

Ubehebe
City

Lippencott Road
severe road
conditions

Ulida Flat

J.O.
Mine

Goldbelt

RH-1c

Harris Grade
possible severe
road conditions

COTTONWOOD

SV-1 Saline Valley Road

Hunter
Mountain
7454ft
2272m

Hunter
Cabin

South Pass

RH-1

Map 13
Racetrack Valley
and Hunter Mountain

N
↑

0   10 km

0   scale approximate   10 mi

RAINBOW

Father Crowley Point

Panamint
Springs

W-2 Highway 190 West

The word "Ubehebe" is used many times in this section. The source of the word is Indian, but the meaning is uncertain and there are many versions of the story. One is that the name comes from "Duhveetah Wahsah," meaning Duhveetah's Carrying-Basket, a term given to the crater because of its shape. In this case, "Ubehebe" is a badly corrupted English version of Duhveetah (who some say was a real person). More correct, perhaps, is a Shoshone term for the crater, "Timpintta Wahsah" (Basket in the Rock).

ROAD LOG MILEAGES	southbound from Ubehebe Crater / northbound from State Highway 190.

0.0 / 59.4	**Ubehebe Crater** is at the end of the paved road 5.7 miles northwest of Grapevine Junction. It, Little Hebe, and other craters in the area are the result of phreatic explosions; that is, "cryptovolcanic eruptions" powered by superheated groundwater flashing to steam because of subsurface magmatic heating. Most of these 16 eruptions probably lasted only a few minutes apiece. Ubehebe itself is the largest and youngest of the craters, having formed only about 300 years ago. The Racetrack Valley Road starts at the bottom of the paved loop road west of Ubehebe Crater.
0.5 / 58.9	**Ubehebe Valley** to the south is bounded by Tin Mountain (elevation 8,953 feet) on the east and Dry Mountain (elevation 8,654 feet) to the west. Both peaks are clad with pinyon-juniper forests near their tops. The road follows the bottom of the valley for about 11 miles to Tin Pass.
~5 / 54	Shrubs are sparse on the gravel desert pavement surfaces along the road, but beavertail, prickly pear, cottontop barrel, golden cholla, and calico hedgehog cacti make this area one of the better "cactus gardens" in the park.
8.1 / 51.3	Southbound drivers encounter the first of many Joshua trees. Most, if not all, of the Joshuas in this region are the short-leaved variety, *Yucca brevifolia jaegeriana*. The rocks in the mountain faces on both sides of the valley are sedimentary rocks of Paleozoic age, mostly limestone.
9.5 / 49.9	The hills just west and southwest of the road are the "monolithologic megabreccia" of the **Tin Mountain Landslide**—they contain angular boulders as much as 8 feet in diameter, most of which are composed of Lost Burro Formation limestone. The source was the face of Tin Mountain to the east, where four slide scars are visible. It is likely that all four happened at the same time, possibly because of an earthquake.

A series of dry lakes, collectively called the **Virginia Lakes**, occupies low areas among the hills.

11.1 / 48.3 **Tin Pass** (elevation about 4,950 feet) separates Ubehebe Valley on the north from Racetrack Valley to the south. Bear poppy (*Arctomecon merriamii*) is a relatively rare Class II endemic wildflower limited to the Death Valley region. It does not bloom in most years, but when conditions are just right, Tin Pass boasts a significant concentration in April or May. Tall stalks with individual yellow-centered white flowers rise above clusters of soft, fuzzy leaves.

12.0 / 47.4 **Tin Pass Lake** is immediately west of the road. Notice the cavernous weathering in the cliffs of Tin Mountain Formation limestone on the east side of the valley.

15.0 / 44.4 The hill west of the road is made of the Ely Springs Formation, a dolomitic limestone of the Ordovician Period. It contains few fossils, but large chert nodules that weather as brownish lumps on exposed surfaces are typical of the formation. The deep canyon through the mountains (east) is called Bighorn Gap.

17.1 / 42.3 **Quartz Spring** (east 2.2 miles; hike) is located up a closed road that is barely visible. Although yielding only 5 gallons of water per hour, the spring is the best water source in the area. It is a hike of about 2.2 miles.

Several rock formations are exposed on the ridge west of the road. First is the Ely Springs Formation. The white rock on the south side of the ridge is Eureka Sandstone and still farther south is the Pogonip Limestone. The three units all date to the Ordovician Period of the Paleozoic Era and are approximately 450 million years old. Fossils are abundant in parts of the Pogonip but are rare in the other formations. Please remember: no collecting within the park.

19.4 / 40.0 **Teakettle Junction** (GPS 36°45.600'N 117°32.539'W, elevation 4,150 feet). The decorations at the sign marking the junction always include several old teakettles; a telephone, an electrical outlet, a coffeemaker, a microwave oven, and a laptop computer with a broken screen have also been seen here. None of these objects work, of course; the nearest power lines are 25 miles away.

Climbing the alluvial fan southeast is the **Hunter Mountain Road**, which cuts through the mountains at Lost Burro Gap. North, the road climbs to Tin Pass and then drops through Ubehebe Valley to the paved road at Ubehebe Crater. **Side Trip RH-1a—The Racetrack** (9.6 miles to Homestake

Dry Camp). This is the southward continuation of the Racetrack Valley Road. The Racetrack with its "sliding rocks" is the prime attraction along this road, but it also leads to several important mines, the Ubehebe Peak Trail, and the very poor Lippincott Road to Saline Valley (a route of questionable quality). Racetrack Valley is a day-use-only area with the exception of the Homestake Dry Camp at the end of the road.

0.0   Teakettle Junction. The road bears southwest from the junction.

1.0   The thin-bedded rocks north of the road are the Racetrack Formation, a dolomite that contains no known fossils but is inferred to date to the early Cambrian Period on the basis of its stratigraphic position among other fossil-bearing rocks.

2.2   **Ubehebe Lead Mine Road** (GPS 36°44.721'N 117°34.526'W, west 0.7 mile; 4WD recommended). The Ubehebe Mine is at the end of the road on the Saline Valley side of the Ubehebe Range. There is one collapsed cabin and a large amount of debris near the mine dumps. A cable tramline leads to several mine openings up and over the mountain.

The Ubehebe Mine was discovered in 1875, but there was little or no mining at the time, even though some of the surface ore was said to contain as much as 67 percent copper by weight. The area was simply too remote to support low-profit copper mining. The electrification of the United States in the late 1890s caused the price of copper to climb. One early Ubehebe investor was famous landscape artist Albert Bierstadt, who bought an option in 1886 but failed to follow through with the purchase.

By 1906 copper was in great demand. The Ubehebe Mine was bought by Jack Salsberry, who was also involved in some of the Greenwater copper promotions and still later had Salsberry Pass named after him while he operated the Carbonate Mine in southern Death Valley. He founded nearby Salina City; built the road from Ubehebe Crater; purchased coal options for his proposed smelter at Bonnie Claire, Nevada; and arranged financial bonds for the construction of the Bonnie Claire & Ubehebe Railroad.

Nevertheless, initial mine production was small, the town was abandoned, and the railroad proposal was dropped in early 1908. Later that year, however, high-grade lead ore was discovered. The Ubehebe became a lead mine with nearly continuous production into 1928. In the 1940s it

Tracks for the ore cars still extend onto the dumps of the Ubehebe Mine.

reopened again, this time as a zinc mine. Ultimately, the Ubehebe District was one of Death Valley's better producers, with recorded total productions (mostly from the Ubehebe Mine itself) of 44,729 ounces of silver, 120,180 pounds of copper, 2,657,559 pounds of lead, and 164,959 pounds of zinc plus a little gold. The last commercial operation ended in 1951.

3.4   **Salina City**, also called Latimer in hopes of attracting a wealthy investor, consisted of about 20 tents, 2 saloons, a company store, 1 lodging tent, and the Kimball Brothers' stage station and feed yard in November 1907. An application for a post office was filed but the town was abandoned before it could be acted on. Essentially no trace of the community remains—scattered rusty cans a few hundred feet east of the road probably mark the site. (See Appendix A.)

5.7   **Grandstand Parking Area**. The Grandstand is the outcrop of granite porphyry that protrudes like an island from the clay surface of The Racetrack lake bed. Some of the famous "sliding rocks" have fallen from the Grandstand, but most are located at the far south end of the lake.

      The **Ubehebe Peak Trail** leads west from the parking area. It is a strenuous climb of about 2 miles to the summit (elevation 5,678 feet; some of the switchbacks are visible high on the north ridge of the peak), but the views into both Racetrack Valley and Saline Valley are tremendous.

7.7 **"Sliding Rocks" interpretive display** (east side of road). The Racetrack is the most famous of several clay lake beds on which rocks occasionally slide across the surface. Some rocks with trails can be seen close to the road, but the best are out on the lake bed toward the prominent cliffs of dolomitic limestone, which are the source of most of the boulders. The Racetrack is, of course, closed to vehicles, but visitors are free to walk on the lakebed to observe the rocks and their trails.

No known person has ever actually seen the rocks move—"they know they're being watched"—but there is no question that they do. Numerous studies have been conducted through the years, but the most thorough and accurate were started in the 1990s by Dr. Paula Messina, of San Jose State University. Using highly precise GPS measurements, 162 rocks were mapped and measured. They were also given names, such as Colette, Mona, Hortense, Cheryl, Goldy, and so on. The largest rock in 1996 was Kitty, weighing in at 1,275 pounds and standing 22 inches tall; the smallest was Hannah, which weighed less than 1 pound.

It is certain that the rocks move when the clay surface is moist and slippery at a time of strong winds; some people think that a frozen layer of thin ice is required too. Winds that blow northeast out of Saline Valley sometimes reach hurricane force and, in fact, most stone movement is toward the northeast. The stones drag tracks into the mud and reach as far as several hundred feet across the slick lake bed; the longest track ever known extended more than 2,400 feet. The trails the rocks leave behind persist for many years. There are cases where a rock moved, rested in a "sitz mark" for perhaps a few years, and then slid again. Some tracks are curved; others follow complex zigzag patterns. See update, page 344.

9.5 **Lippincott Road** (west) is not recommended for travel without first obtaining current information about its condition. It looks like a good road, but once it begins to drop into Saline Valley it becomes one of the worst routes in the park. It is extremely steep and rocky and is often sharply angled outward at the edge of sheer cliffs. In order to provide better access for ranger patrols, the Park Service has occasionally worked to improve the road, but it remains a questionable route.

Exactly how and when rocks move across the lakebed of The Racetrack is unknown—nobody has ever actually seen it happen—but hundred of stones do so and each leaves a long-lasting trail behind it.

9.6	**Homestake Dry Camp** (GPS 36°38.364'N 117°34.485'W). Camping without campfires is permitted in a small area next to the Homestake Mine (small prospect pits explored for talc) below the Lippincott Mine. There is a single chemical toilet but no other facilities.

Ubehebe City was a tent town that briefly competed with Salina City in 1907. Proposed as the terminus of the Bonnie Claire & Ubehebe Railroad, it was located about 2 miles south of The Racetrack and therefore in this general area. Not a trace remains.

10.4	The **Lippincott Mine** is mostly out of sight over the low ridge south of the camping area. The 1-mile road to the workings requires 4WD with extra-high clearance, so hiking from Homestake Dry Camp is recommended. This mine was initially called the Lead King Mine when discovered in 1906, but there was little production until the 1930s. A large operation began in 1942, when the property was leased to George Lippincott. The lead ore was trucked to Bonnie Claire, Nevada, where a mill produced bulk lead concentrate that was further refined in Santa Ana, California. The entire output was used in automobile batteries. The mine closed in 1953.

The little-known **Ubehebe Trail** climbs to Ubehebe Pass southeast of the Lippincott Mine, then drops past several mines, visits Big Dodd Spring and Little Dodd Spring, and ends at the Saline Valley Road in Grapevine Canyon (Chapter 20, Trip Route SV-1). The total distance is about 7.5 miles.
End of The Racetrack side trip.

19.4 / 40.0	Continuing southeast from Teakettle Junction, the **Hunter Mountain Road** is frequently washed by flooding to and through Lost Burro Gap. However, the route is across firm gravel toward the obvious canyon of the gap, and use quickly reestablishes the road when it is washed out.
20.5 / 38.9	The rocks exposed at the west end of Lost Burro Gap are the Tin Mountain Limestone, of early Carboniferous (Mississippian) age. Some beds are highly fossiliferous, especially with brachiopods and crinoid columns. No collecting!
20.8 / 38.6	**Lost Burro Gap** is a water-gap canyon that connects Hidden Valley with Racetrack Valley. The top of the Lost Burro Formation (Devonian age) is in sharp contact with the younger, overlying Tin Mountain Limestone. A prominent brownish layer of limey sandstone contains a wide assortment of fossils, but most are poorly preserved.

21.5 / 37.9	At the east end of Lost Burro Gap, the cliffs south of the road are composed of the Hidden Valley Formation, a Silurian age dolomitic limestone that contains many coral fossils of the common genera *Halysites* and *Favosites*.
22.6 / 36.8	**Lost Burro Junction** (GPS 36°43.774'N 117°30.306'W, elevation 4,863 feet). Two side roads depart the main route at this point.

Lost Burro Mine Road (west 1.1 miles one-way; high-clearance). The site includes 1 cabin, a "Cousin Jack" dugout, an old outhouse, and several flat building sites. The ruins of the mill are on the mountainside to the north, and the large dumps of the mine itself are visible up the canyon beyond the mill. Other mine workings are over the ridge to the west. Camping is not allowed.

The story of the mine's discovery is a classic. In April 1907 Bert Shively picked up a rock to throw at stray burros and its weight caused him to take a close look. It was laced with free gold. The greatest production of the Lost Burro Mine was between 1912 and 1917. The expensive mill was finished in 1917, but it was inefficient and had little production. Water was piped 8 miles from Burro Spring and Rest Spring (see White Top Mountain Road, next). The mill was apparently dismantled before 1922. Mining resumed in 1928, and small operations continued into the late 1970s.

Side Trip RH-1b—White Top Mountain Road (east 11.9 miles one-way to O'Brien Canyon; 4WD required). This road is a little-known delight. Generally in good shape because of a lack of traffic, it gradually climbs through spectacular scenery into a pinyon-juniper forest at an elevation of nearly 7,000 feet. When wet the road may be slippery in the claystone areas, and it is somewhat steep and rocky in Leaning Rock Canyon.

0.0	Lost Burro Junction.
1.5	**Andy Hills** (south of road). The first part of the White Top Mountain Road crosses a gentle alluvial fan with a desert pavement surface toward the Andy Hills (the origin of the name seems to be unknown). Rusty pipe sections beside the road carried water from Burro Spring and Rest Spring to the Lost Burro Mill. The hills are mostly composed of the Hidden Valley Formation, and a low ridge about 0.75 mile south of the road is littered with Silurian age corals and brachiopods.
3.2	A closed road (east) that seemed to have no particular destination provides a decent camping spot.

A cabin, the mill frame, and extensive mine dumps are at the Lost Burro Mine.

4.2   **Rest Spring Gulch**. Tin Mountain Limestone with cavernous weathering is exposed in the lower part of the canyon. Higher up is the Perdido Formation of massive gray limestone interbedded with brown layers of sandstone and shale, and then the soft claystone of the Rest Spring Shale. All three formations date to the Carboniferous Period.

5.2   **Rest Spring** (north; hike) lies 0.6 mile up the sandy wash and **Burro Spring** is 1.9 miles farther over a ridge. Rest Spring is only a seep now, but evidently it had greater discharge around 1917 when it was developed to supply water to the Lost Burro Mill. Burro Spring, called Yetum'ba (possibly "Mountain Water") and used as a campsite by the Shoshone when harvesting pinyon pine nuts, flows perhaps 1 pint of water per minute.

5.5   The smooth hills all around the summit (elevation about 6,800 feet) are composed of the Rest Spring Shale. It is probably of late Carboniferous (Pennsylvanian) age, but it contains only a few brachiopod fossils too poorly preserved for age dating.

6.2   **White Top Mountain** is the jagged summit to the northeast. The prominent mountain to the south is **Leaning Rock Peak**.

6.4   **Dry Bone Canyon** is one of the largest drainages from the Cottonwood Mountains into Death Valley. Rye Grass Spring is a few hundred feet below the road, and there are panels of petroglyphs in the slot canyon about 1.2 miles beyond the spring.

7.1   The road turns north into **Leaning Rock Canyon**, which has been eroded along the Leaning Rock Fault. The rocks exposed on the west wall of the canyon are (in order up-canyon) the Perdido, Tin Mountain, and Lost Burro formation limestones of progressively older Carboniferous and Devonian ages; the rocks in the east wall are older still, starting with the Ely Springs Dolomite of Ordovician age and then the Hidden Valley Formation of Silurian age.

7.2   The mound cactus (*Echinocereus mojavensis*) is also known as the claret cup cactus because of its brilliant scarlet flowers in April or May. It is uncommon in Death Valley, but here numerous large plants grow directly out of cracks in the limestone of the west-facing walls of the canyon.

7.5   The weird "hoodoos" up the east wall of the canyon are erosional remnants of the Hidden Valley Formation. As the road gradually climbs higher, the plants along the wash include desert broom, green Mormon tea, Great Basin sagebrush, indigobush, single-leaf pinyon pine, and Utah juniper.

8.3   A road (northwest, 4WD) leads to some small deposits of tremolite asbestos. Better deposits, which are easier to reach, are farther up the main road.

9.4   **Huntley Mines Cabin** (elevation 6,680 feet). The tremolite asbestos deposits of the Huntley Mines were discovered in 1900. Although the deposits are extensive, little commercial mining ever took place because the asbestos contains too many impurities for most uses. The soft, flexible, pure-white fibers were used in paint products, as a filler and binder in asphalt shingles, and in stucco.

9.5   A network of roads (west; 4WD) leads to some of the asbestos deposits and then drops into the west fork of **O'Brien Canyon** where the small **Lawrence Claims** were developed for copper and fluorite. The primary ore mineral is bornite (copper-iron sulfide) associated with copper carbonates and crystalline masses of violet and green fluorite (calcium fluoride) as much as 3 inches in diameter. The deposits were discovered in 1908, developed with several shafts and tunnels starting in 1917, and explored as recently as the early 1970s, but there never was any commercial production.

9.7   "**Syenite Junction**" (GPS 36°48.140'N 117°24.820'W, elevation 6,915 feet). The rocks in the hills east and northeast of the road are composed of a rare suite of igneous rocks dominated by trachytoid leucosyenites of unusual mineralogy and crystalline texture. ("Trachytoid" means that the crystals tend to lie parallel to one another within the rock mass; "leuco" refers to the exceptionally light color of the rock as a whole.) Among them is California's only known occurrence of nepheline syenite, which can be reached by following the road northeast from the junction into the pinyon forest on the nearby hill, and then walking east a few hundred feet along the slope. The rock is light gray and studded with small black crystals; freshly broken surfaces have a slightly greasy luster.

Nepheline is a rare mineral that is valuable for producing white glazes on porcelain and glass products of exceptional clarity, but tests on this material proved it to be unsuitable for such uses because of the presence of tiny amounts of iron impurities—the black crystals in the rock are the iron-iron garnet, melanite. Several small prospect pits were dug into the syenite but none found rock free of the garnet.

10.0   From Syenite Junction, the road continues northwest across bedrock outcrops of Perdido and Tin Mountain limestones and a stretch of Rest Spring Shale, and then crosses a ridge into the east fork of **O'Brien Canyon**.

11.0 The knob of pale-orange rock, just before a sharp left turn down a steep switchback into O'Brien Canyon, is leucosyenite composed of 97 percent potassium feldspar crystals. Visible far to the east are the white, dry lake beds of Bonnie Claire Playa and Sarcobatus Flat in Nevada, east of Scotty's Castle.

11.9 The **Silver Crown Mines** were discovered in 1912. Masses of small and discontinuous but extremely high-grade copper ore associated with fluorite were found, which led to the development of several mine adits and incline shafts, but actual mine production was minimal.

End of White Top Mountain Road side trip.

22.6 / 36.8 The Hunter Mountain Road continues from Lost Burro Junction.

25.5 / 33.9 **Hidden Valley** has an enclosed drainage. The bottom is well vegetated by saltbushes, including true greasewood (*Sarcobatus*), typical of alkaline clay playas. The road crosses the playa and this is one of the few places in all of Death Valley where the best of 4WD vehicles may get stuck in mud after a rain. The mountains to the west, between Hidden Valley and Racetrack Valley, are the Dutton Range.

27.9 / 31.5 **Ulida Pass** (elevation about 4,900 feet) separates Hidden Valley from the enclosed drainage area of **Ulida Flat**.

28.7 / 30.7 The open-cut mine workings on the low hill east of the road are the **Goldbelt Asbestos Mine**, discovered in 1951. The asbestos here is the chrysotile serpentine form, the best type of asbestos for weaving heat- and sound-insulating materials but also the variety most responsible for health and environmental hazards.

29.1 / 30.3 **Ubehebe Talc Mine Road** (east; 4WD recommended) climbs over the hills 0.9 mile to the mine that produced high-grade steatite talc between 1935 and 1945. The road continues around the mountain to the Keeler Mine and rejoins the Hunter Mountain Road at southbound milepoint 31.1.

The **Ulida Mine Road** (west 1.7 miles; hike on closed road) crosses Ulida Flat to the Ulida Mine. It is believed that the Ulida Mine was the original "Ubehebe Mine," discovered by W. L. Hunter in 1875. There was little mining at that time, but the Ulida was one of the more notable producers early in the greater Ubehebe Mining District boom. It was described as "the queen bee of Ubehebe," but good ore was apparently limited. A 1908 newspaper advertisement announced positions for 40 miners, but then nothing more was heard about the operation. The main tunnel is surrounded by beautiful green (but low-grade) copper-stained rocks. Metal trash and rusty mining equipment are found nearby.

31.1 / 28.3 **Keeler Talc Mine Road** (GPS 36°38.205'N 117°30.122'W, north; 4WD) passes the mine, a small producer of the 1950s, and continues around the mountain to the Ubehebe Talc Mine. It rejoins the main road at northbound milepoint 30.3.

32.3 / 27.1 **Quackenbush Mine Road** (GPS 36°36.949'N 117°27.784'W, east 1.4 miles; 4WD required) loops southeast around the hill to the mine and continues to the Goldbelt Spur Road near Goldbelt Spring. The Quackenbush Mine was called the Irish Mine until it was leased in 1942 by W. J. Quackenbush, who produced 2,000 tons of talc from the mine.

Not quite 0.5 mile along this road is the start of the **Lost Burro Tail Mine Road** (GPS 36°36.782'N 117°27.304'W, north). Although this road was listed as impassable in 1995, it is now open as an exceedingly rugged 3.8-mile 4WD route. The Lost Burro Tail Mine (also called the Mule Tail Mine) was primarily a talc mine, but it was initially located for its tungsten and gold mineralization. It is probably the 1904 discovery by Frank "Shorty" Harris that started the first "rush" of prospectors to Goldbelt Spring.

33.1 / 26.3 "**North Goldbelt Junction**." The road west leads up Hunter Mountain, and the road north goes toward Teakettle Junction. This road log continues south toward Goldbelt Spring.

The bright yellow and black birds common in this high Joshua tree forest in the spring and summer months are Scott's orioles. Many of the shrubs are indigobush, members of the pea family's genus *Dalea*.

33.4 / 26.0 **Goldbelt Spur Road** (south, high-clearance) drops into a small canyon south of "South Goldbelt Junction" and ends at the mining camp of Goldbelt only 0.9 mile distant.

The **Calmet Mine**, just south of the junction, is at the southeastern limit of a belt of contact metamorphic rocks more than 5 miles long. The intrusive magma of the Hunter Mountain quartz monzonite converted the Tin Mountain and Lost Burro limestone formations into almost pure wollastonite, a calcium-silicate mineral with white, bladelike crystals used in a variety of porcelain products. As a whole, the deposits are estimated to contain at least 200 million tons of wollastonite ore, but the Calmet Mine is the only part ever worked. About 10,000 tons were produced during the 1960s.

The **Quackenbush Mine Road** (north, 4WD), 0.6 mile from the junction, leads past the small Quackenbush talc mine and connects with the Hunter Mountain Road at northbound milepoint 27.1.

Goldbelt (GPS 36°36.109'N 117°27.641'W, elevation about 5,000 feet) was a mining camp with three chapters to its history, beginning in 1904 (see Appendix A). The existing structures—4 collapsed cabins, a "Cousin Jack" dugout, miscellaneous junk, and an old truck—date to the talc and wollastonite mining that ended in the early 1960s. **Goldbelt Spring** is just up the small canyon from the ruins, within a dense and very prickly thicket of sweetleaf wild rose, *Rosa woodsii*.

The drainage here is into Death Valley via Marble Canyon. Hikers can go down the canyon to connect with the Cottonwood-Marble loop hike. (See Chapter 8.)

End of Goldbelt side trip.

33.7 / 25.7	From **West Goldbelt Junction**, the road southwest climbs the east face of Hunter Mountain. This is officially named **Harris Grade** but is also called Goldbelt Grade. It is only 3 miles to the summit, but the road is very steep and rocky in places and it may be covered with icy snow in the winter. The road to the southeast goes to the Calmet Mine and Goldbelt, and that to the northeast continues toward Teakettle Junction.
34.6 / 24.8	**Horsetail Springs** are a series of seeps marked by wild rose bushes both above and below the road.
35.0 / 24.4	**Goldbelt Grade Spring** boasts willow trees and wild roses.
35.8 / 23.6	Stop at the pullout for an excellent view southeast into the Mesquite Flat and sand dune portions of Death Valley. The large, dark-green shrubs throughout this area are cliff rose.
36.8 / 22.6	Top of Goldbelt Grade. Northbound drivers should travel cautiously, as parts of the next 3 miles are steep, narrow, and rocky.
36.9 / 22.5	**Side Trip RH-1c—J. O. Mine Road** (GPS 36°34.715'N 117°28.751'W, north 5.2 miles one-way; 4WD required) first crosses the gently rolling plateau of Hunter Mountain but then traverses some steep and tortuous ridges along the very edge of the mountain. There are nearly sheer dropoffs and

spectacular views. The road ends at the J. O. Mine, a wollastonite property of extensive exploration but no commercial production. The road is also the access to Spanish Spring, the Monarch Mine, and the Tourmaline Mine.

0.0 Hunter Mountain Road.

0.8 **Spanish Spring Spur Road** (west about 1.8 miles one-way to the spring). The Monarch Mine may be the oldest mine in the entire Death Valley region (but see the Garibaldi Mine in Chapter 15, Side Trip W-3b), and the Tourmaline Mine was the only producer of gemstones within the national park.

Spanish Spring flows about 2 quarts per minute. It was named because it was the location of an early milling operation. There are the remains of three ore-grinding arrastres and a retort furnace near the spring, all of which apparently were constructed by "Spanish" (in reality, Mexican) miners at least as early as the 1860s when they worked the nearby Monarch Mine. The spring was also used in milling tungsten ore around 1915 and now has a watering trough for open-range cattle.

The **Monarch Mine** is a hike of less than 1 mile along the canyon west of the spring. It was unquestionably mined by Mexican miners in the 1860s, and it is believed that they originally worked the property in 1838 or before. The ore contained silver-bearing tetrahedrite, a copper arsenide-sulfide mineral that sometimes forms beautiful pyramidal crystals but here is only a sooty black powder.

From Spanish Spring, a poor road continues southwest another 2.3 miles to end at the edge of Quail Canyon. Along the way is the **Tourmaline Mine**, which developed pods of granite pegmatite for the production of gem- and specimen-quality tourmaline. Some of the pink crystals were 3 inches long and 1 inch in diameter, but little of quality can be seen now.

1.9 The J. O. Mine Road drops steeply toward the rim of Hunter Mountain.

2.8 The outstanding view north is across Ulida Flat and Hidden Valley toward Tin Mountain.

3.2 There is another excellent viewpoint near some open cuts in a wollastonite ore body. The wollastonite was formed by metamorphism when the Hunter Mountain quartz monzonite intruded into the Tin Mountain and Lost Burro limestone rocks. Wollastonite is a calcium-silicate mineral used in porcelain and whiteware. This contact zone is more than

The view north from the J. O. Mine Road is spectacular, with the Hunter Mountain Road wandering north across Ulida Flat toward Hidden Valley and Lost Burro Gap.

5 miles long, extending from the Calmet Mine near Goldbelt Spring to the J. O. Mine at the end of this road.

4.1 Another outstanding view takes in part of the lake bed of The Racetrack. The last mile of the road beyond this point is very rough and driving it is probably pointless as it reveals nothing other than what has already been seen.

5.2 The J. O. Mine at the end of the road is a series of open cuts and surface scrapes that expose a large body of wollastonite.

End of J. O. Mine Road side trip.

38.5 / 20.9 **Hunter Cabin Road** (GPS 36°33.444'N 117°29.060'W, south 0.8 mile; high-clearance recommended). William L. Hunter settled the Hunter Mountain area in the early 1870s. Hunter Canyon in Saline Valley is also named for him and his brother, and their descendants still graze cattle on the mountain. Hunter built a cabin at this spot in 1875, but it apparently was destroyed by fire in either 1906 or 1910. The existing cabin, made of pinyon pine logs, replaced the original at that time. It was from here, the Hunter Mountain Ranch by name, that Hunter discovered the Ulida Mine, more than 12 miles away by road but only about half as distant directly overland. In

The Hunter Cabin was probably built around 1910 to replace an original 1875 building that burned.

the later 1800s the ranch was regularly used as a camp by U.S. Army patrols. Hunter Cabin Spring (5 gallons per minute) is on the slope just above the building, and Hunter Corral Spring (3 gallons per minute) is at the willow-crowded marsh in the shallow valley below the cabin.

40.9 / 18.5 The road crosses a high point at an elevation of about 7,150 feet within an extensive forest of pinyon pines and Utah juniper trees. Mountain lion, black bear, and mule deer live here; a few wild horses and feral burros also roam the area, and there are some open-range cattle.

42.2 / 17.2 **Jackass Springs** (elevation 6,820 feet at the old water tank) is a series of seeps and flowing springs that support a number of small pools amid wildroses, willows, and reeds. The water is piped to cattle water troughs near Lee Flat, 5 miles west. Although the pools are inviting, the water must be treated before drinking. The road here is often icy and may be impassable in the winter.

42.8 / 16.6 **Lee Pump** (old road north into Jackass Canyon) was the site of a water pumping plant that sent the water from Jackass Springs and other water sources over the hill toward the Lee Mines several miles away. The earliest developments took place in the 1870s.

43.8 / 15.6	The large shrubs growing along the roadcuts are silver lupine (*Lupinus caudatus*), a plant common in the mountains of central Nevada but rare in the park. It bears long flower spikes in the spring months. Great Basin sagebrush, indigo bush, cliffrose, several kinds of saltbush, and at least two species of Mormon tea also grow on these slopes.
43.9 / 15.5	**South Pass** is the divide between Panamint Valley (Mill Canyon) and Saline Valley (Grapevine Canyon). This is the end of the Hunter Mountain Road, and the southernmost 15.5 miles of this trip route out to State Highway 190 is along the Saline Valley Road (see Trip Route SV-1). Northbound travelers going to Hunter Mountain from State Highway 190 should take the turn up the mountain from South Pass rather than continuing down into Grapevine Canyon.
59.4 / 0.0	The **Saline Valley Road** meets State Highway 190 at a point approximately 30 miles east of the nearest full services at either Olancha or Lone Pine in Owens Valley, or 13.5 miles west of the Panamint Springs Resort. See Chapter 20, Trip Route SV-1 for the first 15.5 miles of this road log.

The mystery of the sliding rocks on The Racetrack (page 331) appears to have been solved. In January 2014, a tourist reported seeing the rocks move to the National Park Service. Park rangers then notified two teams of researchers who had been studying The Racetrack under NPS permits. The teams, one from the John Hopkins University Applied Physics Laboratory and one from the Scripps Institute of Oceanography, both observed the movements and quantified them using weather sensors, time-lapse photography, and GPS motion recorders.

What they saw was a flooded lakebed covered with a thin layer of ice that broke into sheets in the warm morning sun. A gust of wind measuring less than 10 miles per hour started the sheets gliding across the lakebed. Some rocks were moved as far as 230 feet at speeds of only 10 feet per minute. The caveat: none of the larger rocks were moved and some of the smaller ones stay fixed, too. So, perhaps something more—thicker ice, stronger wind, or yet another factor—is still needed to fully explain the mystery.

CHAPTER TWENTY

Saline Valley Road, including Lee Flat

Saline Valley is a remote area. From one end to the other, the Saline Valley Road is 78 miles long, and each end is several miles from the nearest services; there are no services whatsoever in Saline Valley. This is, however, a popular area, especially because of the camping and soaking at the informal spas at Lower Warm Spring and Palm Spring. There are also numerous important historic sites throughout the area, and Lee Flat, near the south end of this road, hosts the national park's most extensive stand of Joshua trees.

Saline Valley Road, Trip Route SV-1—Saline Valley Road

FROM: State Highway 190 between Panamint Valley and Owens Valley.

TO: Big Pine Road in the Inyo Mountains.

ROAD CONDITIONS: 78.3 miles one-way, mostly dirt road that is occasionally maintained. The South Pass entrance is usually suitable for any vehicle driven with caution; the North Pass entrance often requires 4WD vehicles. In any case, high-clearance vehicles with durable tires are recommended, and snow sometimes closes both passes to all vehicles.

SIDE TRIPS: Santa Rosa Flat (high-clearance), Lee Mines Road (4WD), Lee Flat Road (Side Trip SV-1a; high-clearance and 4WD), Lippincott Road (4WD), Saline Valley Marsh (walk), Conn & Trudo Borax Works (walk), Artesian Well Road (high-clearance), Warm Spring Road–Steel Pass Road (Side Trip SV-1b; all vehicles, then 4WD), Lead Canyon (Bunker Hill Mine) Road (4WD), Waucoba Mine Road (4WD), and Jackass Flats Road (4WD); access to Hunter Mountain Road (Chapter 19, Trip Route RH-1; 4WD).

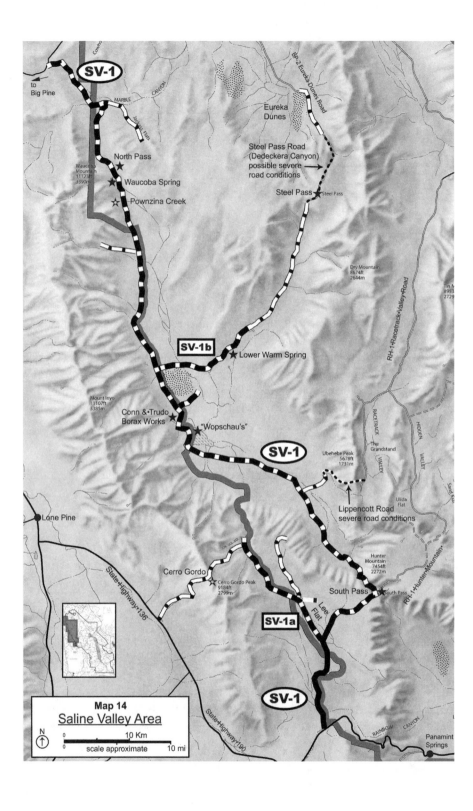

SV-1

to
Big Pine

MARBLE

Jackass Flats

North Pass

Waucoba
Mountain
11123ft
3390m

Waucoba Spring

Pownzina Creek

Eureka
Dunes

BP-2 Eureka Dunes Road

Steel Pass Road
(Dedeckera Canyon)
possible severe
road conditions

Steel Pass   Steel Pass

Dry Mountain
8674ft
2644m

RH-1-Racetrack Valley Road

Tin M
8953
2729

SV-1b   Lower Warm Spring

Mount Inyo
11107ft
3385m

Conn & Trudo
Borax Works

"Wopschau's"

SV-1

Ubehebe Peak
5678ft
1731m

The
Grandstand

RACETRACK

HIDDEN

VALLEY

VALLEY

Ulida
Flat

Sand Fla

Lone Pine

Lippencott Road
severe road conditions

Cerro Gordo

Cerro Gordo Peak
9184ft
2799m

Hunter
Mountain
7454ft
2272m

South Pass   South Pass

RH-1-Hunter Mountain

State Highway 136

SV-1a

Lee
Flat

SV-1

RAINBOW   CANYON

Panamint
Springs

State Highway 190

Map 14
Saline Valley Area

N

0   10 Km
0   scale approximate   10 mi

GENERAL DESCRIPTION: Saline Valley is a special place in many ways. It is one of the most remote spots in California. No services of any kind are available, and a distance of more than 100 miles separates the closest facilities at Panamint Springs on the south and Big Pine on the north. The valley's permanent inhabitants can be counted on one hand, yet a seasonal and holiday population, attracted mostly by the warm springs, may reach more than 100 people.

The name is properly pronounced "suh-LEEN" rather than "SAY-leen." The original name was Salinas Valley, given by the Wheeler Survey in 1871. There has been a long history of mining in the area—gold at Marble Canyon; borax and salt on the valley floor; lead-silver, tungsten, and talc on the east face of the Inyo Mountains; numerous metals and commodities in the Nelson Range; and copper and lead in the Ubehebe Range near Racetrack Valley—starting as early as 1872 and continuing to the present time.

The floor of Saline Valley is more than 1,000 feet higher than that of Death Valley, but because the valley is enclosed on the north and south as well as the east and west, it is as hot as Death Valley in the summer. In fact, quality thermometers at both Willow Creek and Lower Warm Spring often record temperatures several degrees higher than those in Death Valley on the same day.

The Saline Valley Road is maintained by Inyo County. The grading, however, is done only once or twice each year, and in between the road develops rough washboard surfaces. The road over North Pass is steeper and sometimes requires high-clearance or even 4WD vehicles. Also, heavy winter snow may fall on both passes. Clearing them is not a high priority, so the valley is sometimes isolated for days at a time.

ROAD LOG MILEAGES	northbound from State Highway 190 / southbound from Big Pine Road.
0.0 / 78.3	The turnoff from State Highway 190 (Chapter 15, Trip Route W-2) is well marked, 13.5 miles west of Panamint Springs or 30 miles east of Olancha and Lone Pine. The southernmost 8 miles of the Saline Valley Road is paved, but the thin asphalt is badly broken.
1.3 / 77.0	**Santa Rosa Wash** drains a large area to the north and northwest and sometimes produces huge floods.
4.7 / 73.6	**Santa Rosa Road** (west; 4WD recommended) either cuts back to State Highway 190 or west 7.8 miles to the Santa Rosa Mine. The mine was discovered as part of the Darwin mining boom in the 1870s, but it was most active as a producer of lead-silver-zinc ore during the 1920s and 1940s.
5.3 / 73.0	The Santa Rosa Hills consist of Darwin Hills Volcanics lava flows on top of Paleozoic age sedimentary rocks.

6.0 / 72.3	**Lee Mine Road** (GPS 36°26.099'N 117°37.387'W, east 1 mile; 4WD recommended) leads through a small pass to the mines that consist of tunnels and open cuts on the east side of the hill beyond the valley. The major operations at the Lee and Silver Reid mines were during the 1870s and early 1880s. The ore is a discontinuous series of high-grade pockets that contained large amounts of cerargyrite (silver chloride). Even in the waning days of production during the 1950s, sorted ore was as rich as 60 ounces of silver per ton. The sedimentary rock exposed along the road in this little valley is the Lee Flat Limestone of the Carboniferous Period.
6.5 / 71.8	The sedimentary rock just under basalt lava flows low on the ridge west of the road is the Lost Burro Formation, which contains poor fossils of Devonian age.
7.0 / 71.3	Death Valley National Park boundary.
8.2 / 70.1	**Side Trip SV-1a—Lee Flat Road** (GPS 36°27.899'N 117°37.601'W, northwest 11.3 miles to Cerro Gordo Road; high-clearance recommended, 4WD required on side roads) is the access to a wide area of the Inyo Mountains and Nelson Range, with Lee Flat in between. Along the way, a network of routes of variable quality reach talc and lead-silver mines in the mountains. The main road ends at the upper part of Saline Valley's San Lucas Canyon.
0.0	Turnoff from Saline Valley Road. Lee Flat hosts Death Valley National Park's most extensive forest of Joshua trees. These are the short-leaved variety, *Yucca brevifolia jaegeriana*. Most of the shrubs here are shadscale, a member of the saltbush family.
3.4	The road northeast almost immediately splits. The branch straight ahead leads to some small mine prospects and that to the east ends at **Blackrock Well**, which provides water for the cattle that still range this area.
3.5	**Lee Flat Overlook Road** (GPS 36°30.786'N 117°39.675'W, northeast 5.4 miles one-way to end of road; 4WD required) cuts 2.7 miles across Lee Flat and then into the mountains of the Nelson Range where there are several mines. Most of these mines were initially prospected for copper and/or silver-lead-zinc; the most prolific was the Cerussite Mine, but even there production was minimal. These deposits occupy a zone of high-grade metamorphic rocks that in places are composed of industrial-grade garnet and tungsten minerals. As recently as the early 1990s, Union Carbide Corporation held an option on these deposits.

A short spur road (east) at the base of the mountains leads up to "Lee Overlook" and several of the mines. The main road reaches a pass through the mountains to still more mines near an expansive view into Saline Valley.

6.7 The road crosses out of the national park but serves as the western park boundary for the next 6 miles.

11.3 **Cerro Gordo Road** (west; 4WD recommended) crosses over the Inyo Mountains and drops past the Cerro Gordo ghost town (Appendix A) to reach California State Highway 136 near Keeler, 13.0 miles from the Lee Flat Road.

Beyond the Cerro Gordo Road, the Lee Flat Road continues about 1.5 miles farther. It ends at the head of San Lucas Canyon. A spur road (west) near San Lucas Canyon leads to the Bonham Talc Mine and other 4WD roads that wind high into the Inyo Mountains.

End Lee Flat Road side trip.

8.5 / 69.8 The park's most extensive Joshua tree forest covers **Lee Flat**. A large proportion of the shrubs around the trees are shadscale. Although shadscale has the widest distribution of any of the saltbushes, the concentration of the plants on Lee Flat might be greater than anywhere else. This is open cattle range, and a few feral burros are also found in the area.

11.5 / 66.8 The rocks exposed on these hills are all olivine basalt lava flows of the Darwin Hills Volcanics, 2 to 6 million years old.

14.4 / 63.9 The road crosses an unnamed summit at an elevation of 6,225 feet. The open, dry slopes support Utah juniper trees, and the shrubs include Great Basin sagebrush, Mormon tea, burro brush, and scatterings of indigobush and cliffrose.

14.8 / 63.5 This small valley is more sheltered than the open hills to the west, and the greater soil moisture supports a dense grove of single-leaved pinyon pines and Utah junipers.

15.3 / 63.0 A wide pullout provides a spectacular view down precipitous Mill Canyon into Panamint Valley. The Panamint Dunes, up to 250 feet high, are at the near end of the valley. State Highway 190 can be seen crossing the playa of Upper Panamint Lake beyond Lake Hill. Lower Panamint Valley, which is bounded by the Panamint Mountains (east) and Argus Range (west), is in the distance. Note the large cliffrose bushes on the slopes above the road.

15.5 / 62.8 **South Pass** (elevation 5,977 feet). The Hunter Mountain Road (east; 4WD recommended) climbs steeply onto Hunter Mountain; then drops to Goldbelt Spring, Hidden Valley, and

Racetrack Valley; and finally ends at Ubehebe Crater. (It is described as Trip Route RH-1 in Chapter 19.) Northbound travelers begin the steep grade down into Grapevine Canyon. Portions of this road may be slick and muddy when wet, snow-covered in winter, and occasionally blocked by rockfalls.

16.3 / 62.0 A series of springs is scattered along Grapevine Canyon. The small grove of trees near this corral is at the uppermost spring.

17.5 / 60.8 **Grapevine Canyon** is carved into the Hunter Mountain quartz monzonite, a rock similar to granite. It makes up most of the mass of Hunter Mountain to the east and some of the Nelson Range to the northwest. The canyon formed along the trace of the Hunter Mountain Fault Zone, an active fault that connects the faults of Panamint and Saline valleys. This is one of two canyons named Grapevine within the national park; the other is the location of Scotty's Castle.

18.2 / 60.1 Willow trees festooned with wild grapevines (*Vitis girardiana*) grow near the largest of the Grapevine Canyon Springs. A considerable stream often forms in this part of the canyon, and deep gullies sometimes cross the road. The **Ubehebe Trail** (approximate GPS 36°33.450'N 117°34.810'W) is difficult to find but climbs up the canyon wall just up-canyon from a cluster of springs and heads northeast 2.6 miles to **Big Dodd Spring** (GPS 36°35.110'N 117°34.388'W; water flow about 2 gallons per minute) and several small tungsten mines. The trail eventually reaches Racetrack Valley near the Lippincott Mine, about 7.5 miles away.

~20 / 58 Northbound drivers get their first open view into Saline Valley; southbound travelers are about to climb into Grapevine Canyon.

21.9 / 56.4 The square, fenced area east of the road is a burro exclosure. It was intended to show the difference in plant growth between the land outside the fence versus that inside the fence as a result of overgrazing by wild burros. In fact, after many years there is little perceptible difference. Most of the burros have been removed from the area, but a few are still occasionally seen here and on nearby Hunter Mountain.

25.8 / 52.5 **Lippincott Road** (east about 7 miles one-way to the Racetrack Valley [Chapter 19, Side Trip RH-1a]; 4WD absolutely required). The first trail through Lippincott Canyon was built in the 1870s, during the earliest mining activity near the Racetrack Valley, and it was reconstructed as a wagon road during the Ubehebe District copper boom around

1907. It was hardly maintained from then until this area was included within the national park. The National Park Service has done some work to improve the road, but it is extremely steep and rocky, car-width narrow in spots, and lined with sheer cliffs both above and below. It is a route recommended only for narrow, short-wheelbase 4WD cars and motorbikes. Always investigate the current condition of the road before attempting it.

34.1 / 44.2   **San Lucas Canyon** slicing out of the Nelson Range (south) was the original route of the Saline Valley Road. It was very steep, narrow, and winding. Only traces of it remain in the canyon, and it has almost entirely washed away on the alluvial fan at the Saline Valley end.

36.9 / 41.4   **Saline Valley Salt Tram** (GPS 36°41.067'N 117°48.958'W). A few of the wooden tramway towers are still standing near the lake bed northeast of the road and up in the mountains to the west, but large towers that once stood near the road have partially collapsed because of both age and vandalism. More about the tram, once the largest of its kind in the world, is given in Appendix B. Binoculars reveal trenches, collecting ponds, and salt piles in and near the permanent lake of salt water to the east, beyond the last of the towers. The last mining took place in 1933. Both the tram and salt works were entered into the National Register of Historic Places in 1973.

     Big Silver Mine Road (west, 4WD) curves northwest 1.6 miles to the mine at the base of the mountains. With 2,800 feet of tunnels, two tramlines, and several collapsing buildings, this mine may be the largest historic source of silver within Saline Valley. Most of the mining took place during the 1920s, but it is still an active claim that is barely outside the national park boundary.

37.9 / 40.4   View of Saline Valley Marsh. A large area surrounding the freshwater marsh and ponds is fenced to keep nonnative animals (especially burros) from fouling the water and trampling the vegetation. It is at about this point that the road leaves national park land. For the next 20 miles northbound, the road serves as the park boundary: all land east of the road is within Death Valley National Park and that to the west is managed by the Bureau of Land Management.

38.3 / 40.0   **Saline Valley Marsh** (east, short road across cattle guard), with its fresh water and dense groves of mesquite trees, is one of the lushest places in the entire Death Valley region. The largest permanent population of Indians, both Shoshone

The salt works at the edge of the Saline Salt Marsh.

and Paiute, lived near the marsh. The village was called Ko'o, meaning "deep place" in allusion to the lowest spot in Saline Valley. At least 27 significant archaeological sites have been excavated within the marsh, and as many more on the alluvial fan near Hunter Canyon.

During 1907 and 1908, when borax and salt mining were occurring nearby and the Ubehebe copper and lead mining boom was underway in the mountains east of Saline Valley, a store and boardinghouse complex was located somewhere near the marsh. It may have been at Wopschau Spring, which bubbles clean water from a concrete trough. The spring was named for the man who sold the land to the California Department of Fish and Game about 1971, and the marsh area is commonly known as "**Wopschau's**" (sometimes pronounced "WAH-p'shaws").

At least 124 species of birds have been sighted at the Saline Valley Marsh. The water is populated by the red-spotted toad plus introduced bullfrogs and crayfish and chub, bullhead, and bluegill fish. Numerous small mammals live at or visit the marsh, and both bighorn sheep and black bear (one yearling cub) have been seen. Unfortunately, the wildlife also includes swarms of biting flies and mosquitoes.

The Conn & Trudo Borax Works were constructed in 1889, apparently as an enlarged replacement of a smaller processing plant built as early as 1875.

<table>
<tr><td>39.2 / 39.1</td><td>Hunter Canyon Road (west) leads up a short alluvial fan to the mouth of Hunter Canyon, where private Camp Vega is sometimes occupied. The visitor theoretically can scramble the hillside around the camp and into the canyon, where there is a permanent stream.</td></tr>
<tr><td>39.9 / 38.4</td><td>Conn & Trudo Borax Works (both sides of the road). Borax was discovered on the Saline Valley salt pan in 1874 (possibly even 1864, when the salt beds were first described), and apparently some minor production by the Saline Valley Borax Works took place at about that time, several years before the first borax mining in Death Valley. One of the advantages to the Saline Valley deposits was that they were largely composed of actual mineral borax (sodium borate); most so-called borax deposits, including those of Death Valley, were actually cottonball ulexite (sodium-calcium borate), which required complex processing to eliminate the calcium. However, it was left to Frederick Conn and Edward Trudo to establish a commercially successful operation to process the Saline Valley deposits. Residents of Big Pine, California, they claimed 1,200 acres of the salt beds. Beginning in April 1889, their works produced commercial-grade borax continuously</td></tr>
</table>

until 1895, and then intermittently into 1907. For a time in the early 1890s, this was the largest single source of borax in the United States. Thirty men were employed and they produced up to 40 tons of borax each month.

The major part of the facility, where the 3,000-gallon dissolving tank was located, was built on the earthen mound faced with rock walls west of the road. Below that (now on both sides of the road) are the 18 rock-lined settling tanks and evaporation ponds where the borax was crystallized for harvesting and shipment. (Note: the ruins west of the road are on private property but those to the east are within the national park.)

The Conn & Trudo ruins are only the largest and most accessible of Saline Valley's borax works. There were at least three other operations during the 1890s. One was owned by a Mr. Bush, who had claim to 160 acres and made at least some production in 1890; another was a partnership of men named Stoutenborough, Millner, Lent, and Cox; and unknown persons laid claim to cottonball ulexite ground along the south edge of the dry lake. None of these operations lasted longer than a few months.

40.0 / 38.3   **Artesian Well Road** (GPS 36°42.823'N 117°50.034'W, northeast 2.0 miles; high-clearance recommended) used to lead to the warm springs across the valley. It is now closed at the freshwater source of Saline Valley Well, commonly known as "the artesian well," which was dug by Conn and Trudo in the late 1880s. Beyond the well, the old road crossed ground composed of exceptionally fine lake bed clay that turns into sticky, alkaline mud with any rain.

40.2 / 38.1   Much of the land along the main road in this area is private property, largely undeveloped but posted against trespassing. This was the **Saline Valley Indian Ranch** that supplied fruits, vegetables, and mule-breeding services to the mining districts of Cerro Gordo and Waucoba, and later to the borax companies. The Saline Shoshone used mechanized farming equipment as early as the 1870s and worked their land for considerable profit—in 1875, a mine report stated that "experiment has already demonstrated that an abundant supply of vegetables and tropical fruit, as well as those of a more temperate climate, can be raised." In an event unusual for the time, the Indians were granted full possession of the property by the Saline Valley Indian Ranch Homestead Land Grant, signed by President Benjamin Harrison on June 30, 1892.

Their population was as great as 125. However, the Indians lost their water rights following an unfortunate shooting at the Hunter Canyon millsite in 1952. No Indians have lived in the valley since then, and at least some of the private property is now owned by non-Indians.

42.6 / 35.7 **Morning Sun Ranch** (buildings east of the road) is almost hidden behind mesquite trees. It is private property that is patented as a millsite claim related to the Big Silver Mine south of the Saline Valley Marsh.

42.8 / 35.5 **Beveridge Canyon Road** (west; 4WD) climbs to the mouth of Beveridge Canyon. The canyon contains a year-round stream that drops over a series of waterfalls. Climbing skills are needed to hike more than a mile or so up the canyon. Backpackers with a great deal of stamina can eventually reach the ghost town of Beveridge, a climb of several thousand feet into the mountains. Beveridge was occupied from 1877 to 1904. It was a small but successful mining camp whose remoteness has helped preserve several buildings.

43.2 / 35.1 **Sand Dunes Cutoff Road** for northbound travelers. This straight road rejoins the main Saline Valley Road at the far side of a wide curve. It is not much of a shortcut but does give close access to the Saline Valley Sand Dunes. Unlike the dunes in Eureka, Panamint, Death, and Ibex valleys, the dunes in Saline Valley do not form high peaks of sand. Instead, they are spread across a wide area as a blanket of mesquite-locked dunes. Like dunes anywhere, they are delicate and support amazingly diverse wildlife.

44.1 / 34.2 The **Snowflake Mine Road** (west) climbs the alluvial fan and then is visible as a series of switchbacks on the mountain face. The Snowflake Mine produced small tonnages of high-grade steatite talc starting in the 1950s. The International Talc and Steatite Corporation reopened it in 1994, and the road is private.

44.4 / 33.9 Sand Dunes Cutoff Road for southbound travelers (see southbound milepoint 35.1).

45.1 / 33.2 **McElvoy Canyon Road** (west; high-clearance recommended). This "high road" to McElvoy Canyon crosses a short but rocky alluvial fan to a gravel bench perched above the mouth of the canyon. Like many of the canyons draining the east face of the Inyo Mountains, there is a permanent stream that cascades down a series of waterfalls. There are lush grottoes of fern, moss, horsetails, and seasonal wildflowers—including orchids—along the way. It is fairly easy to climb past the first two waterfalls, but going farther requires climbing equipment or dangerous scrambling.

45.4 / 32.9 **McElvoy Canyon Road** (west; 4WD recommended). This is the "low road" to McElvoy Canyon, following the active wash directly to the mouth of the canyon. See the description above.

45.9 / 32.4 **Side Trip SV-1b—Lower Warm Spring Road** (GPS 36°46.698'N 117°52.744'W; east 6.8 miles one-way to Lower Warm Spring and 9.9 miles to start of 4WD Steel Pass Road; high-clearance recommended). The warm springs near the end of the good road are the destination for most visitors to Saline Valley. The camps and soaking pools at Lower Warm Spring and Palm Spring are "clothing-optional" places where full nudity is common. Camping is limited to 30 days. In 2014 the park service issued a Saline Valley Warm Springs Management Plan EIS, and camping and clothing policies may change by 2016.

0.0 Turnoff from the Saline Valley Road. The road has never been formally maintained but is generally in good condition. There are areas of washboard on the flat valley floor and gravel stretches in the wash below Lower Warm Spring. However, motor homes and trailer units as well as standard automobiles routinely make this dusty trip.

3.5 After crossing the gentle drainage of Waucoba Wash, the road approaches the sand dunes and their groves of honey mesquite trees.

4.4 The road makes a sharp left turn where the Artesian Well Road (now closed) used to merge with Lower Warm Spring Road.

6.8 **Lower Warm Spring** rises from a cavernous crater and flows several gallons of water between 110°F and 114°F per minute. The exact temperature varies with time. The rate of water flow is constant except following regional earthquakes that sometimes temporarily reduce it to near zero. The most recent cases occurred following the magnitude 6.2 Eureka Valley earthquake on May 17, 1993, when it was more than a year before the flow completely recovered; in the fall of 2005 when small, local tremors again decreased the flow for more than a year; and in late 2007 when all flow was stopped for several weeks. It is believed that the alignment of Lower Warm, Palm, and Upper Warm springs plus the existence of mercury and manganese deposits farther up the valley mark the trace of the **Steel Pass Fault Zone.**

Mesquite and arrowweed thickets surround Saline Valley's Lower Warm Spring.

The water is highly mineralized and deposits travertine (calcium carbonate). There is a series of small, cool seeps along the base of a travertine terrace just east of the main spring. The natural setting was marked by groves of screwbean mesquite trees and arrowweed thickets. Indians of prehistory must have spent considerable time here—the Saline Timbisha name was Puigetü ("Green Rock")—as arrowheads and pottery shards are occasionally found on top of the travertine terrace. (Keeping such a find is illegal.)

These springs were first described in the 1870s, and the development of Lower Warm Spring for recreation began at least as early as 1928. Constructed pools were in regular use by 1947. The water (when there is sufficient volume) is piped to 2 soaking pools, a concrete bathtub, and a dishwashing sink. The water flow can be adjusted to control the temperature of the pools. The runoff discharges into a pond and then percolates through a thicket of mesquite and arrowweed. In the main camp next to the largest soaking pool is a lawn shaded by mesquites and California fan palms, a fire pit surrounded by benches, picnic tables, and a library. Undesignated campsites are available both above and below the spring. The stay limit is 30 days. The entire facility, including pit toilets, is maintained by the users.

There are three popular hiking destinations from Lower Warm Spring: (1) to Peace Sign Mountain, a cinder cone volcano that is part of the Saline Range Volcanics; (2) to the Seven Sisters Springs where there are water seeps and mesquite groves; and (3) along the Black Mountain Loop Trail, a 5-mile hike in the Saline Range. These hikes are described in Chapter 8.

7.5   **Palm Spring** is a warm spring similar to Lower Warm Spring, but its water flow is somewhat less. Most of the recreational developments date to the 1970s or later and again consist of soaking and washing pools. Several fan palms have been planted, but the camping is in unshaded areas among creosote bushes.

Beyond Palm Spring, the road mostly follows gravel washes and deteriorates to the point that 4WD vehicles are recommended.

8.4   The red rocks on the hillside to the north are the remnants of a cinder cone volcano.

9.4   Just after climbing a rough travertine terrace is a series of pits and trenches. These are the **Black Diamond Mine**, a prospect developed in low-grade manganese ore that contains traces of tungsten and silver.

9.9   **Upper Warm Spring** has an exclosure fence around it to help preserve the purity of the water. There are two pools of water and a short runoff stream among screwbean mesquite trees and arrowweed bushes. The pools were stocked with pupfish in the late 1970s. The plan was for Upper Warm Spring to be a pupfish refuge, but the fish did not survive the warm water.

Steel Pass Road (4WD required). Beyond Upper Warm Spring, the road is officially called the Steel Pass Road. It follows a gravel wash to the base of the mountains, beyond which 4WD is definitely required.

10.4   A faint, closed road southeast leads to the **Lucky Rich Mine**, a small prospect developed for copper.

10.9   On the slope to the northeast is the **Coffee Stop Mine**, a prospect developed at a low-grade cinnabar (mercury sulfide) deposit.

14.5   The road passes the edge of a basalt lava flow. This was an *aa* flow, nearly solid but it still moved so that large, angular blocks of lava were tumbled inside it. (Hotter lava produces smoother flows called *pahoehoe*, and some of these flows can be found by hiking up into the Saline Range.)

Upper Warm Spring in Saline Valley was fenced when it was designed as a pupfish recovery habitat, an experiment that was not successful.

16.5   **Chalk Canyon** (north; road closed to vehicles) exposes pure-white volcanic ash and pumice, not chalk. Some of these rocks were explored as a source of *pozzolan*, which can be used as both a building stone and lightweight concrete aggregate. Production at the **White Cliffs Mine** was slight. The ash was also examined for potential zeolite minerals, which are used as water and chemical filters, but was found to be too impure for production.

17.5   One of the best "cactus gardens" in all of the national park grows on these alluvial fans. Included are cottontop barrels, beavertail, and calico hedgehog cacti among stands of creosote bush, Mormon tea, indigobush, shadscale, Dedeckera buckwheat, and burrobrush.

20.9   Shortly after the road leaves the wash and begins to climb toward the summit at **Steel Pass**, it develops a "serious character," with large rocks, deep holes and dropoffs, and steep grades with sharp turns. Proceed with caution.

Some maps indicate a "Marble Bath" near the pass, but few people agree on where or what it is; there is no spring or even pothole of water anywhere in the area. Over the summit is a canyon with bright-red rocks at its mouth that contains both petroglyphs and pictographs. Eventually the route passes through **Dedeckera Canyon**, where there are some bedrock cascades to be negotiated, and into Eureka Valley near the Eureka Sand Dunes (Chapter 18, Trip Route BP-2). The route can be driven in most 4WD vehicles but requires time and patience.

End of Lower Warm Spring Road side trip.

46.2 / 32.1   **Pat Keyes Canyon Road** (west, high-clearance) contains a small, permanent stream. A high waterfall a short way into the canyon blocks further access without climbing equipment or a steep scramble up the ridges.

46.7 / 31.6   **Badwater Spring Road** ends at the small grove of trees west of the road. A cabin associated with a small gold prospect was occupied as recently as 1992. The water is undrinkable.

49.3 / 29.0   **The Doris Dee Mine Road** (west) is private and leads to a small talc mine.

50.4 / 27.9   **The Gray Eagle Mine Road** (west) is a private road to the largest historic producer of high-grade steatite talc in Saline Valley.

50.5 / 27.8   **Willow Creek** (west of road) looks like a small town on some maps, but it is a private, gated mining camp. No services are available. The camp was the mining headquarters of the International Talc and Steatite Corporation, which operated the Snowflake, Doris Dee, Gray Eagle, and White Eagle mines.

56.0 / 22.3   **Bunker Hill Mine Road** (GPS 36°54.688'N 117°54.548'W, west 2.7 miles; high-clearance, then 4WD) leads into **Lead Canyon**, where there are several mines. The largest is the **Bunker Hill Mine**. It was a source of considerable silver, lead, and zinc at least as early as 1907 and probably was worked in the early 1870s. In recent years it has been mined for gold and is posted, guarded property. The road continues up the canyon beyond the Bunker Hill Mine to other mining properties as far as 5 miles from Saline Valley Road. Another road branches south from the Bunker Hill Mine. It goes to the Blue Monster, Lucky Boy, and other silver-lead mines that also were first worked in the 1870s and more extensively around 1907.

~57 / 21   This long, straight section of the road is known as "Three-Mile Grade."

~58 / 20   For northbound travelers, the national park boundary crosses the road so that the land both east and west is within the park; for southbound travelers, only the land east of the road is within the park for about the next 20 miles.

59.5 / 18.8 **Crystal Ridge** is northwest of the road. Clay-filled fractures within the Cambrian age Harkless Formation quartzite contain well-formed quartz crystals. Most are fairly small, but some as large as 8 by 3 inches have been recovered. They often contain inclusions of fluid-filled bubbles, stibnite (antimony sulfide), or pyrite (iron sulfide). Many also have a rare seventh crystal face along the side of the prism. Some of these crystals were incorporated into the concrete work at Lower Warm Spring, but since this is within the national park, specimen collecting is no longer allowed.

59.9 / 18.4 Just south of a local summit (elevation 4,944 feet) are extensive rock works along the original road, built not later than 1907 and probably as early as 1872–1875. This pass has developed on a fault that separates siltstone and quartzite of the Saline Valley Formation on the west from thinly bedded limestone of the Mule Spring Formation east of the road. Both date to the Cambrian Period.

60.7 / 17.6 **Waucoba Mine Road** (west; 4WD) ends at the Waucoba Mine less than 0.5 mile from the main road. The mines in this area, like those of Lead Canyon to the south, were initially located in January or February 1872 and caused a significant rush to the Waucoba Mining District.

Someplace in this area was a settlement called **Pownzina Creek**, described as "the camp at the Wacuba [*sic*] Mining and Smelting Co." in a report written by the owner of the Waucoba Mine. In July 1872, only 6 months after mines in the area were located, the community was active enough that the *Inyo Independent* newspaper suggested that the county seat might need to be moved here, and in 1875 it was suggested that the Los Angeles & Independence Railroad (see Appendix B) terminate here rather than at Independence. Interestingly, the exact location of Pownzina Creek seems to have been forgotten—it was about 4 miles north of what are probably the mines of the Lead Canyon area and therefore in this vicinity—and there seems to be no record of any commercial businesses in the community. The name "Pownzina," was probably derived from Pau'önzi, the Indian name of a spring near the mines in Lead Canyon, or from Pauwü'ji, the village at Waucoba Spring.

Years later, the Waucoba Mine produced a fair tonnage of tungsten (scheelite) ore between 1938 and 1941 from a related deposit in a contact metamorphic zone between Cambrian limestones and a small, intrusive igneous rock body.

62.7 / 15.6   **Waucoba Spring Road** (GPS 37°00.175'N 117°56.548'W, west 0.3 mile; high-clearance recommended) ends at Waucoba Spring. The spring forms only a trickle of water. Waucoba is Paiute Indian for the pinyon pine tree (specifically the tree and not its edible nut); to the Shoshone this place was Icam'bah ("Coyote Water").

The rocks here—from high in the Inyo Mountains, down Waucoba Canyon, past the spring, and east across Saline Valley Road—are almost entirely Cambrian age limestones and claystones that in places are highly fossiliferous with trilobites, brachiopods, archaeocyathids, and primitive echinoderms. It is such an outstanding fossil assemblage that worldwide it is sometimes referred to as the Waucoban Fauna. Look, but do not collect.

65.1 / 13.2   **Whippoorwill Canyon** has been carved into hard, metamorphosed Reed Dolomite of late Precambrian or early Cambrian age. Not here but in Nevada, the Reed Dolomite has yielded mollusk fossils that might be the oldest found anywhere.

66.0 / 12.3   **North Pass** is an indistinct summit at elevation 7,380 feet within a pinyon pine forest. This is a wonderful camping area in the summer (campfires not permitted), but Whippoorwill Canyon, North Pass, and Whippoorwill Flat often receive heavy snow in winter, so the road here may be closed for days or even weeks at a time.

~67 / 11   **Whippoorwill Flat** is a small, open valley covered with small shrubs of Great Basin sagebrush, *Artemisia tridentata*.

~69 / 9   **Opal Canyon** is carved into exposures of the Wyman Formation, a mixed sandstone-claystone-limestone rock that has been metamorphosed to variable degrees. Of Precambrian age, it is the oldest sedimentary rock formation exposed in this part of the Inyo Mountains. The poor dirt road leading west from the head of the canyon ends at the Silver Spur and Opal mines, both worked for lead and silver beginning around 1900.

70.5 / 7.8   The **Jackass Flats Road** (GPS 37°05.471'N 117°57.876'W, east 6 miles; 4WD required) starts where the Saline Valley Road reaches the bottom of Marble Canyon. It runs down Marble Canyon for 1.7 miles and then climbs south onto Jackass Flats. It effectively ends 6 miles from the Saline Valley

Road, where several closed roads lead to a number of mine prospects that were explored for silver and lead in the 1870s and again in the early 1900s. The largest of these mines is the **Morning Star**, which underwent minor production of high-grade ore in 1968. And yes, a few jackasses—that is, burros—still roam this area.

Northbound drivers turn left (west) up Marble Canyon; southbound travelers turn right (south) up the hill.

The **Marble Canyon Mines** and miscellaneous head-frames, ore bins, and cabins are scattered for about a mile along the road and also up and down the canyon beyond the road over a total length of 9 miles. Some placer mining took place here as early as 1882 when Marble Canyon is said to have had a population as great as 200, and more mining occurred around 1907. The most significant development of the properties started in 1934, when it was realized that rich values in large gold nuggets existed on the bedrock beneath the gravels, 70 to 115 feet below the surface. Most mining ended in 1960, but a few of the claims are still active. The gold probably did not originate at the head of Marble Canyon. Instead, through fault movements and regional extension, it may have been moved from a source area in the White Mountains about 30 miles to the north, where there are similar gold-bearing gravels.

71.7 / 6.6 Northbound, the road turns right (north) and leaves the bottom of Marble Canyon, and leaves national park land to enter Inyo National Forest; southbound drivers turn left (east) down the canyon.

72.5 / 5.8 The top of the "Marble Canyon Switchbacks" are at an unnamed summit, elevation 6,582 feet.

75.5 / 2.8 The road (east, high-clearance) ends in a pinyon pine grove at the **Try Again Mine**, a small, low-grade talc prospect.

~76 / 2 The view east is into Cowhorn Valley.

78.3 / 0.0 **Big Pine Road.** Southbound, the turnoff toward Saline Valley is well marked and signed as "Waucoba–Saline Road." This is 15.3 miles east of State Highway 168 near the full-service town of Big Pine, or 57.1 miles northwest from the Ubehebe Crater Road near Grapevine Junction in Death Valley. The Big Pine Road is described as Trip Route BP-1 in Chapter 18.

CHAPTER TWENTY-ONE

Nevada Triangle

The Nevada Triangle was added to Death Valley National Monument by a proclamation by President Roosevelt in 1937. It encompasses most of the higher elevations
of the Grapevine Mountains and much of the Bullfrog Mining District. Although
many people visit the Rhyolite ghost town, few venture onto the back roads, and this
is one of the least-visited parts of the national park.

Nevada Triangle, Trip Route NT-1—Phinney Canyon Road and Strozzi Ranch Road

FROM: U.S. Highway 95, at a point 11.8 miles north of Beatty, Nevada, or 23.7 miles
south of Scotty's Junction, Nevada.

TO: Strozzi Ranch, at the end of the south branch, or Phinney Canyon, at the end of
the north branch.

ROAD CONDITIONS: 19.2 miles one-way to Strozzi Ranch or 20.8 miles to Phinney
Canyon, unmaintained dirt roads, high-clearance recommended first 12.2 miles to
"Strozzi-Phinney Junction," then 4WD recommended beyond into both canyons

SIDE TRIPS: Woodcutter Spring (4WD) and Phinney Mine (hike); access to Mud
Summit Road (Trip Route NT-3).

GENERAL DESCRIPTION: This road starts by crossing gentle hills and the flat, open
valley of Sarcobatus Flat. As it begins to climb into the Grapevine Mountains, the
road splits into two branches. The south branch ends at the Strozzi Ranch and is
generally in good condition except for a few rocky, high centers near the ranch that
make 4WD desirable. The north branch leads into Phinney Canyon where 4WD is
required. This road deteriorates badly as it climbs high into a pinyon pine forest to
end at a steep bedrock cascade. These beautiful areas receive little visitation and are
quite different from the other parts of Death Valley National Park.

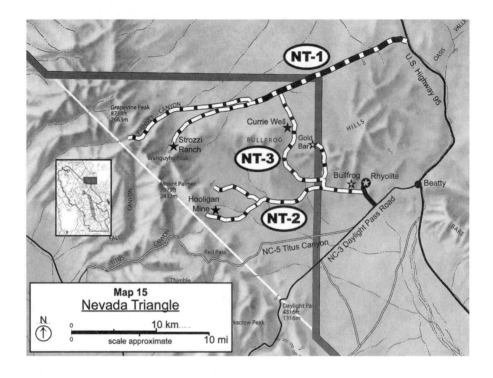

Map 15
Nevada Triangle

N.
0   10 km....
0   scale approximate   10 mi

ROAD LOG MILEAGE   westbound from U.S. Highway 95.

0.0   The turnoff from U.S. Highway 95 is not marked. It leaves
the pavement at a northwest angle between highway mile
markers 71 and 72 (GPS 37°02.954'N 116°46.304'W). A gate
must be opened (and closed behind you) by working a metal
lever on top of the wooden post. Across the wash east of
the highway is the raised dirt grade of the Bullfrog Goldfield
Railroad.

3.8   A dirt road (south) runs to Triple J Spring, named for a ranch.
Several additional roads in the next 3 miles are also related
to ranching and have no particular destinations. Maps show
these roads merging through the Bullfrog Hills to the south,
but because they are outside the national park boundary, they
may be closed with locked gates. This public land is open
cattle range and also supports a population of wild burros.

6.9   **Death Valley National Park** boundary fence and cattle
guard. At the fork in the road, take the left branch. The next
few miles of road are smooth and straight across **Sarcobatus
Flat**. *Sarcobatus vermiculatus* is the true greasewood, a name
often incorrectly given to the creosote bush. Greasewood

366   NEVADA TRIANGLE

Among the most imposing of the ruins at Rhyolite is the façade of the J. S. Cook Bank building.

is a member of the saltbush family that favors the alkaline, clay-rich soil found in this valley. Along this road, however, the related shadscale and hopsage, plus buckwheat, burrobush, Mormon tea, and rabbitbrush are more common.

10.6   **Mud Summit Road** (GPS 36°59.777'N 116°56.891'W, south; 4WD recommended because of sandy washes south of Mud Summit) is a good cutoff route between the Phinney Canyon Road and Rhyolite. It is described as Trip Route NT-3. The north extension of the road reaches the park boundary after 1.7 miles. It is in very bad condition as it crosses about 30 miles of the alkaline clay of Sarcobatus Flat. It is not a recommended route, but it eventually reaches Bonnie Claire on Nevada State Highway 267 (Trip Route N–2).

11.1   The **Las Vegas & Tonopah Railroad** (LV&T) cuts a straight line north-south across the road. It is a bit difficult to see when driving but is just west of a barricade on a side road and next to a large dirt mound. This extension of the LV&T was built between Rhyolite and Goldfield in 1908 and 1909. By that time, the Bullfrog Goldfield Railroad was in operation and there was not enough business for both. In 1914, the LV&T took over the operation of the Bullfrog Goldfield, and these tracks were abandoned less than seven years after they were completed. Fuller histories of both railroads are given in Appendix B.

12.2 "**Strozzi-Phinney Junction**" (GPS 36°59.325'N 116°58.533'W). The south fork drops into Strozzi Wash and then gradually climbs up the canyon to the Strozzi Ranch. The north fork keeps to the elevated alluvial fan for some distance before entering Phinney Canyon. This road log deals with the Strozzi Ranch Road first and then returns to this junction to describe the Phinney Canyon Road.

Branching southwest from this point is a third, faint 4WD road that curves past **Woodcutter Spring** and rejoins the Strozzi Ranch Road at milepoint 15.3.

During the earliest mining at Rhyolite, before there were railroads, wood for mine timbers and buildings was obtained in the local mountains. Extensive logging of pinyon pines was done in the Grapevine Mountains; in some places the mountains were stripped almost bare. A few miles into the Grapevines from Woodcutter Spring was **Mexican Camp** (no road). A National Park Service historical study stated, "The site of Mexican Camp apparently remained on U.S. Geological Survey maps because no one knew what it was and thus dared not take it off the maps." In fact, it was a busy campsite for the Mexican laborers who produced those mine timbers from late 1904 into 1907. Although shown on topographic maps, there is nothing at the site.

4.6 Continuing up the wash on the Strozzi Ranch Road, a scattering of Joshua trees begins to appear on hillsides covered with Great Basin sagebrush, burrobrush, indigobush, spiny menodora, and the regionally endemic Death Valley Mormon tea.

15.3 The poor road that loops past Woodcutter Spring rejoins Strozzi Ranch Road.

15.4 "Strozzi-Phinney Connector Road" (GPS 36°58.506'N 117°01.847'W, north; 4WD required) climbs out of the wash and connects with the Phinney Canyon Road in only 0.4 mile.

16.0 The environment grows wetter as the road climbs into the mountains, and the plants along the wash are joined by large bushes of cliffrose. Soon there are also bright-green mountain joint fir and small pinyon pines.

18.3 The rocks along the canyon are thick beds of volcanic ash, erupted by titanic explosions near Timber Mountain within the Nevada Test Site beginning about 28 million years ago.

19.0 **Strozzi Ranch** (elevation about 6,220 feet) was established by Caesar Strozzi in 1931 as a summer headquarters for

Several buildings, dugouts, and chicken coops remain at Strozzi Ranch.

his cattle- and goat-grazing ranch (he wintered in Beatty). He also raised chickens and vegetables until the property was vacated in 1947. There are remains of two buildings, a "Cousin Jack" dugout, and chicken coops.

19.2 Just above the ranch ruins is a picnic area. Surprising for its remoteness, this area has picnic tables, trash cans, and a chemical toilet. A small nearby spring is marked (the water must be treated before drinking). The better water source of Brier Spring, which yields about 30 gallons per minute, is within the dense grove of willow trees beyond the end of the road.

End of Strozzi Ranch Road; return to Strozzi-Phinney Junction at milepoint 12.2 to continue with the description of Phinney Canyon.

12.2 "**Strozzi-Phinney Junction**." The Phinney Canyon Road branches to the right and for almost 5 miles continues across an old alluvial fan between the two canyons.

15.6 "Strozzi-Phinney Connector Road" (south, 4WD required) provides a convenient connection between the two canyons, saving several miles of backtracking for those who want to explore both.

17.1	The road drops into the wash of **Phinney Canyon** and gets rougher. It deteriorates badly when it reaches the pinyon pine forest and becomes very steep and rocky near its end.
20.5	The **Phinney Mine** (GPS 36°57.390'N 117°06.273'W, north 0.25 mile; hike) is a short walk up a side canyon. It was a two-person operation between 1930 and 1938. The owners put in a tremendous effort. The tunnel penetrates several hundred feet into the mountain. An ore car was run over tracks that extend out of the mine to the end of the dump, and there was a large cabin. Yet the mine was not a success, with a total recorded gold production of only $850.
20.8	The road is closed just beyond a nice campsite at the bottom of a steep, dry cascade with large bedrock boulders. The road used to continue about another 1.2 miles past a mine shaft to the 7,500-foot crest of the Grapevine Mountains (and a spectacular view over northern Death Valley) and then down the canyon past Doe Spring to a small mine.

Grapevine Peak, the highest point in the Grapevine Mountains at elevation 8,738 feet, can be climbed from the pass. The cross-country route (no trail) of about 2.6 miles is north over two false summits, and the peak is indistinct until you reach its top. A similar hike about the same distance south ends at **Wahguyhe Peak** (a Shoshone name that translates as "Pinyon Pine Summit"), the second-highest summit in the Grapevines (elevation 8,628 feet).

End of Phinney Canyon Road.

Nevada Triangle, Trip Route NT-2—McDonald Spring Road

FROM: Bullfrog turnoff on Rhyolite Road, between Nevada State Highway 373 and Rhyolite.

TO: McDonald Spring or Hooligan Mine.

ROAD CONDITIONS: 11.9 miles one-way to McDonald Spring or 12.0 miles one-way to Cave Rock Spring beyond Hooligan Mine, dirt roads with 4WD required.

SIDE TRIPS: None.

GENERAL DESCRIPTION: This is a one-way trip that does not connect with any other through road; it is the same as the southernmost 2 miles of the Mud Summit Road (Trip Route NT-3). It runs through the western Bullfrog Hills into a large wash, where it splits into two branches. Four-wheel-drive vehicles are recommended because of sand in the wash. The north fork ends near McDonald Spring, and the south fork at Cave Rock Spring beyond Hooligan Mine.

The only significant remains at Bullfrog are the walls of the ice house.

ROAD LOG MILEAGE	westbound from Rhyolite Road.
0.0	The turnoff (west) onto Bullfrog Road from paved Rhyolite Road is marked, and the first 0.5 mile to the site of Bullfrog is paved.
0.5	**Bullfrog** was the first big city of the Rhyolite gold rush, but it declined somewhat as Rhyolite grew into the regional metropolis. Even so, Bullfrog had a population of more than 1,000 people during 1907. The only significant ruins are the walls of the Bullfrog Ice House.
1.3	A dirt road (northeast) leads to a miscellany of small gold mines.
1.8	The **McDonald Spring Road** is straight ahead. The wide, graded Mud Summit Road (Trip Route NT-3) curves to the north.
	Located somewhere near this intersection was **Amargosa City**, the first actual town to be established in the Bullfrog Mining District. Never more than a collection of tents, it was soon abandoned in favor of Bullfrog and Rhyolite.
2.6	The east boundary of the national park is at this fence line. The large cuts on the mountainside to the north are at the Original Bullfrog Mine, the discovery location that set off

the Rhyolite gold rush in 1904. Open-cut mining in the 1990s obliterated much of the original mine.

5.3   A dirt road (north; 4WD) connects with the Mud Summit Road but is in very bad condition.

5.5   The prominent cut through the hill a short distance north of the road is the grade of the Las Vegas & Tonopah Railroad (see Appendix B). The large waste dump of the Gold Bar Mine is visible on the mountain on the northeast horizon.

8.2   "**Hooligan Junction**" (GPS 36°53.905'N 116°57.458'W). After winding through the western Bullfrog Hills, the road reaches this junction in the bottom of an unnamed wash. The **Cave Rock Spring Road** (southwest) to the Hooligan Mine and Cave Rock Spring is described first, and the fork to McDonald Spring is then described restarting at this point.

8.5   The majority of the plants in this small canyon are Great Basin sagebrush (*Artemisia tridentata*), commonly but incorrectly called white sage.

10.0   The sagebrush is joined by a dense growth that includes shadscale, hopsage, spiny menodora, burrobrush, Nevada ephedra, and perennial buckwheat.

10.9   **Hooligan Mine** (GPS 36°53.905'N 116°57.458'W, elevation about 4,860 feet), originally called the Happy Hooligan Mine, was part of the Rhyolite boom. The deposit was discovered in May 1905, and by early 1906 the mine supported its own camp, with a boardinghouse, a blacksmith shop, and a store-saloon. A road for high-speed auto stages was constructed, and a nationwide promotion drew investors. However, the ore was high-grade surface enrichment that was quickly worked out, and the Hooligan Mine was abandoned before the end of 1907. Only the mine dumps, sparse wood ruins, and miscellaneous debris remain.

12.0   The road continues beyond the mine up the canyon to the southwest. After passing some stone foundations, it ends about 0.25 mile below **Cave Rock Spring**, a small seep surrounded by a dense thicket of desert broom.

End of Cave Rock Spring Road; return to Hooligan Junction.

8.2   The road to McDonald Spring follows the wash northwest from "Hooligan Junction."

11.5   The variety of plant life along this road is less diverse than that along the Hooligan Mine Road. It is dominated by Great Basin sagebrush and rabbitbrush, with gardens of golden cholla cactus.

11.9   **McDonald Spring** (GPS 36°54.272'N 117°01.060'W, elevation about 5,590 feet). The last 0.3 mile of the road up a small canyon is closed to vehicles. The spring is barely more than a seep, just enough to maintain 2 or 3 shallow pools that are thoroughly fouled by feral burros. Evidently there was once much more water here, as the remains of at least 3 wooden watering troughs and a large metal tank can be seen, all partially covered by a dense stand of desert broom. There are no trees.

End of McDonald Spring Road.

Nevada Triangle, Trip Route NT-3—Mud Summit Road

FROM: Bullfrog turnoff on Rhyolite Road (same as Trip Route NT-2).

TO: Phinney Canyon Road at a point 10.6 miles west of U.S. Highway 95.

ROAD CONDITIONS: 11.6 miles one-way; dirt road generally suitable for high-clearance vehicles but with some deep, sandy washes that may require 4WD.

SIDE TRIPS: Gold Bar Mine area (4WD recommended) and Currie Well (high-clearance).

GENERAL DESCRIPTION: The Mud Summit Road parallels the route of the Las Vegas & Tonopah Railroad. It is a convenient cutoff route between the Rhyolite-Bullfrog mining area and the Phinney Canyon Road to the north.

ROAD LOG MILEAGES	northbound from Rhyolite Road / southbound from Phinney Canyon Road.
0.0 / 11.6	The turnoff at the Bullfrog Road is well marked, and the road is paved to the site of Bullfrog.
0.4 / 11.2	**Bullfrog** was the first big town established at the beginning of the Rhyolite gold rush in 1904. Most of its businesses had moved to Rhyolite by 1907, but it remained as a residential community with a population as great as 1,000 people until the decline in mining in 1908. The only significant ruins are the walls of the ice company.
1.8 / 9.8	The **McDonald Spring Road** (west) is described as Trip Route NT-2. The Mud Summit Road curves north toward the Bullfrog Hills.

                 Located somewhere near this intersection was **Amargosa City**, the first actual town to be established in the Bullfrog Mining District. Never more than a collection of tents, it was soon abandoned in favor of Bullfrog and Rhyolite.

2.2 / 9.4		The Mud Summit Road bears to the west along the hills. The **Gold Bar Road** continues north.

The community of **Gold Bar** (see Appendix A) housed the employees and a few businesses at the Gold Bar Mine and Homestake-King Mine between 1906 and 1909. The two mines shared the same ore body. They eventually merged into a single operation, but as separate operations early in the Rhyolite rush, both built stamp mills. The owners of the Gold Bar were more interested in making speculative money out of investors' pocketbooks than mining, and their mine never showed a profit. The Homestake-King's operators were more serious about mining and made some profit. Modern mining affiliated with the huge LAC/Bullfrog mine near Rhyolite disrupted much of this area and there is little to see except the foundations of the Homestake-King Mill.

0.0   The Gold Bar Road is straight north at the point where Mud Summit Road turns west. The road curves around the east side of Bullfrog Mountain and enters the national park.

3.2   Death Valley National Park boundary.

3.6   At this intersection (GPS 36°55.932'N 116°53.040'W), the road straight ahead led to the recent open-pit mining operation that consumed the Gold Bar Mine ending in 1998. The Gold Bar Road turns to the north.

4.0   On the hillside to the northwest are the extensive concrete foundations of the Homestake-King Mill. For all its huge size, the mill operated for only nine months during 1909.

Not far beyond the mill, the road crosses a gentle summit. About 0.8 mile farther north is an intersection. The road to the northwest encounters a number of sandy washes as it cuts across the slope to reach the Mud Summit Road in 2.5 miles. The road to the northeast leaves the national park and continues past Mud Spring and on to the Phinney Canyon Road after 5.7 miles; explorers might find a locked gate along this road.

End Gold Bar Road.

~3 / 9   This 1.5-mile portion of the road is actually on top of the Las Vegas & Tonopah Railroad (LV&T) grade. Imagine that locomotives pulling Pullman cars once chugged along this hillside.

2.9 / 8.7   Death Valley National Park boundary.

3.0 / 8.6   The **Original Bullfrog Mine** is the series of cuts on the hill north of the road. Its discovery by Frank "Shorty" Harris and Ed Cross set off the Rhyolite gold rush starting in 1904. The ore was phenomenally rich—as much as $4,000 per ton, with masses of free gold studding a lumpy greenish rock that looked sort of like a bullfrog. As was so often the case, the rich ore was confined to the near surface, and the Bullfrog Mine was a relatively minor player in the Rhyolite story. A better producer was the Bullfrog West Extension Mine just to the west. Both properties were scarred by open-strip mining related to the LAC/Bullfrog Mine operation near Rhyolite. That mining ended in 1998.

4.4 / 7.2 The railroad grade curves to the west and is abandoned by the road, which drops into a deep wash. This is the only part of the road that may require 4WD.

~5 / 7 The dumps of the Gold Bar Mine are visible on the mountain to the northeast. Next to the Gold Bar was the Homestake-King Mine.

5.5 / 6.1 A poor road (northeast) ends at a small mine.

6.7 / 4.9 **Mud Summit** (elevation 4,639 feet). The LV&T trains had a stiff climb from Beatty through Rhyolite to this summit and needed extra locomotives to pull the load. The road crosses a railroad spur, where the additional engines used a wye to turn around for the return to Beatty. The main grade of the LV&T is just west of the road.

The long valley north of the summit is Sarcobatus Flat, named for its local concentrations of true greasewood, *Sarcobatus vermiculatus*, a member of the saltbush family. To the south is the Amargosa Valley.

9.1 / 2.5 The road that angles to the southeast reaches the Gold Bar Road after 2.5 miles. Along the way it drops into several deep washes where 4WD may be required.

9.4 / 2.2 **Currie Well** (GPS 36° 58.344'N 116° 55.290'W, west 0.4 mile). Once a stage station, later it was a construction camp and water stop for the LV&T trains. The well is surrounded by a concrete casing but contains only a little stagnant water. The surroundings are littered with trash.

10.2 / 1.4 The **Strozzi's Connector Road** angles to the northwest (4WD) to connect with the Phinney Road near the "Strozzi-Phinney Junction." There are two bad washouts along it and it is not a recommended route.

11.6 / 0.0 **Phinney Canyon Road.** U.S. Highway 95 is 10.6 miles to the east, across Sarcobatus Flat and some low hills. The road west branches to Strozzi Ranch and Phinney Canyon Roads. (See Trip Route NT-1.) The northward continuation of the road reaches Nevada State Highway 267 at the site of Bonnie Claire. It covers 30 miles of very rough and dusty travel and exists only because of the former LV&T. It is not recommended for travel.

Ghost Towns and Mining Camps

Ghost towns and mining camps are numerous in the Death Valley region. To many authorities, the difference between "town" and "camp" is whether or not there was a post office. In either case, these are places where people from diverse backgrounds gathered together to live in hopes of making a living. Often there were commercial businesses such as stores, hotels, saloons, newspapers, and stage lines; services were provided by doctors, barbers, butchers, blacksmiths, and "ladies of the night." Most of these communities existed for only a few months, but a few persisted for several years. They were exciting places to be, filled with hopes and dreams. Now they are abandoned or are bare shadows of what they once were. Sometimes it is difficult to imagine that a remote and quiet mountain valley was home to hundreds of people. Listen for the echoes. See Map 16 for the locations.

■ HOW TO "AGE DATE" A MINING CAMP

In much the same way that a geologist uses fossils to pinpoint the age of a rock, the explorer can date ghost towns and mining camps by their historical debris—the trash of another era. It is rare to find something like a scrap of newspaper that gives a specific date, but bottles, tin cans, and other items exist by the thousands. Like the index fossils of geology, each type was in use for a specific span of time. By comparing a number of pieces of this litter, one can often date a site to within a handful of years.

Bottles are probably the best-known artifacts. Prior to 1902, bottles were formed entirely by hand. The seam from the blowing iron mold ends on the neck of the bottle, and because the glass top was added later by melting and twisting, the seam often curves near the upper end. The Owens Bottle Machine was invented in 1902. It allowed bottles, complete with tops, to be made in one operation, so the seam runs all the way from the bottom of the bottle straight across the top of the

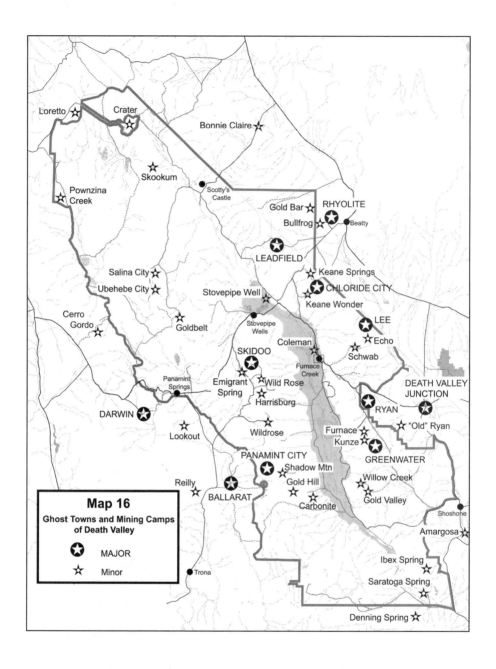

Map 16

Ghost Towns and Mining Camps of Death Valley

⊛ MAJOR

☆ Minor

crown. These bottles gradually replaced the handmade type and were not abundant until 1915.

A second change in bottle style also took place around 1902. Before then the bottle tops were smooth, designed for cork stoppers. After 1902 the tops had enlarged crowns to hold metal caps.

Most of the glass was either brown or green. The famous purple glass was colorless when new but developed the color on exposure to sunlight because of its manganese oxide content. Neither the color itself nor its depth of tint is diagnostic for age, except that this glass chemistry was more common before World War I than it was after the war.

Tin cans changed abruptly around 1915. Before then they were sealed with solder, and a plug in the end of the can is obvious. Lead and tin (the ingredients of solder) were needed for the military efforts of World War I, and the modern way of sealing cans by crimping the seams and lids was developed as a way of conserving the metals.

The change from square to round nails occurred about 1900, as did a switch from thick and soft to thin and hard baling wire.

Most automobiles that existed around mining towns in the earliest 1900s were used as commercial stages. Their owners were excellent and frugal mechanics who rarely threw old parts away. It was not until the 1920s, when cheaper cars became common, that auto parts were dumped. Junked cars were not left behind until the 1930s.

Beer was always bottled until the 1930s. Around 1935 the first beer cans designed to be opened with a large metal "church key" became common. The openers became much smaller about 1950.

As you explore ghost towns and mining camps, see if you can confirm the dates given in this book, or perhaps show that there was activity at the site sometime after it was a living town. Remember, though, that the trash of yesteryear is a valuable resource today. It is as fully protected by the law of the Antiquities Act of 1906 as are Indian artifacts.

Amargosa (no post office)

Amargosa was the company settlement at the Amargosa Borax Works, where borax was produced during the summer months of 1884–1888, when it was too hot to operate the Harmony Borax Works in Death Valley. It is located next to the Amargosa River between the modern towns of Shoshone and Tecopa. It is likely that the employees lived in tents, but a few substantial buildings were constructed too. The remains of adobe brick walls can be seen on both sides of State Highway 178 where there is an interpretive sign just south of the road to Tecopa Hot Springs. **Location**: Trip Route S-3.

Ballarat (post office 1897 to 1917)

There was some settlement at nearby Post Office Spring during the Panamint silver rush in the 1870s, but Ballarat did not become a town in its own right until the Ratcliff, Porter, World Beater, and other gold mines were located in the late 1890s. By 1900 at least 400 people made Ballarat their home. There were several stores, 2

Ballarat was still an active, although fading, community in 1913. (California Division of Mines, courtesy National Park Service, Death Valley National Park)

restaurants, 2 hotels (including the 2-story Calloway Hotel), 3 feed yards, livery and blacksmith shops, and 7 saloons. Ballarat began to decline in 1907, but it has seldom and only briefly been totally vacated. Much of the town is private property and a small store has operated in recent years. Several adobe-wood buildings remain in various states of repair. **Location**: Trip Route PV-2.

Bonnie Claire (post office named Thorp 1905, changed to Bonnie Clare 1906 to 1931)

Established in 1904 as a gold milling settlement at Thorp's Well, Bonnie Claire grew into a major station on the Bullfrog Goldfield Railroad and the Las Vegas & Tonopah Railroad. (The railroads and mining companies spelled the name "Bonnie Claire" whereas the post office used "Bonnie Clare.") The population peaked at about 100 residents in 1907 and then rapidly declined as railroad traffic decreased following the Rhyolite boom. The town thrived again as the shipping point for the Scotty's Castle construction in the 1920s but ceased to exist when the Bullfrog Goldfield rails were removed in 1931. There are only scant remains of the town. The large ruins on the hillside to the northwest are from the more recent Lippincott Lead Smelter (posted private property). **Location**: Trip Route N-2.

Bullfrog (post office 1905 to 1909)

Bullfrog was the first big town established as part of the Rhyolite gold rush. By 1906 it had a population of 1,000 residents supporting its own water company, bank, telephone line, hotels, and chamber of commerce. The growth of Rhyolite nearer the more important mines caused most businesses to abandon Bullfrog by the end of 1906, but it persisted as a residential community into 1909. Collapsed stone walls are scattered around the substantial ruins of the ice house. **Location**: Trip Routes NC-3, or NT-2 and NT-3.

Carbonite (no post office)

It seems that the name would be more correct as "Carbonate," after the Carbonate Mine that was discovered in 1907, but Death Valley archive records show that the name was not applied until the adjacent Carbonite Mine was opened in 1908. The ore was rich silver-bearing cerussite (lead carbonate). Jack Salsberry, of the Greenwater and Ubehebe districts, bought the mines, merged and incorporated them as a single operation, and built a road over Salsberry Pass to the Tonopah & Tidewater Railroad. The town was described in a Goldfield, Nevada, newspaper as "a desert metropolis constructed with tents, rocks, tin cans, dry goods boxes, whiskey bottles, and anything that comes handy." There were a few stores, and famous "Tex" Rickard of Goldfield proposed building a hotel-saloon complex at this "latest sensation of the Western mining world." The mining declined around 1913 and then boomed again as a source of lead during World War I. The property was reorganized in 1923, and the Queen of Sheba Mine farther south on the same ridge became more important. It was worked as recently as 1972. The existing ruins date from the 1930s or later. **Location**: Trip Route SC-3, Side Trip SC-3e.

Cerro Gordo (post office 1869 to 1887, reestablished 1889 to 1895)

The silver deposits at Cerro Gordo were discovered and worked by Mexican miners in 1865, but the boom began in 1867 when the properties were fully developed by Mortimer Belshaw and Victor Beaudry. By 1872 as many as 150 ingots *per day* of smelted silver-lead concentrate were being shipped to the port of San Pedro near Los Angeles. To avoid wagon transport through the sandy ground along the south shore of Owens Lake, two small steamboats, the *Bessie Brady* and *Mollie Stevens*, transported goods across the lake. Mining began to decline in 1879 after more than $17 million of ore had been produced. Minor production continued until a second boom of zinc mining began in 1912. Some production continued into the 1970s. The property is privately owned. The American Hotel, built in 1871, has been restored and is operated as a bed and breakfast, and the old general store sells curios and snacks. Profits are used by the Cerro Gordo Historical Society, a nonprofit 501(c)(3) organization, to maintain the town for "restorative reuse." **Location**: Trip

Route SV-1, Side Trip SV-1a, but better access via the Yellow Grade Road from State Highway 136 near Keeler, California.

Chloride City (no post office)

Silver was discovered on Chloride Cliff in 1871 by A. J. Franklin, and although "Franklin Mines" was never a town as such (there were only seven employees), it merited a constructed road that ran through the south end of Death Valley and on to Daggett on the Mojave River (the same route was adopted by the 20-mule team borax wagons a decade later). Mining ended in 1873 because the distance to market made the operation unprofitable. Franklin held his claims and faithfully did the annual assessment work for 30 years and was finally rewarded when his mine became part of the South Bullfrog Mining District during the Rhyolite boom. As many as 100 people lived in the new town of Chloride City by early 1906. The town's life was brief, however. Much of the financial backing came from San Francisco, and the earthquake of April 1906 led to an almost complete closure of Chloride City's mines by that summer. Sporadic mining continued into 1941. The last of the original wooden buildings collapsed in the early 1970s, but foundations, "Cousin Jack" ruins, leveled tent sites, and debris, plus corrugated metal shacks from later years, remain scattered over a wide area. **Location**: Trip Route NC-4.

Coleman (no post office)

Largely forgotten is Coleman, the residential settlement adjacent to Harmony Borax Works for the Chinese miners who harvested borax ore on the salt flats; the non-Chinese workers who operated the processing plant apparently all lived at Furnace Creek Ranch (then known as Greenland Ranch). The adobe walls are the remains of two of the only three actual buildings in the town. One was a warehouse, the other an office. All the other structures at Coleman were flimsy tents and tent cabins, and there is no trace of their having been here. **Location**: Trip Route NC-1.

Crater (no post office)

Mining for sulfur began in the northern end of the Last Chance Range in 1929. Much of the product dug right out of the ground was more than 40 percent sulfur and easy to process into a 99 percent–pure shipping product. A small company camp with as many as three dozen permanent employees existed from 1929 into 1931. Talk of a railroad led some people to lay claim to potential business sites nearby, but mining was temporarily suspended in late 1930 and there were numerous changes of ownership in the following years. Minor production resumed in the later 1930s and again in the 1950s until sulfur dust exploded and destroyed the processing plant. The Crater Mine was most recently operated in the mid-1990s. It is now inactive and not expected to ever be worked again. Some reclamation has been performed, and this property, deleted from the national park expansion in 1994, will probably be quitclaimed and added to the park area in 2010. None of the old buildings remain but there are some collapsed structures and rusting machinery. **Location**: Trip Route BP-1.

Darwin (post office 1875 to 1953)

Darwin was a true city almost as soon as it was established after the 1874 discovery of silver. At the end of 1875, the town had wide, finished streets, pressurized fire hydrants, a thriving newspaper, and 78 registered businesses supported by as many as 1,400 people (one government report claimed a population of 5,000). Two smelters were operating and a third was added by 1878, but as was so often the case, mining soon declined. Comparatively little production took place from 1880 until 1937, when the Anaconda Corporation began working the Darwin–Mt. Ophir Mine for lead and zinc. That operation continued into 1952. More small-scale mining took place as recently as the 1990s. Darwin has never been completely abandoned and had a census population of 54 in 2000. Buildings that date as far back as 1876 remain, but most of them are on private property. There are no commercial services. **Location**: Trip Route W-2.

Death Valley Junction (no post office; mail via Ryan post offices 1907 to 1930 and via Death Valley post office 1930 to present)

Death Valley Junction owes its existence to the Tonopah & Tidewater Railroad and borate mining. It was established in 1907 when a branch line of the T&T was built west to Ryan and the Lila C. Mine. The town reached its peak population of about 100 residents after the borax mill was moved from Ryan. In 1923, in response to strongly negative publicity generated by a magazine article by famous author Zane Grey, the company built a large civic center to house corporate offices, a sleeping dormitory, gymnasium, billiard room, ice cream parlor, and the Corkhill Hall theater. When the mines at Ryan shut down around 1927, much of the building was remodeled into the Amargosa Hotel to serve tourists arriving on the T&T. More recently, Corkhill Hall was renovated into the Amargosa Opera House. It, the hotel, and a gift shop are the only commercial enterprises in Death Valley Junction. **Location**: Trip Routes E-1, E-4, or E-5.

Denning Springs (no post office; mail via Crackerjack post office 1907 to 1909)

At about the same time as the Greenwater copper boom, similar deposits containing a bonus of silver were found in the Avawatz Mountains south of Death Valley. Several competing towns sprang up, of which Crackerjack was the most important. Denning Springs is the only one of these communities now accessible on public land (all the others are within the Fort Irwin National Training Center of the U.S. Army). It has been reported that as many as 60 people lived at Denning Springs between 1907 and 1912, although it seems clear that the population was much smaller than that most of the time. The place was intermittently occupied as a millsite until 1937. Dugouts, 2 or 3 fallen rock walls, a few leveled tent sites, and litter remain. Denning Spring itself is little more than a seep. The official name is "Denning," after Frank Denning, who discovered the Ibex Mine in 1883. However, the spring apparently was originally named after Andrew Demming, a member of the government boundary survey of 1861. It is curious that two names so similar should be associated with such a remote place. **Location**: Trip Route S-2, Side Trip S-2b.

Echo (post office applied for but not established)

Echo hardly merits mention, as it barely existed as a tent town before being abandoned. Official announcement of the townsite was made in March 1907, and an application for a post office was submitted immediately. Although a few people settled there, the community lasted no longer than a few weeks. The location was near the pass at the top of Echo Canyon, between the towns of Schwab and Lee. There are no remains other than a sparse scattering of old cans. **Location**: Trip Route E-1, Side Trip E-1a; or Trip Route E-6.

Emigrant Springs (no post office)

Shortly after the discovery of the Cashier and Eureka mines at Harrisburg in 1905, numerous prospectors congregated at Emigrant Spring and Upper Emigrant Spring, which were then and still are among the best and most convenient water sources in Emigrant Canyon. A few businesses at the upper spring, including a restaurant-saloon, a boardinghouse, and a store, served a loose population said to have briefly reached as high as 200 (although that figure seems extreme). Everything in the town occupied tents on the canyon floor, so not a trace remains. **Location**: Trip Route W-3.

Furnace (post office 1907)

Furnace was established near the copper mines about 5.5 miles northwest of Greenwater. It was initially intended only as the mine camp for the Furnace Creek Copper Company. It never was much more than a tent city, but in February 1907 it did boast several stores and restaurants, a saloon, a hotel, and its own post office to serve a population said to have been as high as 500. The town was abandoned within months of its founding. Sparse wooden debris, a few dugouts, and a collapsed mine frame mark the site. **Location**: Trip Route E-3, Side Trip E-3a.

Gold Bar (no post office)

Less than three months after the discovery of the Original Bullfrog Mine that set off the rush to Rhyolite, the Gold Bar Mine was located on the next mountain to the north. A few months later, the Homestake and Gold King mines were claimed immediately north of the Gold Bar. Mills were constructed at both mines, and the workers and their families lived in the community of Gold Bar. By early 1907 the town consisted of numerous tents and at least 15 wooden buildings that included a restaurant-saloon, boardinghouse, and feed yard. The presence of 18 school-age children led to a fund-raising campaign to establish a school. However, the Gold Bar Mine shut down in April 1908 and the merged Homestake-King Mine in 1909, and Gold Bar was no more. Much of the site was encompassed by open-pit mining in the 1990s, and nothing remains of the town. The massive concrete foundations of the Homestake-King Mill are on the hillside to the northeast. **Location**: Trip Route NT-3.

Goldbelt (no post office)

Goldbelt hardly qualifies as a bona fide town, but it was the center of three mining episodes that attracted small populations. The first two lasted only a few weeks each. In 1904, only months after finding and then selling his share of the Original Bullfrog Mine that set off the Rhyolite gold rush, "Shorty" Harris located rich gold ore near Goldbelt Spring. It proved to be a tiny deposit, but it attracted enough attention for the Gold Belt Mining District to be established, and paper plans for a city of Goldbelt were drafted by a Goldfield, Nevada, promoter. Eleven years later, in 1915, Harris found tungsten ore in the same area, as did Bob Eichbaum, who later founded the Stovepipe Wells Hotel. Tungsten was needed because of World War I, so these discoveries attracted considerable attention. A few people settled at Goldbelt and a store-saloon operated for several weeks in 1915. Again, the deposits were small and the excitement was brief. Years later the site was occupied by a talc mining company, and the collapsed wooden buildings remain from that development. **Location**: Trip Route RH-1.

Gold Hill (no post office)

Gold was found near the upper end of Warm Spring Canyon in the 1870s, but there was no significant development of the properties until 1889. Gold Hill then enjoyed a brief existence when "jewelry-rock" was found in some of the prospects and attracted several dozen prospectors to the area. As was so often the case, most of the deposits proved to be small except those of the Death Valley Mining Company, which continued to operate for several years. Whether any actual businesses ever operated at Gold Hill is unlikely, but at least there was a company boardinghouse with food service. A few rock walls and level tent pads mark the townsite but probably date to the 1920s. **Location**: Trip Route SC-3, Side Trip SC-3f.

Why these men were standing in Greenwater's main street in late 1906 or early 1907 is unknown. The town was at its peak despite the thin scattering of buildings and desolate appearance. (Unknown photographer, courtesy National Park Service, Death Valley National Park)

Gold Valley (post office approved but not established)

Copper was located a few miles south of Greenwater early during the Greenwater excitement. The "rush" to the mining camp of Willow Creek was brief, but in June 1907 placer gold and then lode deposits were found in the same valley. By 1908, the town of Gold Valley, with 96 surveyed city blocks and 1,200 lots for sale, welcomed several businesses including a store, saloon, barber, and lodging house. The Death Valley Chug Line auto stage provided transportation. The population reached as high as 200 people before the gold played out later in 1908. Small dumps of tin cans and bottles amid leveled tent sites and low stone walls remain at Gold Valley, and a view from the hill east of the townsite reveals the faint grid of the city's streets. **Location**: Trip Route E-3, Side Trip E-3c.

Greenwater (post office 1907 to 1908)

The copper deposits at Greenwater were actually discovered during the 1880s, but they were ignored at that time, probably because those prospectors realized that copper in that remote place could not be mined for a profit. However, by 1904 the electrification of the world made copper much more valuable. New claims were

filed and the mines were promoted as the richest in the world. Among the owners were famous industrialists Charles Schwab, John Brock, and William Clark. Those names were all it took to attract millions of dollars in investments. By mid-1906 the Greenwater district had a population of more than 1,000 and was growing rapidly. Initially, Ramsey (also called Copperfield) was just one of several camps. Kunze was the largest of the growing towns, but because it was in a narrow canyon that left little room for growth, the entire population moved to Ramsey—renamed Greenwater—starting in November 1906. The city that expected to be the richest in the world had streets 150 feet wide, the *Times* and *Miner* newspapers, and the *Death Valley Chuck-Walla* magazine. "Tiger Lil's" popular den of infamy was "conveniently" located next door to the post office. Three different railroads were proposed, and surveys for the Greenwater Death Valley Copper Mines & Smelter Company Railroad and for the Tonopah & Greenwater Railroad were actually completed. But everything was built on promotion. Although the discovery ore was very rich, it was supergene and limited to the surface. Only a single shipment of ore ever left the district, and it was worth less than $3,000. The boom was quickly over, and by July 1908 only one store remained when the post office was closed. Almost nothing but a sign marks the townsite. **Location**: Trip Route E-3, Side Trip E-3a.

The old Emigrant Springs restaurant tent had been moved to someplace near Harrisburg when this photo was taken in May 1908. Compare with the Emigrant Springs photo in Chapter 15, Trip Route W-3. (Author's collection)

Harrisburg (no post office)

Frank "Shorty" Harris and Jean Pierre ("Pete") Aguereberry, en route to the Fourth of July celebration in Ballarat, discovered the Eureka and Cashier mines on July 1, 1905. Harris let word of the discovery slip out, and by September "Harrisberry" had a population in excess of 300 people (note the town's original name). However, there were only two deposits of merit, and the discovery of richer gold at Skidoo in January 1906 led to the gradual abandonment of Harrisburg. Harris sold out a year later. Aguereberry became the sole owner of both mines, and he worked in and lived near the mines until 1938. Three cabins remain at his Aguereberry Camp, and there are some dugouts at Harrisburg. **Location:** Trip Route W-3, Side Trip W-3c.

Ibex Spring (no post office)

There were three distinct episodes in the history of Ibex Spring. First, in 1883 it began service as the millsite for the Ibex Mine, a silver deposit located a few miles away in Buckwheat Wash. Around 1907, people searching for the "Lost Bethune Mine" found new deposits of silver rich enough to warrant what was described as "a fine camp," with several buildings and a few businesses. The heyday of Ibex Spring was during the 1950s and 1960s, when it was a residential town during talc mining

The Keane Wonder Mill was one of the few in the Death Valley region to have had a long and successful life, operating intermittently from 1907 into 1942. (Unknown photographer [Gordon Chappell files], courtesy National Park Service, Death Valley National Park)

in the mountains to the north. The decaying buildings and exotic fan palm trees date to that time. **Location**: Trip Route S-4, Side Trip S-4a.

Keane Springs (post office approved in 1906 but not established)

As part of the Rhyolite boom, the central Funeral Mountains area was organized as the South Bullfrog Mining District. Being the only reliable water source in the district, Keane Spring became a center of activity. The first to start a business was S.A.C. Nelson, who put up a large tent in February 1906 to house his Death Valley Mercantile Company; the Porter brothers, of Rhyolite, soon provided competition with a general store. By May the town consisted of those 2 stores plus 2 office buildings, a boardinghouse, a saloon, a corral and stable, and numerous tent houses. Kimball's Stage provided daily transportation to Rhyolite. Lots were being sold by the Keane Springs Land Company for $25 to $100 each, with water guaranteed to every doorstep. Improved streets had been put in, and tents were available for rent. But the boom did not last. Even though it had the water, Keane Springs lost out to larger and better-developed Chloride City and Keane Wonder. Only 2 wood-frame buildings were erected and they, along with nearly everything else in the town, were washed away by a flash flood in 1909. A few leveled building sites and rock walls remain. **Location**: Trip Route NC-4.

Keane Wonder (post office 1912 to 1914)

The gold deposit at the Keane Wonder Mine was discovered in January 1904. The ore was so rich that the property was sold three times before large-scale mining got underway. A tramway between the mine on the mountain and the 20-stamp mill at the townsite was completed in 1907. The peak of the activity was prior to 1912, but a post office, a school, and 2 or 3 businesses operated until 1914 at the mouth of the canyon below the Keane Wonder Mill. Additional mining extended into 1942, and a total of more than $1 million in gold was produced. Extensive ruins of the mill, mine, and tramway remain. **Location**: Trip Route NC-2 but temporarily closed to public entry as of September 2008 because of dangerous collapsing structures and heavy-metal contamination at the millsite area.

Kunze (no post office by this name; site of original "Greenwater" post office 1906 to 1907)

Kunze was the most important original townsite of the Greenwater boom and the first location of the Greenwater post office and newspapers. By late 1906 it boasted 5 restaurants, 5 saloons, 2 general merchandise stores, 2 barbers, a shoe repair, a lawyer, 3 lodging houses, several commercial corrals, the *Greenwater Times* newspaper, and a post office. Located in a canyon between the towns of Furnace and Ramsey, Kunze was abandoned starting in November 1906—because the canyon left no room to grow, the entire population moved to Ramsey, which by then had been renamed Greenwater. The canyon has helped preserve the site, for there are more remains at Kunze than at either Greenwater or Furnace. **Location**: Trip Route E-3, Side Trip E-3a.

Leadfield (post office 1926 to 1927)

Published stories about Leadfield and promoter Charles C. Julian, claiming a lack of ore and stock swindles, have almost always been wrong (including the one in the first edition of this book). In fact, Leadfield could well have been a real town with a significant lifetime. It was established on the basis of good lead ore with a significant silver content, and Julian's promotions were completely honest in their assessments about the mine and its risks to investors. The ore was initially found in 1905 but at that time was judged too low in grade to justify shipping. The property was relocated as the Western Lead Company in 1924. Well-known mine owner and promoter Jack Salsberry became the company president in 1925 and started the construction of the Titus Canyon Road. By the end of 1925 Ramsey Street boasted several businesses including a 16-room boardinghouse, and people were rapidly buying residential lots on Salsberry and Brundage streets. In February 1926 C. C. Julian bought a controlling interest in the mine, which had 140 employees. He put together a promotional package, and on March 15 more than 1,180 people arrived on 94 auto stages for a luncheon, speeches, and tours, and the boom was

Leadfield was near its peak when photographed by Alan Ramsey in early 1926. (County of Inyo, Eastern California Museum)

underway. By that time, six companies other than Western Lead were also mining properties that extended 2 miles both north and south of the growing town. The *Leadfield Chronicle* newspaper began publication in late March (although it was actually printed in Tonopah, Nevada), the town plat of 93 city blocks with 1,749 lots was officially approved in May, and the post office had mail for 200 people the day it opened in August 1926. There were even plans for an airport with daily Los Angeles–Leadfield service. Unfortunately, that was nearly the end. In October, when the tunnel of the Western Lead Company reached the ledge of lead-silver ore, what it found was nearly barren. Coupled with the financial problems of C. C. Julian, the company shut down and the other mines quickly followed. On the post office's last day of business in January 1927, there was mail for only one person. Numerous stone and concrete foundations and several corrugated metal buildings remain. **Location:** Trip Route NC-5.

Lee (post office 1907 to 1912)

Lee was an important sidelight of the Rhyolite boom. Gold was discovered on the east face of the Funeral Mountains in 1905, and a town was quickly established. The approaching Tonopah & Tidewater Railroad no doubt helped, because the tracks were to pass only a few miles away. Lee quickly became the commercial center for the entire Funeral Mountain mining area. By mid-1907, the city boasted a population of more than 500 people who supported a telephone service, the *Lee Herald* newspaper, a post office, 4 restaurants, a meat market, 4 dry-goods stores, the 2-story Lee Hotel, 3 feed yards, 4 office buildings, 4 saloons, an assay office, an ice house, a miner's supply shop, a barbershop, a civil surveyor, a stockbroker, 2 lumberyards, 2 lodging houses, a stage station, a Miner's Union hall, and 2 doctors. (Especially interesting was "Mrs. Dr. Sellier [who] uses electricity in her profession . . . and is also a phrenologist, palmist and telepathist, and is endowed with physic and magnetic power to a wonderful degree.") The T&T announced that it would build a spur line into town from the station at Leeland, Nevada. But when the financial panic of 1907 hit, the boom was over. By June 1908 the business community was down to only 3 stores, 1 saloon, and 1 restaurant. Lee was completely abandoned by January 1912. Extensive debris of tin cans and bottles, stone walls, dugouts, and leveled building sites mark Lee. There are additional remains at Lee Annex, a suburb astride the state line about a mile east of Lee. **Location**: Trip Route E-6.

Lookout City (post office as Modock 1875 to 1879) and Minnietta (no post office)

The Modoc Mine was located in 1875 and the town of Lookout was established on the adjacent ridge, high above Panamint Valley. By the end of 1875 there were 2 general stores, 3 saloons, a slaughterhouse, a hotel, and the post office of Modock (so named to avoid confusion with Modoc County in northern California, and because there was already a town of "Lookout" in Mono County, California). One of the owners of the mine was Senator George Hearst, the father of more famous William Randolph Hearst. The silver ore was smelted on site, using charcoal produced at the Wildrose Charcoal Kilns (Trip Route W-3, Side Trip W-3d), and transported across the valley via the Lookout Coal & Transportation Company. Production decreased and the town was practically vacated in 1879, leaving behind the usual assortment of foundations, wooden debris, and trash. Small-scale mining at the Modoc continued into 1897.

Just over the ridge south of Lookout was the Minnietta Mine. Although discovered in 1876 as part of the Modoc excitement, it was not extensively worked until 1895. The Minnietta turned out to be a better mine property than was the Modoc. Production was continuous into the 1920s, and for a while enough people were in the area to support 2 or 3 stores and 1 saloon in the community of **Minnietta**, on the canyon floor below the mine. Rock walls remain of that settlement, and there is 1 remaining building and extensive ruins at the Minnietta Mine. **Location**: Trip Route PV-1.

Loretto (no post office)

At the turn of the twentieth century, the use of electricity and the wiring that goes with it, plus new metallurgical needs, produced a demand for copper that existing mines could not meet. Any rich deposit was subject to great excitement and promotion. Loretto's deposits had been found before 1888, but it was not until

The twenty-stamp Surprise Valley Mill and smelter at Panamint City could process 40 tons of ore per day. The silver was cast into large ingots that weighted several hundred pounds apiece and could be shipped across the desert without fear of robbery. The mill started operating in June 1875, but there was little ore and it shut down less than two years later. One of the brick smokestacks, the stub of another, and stone foundations are still standing above the remote ghost town. (U.S. Borax [Rio Tinto] Collection, courtesy National Park Service, Death Valley National Park)

1906, when Charles Schwab bought a controlling interest, that there was much development. A town of solid stone buildings, with businesses supported by 150 people, was erected along Loretto Wash. The company built a smelter for $2 million. However, although the ore was tremendously rich, it was limited to the near surface. The official value of mine production was zero, and Loretto was all but abandoned by the end of 1907. Fallen stone walls and level building sites are scattered along the wash on the south side of the road in northwestern Eureka Valley. **Location**: Trip Route BP-1.

Panamint City (post office 1874 to 1877 and 1887 to 1895)

Silver ore, rich enough to attract the attention of important mine owners at Virginia City, Nevada, was discovered high in Surprise Canyon of the Panamint Mountains in 1873. Panamint City grew in the narrow canyon below the mines.

Only wide enough for one main street, the town was more than a mile long. A population of 2,000 residents was reached by February 1874, when the city had numerous businesses including stores, hotels, restaurants, a brewery, and the *Panamint News* newspaper. There were more than two dozen saloons and Martha Camp's "girls," but no church. The Los Angeles & Independence Railroad was being surveyed from Los Angeles, and Shermantown was established on the floor of Panamint Valley to serve as the railway station. But although the large Surprise Valley Mill started up in 1875, the ore was shallow and most of the mines had closed by 1877. Numerous foundations are scattered along Surprise Canyon, and extensive walls and the tall, brick smokestack of the smelter dominate the head of the canyon. **Location**: Trip Route PV-2.

Pownzina Creek (no post office)

The community of Pownzina Creek is something of a mystery. The mines of the widespread Waucoba Mining District were discovered in early 1872, and within six months the settlement near the Waucoba Mine was busy enough that the *Inyo Independent* newspaper suggested that it might eventually become the location of the Inyo county seat. The settlement still existed and was called Pownzina Creek in 1875, when a mine report referred to it by name, saying it was "the camp and center of activity" 4 miles north of mines referred to as the "Waverley Group" (probably the same as the Bunker Hill and other mines) and that it would probably be the mainline destination of the Los Angeles & Independence Railroad (which was never constructed; see Appendix B). With that, however, information about the place came to an end. Whether any commercial businesses ever operated at Pownzina Creek is unknown. Indeed, although it was probably near Waucoba Spring, even the town's exact location is uncertain. **Location**: Trip Route SV-1.

Reilly (post office 1883)

Silver was discovered here in 1875 but no developments took place until Edward Reilly founded the Argus Range Silver Mining Company in February 1882. He spent about $200,000 on developments before he sold out the following December for $500,000. Construction of a mill had just started at that time. The town was company owned and included a boardinghouse, general store, corral and stable, and post office; the 60 or more workers lived in rock structures they built themselves. Amid many delays, the mill did not operate until October 1883, and the short-lived post office had closed even before the mill was completed. By that time it was clear that the rich silver ore was confined to small near-surface pockets. Ultimately, the mine and mill yielded only about $21,000, and the property was on the auction block in February 1884. Minor operations continued for a few more years under new owners, but production was never significant. The stone walls of two dozen small buildings and the foundation of the mill remain. **Location**: Trip Route PV-1.

Rhyolite (post office 1905 to 1919)

Frank "Shorty" Harris and Ed Cross discovered the Bullfrog Mine in 1904, and the rich ore led to the last great American gold rush. By 1907 the Bullfrog District had a population of around 10,000 people, more than half of whom lived in the modern city of Rhyolite. Three railroads—the Bullfrog Goldfield, Las Vegas & Tonopah, and Tonopah & Tidewater—crossed the desert to serve the mines. Nearby towns included Amargosa City, Aurum, Beatty, Bonanza, Bullfrog, Gold Bar, Gold Center, and Pioneer. The financial panic of 1907 caused mines to close nationwide, but Rhyolite felt little impact until 1909. By the 1910 census, Rhyolite's population was just 611; in 1922 it was reported as 1. There are a few imposing ruins, most notably the 3-story J. S. Cook Bank building, which partially remained in use until 1919 because it contained the post office. **Location**: Trip Routes NC-3 or NT-2.

Ryan (post office at "Old" Ryan 1907 to 1915, at "New" Ryan 1915 to 1930)

There were two towns named after John Ryan, a long-time Pacific Coast Borax employee and then the general manager of the Tonopah & Tidewater Railroad. The first, "Old" Ryan, was at the Lila C. Mine, about 6 miles southwest of Death Valley Junction. It had a population as great as 300 people from 1907 to 1915. When new mines were opened above Furnace Creek on the west side of the Greenwater Range and the Death Valley Railroad was built to serve them, the Lila C. shut down and Old Ryan was abandoned. "New" Ryan grew to support a population of 250. After those mines closed in 1927, Ryan was renamed Devar, and some of the buildings were remodeled as the Death Valley View Hotel. The hotel, post office, and railroad ceased operations in 1930. With no future use for mining, Rio Tinto Borax has donated the "New" Ryan townsite to the non-profit Death Valley Conservancy. In the future, the ghost town is expected to become a science and education center. **Locations**: Old Ryan on Trip Route E-1, Side Trip E-1c; New Ryan on gated private property visible from Trip Route E-2.

Salina City (post office applied for but not established) and Ubehebe City (no post office)

The Ubehebe Copper Mine was found in 1875, but there was no mining or promotion of the deposit until the Greenwater copper rush of 1906. Jack Salsberry claimed that in a shaft only 85 feet deep he could prove the existence of 50 million tons of high-grade copper ore worth more than a billion dollars. The town of Salina City (also called Latimer) was founded about 2 miles northwest of The Racetrack dry lake. By late 1906 there were 20 tents near a company store, a tent hotel, a feed yard, and 2 saloons, and an application for a post office had been filed. The rival town of Ubehebe City was established closer to the Lead King (Lippincott) Mine south of The Racetrack. The Ubehebe boom was over before the summer of 1908,

The volunteer fire department was showing off its fire hoses on Rhyolite's Golden Street during the Independence Day parade of July 4, 1908. Note the three-storey J. S. Cook Bank building in the center background of the photo. (Photograph by A. E. Holt, courtesy National Park Service, Death Valley National Park)

Rhyolite's Golden Street had a forlorn appearance when Frank "Shorty" Harris took this photograph in the late 1920s. The J. S. Cook Bank is the three-storey building in the right background. (Special Collections & Archives, Merrill-Cazier Library, Utah State University

and essentially nothing remains of either tent camp. **Locations**: Trip Route RH-1, Side Trip RH-1a.

Saratoga Springs (no post office)

Saratoga Springs was a major water stop for the summertime 20-mule-team borax wagons operating out of the Amargosa Borax Works from 1883 to 1888. A combination saloon-store and a blacksmith shop were established to serve the teamsters. Between 1902 and World War I, exploration for nitrate deposits took place in southern Death Valley, and the freshwater pools at Saratoga Springs were the most likely place for a new settlement. A population as great as 50 people frequented a couple of stores, a livery stable, and at least 1 saloon. Finally, in the 1930s the Saratoga Water Company operated a bottling plant and health resort at the springs. A dugout with ruined stone walls dates to the borax days of the 1880s, faint foundations scattered along the old road at the base of the hill north of the springs are left from the nitrate prospecting circa 1909, and leveled tent cabin sites remain from the health resort. **Location**: Trip Route S-2, Side Trip S-2c.

Schwab (post office 1907)

Schwab was another result of the Rhyolite boom. After its initial founding, the townsite was owned by three enterprising women—Gertrude Fessler, a stockbroker from Chicago; Mrs. F. W. Dunn, a wealthy matron from San Bernardino; and her daughter, Mrs. Helen H. Black—who incorporated the town by issuing 30,000 shares of stock. It was not a lasting success. Located in Echo Canyon on the Death Valley side of the Funeral Mountains, the population reached 200 residents in early 1907 but nearly everyone was gone by the end of that year. Part of the town's trouble was its remote location. Lee, on the other side of the mountains, was much more accessible. That Schwab's owners disliked saloons, gamblers, and "ladies of the night" did not help either. A few leveled but overgrown tent pads, broken bottles, and rusty cans serve to locate the site. Farther up Echo Canyon is the Inyo Mine, where structures sometimes misidentified as Schwab date to mining between 1928 and 1940. **Location**: Trip Route E-1, Side Trip E-1a.

Shadow Mountain (no post office)

Mineral deposits that contained free-milling gold plus silver and copper were discovered in early summer 1907 in the upper reaches of Johnson Canyon. Prospectors flocked to the area, given the claims that Shadow Mountain was bound to surpass both Skidoo and Lee, and perhaps even Greenwater and Rhyolite, in fame and fortune. Well more than 100 mining claims were filed, and at least two companies capitalized for $1.5 million each were founded. By the fall of 1907, Shadow Mountain (which some wanted to rename as "Panamint") was described as a camp

A fine cookhouse and other buildings were put up at Saratoga Springs by the Pacific Nitrate Company in 1909, but they were soon abandoned when it was realized that the nitrate deposits were of unmineable low grade. (Photograph attributed to A. W. Scott Jr., courtesy National Park Service, Death Valley National Park)

whose development proceeded "full steam," and an application for a post office was anticipated. And then came the bust, when one of the mines was professionally examined and declared to be "a fake, pure and simple." Almost nothing other than small mine prospects remains in the canyon, near Panamint Pass above Hungry Bill's Ranch. **Location**: Trip route SC-3, Side Trip SC-3c.

Skidoo (post office 1906 to 1917)

Prospectors trekking between Rhyolite and Harrisburg found gold veins in 1906, and a town quickly grew in the gentle valley to the north. The population by early 1907 was around 500 people, and the town's 100 buildings included several stores, the *Skidoo News* newspaper, a bank, telephone and electric companies, and a brewery. Litigation and the financial panic of 1907 led to Skidoo becoming a one-company town, and there was a slow decline in production and population until 1917. There are almost no remains of the town—Skidoo has been picked clean of "souvenirs." The Skidoo Mill west of the town has undergone restorative stabilization by the National Park Service but is not safe to enter. **Location**: Trip Route W-3, Side Trip W-3b.

Skookum (no post office)

Mining claims were located and some placer gold production took place on Chuckawalla Hill in the Last Chance Range in 1909, but real development of the Skookum Mining District did not take place until the properties were taken over by the Death Valley Gold Mining Company in January 1927. Many people disappointed by the Leadfield promotions headed for Skookum. By March 1927 the town boasted 4 wooden buildings and 20 tents along with many prospectors living in cars. Apparently there were as many as 150 people at the site. The only business in town was a saloon in the back of a truck, but a store and service station (apparently called Desert Gold) operated at Sand Spring, the closest permanent water source about 10 miles to the north. The company produced a small amount of high-grade gold ore, but Skookum was another place built mostly on promotion. Death Valley's last gold flash-in-the-pan was abandoned before 1928. Nothing other than mine dumps and sparse trash remain at the site (GPS 37°02.387 N 117°34.502 W), which is not accessible by vehicle since the road washed away long ago. **Location**: Trip Route BP-1.

Stovepipe Well (no post office)

From 1906 into 1908, when the cities of Rhyolite and Skidoo were both booming, the road between them was very busy. The only source of water on the floor of Death Valley was at Stovepipe Well, a hole with marginally palatable water at the east edge of the sand dunes. By February 1907 the Stovepipe Well Road House was in operation. A pump was installed at the well, and water "of the best quality" was made available to all who arrived there. The settlement was served by Tucki Consolidated Telephone and Telegraph Company (the first telephone in Death Valley itself) and the Kimball Brothers stage. At its peak in 1907, it included a boardinghouse, grocery store, restaurant, saloon, feedstore and corral, and bathhouse. In commenting about a proposed resort, the *Rhyolite Herald* newspaper noted, "If the sun cure has merit, it could be worked to the limit at Stovepipe." Meals and beds were available for 75 cents each. As mining declined, so did business, and the Stovepipe Well Road House faded away. Nothing remains of the community at the end of Old Stovepipe Road. **Location**: Trip Route N-1, Side Trip N-1a.

Wild Rose (no post office)

Wild Rose had a brief existence in mid-1906. The gold discoveries drew hundreds of prospectors to the area around Harrisburg Flat, and the competing towns of Harrisburg and Emigrant Springs were established. Then, after the founding of

Skidoo, the promoters of Wild Rose hoped to replace the other two towns with one community along the road to Skidoo. The town was surveyed, a few lots were sold, and perhaps one or two businesses were opened, but the community was abandoned within a few weeks. The town left no remains and, in fact, its exact site is unknown except that it was near the base of the hills just south of the Skidoo Road. **Location**: Trip Route W-3, Side Trip W-3b.

Wildrose (no post office)

Mining began at the Modoc Mine on the west side of Panamint Valley in 1875. The ore was very rich—some people contend that if the "Lost Gunsight Lode" was ever found, then it was at the Modoc—but to properly smelt the ore, large tonnages of charcoal were needed. The Wildrose Charcoal Kilns were built by James Honan and O. B. Morrison for the Lookout Coal & Transportation Company, and the town of Wildrose served the kiln operators. In 1877, when the population bolstered by prospectors reached more than 100 people, the town boasted a boardinghouse, store, blacksmith and livery, and saloon; a teacher was hired to tutor several school-age children. The charcoal kilns remain but the town is completely gone. **Location**: Trip Route W-3, Side Trip W-3d.

Willow Creek (post office applied for but not established)

As part of the Greenwater boom, in July 1906 copper was located in a deep valley several miles south of Greenwater. A camp called Copper Basin was established but quickly abandoned (apparently in part because its Mormon founder would not allow a saloon); it had such a brief existence that nobody knows exactly where Copper Basin was located. In its place was nearby Willow Creek, located just above Willow Springs, then and now the best water source in the southern Black Mountains. By the end of 1906 Willow Creek had 3 stores, 3 saloons, 2 lodging houses, and a corral. When paying silver values were discovered in some of the mines in May 1907, the town grew even more. A plat map showing 31 city blocks with 300 lots for sale was approved by Inyo County, and a post office was applied for. But then gold was found a few miles away in the same valley. The town of Gold Valley came into existence and Willow Creek was largely abandoned within weeks. Foundations of what was probably the first, largest, and last store remain but there is little else at the site. **Location**: Trip Route E-3, Side Trip E-3c.

Railroads of Death Valley

The silver and gold discoveries at Tonopah, Goldfield, and Rhyolite, Nevada, created the last great mining rushes in U.S. history. Beginning in 1900, people flocked to the desert in and around Death Valley, locating uncountable numbers of mining claims and creating a regional population in the tens of thousands. Large-scale mining operations always required efficient transportation. Great tonnages of mining supplies were required, ore had to be shipped, and people moved in and out of the cities. In the days before highways, the only realistic transportation option was the railroad.

Between 1873 and 1922, 14 different railroads, 1 monorail, and 1 large tram were constructed or proposed in the immediate Death Valley area. Only some of them actually entered into what is now the national park area, but they all had a strong effect on Death Valley's history. The routes of all of these lines are shown on Map 17.

■ CONSTRUCTED RAILROADS
Bullfrog Goldfield Railroad (BGRR)

In the early days of the Rhyolite gold rush, financial and mining interests at Tonopah sought to ensure their position by building a rail line south from Goldfield. Despite the numerous active mines, however, neither of the existing railroads—the Tonopah Railroad and the Goldfield Railroad (soon merged into the single Tonopah & Goldfield Railroad)—was doing well. The promoters of the new Bullfrog Goldfield Railroad had difficulty arranging the financial support needed to build the new line. Work did not begin until May 1906, and it took almost a year for the rails to reach Rhyolite.

Had construction been more efficient, the BGRR story might have had a happier ending, but by the time the railroad arrived in Rhyolite, the Las Vegas & Tonopah

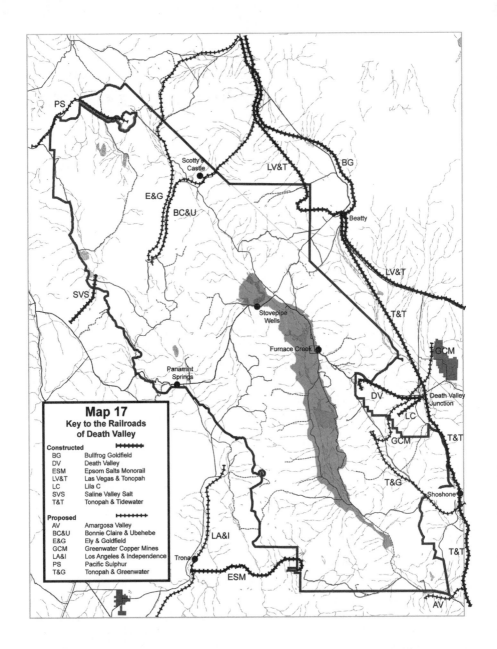

Map 17
Key to the Railroads of Death Valley

Constructed
BG	Bullfrog Goldfield
DV	Death Valley
ESM	Epsom Salts Monorail
LV&T	Las Vegas & Tonopah
LC	Lila C
SVS	Saline Valley Salt
T&T	Tonopah & Tidewater

Proposed
AV	Amargosa Valley
BC&U	Bonnie Claire & Ubehebe
E&G	Ely & Goldfield
GCM	Greenwater Copper Mines
LA&I	Los Angeles & Independence
PS	Pacific Sulphur
T&G	Tonopah & Greenwater

Railroad (LV&T) had already been serving the town for 6 months. There really was not enough traffic to support even one railroad, and the situation deteriorated further when the Tonopah & Tidewater Railroad (T&T) arrived later in 1907. The BGRR was a resounding failure.

The T&T took over the operation of the BGRR in 1908. Although the BGRR was still officially a separate entity, the phrase "T&T all the way [to Goldfield]" was advertised. Through complex financial wrangling, including a reissue of BGRR stock, the LV&T assumed the operation in 1914. The LV&T abandoned its own rails between Rhyolite and Goldfield, and for a brief time the BGRR (and therefore, the LV&T) actually made a profit.

During World War I, all of the railroads in the United States were taken over by the U.S. Railway Administration. In 1918 the administration judged the LV&T to be an unnecessary route. The LV&T was dismantled the next year, and a new agreement was drafted for the BGRR to once again be operated by the T&T.

The BGRR was still a separate entity, but it no longer owned any rolling stock of its own. All locomotives and cars bore the T&T insignia as the line muddled through the 1920s. There was a brief surge in business while Scotty's Castle was being built, but it was not enough to sustain the railroad. The last train ran in January 1928. When the tracks were torn up, many of the crossties were hauled to Scotty's Castle for firewood. They can still be seen in "Tie Canyon" along the interpretive trail at the Castle. Otherwise, only traces of the grade can be found at Rhyolite, along Oasis Valley near Springdale north of Beatty, and southeast of Goldfield.

Death Valley Railroad (DVRR)

Death Valley's borax mining operations were completely shut down in 1893 to allow new discoveries to be worked in the Calico Mountains near Barstow, California, much closer to market. The Calico deposits were quite small, however, and they were nearly exhausted by the early 1900s. F. M. "Borax" Smith and his Pacific Coast Borax Company returned to Death Valley. The first new producer was the Lila C. Mine in the foothills of the Greenwater Range. When Smith's Tonopah & Tidewater Railroad (T&T) reached Death Valley Junction, a branch line was built to serve the Lila C.

From its beginning, the Lila C. was only temporary. Larger and richer deposits lay in the mountains farther west, at the head of Furnace Creek Wash overlooking Death Valley. The T&T applied for permission to issue construction bonds on a new branch, but the request was denied, in part because of Smith's personal financial difficulties. He was virtually bankrupt as a result of poor land investments in Oakland, California, and he lost control of both the mining company and the railroad as a result. New management took over and incorporated the Death Valley Railroad Company in early 1914. The 20-mile line was in operation before the end of that year. The route of the DVRR crossed the same summit that is now followed by State Highway 190, dropped into Dead Horse Canyon, wound around the north end of the Greenwater Range, and ended at the new town of Ryan. To serve the mines, a "Baby Gauge Railroad" with tracks only 2 feet apart was extended beyond the end of the DVRR.

The DVRR was successful, and the colemanite borax ore it hauled ensured business for the T&T as well. But the death knell had begun to ring even before

Death Valley Railroad #1 was photographed near Pyramid Pass in August 1914, when the railroad was still under construction. Identical locomotive #2 is now on display at the Furnace Creek Ranch Borax Museum. (County of Inyo, Eastern California Museum, Harry Holgate Collection)

the DVRR had been built. A huge deposit of pure borax was discovered in 1913 at Kramer (now Boron) on the Mojave Desert. That deposit was deep underground and required substantial development, but when full production began in 1925, the end of the Death Valley operation was near. The last ore train ran to Death Valley Junction in October 1927.

In an effort to replace the mineral revenue with tourist dollars, Pacific Coast Borax built the Furnace Creek Inn below the mines near the floor of Death Valley. Ryan was renamed Devar (an acronym for **De**ath **Va**lley **R**ailroad), and some of its buildings were remodeled into the Death Valley View Hotel. By arrangement with the Union Pacific Railroad (UP), packaged tours were put together, with transportation via the UP, T&T, and DVRR, and accommodations at one of the two hotels. The visitors toured Death Valley on busses borrowed from Zion National Park in Utah, and they could see the mines by riding the Baby Gauge. Unfortunately, the tourist traffic did not match expectations. The Union Pacific terminated its part of the agreement in 1930, and the DVRR was left with no business at all.

The last train ran on March 15, 1931, and the railroad was dismantled. Some of the timbers from a large trestle in Dead Horse Canyon were used in an expansion of the Furnace Creek Inn. Today, the grade of the DVRR can be seen south of State Highway 190 on both sides of Pyramid Pass 10 miles west of Death Valley Junction, and also from the Dante's View Road near State Highway 190. Although it had interim service elsewhere, Locomotive No. 2 is now on display behind the Borax Museum at the Furnace Creek Ranch.

The "Baby Gauge Railroad" connected borate mines to the Death Valley Railroad at Ryan. After mining ended, it was used to carry tourists around the mining district until 1950. (Photograph by Dwight Bentel, courtesy National Park Service, Death Valley National Park)

The Baby Gauge fared somewhat better. It continued to ferry tourists among the mines until an expensive liability lawsuit forced it to stop running in 1950. Plans to reopen it around 1960 did not materialize. Some rails are still in place, and the numerous switchbacks and rockworks of the line are visible northeast of the Dante's View Road 7 to 8 miles south of State Highway 190.

Epsom Salts Monorail (ESM)

Thomas Wright, a florist and part-time prospector from Los Angeles, found a rich deposit of Epsom salt (magnesium sulfate) in the Crystal Hills near Wingate Pass in southern Death Valley in 1917. Epsom salt was quite valuable at the time, but transportation from the remote site was needed. The first solution to be considered was a railroad across Death Valley to a connection with the Tonopah & Tidewater Railroad. A second plan was for another railroad, this one running west to a connection with the Trona Railway, which was (and still is) serving the mineral operation at Searles Lake. Although that route was only 28 miles long, it included prohibitive grades. Something different was necessary.

The Epsom Salts Monorail was innovative but ultimately unsuccessful as the weight of the ore overburdened the monorail's engines. Here it was near Layton Pass in 1924, in the Slate Range within what is now Range B of the Naval Weapons Station–China Lake. (Photograph by James Boyles, Trona, CA, courtesy National Park Service, Death Valley National Park)

Wright investigated a monorail system, which was not unique but still was innovative at the time. He tinkered with several designs, one of which was granted a patent in 1923. By then the actual construction was underway, and the Epsom Salts Monorail was put into operation in 1924.

The mining operation was successful at first, when nearly pure Epsom salt could be scraped from the ground with garden hoes. The workers lived in Crystal Camp, where there was a substantial stone house and 5 frame buildings. The ore was simply shoveled into balanced bins on the sides of the monorail cars. Unfortunately, two problems soon developed. The ore became increasingly impure within a few feet of the ground surface, and the monorail engines suffered repeated breakdowns because of the heavy loads. Over $1 million had gone into the construction, but the last train ran in June 1926 after just two years of operation.

Attempts to sell the mine and monorail were unsuccessful. The rail and most side timbers of the ESM were removed sometime during 1934. Some of the wooden A-frames apparently remain in the Slate Range and near Wingate Pass, both areas that are off limits within the Naval Air Weapons Station–China Lake Range B. The mine, Crystal Camp, and the easternmost portion of the monorail are within the national park and accessible to hikers, but there is little to see.

Las Vegas & Tonopah Railroad (LV&T)

In the early 1900s, Montana Senator William A. Clark and his brother J. Ross Clark were building the San Pedro, Los Angeles & Salt Lake Railroad (commonly known as the "Salt Lake Route" and later part of the Union Pacific) through southern Nevada. It was completed in 1905, just as the Rhyolite boom was getting underway.

Francis M. "Borax" Smith proposed building a line called the Tonopah & Tidewater (T&T) between Las Vegas and Rhyolite. The Clarks' transcontinental rails would provide the connection to the outside world. Their verbal agreement seemed firm enough for Smith to begin construction. But then Senator Clark reneged on the deal by refusing to let the T&T rails join those of the Salt Lake Route. Smith was forced to relocate the T&T. Clark purchased everything the T&T had built and started the construction of his own Las Vegas & Tonopah Railroad in late 1905.

Construction progressed with few delays, and the first train made the entire 117-mile run between Las Vegas and Beatty in October 1906, and the rails were pushed over the steep Doris Montgomery Summit into Rhyolite by mid-December. The LV&T found itself with relatively little business, however, and the route was not extended farther north to Goldfield until late 1907. By that time both the Bullfrog Goldfield Railroad (BGRR) and the T&T were also serving Rhyolite. There was hardly enough business for one railroad. Miners' strikes further reduced business, and the nationwide financial panic of October 1907 forced many mines to close. Within months of its completion, most of the traffic on the LV&T consisted of people leaving town.

In 1914, through complex financial arrangements, the LV&T took over the operation of the BGRR. Since the two railroads had duplicate routes between Beatty and Goldfield, the LV&T rails were abandoned. For a brief time the combined BG–

LV&T was able to turn a profit, but the end of the LV&T was near. With the U.S. entry into World War I, all American railroad operations were assumed by the U.S. Railway Administration. The LV&T was judged to be unnecessary—its Tonopah & Tidewater nemesis followed a shorter route to the large market of Los Angeles. The LV&T ceased all operations in October 1918 and was dismantled during 1919. The first railroad to reach Rhyolite was the first to disappear.

Little remains of the LV&T. Its alignment between Las Vegas and Beatty is almost completely covered by U.S. Highway 95. The grade is visible north of Nevada State Highway 373 just west of Beatty, cutting across the hillsides northwest of Rhyolite, and in the hills south of Goldfield; long but remote stretches of the grade slice across Sarcobatus Flat within and north of the park's Nevada Triangle. The fancy LV&T station building in Rhyolite stands at the head of the city's main street, but it is closed and fenced.

Lila C. Railroad (LCRR)

The Lila C. Railroad was a legal entity. After the Death Valley borax operations were moved from the Lila C. Mine to "New" Ryan in 1915, the old Tonopah & Tidewater rails that had served the Lila C. were taken up. It was later decided that a sufficient borate stockpile remained at the Lila C. to merit rebuilding the line. Using very light, temporary rails, the Lila C. Railroad was built on top of the old T&T grade in 1920. It survived for three years as a secondary route operated by the Death Valley Railroad.

Saline Valley Salt Company Tram (SVSCT)

The Saline Valley Salt Company Tram was not a railroad, but it deserves mention here. Constructed because a railroad into Saline Valley was impractical because of steep grades, it was a technological masterpiece at the time, larger and more elaborate than any other tram in the world.

To this day, Saline Valley does not contain a paved road, but in the 1870s and 1880s it was "just over the hill" from the major mining areas of Cerro Gordo and Darwin and was extensively prospected. People flocked to the Waucoba District in 1872, and a brief gold rush at Marble Canyon just north of the valley led to a temporary population of around 200 people around 1882. More significant were borax and salt deposits that had been discovered on the floor of Saline Valley in 1874. Men named Conn and Trudo built a borax-processing plant in 1889. Small but successful (it was the most prolific source of borax in the United States in the early 1890s), the plant produced borax continuously until 1895 and then sporadically into 1907.

Near the borates were extensive flats of 100 percent pure salt. Various people tried to devise an economical way to work them. A railroad was proposed as early as 1882, but it would have been prohibitively expensive to negotiate the steep mountain canyons. Not until 1911, when the Saline Valley Salt Company decided to build the tramway over the Inyo Mountain to Owens Valley, did significant developments occur.

The tram climbed more than 7,000 feet up tortuous Daisy Canyon to the crest of the mountains and then down more than 5,000 feet to the Owens Valley terminus, all in a distance of less than 13 miles. There were 265,000 feet (more than 50 miles) of cable, 1.3 million board feet of timbers, 650 tons of metal bolts and braces, and 5,000 large sacks of cement. There were 286 steel buckets, each with a capacity of 12 cubic feet, strung on the cables between 39 major and 120 secondary towers. And it worked! The first load of salt was shipped in 1913, and the tram was also used in 1914 to ship copper ore from the Blue Jay Mine in the Ubehebe District on the east side of Saline Valley.

Unfortunately, the costs of construction overburdened to company, which was unable to make a profit and pay the bills. By 1920 the salt fields and tram were owned by U.S. Steel in lieu of payment for the tram's cables. Subsequent lessees built the first road into Saline Valley in the early 1920s, but the use of trucks also proved overly expensive. Finally, in 1928 the Sierra Salt Company purchased all the holdings from U.S. Steel. The tram was refurbished and put back into use that December, but the operation ceased in 1933.

The metal cables and buckets were removed years ago, and most of the woodwork and buildings disappeared through time and vandalism. A few of the towers still stand in the mountains, especially along Daisy Canyon, and near the Saline Valley terminus.

Tonopah & Tidewater Railroad (T&T)

The last of Death Valley's railroads alphabetically, the Tonopah & Tidewater was also the last of the lines to be completed and the last to be abandoned. When borax mining returned to Death Valley at the Lila C. Mine in 1904, Francis M. "Borax" Smith first tried to use a steam-traction engine to serve the mine. When that failed, a railroad seemed to be the only solution. The Tonopah & Tidewater Railroad was incorporated in July 1904, one month *before* the discovery of the Original Bullfrog Mine that precipitated the Rhyolite gold rush. Smith arranged for the T&T to connect at Las Vegas with the Clark brothers' transcontinental San Pedro, Los Angeles, and Salt Lake Railroad (the "Salt Lake Route," now the Union Pacific), which was nearing completion. It was a gentlemen's agreement, and the arrangement seemed firm enough. Smith's crews prepared about 30 miles of grade before the Clarks reneged on the deal by refusing to allow the rails to join. The sudden rush to Rhyolite had attracted Senator Clark's attention. He took over the grade already completed by the T&T and used it as the beginning of his own Las Vegas & Tonopah Railroad (LV&T).

Smith was forced to relocate his T&T. With a new agreement between the Atlantic & Pacific Railroad (later the Santa Fe), the T&T construction was restarted at Ludlow, California. Progress was rapid at first, and the rails reached 75 miles north to Dumont (near what is now the southeastern corner of Death Valley National Park) in May 1906. The T&T seemed to be keeping pace with the competitive LV&T. But the rugged gorge of the Amargosa River lay between Dumont and Tecopa. In the summertime heat, progress through the canyon was excruciatingly slow—barely 1 mile per month. The T&T did not reach Tecopa until February 1907. By then, the LV&T was already running into Rhyolite. Smith had lost the race, but he pressed on. The T&T finally reached Gold Center (just south of Beatty and Rhyolite) in October 1907, a full year after the LV&T and 6 months behind the Bullfrog Goldfield Railroad (BGRR). All three lines suffered from a serious lack of business, which was exacerbated by the financial panic that also happened in October 1907. However, the T&T had one great benefit over the LV&T and other regional railroads—the Death Valley borate deposits that had been its original goal.

A side spur had been shipping ore from the Lila C. Mine since August 1907, and it continued to provide regular business until 1914, when the company began to develop larger deposits on the Death Valley side of the mountains. The intention was for the T&T to extend the Lila C. branch on to the new mines, but permission to issue construction bonds was denied by the government because of Smith's personal financial problems. The reorganized mining company countered by incorporating the new Death Valley Railroad (DVRR). The DVRR hauled ore to Death Valley Junction, where it was partially processed before shipment toward Los Angeles via the T&T. At times there was additional revenue in clay, marble, salt, and other borates, but when the Death Valley mines shut down in 1927 the T&T was near its end. The railroad was able to muddle through the 1930s, but the last train ran south on June 14, 1940.

Remains of the Tonopah & Tidewater Railroad are abundant along much of its route. The grade parallels State Highway 127 much of the way from Baker, California, to Nevada. It is especially visible as a straight line across Silver Lake a few miles north of Baker and between Shoshone and Death Valley Junction where the raised grade is often only a few feet from the pavement. The ruins of concrete bridge abutments and wooden drainage culverts exist all along the route, but little else remains. Any rail spikes, station walls, and other remnants that might have been left behind were removed by collectors long ago.

■ PROPOSED RAILROADS

At least seven other railroads that would have penetrated into or very near modern Death Valley National Park were proposed. Five reached the official paperwork stage, some issued financial bonds, and a few began actual construction. Briefly, these rail lines are as follows.

The raised dirt grade of the Tonopah & Tidewater Railroad runs beside State Highway 127 for much of the distance between Death Valley Junction and Shoshone.

Amargosa Valley Railroad (AVRR)

It seems that "Avawatz" would have been a more geographically accurate name than "Amargosa." Salt, gypsum, and celestite (strontium sulfate) deposits at the base of the Avawatz Mountains at the south end of Death Valley were located 1906 by W. A. "Whispering" Kelly and Thomas Osborne, who founded the Death Valley Salt Company. Exploration of the deposits was conducted during 1909 by the United States Smelting Company, but there was no sale because the salt was judged too impure for use as a smelting flux. In 1912, W. G. Kerckhoff bought the property and established the Avawatz Salt and Gypsum Company, and he proposed the construction of the Amargosa Valley Railroad to extend 18 miles to a connection with the Tonopah & Tidewater Railroad. No construction took place then, nor when the T&T considered building its own branch line in 1921.

Bonnie Claire & Ubehebe Railroad (BC&U)

The 1906 development of copper properties near The Racetrack began a mining rush similar to that at Greenwater. John Salsberry developed the Ubehebe Mine, established the town of Salina City, and had construction bonds worth more than $1 million issued to finance the Bonnie Claire & Ubehebe Railroad. Surveying of the 48-mile line was accomplished and some grading on the route was done near

Bonnie Claire, Nevada, but the project was dropped after the financial panic of 1907.

Bonnie Claire was the proposed terminus of three other railroads, in addition to the BC&U. All three followed the same route north from Bonnie Claire. The Bonnie Claire and Gold Mountain Railroad apparently actually constructed (or at least graded) three miles of its 7-mile route during 1907, and the Gold Mountain Railway was separately proposed later that year. In 1910, the Bonnie Clare & Gold Mountain Railroad (note the change in spelling, "Clare" versus "Claire") actually purchased rails and a locomotive from the defunct Mohave & Milltown Railroad (in Arizona), but it performed no groundwork before folding.

Ely & Goldfield Railroad (E&G)

The mineral deposits of the Ubehebe Mining District were so rich in lead that in late 1908 (about 1 year after the demise of the Bonnie Claire & Ubehebe Railroad) the ownership of the Tonopah & Tidewater Railroad (T&T) proposed the new Ely & Goldfield Railroad to ship ore all the way across Nevada to the smelter at Ely, Nevada, which needed lead-bearing ore as a flux. The proposed route from Goldfield, Nevada, went across Lida Valley and dropped through Tule Canyon to reach upper Death Valley Wash, which then was followed south past Ubehebe Crater and on to Racetrack Valley. Like many other financial propositions, these plans did not progress and no physical construction took place.

Greenwater Death Valley Copper Mines & Smelter Company Railroad (GCM)

The copper ore at Greenwater was said to be the richest known in the world. To process the ore, the Greenwater Death Valley Copper Mines & Smelter Company expected to build a mill at Ash Meadows, Nevada, where water is abundant. The company's anticipated railroad through Greenwater Canyon was surveyed at a cost of $11,073. At the same time, the Las Vegas & Tonopah Railroad (LV&T) modified its incorporation papers to allow a branch line to connect at the smelter. Nearly as quickly as these moves were accomplished, the supergene, surface-enrichment nature of the ore had been proven. No construction took place.

Los Angeles & Independence Railroad (LA&I)

Had its construction been completed, the Los Angeles & Independence Railroad (also known as the Panamint Railroad) would have been the first to reach the Death Valley mining country. Its basis was the silver of Panamint City with an extension to Owens Valley, and in 1875 it was also suggested that the actual terminus would be in the Waucoba Mining District of northern Saline Valley. Surveying began in 1874 and reached from Santa Monica, through Los Angeles, and over Cajon Pass to the vicinity of Victorville before the project was abandoned. Tracks were actually laid between Santa Monica and downtown Los Angeles, and that alignment was later purchased by the Southern Pacific Railway Company.

Pacific Sulfur Railroad (PS)

The construction of a rail line to connect the sulfur mines at Crater, in the Last Chance Range of far northern Death Valley, with the Carson & Colorado Railroad in Owens Valley was considered in 1930. It was probably never more than a passing thought, since the mines themselves were temporarily shut down later in 1930.

Tonopah & Greenwater Railroad (T&G)

As one of the many developments that were part of the brief Greenwater copper boom in 1906–1907, the Tonopah & Tidewater Railroad planned a semi-independent, connecting line that was to run 37 miles between the T&T station at Zabriskie (between modern Shoshone and Tecopa) and Greenwater. Although the line was formally incorporated in 1907 and surveying determined two possible routes, no construction took place.

Visitor Services and Activities

This land and its resources belong to everyone, and you share the responsibility for their protection. There are a few basic but critical rules that must be obeyed by everyone who visits Death Valley National Park.

- It is illegal to collect or disturb any animal, plant, fossil, or other natural, historical, or archaeological feature. These are irreplaceable resources.

- Never feed any of the wildlife. Unnatural food is harmful, and habituated animals are more dangerous than are fully wild animals.

- All vehicles—including bicycles, motorcycles, 4WD vehicles, all-terrain vehicles (ATVs), and motor homes—must stay on designated roads. The desert landscape is fragile, and tire tracks remain visible for decades. All motorized vehicles and their drivers must be properly licensed and street-legal; unlicensed dirt bikes and ATVs are not allowed under any circumstances.

- Pets must be either confined or leashed (maximum 6-foot leash length) at all times.

Persons who fail to abide by these rules may be penalized by severe fines and/or jail sentences.

Note: in the following sections, all prices and dates are provided only to serve as a guide as to what you may expect when you visit the park. They are correct as of Spring 2014 but are subject to change.

■ NATIONAL PARK SERVICES

Entrance Fees

Per Vehicle (for 7 days) **$20**

Individual (bus passenger, bicycle, walk-in for 7 days) **$10**

America the Beautiful Pass (annual free admission to all national parks) **$80**

Senior Pass (62 years or older and U.S. citizen; lifetime free admission) **$10**

Medical Emergencies

Dial 911 from any local telephone. Only basic first aid is available within Death Valley. There is no physician in residence, and a nurse only may (or may not) be available through the Furnace Creek Resorts. As needed, ambulance and helicopter life-support services provide at-cost emergency transportation to regional hospitals.

Furnace Creek Visitor Center

Open: All year, 8:00 AM to 5:00 PM daily; evening hours for special events

Park Headquarters (adjacent to Visitor Center), Monday through Friday, 8:00 AM to 4:00 PM

Telephone: (760) 786-3200 (recording after hours)

Web site: www.nps.gov/deva

Orientation Programs: An introductory 12-minute slide program is presented every 30 minutes at the Visitor Center Auditorium.

Evening Programs: November through April, presented nightly in the Visitor Center Auditorium. Check at the Visitor Center for current topics and schedules.

Daytime Activities: November through April, Park Service rangers present a wide variety of walks, talks, and slide presentations about Death Valley's cultural and natural history. Times and locations vary; check at the Visitor Center for the current schedule.

Book Sales: The Death Valley Natural History Association operates a bookstore that offers an extensive range of books and other park-related materials.

Death Valley Natural History Association (DVNHA)

The DVNHA is a nonprofit organization dedicated to the preservation and interpretation of the natural and human history of Death Valley National Park. The organization publishes and distributes park literature; sells books by other publishers; rents the "GPS Ranger" self-guided tour device; and provides personnel, supplies, and equipment to the National Park Service in support of interpretation. The DVNHA also operates book sales at the Scotty's Castle Visitor Center and the Stovepipe Wells Ranger Station.

The Death Valley '49ers art show at the Furnace Creek Museum and Visitor Center.

Ranger-led hikes are among the many interpretive activities offered by the National Park Service.

Web site: www.dvnha.org
Telephone: (800) 478-8564 or (760) 786-2146
Mailing Address: P.O. Box 188, Death Valley, CA 92328
Membership: $20 and up, provides a 15 percent discount on all purchases.

Park visitors can tour the grounds of Scotty's Castle on their own and take ranger-led tours of the house.

Scotty's Castle (Death Valley Ranch)

Scotty's Castle and the Scotty's Castle Visitor Center and Museum operate year-around. Admission to the grounds is free during operating hours. There are fees for tours; the prices given are as of Spring 2014.

Winter Hours: 8:30 AM to 5:00 PM
Summer Hours: 9:00 AM to 4:30 PM
Telephone: (760) 786-2392

House Tour: Available on a first-come, first-serve basis on the day of the tour (advance reservations for groups only). Tours last approximately 50 minutes.

Adults (under age 62 or without Senior Pass)   **$15**
Adults with Senior Pass or Access Pass   **$7.50**
Children (ages 6 to 15)   **$7.50**
Children (under age 6)   **Free**

Underground Tour: Available on a first-come, first-serve basis on the day of the tour, November through April (summer tours dependent on staff availability). Tours last approximately 1 hour. This tour is not handicap-accessible.

Adults (under age 62 or without Senior Pass)   **$15**
Adults with Senior Pass or Access Pass   **$7.50**
Children (ages 6 to 15)   **$7.50**
Children (under age 6)   **Free**

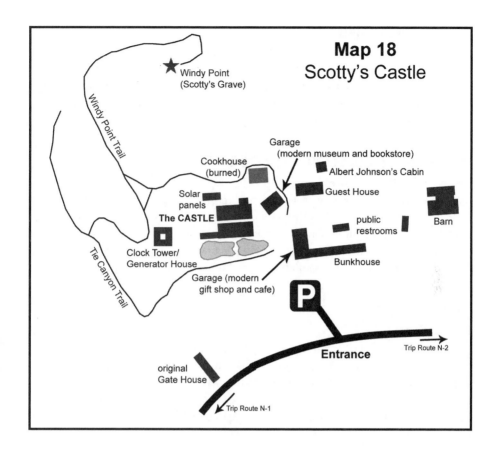

Map 18
Scotty's Castle

Windy Point
(Scotty's Grave)

Windy Point Trail

Garage
(modern museum and bookstore)

Cookhouse
(burned)

Albert Johnson's Cabin

Solar
panels

Guest House

The CASTLE

public
restrooms

Barn

Clock Tower/
Generator House

Bunkhouse

The Canyon Trail

Garage (modern
gift shop and cafe)

P

original
Gate House

Entrance

Trip Route N-2

Trip Route N-1

Lower Vine Ranch Tours: Lower Vine Ranch, the actual residence of Death Valley Scotty, is normally closed to the public. However, special tours are sometimes offered on a limited basis. Tours last 2.5 hours and cover 2+ miles of walking in the open over rough ground (not handicap-accessible); restrooms and other facilities are not available during the tour. When available, advance reservations via the Scotty's Castle telephone are strongly recommended.

Fee: **$20**, limited to 15 people per tour.

Other Facilities: Self-guided walking tours of the Castle grounds are available at no charge; a guidebook is available at the ticket office or Visitor Center. Entry to the Visitor Center and Museum is free; includes a DVNHA outlet.

Beatty Information Center

The Beatty Information Center, formerly located in the town of Beatty, Nevada, no longer exists.

Stovepipe Wells Ranger Station

A ranger station is located on State Highway 190 just east of Stovepipe Wells Village. Open daily from mid-October through April but infrequently during the summer; hours vary, depending on staff availability. The staff can provide general information, activity schedules, and maps and accept park entry fees. A small selection of books is for sale by the DVNHA.

■ NATIONAL PARK SERVICE CAMPGROUNDS

The National Park Service operates nine developed campgrounds plus three other designated camping areas, as follows. The camping limit is 14 days at the Furnace Creek Campground, which is the only campground that accepts reservations (see below); the camping limit in all other parts of Death Valley National Park is 30 days per calendar year. Note that there are no RV hookups in any NPS campground; campsites with hookups are available only at Stovepipe Wells Village and Panamint Springs Resort.

Reservations:

For Furnace Creek Campground (all sites) and Texas Spring Campground (group sites only), campsites can be reserved through the federal system either by telephone at (877) 444-6777 or via the Web site www.recreation.gov. Fees are $18 per night ($12 per night in summer) at Furnace Creek Campground, and $40 per night for group sites at Texas Spring Campground. All other campgrounds are first-come, first-serve.

Campground Regulations:

Quiet hours are from 10:00 PM to 6:00 AM. Generators may be operated between 7:00 AM and 7:00 PM, but are prohibited at all times at the Texas Spring Campground.

Fires are permitted only where fireplaces or campfire rings are provided. Where none are provided, fires are restricted to portable stoves or barbecues kept off the ground. Ground fires are prohibited everywhere in the park. Wood gathering is not permitted; firewood is generally available for sale at the general stores at Furnace Creek Ranch and Stovepipe Wells Village.

Pets must be kept on a leash no longer than 6 feet at all times, or otherwise confined. There is a maximum of 4 pets per campsite.

EMIGRANT CAMPGROUND

Elevation: 2,100 feet. 10 sites, tents only. Fee: free. Season: open all year. Location: at Emigrant Junction on State Highway 190, 9 miles west of Stovepipe Wells Village. Facilities: Water and flush toilets; no fires.

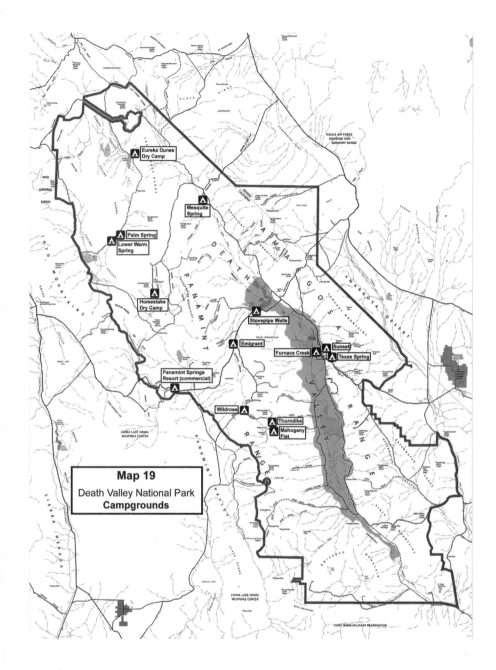

Map 19
Death Valley National Park
Campgrounds

EUREKA DUNES DRY CAMP

Elevation: 3,200 feet. 10 informal sites at picnic tables. Fee: free. Season: open all year. Location: adjacent to the Eureka Dunes, 9.6 miles south of Big Pine Road. Facilities: chemical toilet, tables, trash cans, and fire grates. Camping also permitted on spur roads 0.5 mile southeast with no facilities and no fires.

FURNACE CREEK CAMPGROUND

Elevation: –196 feet. 136 sites. Fee: $18; $12 mid-April to mid-October. Season: open all year, stay limit 14 days. Location: near Furnace Creek Visitor Center. Trailer, motor home, and tent-only sites. Facilities: Water, tables, fire pits, flush and pit toilets, and dump station. Some sites are shaded by trees. See reservation information at the start of this section.

HOMESTAKE DRY CAMP

Elevation: 3,770 feet. No set sites. Fee: free. Season: open all year. Location: near the end of Racetrack Valley Road, 29 miles south of Ubehebe Crater and 9.6 miles south of Teakettle Junction. Facilities: chemical toilet but no other facilities; no fires.

LOWER WARM SPRING CAMPGROUND

Elevation: 1,380 feet. No set sites. Fee: free. Season: open all year, depending on road conditions. Location: 45.9 miles north of State Highway 190 or 32.4 miles south of Big Pine Road via Saline Valley Road, then 6.8 miles east on Warm Spring Road; roads usually suitable for any vehicle driven with caution. Note: this is a clothing-optional area with hot pools that are user-maintained. Some shade. Services: pit toilets but no other facilities. Rules for the use of this area may change.

MAHOGANY FLAT CAMPGROUND

Elevation: 8,133 feet. 10 sites. Fee: free. Season: March through November; winter depending on snow conditions. Location: at the end of Upper Wildrose Canyon Road, then to the end of Mahogany Flat Road 1.6 miles beyond Wildrose Charcoal Kilns; high-clearance required and 4WD may be necessary. Facilities: tables, fire pits, and pit toilets; no water.

MESQUITE SPRING CAMPGROUND

Elevation: 1,800 feet. 30 sites. Fee: $12. Season: open all year. Location: near Grapevine Ranger Station 4 miles south of Scotty's Castle. Sites for most recreational vehicles and tents, plus group sites. Facilities: water, tables, flush toilets, and dump station. This is a very popular campground because of its higher elevation and proximity to Scotty's Castle.

PALM SPRING CAMPGROUND

Elevation: 1,460 feet. No set sites. Fee: free. Season: open all year, depending on road conditions. Location: 45.9 miles north from State Highway 190 or 32.4 miles south of Big Pine Road via Saline Valley Road, then 7.5 miles east on Warm Spring Road. Note: this is a clothing-optional area with hot pools. No shade. Facilities: pit toilets but no other services. Rules for the use of this area may change.

STOVEPIPE WELLS CAMPGROUND

Elevation: sea level. 190 sites. Fee: $12. Season: October through April. Location: on State Highway 190 adjacent to Stovepipe Wells Village. Trailer, motor home, and tent-only sites. Facilities: water, flush toilets, some tables and fire pits, and dump station; showers available at Stovepipe Wells Village. No shade; this is essentially a parking lot campground that is open to the wind and, therefore, occasionally very dusty.

SUNSET CAMPGROUND

Elevation: –196 feet. 270 sites. Fee: $12. Season: October through April. Location: at Furnace Creek, the entrance 1 mile south of the Visitor Center. Primarily for recreational vehicles. Facilities: water, flush toilets, and dump station; no tables or fire pits. Has the ambiance of a large parking lot with the advantage of all services being available across the highway at Furnace Creek Ranch.

TEXAS SPRING CAMPGROUND

Elevation: sea level. 92 sites. Fee: $14. Season: October through April. Location: at Furnace Creek, the entrance 1 mile south of the Visitor Center via the same road to but beyond the Sunset Campground. Trailer, motor home, tent-only, and by-reservation group sites. No generators permitted. Facilities: water, flush toilets, tables, fire pits, and dump station.

THORNDIKE CAMPGROUND

Elevation: 7,500 feet. 6 sites. Fee: free. Season: March through November; winter depending on snow conditions. Location: at the end of Upper Wildrose Canyon Road, then Mahogany Flat Road 0.7 mile beyond Wildrose Charcoal Kilns; high-clearance required and 4WD may be necessary. Facilities: tables, fire pits, and pit toilets; no water.

WILDROSE CAMPGROUND

Elevation: 4,100 feet. 23 sites. Fee: free. Season: open all year. Location: on Upper Wildrose Canyon Road just east of Wildrose Junction. Sites for smaller recreational vehicles and tents. Facilities: water (may be turned off in winter), tables, fire pits, and chemical toilet.

Backcountry Camping

Backcountry camping is permitted in most of Death Valley National Park, provided that:

- Overnight sites must be at least 1 mile from any developed area or the nearest paved or "day-use-only" road and at least 100 feet from any open water source.

The Thorndike Campground is within the pinyon-juniper forest of upper Wildrose Canyon.

- "Day-use-only" areas include all below-sea-level parts of the floor of Death Valley, all of Racetrack Valley except the Homestake Dry Camp, all of Titus Canyon Road, and abandoned mining areas and ghost town sites. Check with the National Park Service if unsure about the location.

- Groups are limited to 12 people and 4 vehicles; larger groups must obtain a Special Use Permit and separate into smaller groups that camp at least 1 mile apart.

- Be sure you are properly equipped to take care of emergencies, and carry at least 1 gallon of water per person per day (more in summer) to be used for drinking only (remember your pets).

- Remember that most backcountry areas are infrequently patrolled. It is recommended that you complete a voluntary backcountry registration form and then check back in upon your return.

■ LODGING SERVICES

Xanterra Parks and Resorts, Inc. maintains an inholding of 342 acres of private land at Furnace Creek, where it operates the Furnace Creek Inn and Ranch Resort. Stovepipe Wells Village is run by the Death Valley Lodging Company as a

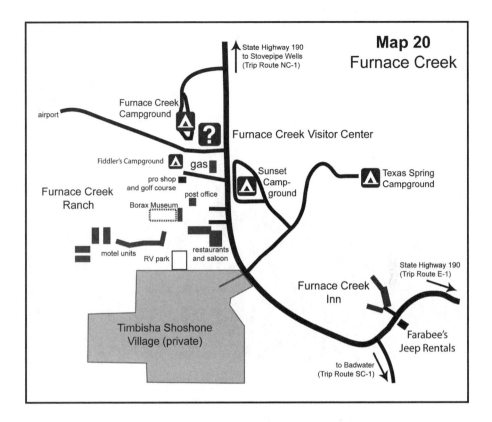

Map 20
Furnace Creek

State Highway 190
to Stovepipe Wells
(Trip Route NC-1)

airport

Furnace Creek
Campground

Furnace Creek Visitor Center

Fiddler's Campground

gas

Sunset
Camp-
ground

Texas Spring
Campground

Furnace Creek
Ranch

pro shop
and golf course

post office

Borax Museum

motel units

RV park

restaurants
and saloon

State Highway 190
(Trip Route E-1)

Furnace Creek
Inn

Timbisha Shoshone
Village (private)

Farabee's
Jeep Rentals

to Badwater
(Trip Route SC-1)

National Park Service concession. Panamint Springs Resort, on State Highway 190 in northwestern Panamint Valley, is privately owned. These are the only facilities with overnight lodging within Death Valley National Park; there is no lodging at Scotty's Castle.

Note: In the following sections, prices and dates are provided only to serve as a guide as to what you may expect when you visit the park. As given, all were correct as of Spring 2014.

The Inn at Furnace Creek

Designed by architect Albert C. Martin, this Mission-style resort hotel, located on State Highway 190 about 1.4 miles from the Furnace Creek Visitor Center, was opened to the first tour group on February 1, 1927. Since that time, this desert oasis has offered its guests AAA Four-diamond rated guest rooms, many with private patios, grounds with meandering streams, sheltering palms, terraced lawns, warm spring-fed pools, and lighted tennis courts have combined with the old-time elegance of the Inn to draw not only tours but others who simply want to get away and relax. The dining room enforces a "casual elegance" dress code for dinner (no

The Furnace Creek Inn.

shorts, jeans, or T-shirts). Season: mid-October to mid-May (closed in summer). 66 rooms. Rates as of 2014: $350 and up (plus tax and Resort Fee), depending on the season and special events. No pets. Reservation deposit required. All major credit cards accepted. Direct phone: (760) 786-2345; fax (760) 786-2514. Xanterra Central Reservations (nationwide): (800) 236-7916. Mail address: P.O. Box 1, Death Valley, CA 92328. Internet Web site: www.furnacecreekresort.com.

The Ranch at Furnace Creek

Located on State Highway 190 near the Furnace Creek Visitor Center, lodging ranging from modest cabins to modern guest rooms is available with wireless internet. Amenities include the 49er Coffee Shop, Wrangler Buffet (breakfast & lunch) and Dinner House, Corkscrew Saloon, 19th Hole Verdana Bar & Grill, gift shop and general store, warm-spring fed swimming pool, and court sports such as bocce ball, basketball, and tennis. Horseback rides, carriage and hay rides. The Borax Museum and Death Valley post office are on the grounds, and a gas station (propane available) is nearby. Golf on the lowest elevation course in North America; green fees seasonal. Park tours available. Shuttle service to/from the Death Valley airport (no aviation fuel, no commercial flights). Season: open all year. A 26-site RV park has full hookups and provides all Ranch amenities for $37 per night. The Fiddler's

The steam tractor called "Old Dinah" is one of the museum pieces at the Furnace Creek Ranch.

The entrance to the Furnace Creek Ranch.

Campground between the Ranch and the Visitor Center has 35 unimproved sites for $17. 208 standard and deluxe guest rooms and 16 cabins. Rates as of 2014: $199 and up (plus tax and resort fee). No pets. Reservation deposit required. All major credit cards accepted. Direct telephone: (760) 786-2345; Fax (760) 786-2514. Xanterra Central Reservations (nationwide): (800) 236-7916. Mail address: P. O. Box 1, Death Valley, CA 92328. Web site: www.furnacecreekresort.com.

Stovepipe Wells Village

The Stovepipe Wells Hotel opened for business on November 1, 1926. Death Valley's first tourist resort, "Bungalow City" consisted of 20 open-air cottages with screened windows and awnings. Now operated by the Death Valley Lodging Company, there is a general store, the Nugget Gift Shop, Tollhouse Restaurant, Badwater Saloon, swimming pool and showers, gas station (no propane), and motel lodging. The National Park Service campground and ranger station are nearby, and a paved airplane landing strip (no services) is just to the west. A 12-site RV park with hookups is adjacent to the store, $32.50. Season: open all year (facility hours vary with the season and special events). 82 motel units. Television and coffee maker in all rooms; refrigerators in deluxe rooms only. No in-room telephones. Rates as of 2014: $100 to $182 (plus tax). Pets OK with deposit. Reservation deposit required. All major credit cards accepted. Telephone: (760) 786-2387; fax (760) 786-2389. Web site: www.escapetodeathvalley.com.

The logo on the door of the old Stovepipe Wells Village fire truck depicts a prospector at the original Stovepipe Well near the sand dunes.

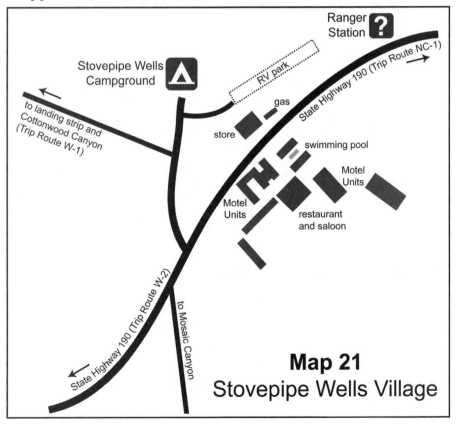

Ranger Station

Stovepipe Wells Campground

RV park

State Highway 190 (Trip Route NC-1)

gas

to landing strip and Cottonwood Canyon (Trip Route W-1)

store

swimming pool

Motel Units

Motel Units

restaurant and saloon

State Highway 190 (Trip Route W-2)

to Mosaic Canyon

Map 21
Stovepipe Wells Village

The Panamint Springs Resort.

Panamint Springs Resort

An oasis of amenities is found here, a friendly, homey touch in an isolated desert location. The Panamint Springs Resort straddles State Highway 190 in northwestern Panamint Valley. Motel, restaurant, bar, general store and gift shop, and gas station (open 8:00 AM to 8:00 PM). A campground across the highway has tent sites ($10), dry RV sites ($20), and full hookup RV sites ($35); showers in the restroom facility are included. Season: open all year. 14 motel units and 1 larger cabin. Rates as of 2014: $79 to $129; cabin $149-$169 (plus tax; ask about AAA and AARP discounts). Pets $5 per night. Satellite TV and evaporative coolers in all rooms. Reservations suggested. Telephone: (775) 482-7680; fax (775) 482-7682. Web site: www.deathvalley.com/psr.

■ FOUR-WHEEL DRIVE JEEP RENTALS

Farabee's Jeep Rentals, located across State Highway 190 from the Furnace Creek Inn, offers four-wheel drive Jeep Wrangler rentals. Prices in 2014: $195 per day for 2-door Jeep, $235 per day for 4-door Jeep. Mileage is limited to 200 miles per day. Drivers must be age 25 or older with valid driver's license, credit card, and proof of full-coverage auto insurance. Farabee's also conducts guided tours that vary from 2 hours to all day; per person tour prices range from $65 to $280. Some custom tours are available on advance request. Telephone: (760) 786-9872 or (877) 970-5337. Web site: www.DeathValleyJeepRentals.com.

Some of the events at the annual Death Valley '49ers Encampment are attended by hundreds of people.

◼ DEATH VALLEY '49ERS ENCAMPMENT

The Death Valley '49ers Encampment (Web site: www.deathvalley49ers.org) is an annual event that since 1949 has commemorated the anniversary of the historic pioneers' entry and crossing of Death Valley. Run by dedicated volunteers, the '49ers sell memberships (most activities are open to all visitors) to help finance the productions. These funds generate scholarships that are granted to qualified graduates of the Death Valley High School District, and money is also donated to Death Valley National Park for sign maintenance and museum work.

The Encampment usually begins the second Wednesday of November and lasts through Sunday morning (this is usually the Veteran's Day holiday weekend). Some of the yearly events are the Invitational Western Art show; sponsored outdoor breakfasts; cowboy poetry, music and stories; the Old Time Fiddlers' Contest; and Old Prospector's Race, and evening campfires with live music. There are also a golf tournament, square dancing under the stars, gold panning, and storyteller's contests. This is *the* annual event in Death Valley, and in some years as many as 50,000 people have been in attendance. Reservations for the Furnace Creek Campground or for any park lodging should be made well in advance.

Suggested Reading

Cunningham, B., and P. Cunningham. 2008. *Hiking Death Valley National Park*. Guilford, CT: Falcon Guides (Globe Pequot Press).

Bagnold, R. A. 1942. *The Physics of Blown Sand and Desert Dunes*. New York: William Morrow and Company.

Benson, L. 1969. *The Native Cacti of California*. Stanford, CA: Stanford University Press.

Borror, D. J., and R. E. White. 1970. *A Field Guide to the Insects of America North of Mexico*. Boston: Houghton Mifflin Company.

Bowers, J. E. 1986. *Seasons of the Wind*. Flagstaff, AZ: Northland Press.

Brockman, F. 1979. *Trees of North American*. New York: Golden Press.

Brogan, G. E., K. S. Kellogg, D. B. Shemmons, and C. L. Terhune. 1991. *Late Quaternary Faulting along the Death Valley–Furnace Creek Fault System, California and Nevada*. Bulletin 1991. Washington, DC: U.S. Geological Survey Bulletin.

Brown, L. 1979. *Grasses: An Identification Guide*. New York: Houghton Mifflin Company.

Burt, W. H., and R. P. Grossenheider. 1964. *A Field Guide to Mammals*. Boston: Houghton Mifflin Company.

Collier, M. 1990. *An Introduction to the Geology of Death Valley*. Death Valley, CA: Death Valley Natural History Association.

Cornett, J. W. 1987. *Wildlife of the North American Deserts*. Palm Springs, CA: Nature Trails Press.

Cronkhite, D. 1977. *Death Valley's Victims—A Descriptive Chronology 1849–1977*. Morongo Valley, CA: Sagebrush Press.

Deal, K. 1994. *Archaeology of Death Valley*. San Bernardino: California State University Desert Studies Program.

DeDecker, M. 1993. *White Smith's Fabulous Salt Tram*. Death Valley, CA: Death Valley '49ers, Inc., Keepsake No. 33.

Digonnet, M. 1997. *Hiking Death Valley*. Palo Alto, CA: published by the author.

———. 2009. *Hiking Western Death Valley National Park: Panamint, Saline, and Eureka Valleys*. Palo Alto, CA: published by the author.

Federal Writer's Project. 1939. *Death Valley: A Guide*. Boston: Houghton Mifflin Company.

Ferris, R. S. 1981. *Death Valley Wildflowers*. Death Valley, CA: Death Valley Natural History Association.

Fife, D. L., and A. R. Brown (eds.). 1980. *Geology and Mineral Wealth of the California Desert*. Annual Field Trip Guidebook No. 8. Santa Ana, CA: South Coast Geological Society.

Foster, L. 1987. *Adventuring in the California Desert*. San Francisco: Sierra Club Books.

Greene, L. W. 1981. *Historic Resource Study: A History of Mining in Death Valley National Monument*. Volume 1, printed in two parts. Denver: Historic Preservation Branch, Denver Service Center, National Park Service.

Gregory, L. W., and E. J. Baldwin (eds.). 1988. *Geology of the Death Valley Region*. Annual Field Trip Guidebook No. 16. Santa Ana, CA: South Coast Geological Society.

Heizer, R. F., and M. A. Whipple. 1971. *The California Indians*. Berkeley: University of California Press.

Hill, M. 1984. *California Landscape—Origin and Evolution*. Berkeley: University of California Press.

Hollon, W. E. 1966. *The Great American Desert*. New York: Oxford University Press.

Hunt, C. B. 1975. *Death Valley: Geology, Ecology, Archaeology*. Berkeley: University of California Press.

Jaeger, E. C. 1941. *Desert Wildflowers*. Stanford, CA: Stanford University Press.

———. 1957 . *A Naturalist's Death Valley*. Death Valley, CA: Death Valley '49ers, Inc., Keepsake No. 5.

———. 1961. *Desert Wildlife*. Stanford, CA: Stanford University Press.

———. 1965. *The North American Deserts*. Stanford, CA: Stanford University Press.

Johnson, J. 2006. *Strolling Stones: The Mystery of Death Valley's Racetrack*. Death Valley, CA: Death Valley '49ers, Inc., Keepsake No. 46.

——— (ed.). 1995. *Proceedings, Fourth Death Valley Conference on History and Prehistory*. Death Valley, CA: Death Valley Natural History Association.

——— (ed.). 1999. *Proceedings, Fifth Death Valley Conference on History and Prehistory*. Death Valley, CA: Death Valley Natural History Association.

——— (ed.). 2002. *Proceedings, Sixth Death Valley Conference on History and Prehistory*. Death Valley, CA: Death Valley Natural History Association.

——— (ed.). 2005. *Proceedings, Seventh Death Valley Conference on History and Prehistory*. Death Valley, CA: Death Valley Natural History Association.

Kirk, R. 1973. *Desert—The American Southwest*. Boston: Houghton Mifflin Company.

Latschar, J. A. 1981. *Historic Resource Study: A History of Mining in Death Valley National Monument*. Volume 2, printed in two parts. Denver: Historic Preservation Branch, Denver Service Center, National Park Service.

Lengner, K. E. (ed.). 2008. *Proceedings, Eighth Death Valley Conference on History and Prehistory*. Death Valley, CA: Death Valley Natural History Association.

Levy, B. 1969. *Death Valley National Monument: Historical Background Study*. Denver: Office of Archaeology and Historic Preservation, Denver Service Center, National Park Service.

Lingenfelter, R. E. 1986. *Death Valley & the Amargosa: A Land of Illusion*. Berkeley: University of California Press.

Machette, M. N., M. L. Johnson, and J. L. Slate (eds.). 2001. *Quaternary and Late Pliocene Geology of the Death Valley Region: Recent Observations on the Tectonics, Stratigraphy, and Lake Cycles*. Guidebook for the 2001 Pacific Cell–Friends of the Pleistocene Fieldtrip. Washington, DC: U.S. Geological Survey, Open-File Report 01-51.

MacMahon, J. A. 1990. *Deserts*. The Audubon Society Nature Guides. New York: Alfred A. Knopf.

McKee, E. H., et al. 1984. *Mineral Resources and Resource Potential of the Hunter Mountain Wilderness Study Area, Inyo County, California*. Washington, DC: U.S. Geological Survey, Open-File Report 84-638.

Miller, M. B, and L. A. Wright. 2004. *Geology of Death Valley National Park*. Dubuque, IA: Kendall/Hunt Publishing Co.

Mitchell, R. 2006. *Death Valley SUV Trails*. Oakhurst, CA: Track & Trail Publications.

Myrick, D. F. 1992. *Railroads of Nevada and Eastern California*. Volume 2: The Southern Roads. Reno: University of Nevada Press.

National Park Service. 1988. *Death Valley National Monument: Draft Environmental Impact Statement and Draft General Management Plan*. Death Valley, CA: National Park Service.

Norman, L. A., and R. M. Stewart. 1951. "Mines and Mineral Resources of Inyo County." *California Journal of Mines and Geology* 47, no. 1: 18–223. Sacramento: California Division of Mines and Geology.

Nyborg, T. G., and V. L. Santucci. 1999. *The Death Valley National Park Paleontological Survey*. Lakewood, CO: National Park Service, Geological Resources Technical Report NPS/NRGRD/GRTDR-99/01.

Paher, S. W. 1970. *Nevada Ghost Towns & Mining Camps*. Berkeley, CA: Howell-North Books.

———. 1973. *Death Valley Ghost Towns*. Volume 1. Las Vegas: Nevada Publications.

———. 1981. *Death Valley Ghost Towns*. Volume 2. Las Vegas: Nevada Publications.

Palmer, T. S. (ed.) 1977. *Place Names of the Death Valley Region in California and Nevada*. Morongo Valley, CA: Sagebrush Press.

Pyle, R. M. 1981. *The Audubon Society Field Guide to North American Butterflies*. New York: Alfred A. Knopf.

Robbins, C. S., D. Bruun, and H. S. Zim. 1983. *Birds of North America: A Guide to Field Identification*. New York: Golden Press.

Rowlands, R. G. 1978. "The Vegetation Dynamics of the Joshua Tree (Yucca brevifolia Engelm.) in the Southwestern United States of America." Ph.D. thesis, University of California, Riverside. Ann Arbor, MI: University Microfilms, Dissertation Information Service.

Sharp, R. P., and A. F. Glazner. 1997. *Geology Underfoot in Death Valley and Owens Valley*. Missoula, MT: Mountain Press.

Skinner, M. W., and B. M. Pavlik (eds.). 1994. *Inventory of Rare and Endangered Vascular Plants of California*. Sacramento: The California Native Plant Society.

Soltz, D. L., and R. J. Naiman. 1978. *The Natural History of Native Fishes in the Death Valley System*. Science Series 30. Los Angeles: Natural History Museum of Los Angeles County in conjunction with Death Valley Natural History Association.

Stebbins, R. C. 1966. *A Field Guide to Western Reptiles and Amphibians*. Boston: Houghton Mifflin Co.

Steward, J. H. 1938. *Basin-Plateau Aboriginal Sociopolitical Groups*. Washington, DC: Smithsonian Institution Bureau of American Ethnology Bulletin 120.

Taylor, G. C. 1993. *Mineral Land Classification of the Ash Meadows, Big Dune, Eagle Mountain, Funeral Peak, Ryan, Pahrump, and Stewart Valley 15-minute Quadrangles and High Peak 7.5-minute Quadrangle, Inyo County, California*. Special Report 167. Sacramento: California Division of Mines and Geology.

Taylor, G. C., and S. E. Joseph. 1992. *Mineral Land Classification of the Eureka–Saline Valley Area*. Special Report 166. Sacramento: California Division of Mines and Geology.

Tucker, H. 1992. *Stove Pipe Wells Village—From Dream to Reality*. Death Valley, CA: Death Valley '49ers, Inc., Keepsake No. 32.

Unrau, H. D. 1997. *A History of the Lands Added to Death Valley National Monument by the California Desert Protection Act of 1994*. Denver: Denver Service Center, National Park Service.

Van Dyke, J. C. 1903. *The Desert*. New York: Charles Scribner's Sons [1976, Phoenix Arizona Historical Society].

Vredenburgh, L. M., G. L. Shumway, and R. D. Hartill. 1981. *Desert Fever*. Canoga Park, CA: The Living West.

Wright, L. A., R. M. Stewart, T. E. Gay Jr., and G. C. Hazenbush. 1953. "Mines and Mineral Deposits of San Bernardino County, California." *California Journal of Mines and Geology*, vol. 49, no. 1: 19–257; no. 2: 1–192. Sacramento: California Division of Mines and Geology.

Betty Tucker-Bryan and T. Scott Bryan. (Photograph by Gina Blair)

The authors met in, of all places, the Badwater Saloon in Death Valley's Stovepipe Wells Village in 1974, just one of the many years and wonderful times spent exploring and learning the secrets of this great desert.

T. Scott Bryan once worked as the National Park Service mining geologist in Death Valley National Monument. He has also been a permanent ranger-naturalist at Glen Canyon National Recreation Area and a seasonal ranger-naturalist in Yellowstone National Park, and held other Park Service positions in Glacier National Park and the Los Angeles Field Office. He received his Bachelor of Science degree in geology at San Diego State University and continued his education at the University of Montana, where he took his Master of Science degree in 1974. He is retired from Victor Valley Community College in Victorville, California, as the emeritus professor of geology, astronomy, and physical science and director of the college planetarium. His published books are *The Geysers of Yellowstone* (4th Edition, University Press of Colorado) and *Geysers: What They Are and How They Work* (2nd Edition, Mountain Press). He has also published several articles on the history and geology of the American West.

Betty Tucker-Bryan was the first woman to solo hike the 140-mile length of Death Valley. She spearheaded the mapping and hiking of the proposed border-to-border Desert Trail between Mexico and Canada and was the founder of the Death Valley Hikers Association. She has served on the board of directors of the Desert Protective Council and as director of the Roadrunner District of California Garden Clubs. As a freelance writer, desert conservationist, and outdoors woman, she has been published in many national magazines. She contributed to the Mountaineers' book *Gorp, Glop & Glue Stew* and to the Sierra Club book *Adventuring in the California Desert*.

Index

Page numbers in italics indicate illustrations

 A

A Canyon, 282
Aguereberry, Jean Pierre ("Pete"), 193, 198, 279, 301, 388
Aguereberry Camp, 279, 388
Aguereberry Point, 280–281; view from, *62*
Aguereberry Point Road, 279–281
Albright, Horace, 43
Alvord, Charles, 196
Alvord's Lost Gold Mine, 196
Amargosa (ghost town), 161, 379
Amargosa Borax Works, 32, 161, 397; ruins, *163*
Amargosa Chaos, 15, 145, 176
Amargosa City (ghost camp), 371, 373
Amargosa Farm Road, 229
Amargosa Hotel, 227
Amargosa Opera House, 225, 227–228, 383
Amargosa pupfish, 90, 153, 167
Amargosa River, 150, 153, 155, 162, 167, 199
Amargosa Valley, Nevada (community), 205, 229
Amargosa Valley Railroad, 154, 411
American Borate Company, 211, 213
American Mine, 147
Anaconda Corporation, 383
Anasazi, paleoindian trade with, 22
Andy Hills, 334
Antelope squirrel, white-tailed, 68
Antimony mining, 36, 283
Antiquities Act of 1906, 26
Ants, rough harvester, *93*
Anvil Spring, 196, *197*
Anvil Spring Canyon, 193

Anvil Spring Junction, 196, 302
Arcan, John, and family, 28, 188, 190
Archaeological Resources Preservation Act of 1979, 26
Argenta Mine, 281
Argus Range, 290
Argus Range Silver Mining Company, 394
Arrastre Spring, 195, 297
Arrowweed, 54, 243
Artesian Well Road, 354
Artists Drive, 173
Artists Palette, 174
Asbestos: chrysotile, 338; tremolite, *337*
Ash Meadows National Wildlife Refuge, 225
Ash Meadows, Nevada, 412
Ashford Canyon, 180
Ashford Junction, 143, 149, 181
Ashford Mill, 180, *181*
Ashton (railroad station site), 231
Atlantic & Pacific Railroad, 409
Automobile Club of Southern California, 41
Avawatz Mountains, 156, 383; origin of name, 159
Avawatz Salt and Gypsum Company, 411
Azizia, Libya, 178

 B

Baby Gauge Railroad, 215, 403, 405; tourist excursion, *405*
Backcountry camping, 423–424

Backpacking: clothing recommendations, 117–118; gear and supply recommendations, 118; overview, 116; photo, *117*; registration, 118; supply caches, 116–117

Badwater Road, 169–178, 202

Badwater Salt Flats short walk, 110

Badwater snail, 90, 178

Badwater Spring (Death Valley), 176, *177*

Badwater Spring (Saline Valley), 360

Badwater turtleback, 176

Baker, California, 163

Ballarat (ghost town), 280, 295, 298, 379–380; in 1913, *295*; ruins, *380*

Ballarat Road, 290

Barker Ranch, 301

Basin and Range, 9, 15

Bats, 75–76, 280; big-eared brown, 280; California myotis, 76; western pipistrel, 76

Battle of Wingate Pass, 42, 198

Batus Mountain, 311

Bear poppy, 328

Bear, black, 343, 352

Beatty, Nevada, 253

Beatty Cutoff Road, 239, 245–249

Beatty Information Center, 253, 419

Beatty Junction, 246

Beaudry, Victor, 381

Beavertail cactus, 55, 211, 327

Becket, Marta, 228

Beetles, darkling, 91

Belshaw, Mortimer, 381

Bennett, Asa, and family, 28, 188, 190

Bennett, Charles, 188

Bennett's Long Camp, 188

Bennett's Well, 29, 188

Bering Land Bridge, 21

Bessie Brady (steamboat), 381

Beveridge (ghost town), 355

Beveridge Canyon Road, 355

Bicycling: difficult roads, 126–128; easy roads, 124–125; moderate roads, 125–126; supplies for, 124

Bierstadt, Albert, 329

Big Bell Mine, 249, 255

Big Dodd Spring, 333, 350

Big-eared brown bat, 280

Big Four Mine, 269

Bighorn Gorge, 308

Bighorn sheep, 72, *73*

Big Pine, California, 321

Big Pine Road, 308, 313–321, 363

Big Silver Mine, 351, 355

Big Talc Mine, 193

Billie Mine, 44, 45, 214

Biological environments chart, 64

Birch Spring, 283

Black cardinal, 78

Black Diamond Mine, 358

Black Magic Mine, 146, 152

Black Mountain Fault Zone, 16, 172, 239

Black Mountain Trail, 358; day hike, 116

Black Point, 267

Black, Mrs. Helen H., 397

Blackrock Well, 348

Blazing star: Panamint, 62; pigmy, 62

Blue Bell Mine Road, 277

Blue Jay Mine, 409

Blue Monster Mine, 360

Bobcat, 72, *72*

Bonham Talc Mine, 349

Bonney Talc Mine, 191

Bonnie Claire (ghost town), 312, 367, 380, 412

Bonnie Claire and Gold Mountain Railroad, 412

Bonnie Claire & Ubehebe Railroad, 329, 333, 411–412

Bonnie Claire Bullfrog Mining Company, 312

Bonnie Claire Playa, 312, 338

Bonnie Claire Road, 311–312

Bonnie Clare, 380

Bonnie Clare & Gold Mountain Railroad, 412

Borate, California, 33

Borate mining, 32–34, 35–36, 44–45, 161, 208–209, 211, 213, 214, 215, 237, 239, 353

Borax Museum: original building site, 209; present site, 426

Borax trenches, 173

Boraxo Mine, 44, 211, 214

Borden, Alexander "Shorty," 185, 275

Boron, California, 36, 404

Boulder Dam, 43, 171

Boundary Canyon, 251, 252

Boundary Canyon Fault, 251

Bradbury Park, 147

Bradbury Well, 146

Breakfast Canyon, 172

Breakneck Canyon, 317

Brewery Spring, 294

Brier, James W., and family, 28, 29

Brier Spring, 368

Briggs Mine, 299

Bristlecone Copper Company, 321

Bristlecone pine, 60

Brock, John, 387

Broken Pick Millsite, 44, 184

Brown-eyed primrose, 61

Brush Stroke Hills, 150

Buckwheat Wash Road, 165, 388
Bullet Mine, 267
Bullfrog (ghost town), 34, 252, 371, 373, 381; ruins, *371*
Bullfrog Goldfield Railroad, 35, 252, 312, 366, 380, 395, 401–403, 407, 410
Bullfrog Mountain, 371, 374
Bullfrog Road, 252
Bullfrog West Extension Mine, 375
Bullock's oriole, 80, *81*
Bull snake, 86
Bulrush, *53*
Bungalow City, 41
Bunker Hill Mine, 360
Bureau of Land Management (BLM), 4, 154, 162, 351
Burned Wagons Point, 28, 241
Burros, wild, 74, *75,* 317, 363, 373
Burro Spring, 336
Butte Valley, 302
Butte Valley Neighborhood Improvement Association, 196
Butte Valley Road, 194–198
Butte Valley Stamp Mill, 197
Butterfly, painted lady, 93

 C

Cacomistle, 73
Cactus, 211, 327, 336, 359; beavertail, 55, 211, cottontop, 55, 211; mound, *56*
Calico Hills, 147
California Desert Protection Act, 45
California juniper, 58
California myotis bat, 76
California Native Plant Society, 50
California Nitrate Development Company, 156
Calmet Mine, 339
Camp Holdout, 181
Camp Vega, 353
Campfire regulations, 102
Campground: list of campgrounds, 420–423; regulations, 101–102, 420; reservations, 420
Carbonate Mine, 192, 329
Carbonite (ghost camp), 192, 381
Carbonite Mine, 192
Carson & Colorado Railroad, 413
Cashier Mill, 280; ruins, *34*
Cashier Mine, 280
Cattle, 74, 317, 343
Cautionary notes, 102–103
Cave Fault, 110

Cave Rock Spring, 372
Cave Rock Spring Road, 372
Celestite, 136, 154
Cell phones, lack of service, 103
Cenozoic Era, 15–17
Centipedes, 91
Cerro Gordo (ghost town), 31, 349, 381–382
Cerro Gordo Historical Society, 381
Cerro Gordo Road, 349
Cerussite Mine, 348
Chalk Canyon, 359
Charcoal Kilns Road, 282
Cheesebush, 52
Chia, 57
Chicory, desert, 61
China Garden Spring, 270
Chloride City (ghost town), 251, 252, 256, 382, 389; James McKay grave at, *257*; ruin, *256*
Chloride Cliff, 239, 256, 382
Chloride Cliff Road, 252, 255–257; historic, 182
Chloride Junction, 255
Chocolate Sundae Mountain, 148
Chris Wicht Camp, 294
Christmas Gift Mine, 282, 283
Christmas Mine, 282
Chuckawalla Canyon, 314
Chuckawalla Hill, 38, 314, 399
Chuckwalla, 82, *84*
Cinder Cone short walk, 113
Cinder Hill, 180, 199
Circus beetles, 91
Civilian Conservation Corp (CCC), 43, 267, 277, 283
Clair Camp, 297
Clark, J. Ross, 407, 409
Clark, Senator William A., 387, 407, 409
Climate, general, 97–99
Clinton, President William J., 45
Closed roads, cautionary note, 102
Coen Corporation, 255
Coffee Stop Mine, 358
Coffin Canyon, 179
Coffin Mine, 179, 218
Coleman (ghost camp), 237, 382
Coleman, William Tell, 32
Communications, cautionary note, 103
Cone Hill Mine, 213
Confidence Hills, 149
Confidence Mill, 148, 149; historic, *151*
Confidence Mine, 148, 149–150
Conn & Trudo Borax Works, 32, 353–354, *353*
Conn, Frederick, 32, 353, 408
Contact Mine, 194

Cooper Mill, 297
Cooper rush, 53
Copper Basin (ghost camp), 400
Copper Canyon, 179
Copper Canyon turtleback, 179
Copperfield, 387
Copper mining, 34, 35, 218–219, 224, 320, 329, 338, 348, 358
Corkscrew Canyon, 210
Corkscrew Peak, 249, 251; day hike, 115
Corona Mine, 293
Coso, 31
Cottonball Marsh pupfish, 89
Cottontop cactus, 55, 211, 327
Cottonwood, 58
Cottonwood Canyon Road, 263–266
Cottonwood Canyon–Marble Canyon backpacking, 121
Cottonwood Creek, 266
Cottonwood Mountains, 308
Cottonwood Wash, 264
Cow Creek Road, 238
Cowhorn Pass, 321
Cowhorn Valley, 363
Coyote, 67, 70; tracks of, 69
Coyote Canyon Road, 299
Coyote Hole, 179
Crankshaft Junction, 317
Crater (ghost camp), 318, 382–383, 413
Crater Road, 318
Creosote bush, 53; King Clone, 53
Crist, George C., 281
Cross, Ernest "Ed, " 34, 35, 252, 375, 395
Crowell Mining and Milling Company, 256
Crowley, Father John J., 270–271
Crowley Point, 270
Crystal Camp, 153, 407
Crystal Hills, 44, 405
Crystal Ridge, 361
Cucomungo Canyon Road, 319
Culverwell, Richard I. A., 30, 45
Curious Butte, 196
Currie Well, 375
Cyty, Johnny, 249, 255
Cyty Mill, 249; short walk, 112

Dante's View, 176, 215, 216
Dante's View Road, 212, 214–126
Darwin (ghost town), 31, 270, 271, 383
Darwin Falls, 269–270
Darwin Falls Road, 269
Darwin Junction, 271
Date palms, 48, 203
Daunet, Isadore, 32, 187, 267
Day hikes, supplies for, 113
Daylight Pass, 251
Daylight Pass Road, 249–254
Daylight Spring, 251
Dayton, Jim, 186
Dayton-Harris graves, 186
Day-use only areas, 102
Dead Horse Canyon, 212, 404
Deadman Canyon, 321
Deadman Pass Road, 224, 228
Death Valley, origin of name, 29–30, 297
Death Valley Buttes, 250
Death Valley Chuck-Walla magazine, 35, 39, 387
Death Valley Chug Line, 386
Death Valley Coyote (train), 249
Death Valley Days radio and television programs, 43
Death Valley '49ers Encampment, 430–431; annual art show, 417 (top); parade, 431
Death Valley Gold Mining Company, 399
Death Valley Humbug, 42
Death Valley joint fir, 55, 148
Death Valley Junction, 214, 225, 227, 383
Death Valley Mercantile Company, 389
Death Valley Mining Company, 195, 385
Death Valley Natural History Association, 416–417
Death Valley phacelia, 61
Death Valley Railroad, 36, 41, 212, 213, 214, 228, 395, 403–405, 408, 410; Locomotive No. 1, 404
Death Valley Ranch, 309, 310, 311
Death Valley sage, 54
Death Valley Salt Company, 411
Death Valley Scotty, 41, 181, 198
Death Valley View Hotel, 41, 395
Death Valley Wash, 315, 412
Dedeckera Canyon, 324, 360
Del Norte Mine, 278
Demming, Andrew, 384
Denning, Frank, 165, 384
Denning Spring Road, 154
Denning Springs (ghost camp), 154, 383–384
Desert broom, 51
Desert fir, 52, 174
Desert five-spot, 60

 D

Daisy Canyon, 409
Daisy, Panamint, 60, 285
Dandelion, desert, 62
Dante's Canyon, 215

Desert Gold (ghost store), 316, 399
Desertgold (plant), 63
Desert holly, 54
Desert Hound Mine, 145
Desert pavement, 174, 183, 242; coarse variety, 183
Desert tortoise, 80, 82
Desert travel precautions, 99–100
Desert trumpet, 54
Desert velvet, 62
Desolation Canyon, 173
Detachment faults, 146, 186
Devar, 41, 395, 404
Devil's Cornfield, 243
Devil's Gate, 321
Devil's Golf Course, 19, 174–175, 175, 182
Devil's Golf Course Road, 174
Devil's Hole, 226, 227; added to monument, 43
Devil's Hole pupfish, 90, 227
Devil's Slide, 265
Devil's Speedway, 182
Dog Spring, 189
Doris Dee Mine, 360
Doris Montgomery Summit, 253
Dripping Blood Mountain, 110
Dry Bone Canyon, 336
Dry Mountain, 327
Dublin Hills, 148
Dumont Dunes Road, 162
Dumont Sand Dunes, 162
Dune primrose, 61
Dunn, Mrs. F. W., 397
DuPont, T. Coleman, 145

E. I. DuPont de Nemours Powder Company, 145
El Capitan Mine, 318
Eleodes beetles, 91; tracks in sand, 92
Ely & Goldfield Railroad, 412
Emigrant Campground, 267, 420
Emigrant Canyon, 29, 30
Emigrant Canyon Road, 267, 271–282
Emigrant Junction, 267, 272
Emigrant Pass, 281
Emigrant Spring, 274, 384
Emigrant Springs (ghost camp), 274, 384; historic newspaper photo, 275; restaurant tent near Harrisburg, 388
Endangered Species Act, 48
Endemic animals, 65–66; list, 66
Endemic plants, 48–50; list, 49–50
Entrance fees, 416
Environmental Quality Act, 48
Epaulet Peak, 147
Epsom salts mining, 37, 153, 405–407
Epsom Salts Monorail, 37, 153, 405–407; near Layton Pass, 406
Eureka dune primrose, 61
Eureka Dunes Dry Camp, 322, 421
Eureka Dunes Road, 322
Eureka Hill, 278
Eureka Mine, 280
Eureka Sand Dunes, 315, 323, 323–324, 360
Eureka Valley Road, 319–320
Eureka Valley Well Road, 322
Evelyn (railroad station site), 229
Evening Star Mine, 165
Exclamation Hill, 145
Eye of the Needle, 203, 205

 E

Eagle Borax Mining Company, 32
Eagle Borax Spring, 29
Eagle Borax Works, 187, 187, 267
Eagle Mountain, 228
Earhart, Henry, Jacob, and John, 28, 29, 193
Earthquakes, general history, 17
East Greenwater (ghost camp), 222
East Side Borax Camp, 239
East Side Road, 178–181, 199
Eastern Sierra Interagency Visitor Center, 4
Ebbetts, John, 317
Echo (ghost camp), 231, 384
Echo Canyon, 397
Echo Canyon Road, 203–206
Echo Pass, 231
Eichbaum, Herman W. "Bob, " 41, 385, 244

F

Fairbanks, Nevada (ghost camp), 317
Fall Canyon, 307; day hike, 115
Fan palms, 203, 306, 357, 358
Father Crowley Point, 270
Fault scarps, 17, 172, 176, 179, 180, 186, 241, 267, 329
Faults, 16; Black Mountain, 172, 239; Cave, 110; detachment, 146, 176; Fish Lake Valley, 315, 316, 319; Furnace Creek, 210, 239; Garlock, 152, 154; Hanaupah, 186; in Johnson Canyon, 18; Keane Wonder, 239, 249, 250; Last Chance Thrust, 322; Leaning Rock, 336; Northern Death Valley, 17, 239, 242, 246, 250, 262, 305, 306, 308, 315; Panamint Valley, 268, 286; Salt Spring, 239; Southern Death Valley, 17; Steel

Pass, 149, 154, 180, 199, 356; Titus Canyon, 261; Towne Pass, 267
Feather Spring, 189
Fessler, Gertrude, 397
Fisch, "Old Man, " 299
Fish Canyon, 299
Fish Lake Valley Fault Zone, 315, 316, 319
Flamingo, 156
Forest Service, U.S., 4, 363
Fort Irwin National Training Center (U.S. Army), 4, 152, 153, 154, 384
49ers, 27–30, 28, 159, 163, 182, 188, 190, 195, 203, 211, 241, 267–268, 291, 292, 297, 298, 299
Four-wing saltbush, 51
Franklin, August J., 382
Franklin Mines, 256
Fred Harvey Corporation, 171
Frémont, John C., 316
French, Dr. Darwin, 269
Frontier Road, 230
Funeral Mountains, 237
Funeral Peak, 222
Furnace (ghost town), 217–218, 384; in 1907, 218
Furnace Creek Badlands, 206; view from Zabriskie Point, 207
Furnace Creek Campground, 237, 422
Furnace Creek Canyon, 215
Furnace Creek Copper Company, 218, 384
Furnace Creek Fault Zone, 210, 239
Furnace Creek Inn, 203, 404; founding, 41; services, 426–426; view of, 426
Furnace Creek Ranch, 169, 201, 382; historic chicken yard, 171; history, 43, 169–171; services, 426; view of, 428
Furnace Creek Visitor Center, 169, 201, 237; services, 416; ranger-led hikes, 417
Furnace Creek Water Management Plan, 50
Furnace Mine Road, 217–218

◼ G

Galena Canyon, 179, 190–191
Garibaldi Mine, 277–278, 341
Garlock Fault, 152, 154
Garnet, industrial grade, 348
Gaylord, E. Burdon, 249
Gecko, banded, 83
Gem Mine, 293
Geoglyphs, described, 26
Geologic time scale chart, 11–12
George, Dr. Samuel G., 283, 293
Georgians (49ers), 28

Gerstley Mine, 43, 148
Ghost-flower, 60
Giant Mine Road, 162
Gnomes' Workshop, 238; short walk, 109
Gold Bar (ghost town), 374, 385
Gold Bar Mine, 374, 385
Gold Bar Road, 374
Goldbelt (ghost camp), 340, 385
Goldbelt Asbestos Mine, 338
Goldbelt Grade Spring, 340
Goldbelt Spring, 340
Goldbelt Spur Road, 339
Gold Bottom Mill, 275
Gold Bug Road, 298
Golden Canyon, 172, 206; short walk, 109, 111
Golden Treasure Mine, 180
Goldfield Railroad, 401
Gold Hill (ghost camp), 195–196, 385
Gold Hill Mill, 194, 195
Gold King Mine (Emigrant Canyon), 276
Gold King Mine (Nevada Triangle), 385
Gold mining, 34, 38, 148, 149, 154, 180, 194, 204, 206, 223, 230, 233, 247, 252, 273, 276, 278, 280, 293, 297, 298, 314, 315, 317, 334, 363, 370, 372–376
Gold Mountain, Nevada (ghost town), 315
Gold Mountain Railway, 412
Gold Point, Nevada, 315
Gold Valley (ghost town), 34, 179, 223, 386, 400
Gold Valley Pass, 223
Gold Valley Road, 222–224
Goler Gulch, 300
Goler Wash Road, 198, 299–302
Goller, John, 300
Gopher snake, 86, 86
Gower Gulch, 172, 208; short walk, 110
Global Positioning System (GPS) coordinates, 6
Grandstand, the, 330
Grantham Mine, 193
Grapevine Canyon (Death Valley), 309; Narrows, 311
Grapevine Canyon (Saline Valley), 350
Grapevine Canyon Springs, 350
Grapevine Mountains, 306, 307, 312
Grapevine Peak climb, 370
Grapevine Ranger Station, 308
Grapevine Springs, 308
Gravel Well, 190
Graves: Death Valley Scotty, 419; James McKay, 256; Jean Lemoigne, 240; Val Nolan, 305
Gray Eagle Mine, 360
Greasewood, 54
Great Automobile Race, 39

Great Basin, 9, 21
Great Drought, The, 22
Greater View Spring, 198, 302
Greenland Borax and Salt Mining Company, 32
Greenland Ranch, 169, 237, 382
Greenleaf Spring, 189
Greenwater (ghost town), 34, 219, 220, 320, 384, 386–387, 390; in 1907, *386–387*
Greenwater Canyon, 213, 220–222
Greenwater Cemetery, 220
Greenwater Copper Company, 218
Greenwater Death Valley Copper Mines and Smelter Company Railroad, 412
Greenwater Road, 220
Greenwater Spring, 220
Greenwater Valley, 228
Greenwater Valley Road, 148, 215, 217–225
Grey, Zane, 39, 227, 383
Grotto Canyon Road, 244
Ground squirrel, round-tailed, 70
Gutache Mountain, 148
Gypsum, 36, 154

 H

Hall Canyon, 290, 293
Halophytic plants, 51
Hanaupah Canyon, origin of name, 186
Hanaupah Canyon Road, 186
Hanaupah Creek, 186
Hanaupah Fault, 186
Hanging Cliff Mine, 277
Hanging Rock Canyon, 319
Hanson, Indian George, 293
Happy Canyon Road, 295
Harmony Borax Works, 32, 187, 237, 239, 379, 382; in 1886, *33*; ruins, *238*; short walk, 108
Harris, Frank "Shorty," 34, 35, 186, 193, 198, 252, 275, 279, 298, 301, 339, 374, 385, 388, 395; as 1920s auto prospector, *37*
Harrisberry, 388
Harrisburg (ghost town), 34, 280, 384, 388, 398–399
Harrisburg Flat, 276, 278, 399
Harris Grade, 340
Harrison, President Benjamin, 354
Harry Wade Monument, 159, 163
Harry Wade Road, 149–160, 163, 181
Haystacks, 237; short walk, 109
Hearst, Senator George, 392
Hearst, William Randolph, 392
Hell's Gate, 249, 250

Hidden Sand Dunes, 322
Hidden Spring, 223
Hidden Valley, 338
Hole-in-the-Rock Spring, 250
Hole-in-the-Wall, 210
Hole-in-the-Wall Road, 209–210
Homestake Dry Camp, 333, 422
Homestake Mine (Nevada Triangle), 385
Homestake Mine (Racetrack Valley), 333
Homestake-King Mill, 374, 385
Homestake-King Mine, 374
Homewood Canyon Road, 291
Honan, James, 400
Honey mesquite, *53*
Honey sweet, 54
Hoodoos, 274, 336
Hooligan Junction, 372
Hooligan Mine, 372
Hoover, President Herbert, 43
Horned lizard, 82, *83*
Horse Bone Camp, 294
Horse Thief Hills, 319
Horses, wild, 74, 343
Horsetail, 53
Horsetail Springs, 340
Hubcap Rock, 301
Hummingbird, Costa's, 78
Hummingbird Spring, 283
Hungry Bill's Ranch, 189, 398; day hike, 114; ruins, *190*
Hunt, Jefferson, 27, 29, 160
Hunter, William L., 338, 342
Hunter Cabin, 342–343, *343*
Hunter Canyon Road, 353
Hunter Mountain, high point, 343
Hunter Mountain Ranch, 342
Hunter Mountain Road, 328, 338–344
Huntley Mines, 337

 I

Ibex Junction, 155, 167
Ibex Mine, 165, 384, 388
Ibex Pass, 162
Ibex Sand Dunes, 162, 167
Ibex Spring (ghost camp), 165, 388–389; ruins, *166*
Ibex Spring Road, 164–165
Ibex Valley Road, 162, 164–167
Ice Age lakes, 19
Indian paintbrush, *63*
Indian Pass, 28

Indian Pass Canyon, 233
Indian Pass Road, 231–233
Indian Pass Trail backpacking, 120
Indian Ranch, 293
Indian Ranch Road, 286, 290, 292–295
Indian reservations, 4
Indian water (plant), 224
Inkweed, 52
International Talc and Steatite Corporation, 355, 360
Inyo Mine, 206, 397
Inyo Mountains, 349
Iron Caps Mine, 291
Isham, William, 299
Isham Canyon, 299

 J

J. O. Mine, 342
J. O. Mine Road, 340–342, *342*
Jackass Flat Road, 362
Jackass Springs, 343
Jackpot Canyon, 297
Jackrabbit, black-tailed, 67, *68*
Jaeger, Dr. Edmund C. (quoted), 1
Jail Canyon, 283
Jail Canyon Road, 283, 292–293
Jayhawker Canyon, 29, *30*, 267
Jayhawkers (49ers), 28, 267
Jimsonweed, 61
Johnson, Albert M., 41, 308, 309
Johnson, William, 188
Johnson Canyon, 188–190, 397
Joint fir, *55*
Joshua Flat, 321
Joshua tree, *58*, 281, 321, 327; Lee Flat forest, *59*, 348, 349
Journigan, Roy, 275
Journigan's Mill, 275, *276*
Jubilee Pass, 145
Jubilee Pass Road, 143–148, 181
Jubilee Spring, 198
Julian, Charles C., 37, 390
Juniper, 58

 K

Kaleidoscope View, 174
Kangaroo rat, Merriam, 66, *67*
Keane Springs (ghost town), 254–255, 389
Keane Springs Land Company, 389

Keane Wonder (ghost town), 247, 389, 390
Keane Wonder Fault, 239, 249, 250
Keane Wonder Mill, 247, 390; historic, *389*; ruins, *248*
Keane Wonder Mine, 247; day hike, 114
Keane Wonder Mine Road, 246–249
Keane Wonder Springs, 249; short walk, 112
Keeler Talc Mine Road, 338, 339
Kelly, W. A. "Whispering," 411
Kerckhoff, W. G., 411
Keys, Bill, 145
Keystone Mine, 300
Kimball Brothers Stage, 389, 399
King Clone creosote, 53
King snake, common or California, 87, *88*
Kit fox, 70, *71*
Kit Fox Hills, 241, 250, 305
Klare Spring, 260; day hike, 115
Kunze (ghost town), 218, 390; in December 1906, *219*

 L

LAC/Bullfrog Mine, 253, 375
Ladd Mountain, 253
Lake Hill, 268, 269, 349
Lake Hill Road, 268–269
Lake Manly, 19, 180, 199, 242, 243, 246
Lake Panamint, 19
Lake Rogers, 314
Lake Tecopa, 19; lakebeds of, 161
Land classification, 3–4
Lane Mill, 256
Las Vegas & Tonopah Railroad, 35, 252, 312, 367, 372, 374, 380, 395, 402, 407–408, 409, 412; Rhyolite Depot building, 253
Last Chance Range, 38, 314, 315, 318, 319, 324, 382, 399
Last Chance Springs, 317
Last Chance Thrust Fault, 322
Laswell, Andrew Jackson "Bellerin' Teck," 169
Latimer, 330, 395
Lawrence Claims, 337
Lead Canyon, 360
Leadfield (ghost town), 37, 260, 390–391, 399; in 1926, *391*; ruins, *261*
Lead Hope Mine, 271
Lead King Mine, 333, 395
Lead mining, 37, 192, 197, 260, 267, 269, 271, 329, 333
Leaning Rock Canyon, 336
Leaning Rock Fault, 336

Leaning Rock Peak, 336
Lee, California (ghost town), 34, 205, 229–231, 384, 391–392
Lee, Nevada (ghost camp), 230, 392
Lee Annex (ghost town), 230, 392
Lee Flat, 343, 349
Lee Flat Overlook Road, 348
Lee Flat Road, 348–349
Leeland (railroad station site), 230
Lee Mine Road, 348
Lee Pump, 343
Legislation: Antiquities Act of 1906, 26; Archaeological Resources Preservation Act of 1979, 26; California Desert Protection Act of 1994, 45; Endangered Species Act, 48; Environmental Quality Act, 48; Mining in Parks Act of 1976, 44, 211, 273; Native Plant Protection Act, 48; Natural Communities Conservation Planning Act, 48; Paleontological Resources Protection Act of 2009, 20; Saline Valley Indian Ranch Homestead Land Grant, 354
Lemoigne, Jean, 267; grave, 240
Lemoigne Canyon Road, 266–267
Lemoigne Mine, 267
Lestro Mountain Mine, 300
Lichen, 57
Life zones, 47
Lila C. Mine, 35, 213, 228, 383, 395, 403, 409, 410
Lila C. Railroad, 408
Limber pine, 60
Lime Hill Summit, 321
Limekiln Spring, 294
Lippincott, George, 333
Lippincott Mine, 333, 395
Lippincott Road, 331, 350
Lippincott Smelter, 312, 380
Little Bridge Canyon, 243
Little Chief granite porphyry, 186
Little Cowhorn Valley, 321
Little Dodd Spring, 333
Little Dumont Sand Dunes, 161
Little Hebe Crater Trail, 112, 309
Little Sand Spring, 315
Little Sand Spring–Stovepipe Wells backpacking, 121
Long Valley, 193, 299
Longstreet Inn and Casino, 228
Lookout (ghost town), 289, 392
Lookout Coal & Transportation Company, 392, 400
Loretto (ghost camp), 320, 392–393
Loretto District, 35

Los Angeles & Independence Railroad, 295, 361, 394, 412–413
Lost Bethune Mine, 388
Lost Burro Gap, 333
Lost Burro Junction, 334
Lost Burro Mill, 334, 336
Lost Burro Mine, 334; ruins, 335
Lost Burro Tail Mine, 339
Lost Goller Mine, 300
Lost Gunsight Lode, 30, 268, 283, 400
Low elevation point, 110, 178
Lower Lotus Spring, 300
Lower Vine Ranch, 308, 419
Lower Warm Spring, 320, 356–358; earthquakes at, 356; view, 357
Lower Warm Spring Campground, 422
Lower Warm Spring Road, 356–358
Lower Wildrose Canyon Road, 285, 290
Lucky Boy Mine, 360
Lucky Find Millsite, 185
Lucky Rich Mine, 358
Lucky Strike Mine, 319
Lyle, Lt. David A., 156

◼ M

Mahogany Flat Campground, 285, 422
Mahogany Flat Road, 282
Mammoth Mine, 191
Manganese mining, 151–152, 358
Manly, William Lewis, 29, 188, 190, 211, 299
Manly Beacon, 206
Manly Fall, 299
Manly Pass, 292, 299
Manson, Charles, 285, 301
Map symbols, 133
Maps, sources of, 5
Marble Bath, 359
Marble Canyon (Death Valley), 121, 265
Marble Canyon (Saline Valley), 363, 408
Marble Canyon Mines, 363
Marble Peak, 314
Martin, Jim, 30, 268
Mather, Stephen Tyng, 33, 42
Maturango Peak, 290
McDonald Spring, 373
McDonald Spring Road, 370–373
McElvoy Canyon, 355, 356
McKay, James, 256
McLean Spring, 240; trading posts at, 241
Medical emergencies, 416
Mengel, Carl, 198, 301

Mengel Pass, 198, 301
Mercury mines, 256, 318, 322, 358
Mesa Negra, 212
Mesozoic Era, 14–15
Mesquite Flat Culture, 22, 221
Mesquite Flat Sand Dunes, 244, *245*
Mesquite Spring Campground, 308, 422
Mesquite Well, 190
Messina, Dr. Paula, 331
Mexican Camp, 368
Microwave Road, 152–153
Middle Panamint Junction, 286, 290
Middle Park, 298
Midges, 92
Midway Well, 306
Military lands, 4, 152, 153, 154, 299, 301, 384, 407
Mill Canyon, 349
Miller, Stanley, 165
Miller Spring (Darwin area), 270
Miller Spring (Greenwater Valley), 224
Minietta (ghost camp), 289, 392
Minietta Mine, 289, 392; ruins, *290*
Minietta Mine Road, 289
Mining areas, cautionary note, 102–103
Mining camp age dating techniques, 377–378
Mining in Parks Act of 1976, 44, 211, 273
Mining World journal, 146
Mississippians (49ers), 28, 268
Mister Mine, 147
Modoc Mine, 31, 283, 289, 392
Modock (post office), 392
Mojave desert mallow, 60
Mojave rattlesnake, 84
Mojave River Valley Museum, 165
Mollie Stevens (steamboat), 381
Molybdenum deposit, 319
Monarch Canyon Mine Road, 255
Monarch Canyon Road, 251, 254–255
Monarch Mine, 341
Monte Blanco, 209
Montgomery, E. A. "Bob," 253, 278
Montgomery-Shoshone Mine, 253
Mormon Gulch Cabin, 297
Mormon Point, 179
Mormon Point turtleback, 179
Mormon tea, 55
Morning Star Mine, 363
Morning Sun Ranch, 355
Morrison, O. B., 400
Mosaic Canyon day hike, 113
Mosaic Canyon Road, 266
Mosquitoes, 93

Mound cactus, *56*
Mountain Girl Mine, 297
Mountain joint fir, 55
Mountain lion, 72, 343
Mountain mahogany, 58
Mount Perry, 215
Mud Canyon Road, 250, 303
Mud Summit, 375
Mud Summit Road, 367, 373–376
Mustard Canyon Road, 237–238
Myer's Ranch, 301

 N

Nadeau, Remi, 291
Nadeau Road, 289, 291
Napoleon Mine, 279
Narrows, The, 149
National Monument creation (1933), 43
National Park: creation (1994), 45; initial proposal, 43; regulations, 415
Native Americans: regional tribes, 21–22; Timbisha Shoshone, 22, 23, 171, 172
Native Plant Protection Act, 48
Natural Bridge, 244; short walk, 110
Natural Bridge Road, 176
Natural Communities Conservation Planning Act, 48
Nature Conservancy, 227
Naval Air Weapons Station, China Lake, 4, 153, 299, 301, 407
Navel Spring, 211
Navel Spring Road, 211
Nelson, S.A.C., 389
Nemo Canyon, 281
Nemo Crest, 281
Nepheline syenite, *337*
Nevada joint fir, 55
Nevada Test Site, 258, 259
Nevada Triangle, added to monument, 43
Nevadan Orogeny, 14
Nevares Spring Culture, 21
New Deal Mine, 152
New Lake Manly, 97
Nikolaus-Eureka Mine, 321
Nitrate minerals, 36, 156, 308
Nitre Beds, 308
Noble Hills, 154
North Pass, 362
Northern Death Valley Fault Zone, 17, 239, 242, 246, 250, 262, 305, 306, 308, 315
Novak Camp, 294

O

O. B. Joyful Mine, 286, 293
O'Brien Canyon, 337, 338
Off-road driving regulations, 102
Oilpan Rock, 301
Old Dependable Mine, 184
Old Dinah steam traction engine, 258; display at Furnace Creek Ranch, 427
Oldest building in Death Valley, 198
Old Spanish Trail Highway, 161, 160, 162
Old Stovepipe Road, 243, 305
Opal Canyon, 362
Opal Mine, 362
Oriental, Nevada (ghost town), 315
Oriental Wash Road, 315
Original Bullfrog Mine, 35, 187, 252, 371, 374, 385, 409
Oriole: Bullock's, 80, 81; Scott's, 80
Osborne, Thomas, 411
Outlaw Cave, 197
Owl, great horned, 79
Owl Dry Lake, 150
Owl Hole Spring, 151
Owl Hole Spring Road, 150–152
Owlshead Mountains, 150, 152, 179
Ox Jump Fall, 299

P

Pacific & Atlantic Railroad survey, 317
Pacific Coast Borax Company, 33, 36, 171, 206, 227, 228, 403
Pacific Nitrate Company, 156; in 1909, 398
Pacific Sulfur Railroad, 413
Pages' Mill, 198
Pagoda buckwheat, 54
Pahrump, Nevada, 161
Painted lady butterfly, 93, 93
Paisano, 77
Paleoindian cultures, 21–22
Paleontological Resources Protection Act of 2009, 20
Paleozoic Era, 12–14; rock exposures, 13
Palisades, The, 274
Palms: date, 48, 203; fan, 203, 306, 357, 358
Palm Spring (Death Valley), 306
Palm Spring (Saline Valley), 358
Palm Spring Campground, 422
Panamint, origin of name, 22
Panamint Butte, 268
Panamint City (ghost town), 31, 169, 188, 277, 281, 290, 294, 393–394, 412; backpacking, 120;

street scene in 1875, 31; Surprise Valley Mill at 1875, 393
Panamint daisy, 60, 285
Panamint Mine, 193
Panamint Mountains, 177, 179, 182, 187
Panamint Pass, 398
Panamint Railroad, 412
Panamint rattlesnake, 86
Panamint Sand Dunes, 268, 348; day hike, 115
Panamint Springs Resort, 269, 430; services, 428–430
Panamint Treasure Mine, 194
Panamint Valley Fault Zone, 268, 286
Panamint Valley Road, 269, 286, 287–290
Panamint-Montgomery Mine, 194
Parachute plant, 63
Park area and dimensions, 1
Pat Keyes Canyon, 360
Peace Sign Mountain, 358; short walk, 113
Pegma Mine, 146
Petro Road, 213, 228
Petroglyph Canyon, 221
Petroglyphs, 115, 206, 221, 261, 265, 336; described, 24; in Echo Canyon, 207
Phacelia, 61
Phainopepla, 78
Phinney Canyon Road, 134, 365–370, 370, 375
Phinney Mine, 370
Pickleweed, 52
Pictographs, 24; in Greenwater Canyon, 24
Pink Elephant Mine, 194
Pinyon Mesa Road, 283
Pinyon pine, 58
Pioneer Point, California, 292
Piper Summit, 319
Pleasant Canyon–South Park Canyon Loop, 296–298
Pleasant City (mine camp), 297
Pluto Salt Pools, 175
Point of Rocks, 144
Poplar Spring, 285
Porter Brothers Store, 389
Porter Mine, 297
Post Office Spring, 298, 379
Pownzina Creek (ghost camp), 361, 394
Precambrian time, 10–12
Price, Bill and Edna, 241
Primrose: brown-eyed, 61; dune, 61; Eureka dune, 61, 324
Private property, 4
Providence Hill, 278
Pupfish: Amargosa, 90, 153, 167; breeding, 89; Cottonball Marsh, 89; Devil's Hole, 90, 227;

general history, 87; Saline Valley refuge plan, 358; Salt Creek, 87, 240–241; Saratoga Springs, 89, 155
Purple mat, 60
Pyramid Pass, 212, 404
Pyramid Peak, 212, 215

 Q

Quackenbush, W. J., 339
Quackenbush Mine Road, 339, 340
Quail, Gambel's, 79, 79
Quartz Spring, 328
Queen of Sheba Mine, 192, 381; ruins, 192
Queen of Sheba Mine Road, 191, 192
Quicksilver, 318

R

Racetrack, The, 309, 328, 331, 395, 411
Racetrack Valley, 301, 312, 350
Racetrack Valley Road, 309, 325–333
Rainbow Canyon, 271
Ramsey, 218, 387, 390
Rancho San Francisco, 29
Ratcliff Mine, 297
Rattlesnake Gulch, 282
Rattlesnake: Mojave, 84, 85; Panamint, 86; sidewinder, 85
Raven, 76, 77
Reagan, Ronald, 43
Red Amphitheater, 210
Red Cathedral, 110
Redlands Canyon, 197
Redlands Canyon Road, 299
Red Pass, 260
Red Wall Canyon, 307
Red-tailed hawk, 76
Regulations, National Park Service, 101–102
Reilly (ghost town), 291, 394
Reilly, Edward, 394
Resting Spring, 161
Rest Spring, 336
Rest Spring Gulch, 336
Rhodes, Albert, 146
Rhodes Spring, 146; ruins, 147
Rhodes Spring Road, 146
Rhodes Wash, 145, 149
Rhyolite (ghost town), 34, 252, 258, 371, 373, 381, 385, 395, 398, 401, 407, 409; Golden Street in1908, 396; Golden Street

in late 1920s, 396; J. S. Cook Bank ruins, 367
Rhyolite Road, 252–253
Rhyolite-Skidoo Road, 258, 305, 399
Rickard, George L. "Tex, " 381
Ringtail cat, 73, 74
Rio Tinto Borax, 45, 213, 215, 395
Road classifications, 4–5, 131–133; symbol chart, 133; view of four-wheel drive road, 134
Road Logs, described, 133–142
Roadrunner, 77, 78
Roadside Spring, 285
Robber's Roost, 197
Rock alignments, 24, 109; color-coded, 25
Rogers, John, 29, 188, 190, 299
Rogers Pass, 297
Rogers Peak, 282
Ronald A. Millsite, 184
Rood, William B., 268
Roosevelt, Nevada (ghost town), 317
Roosevelt, President Franklin D., 43
Rose Springs Mining District, 285
Rothrock, Dr. John T., 57
Round-leaved phacelia, 61
Russell, Asa "Panamint Russ, " 198, 302
Russell Camp, 198, 302
Rusty Pick Mine, 165
Ryan, "New" (ghost town), 36, 41, 215, 395
Ryan, "Old" (ghost town), 36, 213, 228, 383, 395
Ryan Camp Science and Education Center, 395
Ryan Road, 215

 S

Sacred datura, 61
Saddleback Court, 230
Saddle Cabin Junction, 204
Saddle Peak Hills, 162
Salina City (ghost camp), 329, 330, 395–397, 411
Saline Range, 318, 324
Saline Salt Marsh, 19
Saline Valley, 324, 331; origin of name, 347
Saline Valley Borax Works, 32
Saline Valley Indian Ranch, 354; Homestead Land Grant, 354
Saline Valley Marsh, 351
Saline Valley phacelia, 61
Saline Valley Road, 271, 321, 324, 331, 344, 345–363
Saline Valley Salt Company Tram, 351, 408–409; Salt Works, 352
Saline Valley Sand Dunes, 355, 356

Saline Valley Well, 354
Saline-Waucoba Road, 321
Salsberry, Jack, 146, 148, 192, 329, 381, 390, 395, 411
Salsberry Pass, 148
Salsberry Peak, 147
Salt mining, 36, 154, 351, 408
Salt Basin, 154
Salt Basin Road, 154
Salt Creek, 182; Interpretive Trail, 240; pupfish, 87, 240; short walk, 110
Salt Creek Road, 240
Salt Spring Hills, 160, 162
Salt Spring Mine, 29, 160
Salt Spring Mine Road, 162
Salt Springs Fault Scarp, 239
Salt Well, 191
Salty Navel Spring, 211
San Joaquin Company, 27
San Lucas Canyon, 349, 351
San Pedro, Los Angeles & Salt Lake Railroad, 407, 409
Sand Dune Junction, 242, 303
Sand Dunes: display, 244; Dumont, 162; Eureka, 322–324, 323; Hidden, 322; Ibex, 162, 167; Little Dumont, 162; Mesquite, 112, 242, 244; Panamint, 116, 268, 348; Saline Valley, 355–356
Sand Spring, 316, 316, 399
Sand verbena, 61
Sand Walking Company, 27
Santa Rosa Mine, 347
Santa Rosa Wash, 347
Saratoga Spring Culture, 22; hunting blind, 23; settlements, 22
Saratoga Springs, 155–156; aerial view, 158; historical description, 156
Saratoga Springs (ghost camp), 156, 397; Pacific Nitrate Company camp at (1909), 398; ruins of 1880s, 157
Saratoga Springs pupfish, 89, 155
Saratoga Springs Road, 155
Saratoga Water Company, 156, 397; tourist camp in 1930, 159
Sarcobatus Flat, 54, 312, 338, 366, 375
Scheelite Mine, 321
Schwab (ghost town), 34, 205, 384, 397
Schwab, Charles, 320, 387, 393
Schwaub Peak, 215
Schwendener, Simon, 57
Scorpion, giant desert hairy, 91
Scott, Walter E., 41, 308, 309
Scott's oriole, 80
Scotty's Canyon, 180

Scotty's Castle, 41–42, 42, 181, 309, 310, 310, 311, 312, 380, 403, 418; tours and services, 418–419
Scotty's Castle Road, 242, 262, 303–310
Scotty's Junction, Nevada, 312
Screwbean mesquite, 53
Searles Lake, 32, 405
Seepweed, 52
Seep willow, 51
Senner, Nevada (ghost post office), 317
Seven Sisters Springs, 358
Shadow Mountain (ghost camp), 114, 189, 397–398
Sheep Canyon, 179, 223
Sheep Creek Spring Road, 156
Sheephead Mountain and Pass, 147
Shermantown (ghost camp), 294, 394
Shively, Burt, 334
Shoreline Butte, 180, 199
Short walks, supplies for, 108
Shorty's Well, 185
Shoshone (town), 148, 160, 229
Shotgun Road, 291
Shoveltown, 239
Side-blotched lizard, 84
Sidewinder rattlesnake, 85
Sierra Salt Company, 409
Sigma Mine, 44, 215
Silver Crown Mines, 338
Silver Reid Mine, 348
Silver Spur Mine, 362
Silver mining, 30, 31, 34, 146, 147, 197, 256, 260, 267, 271, 277, 281, 282, 283, 289, 291, 293, 294, 347, 348, 351, 358, 360, 361, 363
Skidoo (ghost town), 34, 278, 398–399, 400; in 1907, 279
Skidoo granite, 274, 277
Skidoo Mill, 278, 398
Skidoo Mine, 253
Skidoo Road, 276–278
Skidoo water line, 277, 280, 283
Skookum (ghost camp), 38, 314–315, 399
Slate Range Crossing, 291
Slate Range Road, 289
Slate Ridge, Nevada, 315
Sliding Rocks, 331, 332; display, 331
Smith Mountain turtleback, 179
Smith, Francis M. "Borax," 32, 403, 407, 409
Smith, Orson K., 27
Smoke trees, 120, 150
Snails (springsnails), 90, 178, 308
Snow Canyon Road, 289
Snowfall, 98
Snowflake Talc Mine Road, 355

Sourdough Spring, 300
South Bullfrog Mining District, 382, 389
Southern Death Valley Fault Zone, 149, 154, 180, 199, *356*
South Eureka Road, 319, 322–324
South Greenwater Road, 148, 161
South Park Canyon, 298
South Park Canyon Road, 298
South Pass, 344, 349
Spanish Spring, 341
Spanish Trail, 27, 29
Specimen collecting regulations, 102
Spiny herb, 173
Squaw Springs, 198
Starr Mill, 274
Starvation Canyon, 188
State Highway 127, 148, 213, 225, 227–229; south, 160–163
State Highway 190: Central, 235–245; East, 201–214; West, 266–271
State Line Road, 225
Steel Pass, 324, 359
Steel Pass Fault Zone, 356
Steel Pass Road, 324, 358–360
Steininger, Jacob, 311
Steininger's Springs, 311
Stingbush, 51, *52*
Stink bugs, 91
Stone Corral, 297
Stovepipe Well (ghost camp), 305, 399; Road House, *306*
Stovepipe Wells Campground, 423
Stovepipe Wells Ranger Station, 419
Stovepipe Wells Village, 244; fire truck logo, *429*; founding, 41; services, 428; Stove Pipe original name, 245
Stovepipe Well Toll Road, 41, 269
Striped Butte (mining camp), 197
Striped Butte (mountain), 196
Strozzi, Caesar, 368
Strozzi-Phinney Connector Road, 368, 369
Strozzi-Phinney Junction, 368, 369
Strozzi Ranch, 368–369; view; *369*
Strozzi Ranch Road, 368–369
Strozzi's Connector Road, 375
Suitcase Mine, 298
Sulfur mines, 37, 318, 382
Sullivan, Mike, 249
Summerville, Nevada (ghost camp), 317
Sunset Campground, 423
Supergene enrichment, 31, 35, 218
Superior Mine, 167
Surprise Canyon, *393*; backpacking, 120

Surprise Canyon Road, 294
Surprise Valley Mill, *393, 394*
Surveyors Well, 307
Syenite Junction, 337
Sylvania Mountains, 319

 T

Tafoni, 144, 309
Talc mining, 2, 36, 156, 162, 165, 167, 179, 190, 191, 193, 320, 333, 348, 349, 355, 360, 363
Talc Springs, 191
Tamarisk, 48, 188, 203
Tarantula, desert, 90
Tarantula hawk, 91
Tarantula Mine, 184
Taylor Millsite, 195
Teakettle Junction, 328, 333
Tecopa, 161
Tecopa Hot Springs, 161
Tecopa Lakebeds, 161
Teel's Marsh, Nevada, 32
Telephone Canyon, 272
Telephone Spring, 272–273
Telescope Peak, *177, 187,* 290
Telescope Peak Trail, 285; backpacking, 119
Temperature-Rainfall Table, 99
Tenneco Corporation, 211
Terry Mine Road–Petro Road, 213, 220, 222
Terry Mine, 213
Texas Spring Campground, 423
The Air Mail (movie), 39
Thimble Peak, 260
Thorndike, John, 283–285
Thorndike Campground, 283, 423, *424*
Thorp post office, 380
Three Bare Hills, 239
Three Mile Grade, 360
Through Canyon, 150; backpacking, 120
Tidewater (trailer park site), 212
Timbisha Shoshone Indian Village, 171, 172
Tin Mountain, 308, 314, 327
Tin Mountain Landslide, 327
Tin Pass, 328
Tin Pass Lake, 328
Tiny Mine, 277
Titanothere Canyon backpacking, 120, 259
Titus Canyon, 37, 260
Titus Canyon Fault, 261
Titus Canyon Formation, 259
Titus Canyon Narrows, 261; short walk, 112
Titus Canyon Road, 252, 257–262, 307, 390

Tokop, Nevada (ghost town), 315
Tonopah & Goldfield Railroad, 401
Tonopah & Greenwater Railroad, 413
Tonopah & Tidewater Railroad, 35, 41, 161, 225, 228, 229, 230, 231, 252, 383, 391, 395, 402–403, 405, 407, 409–410, 411, 413; old grade, 411
Tonopah Railroad, 401
Tortoise, desert, 80, 82
Tourmaline Mine, 341
Towne Pass, 29, 268
Towne Pass Fault Zone, 267
Townes, Paschal H., 268
Trail Canyon, 280
Trail Canyon Road, 183–185
Travertine Point, 212
Travertine Springs, 28, 29, 48, 50, 203
Triangle Springs, 306
Trona, California, 292
Trona Railway, 405
Trona-Wildrose Road, 286, 290–292
Trudo, Edward, 32, 353, 408
Truman, President Harry S, 44
Try Again Mine, 363
Tuber Canyon, 293
Tuber Canyon Road, 286
Tucki Consolidated Telephone and Telegraph Company, 399
Tucki Mine, 273, 273
Tucki Mountain, 29, 113, 274
Tucki Mountain Road, 272–274
Tule Canyon, Nevada, 317, 412
Tule Canyon Road, 317
Tule Spring, 29, 185
Tungsten mining, 35, 184, 321, 348, 358, 363, 385
Turtleback (plant), 62
Turtlebacks, 15, 146; Badwater, 146, 176; Copper Canyon, 146, 179; Mormon Point, 146, 179; Smith Mountain, 179
20 Mule Team Borax trademark, 33, 39
Twenty Mule Team Canyon Drive, 208–209

Ubehebe Talc Mine Road, 338
Ubehebe Trail, 333, 350
Ubehebe Valley, 314, 327
Ulida Flat, 338
Ulida Mine, 338, 342
Ulida Pass, 338
Union Carbide Corporation, 348
Union Pacific Railroad, 41
United States Smelting Company, 411
Up & Down Mine, 322
Upper Confidence Wash Road, 147
Upper Echo Canyon Road, 205, 231
Upper Emigrant Spring, 274, 384
Upper Panamint Lake, 269
Upper Sheep Creek Spur Road, 223
Upper Warm Spring, 358, 359; pupfish refuge plan, 358
Upper Wildrose Canyon Road, 282–283
U.S. Fish & Wildlife Service, 227, 227
U.S. Forest Service, 4, 363
U.S. Potash, 43
U.S. Steel, 409
Uranium mining, 319
Utah juniper, 58

 U

Ubehebe, origin of name, 327
Ubehebe City (ghost camp), 333, 395
Ubehebe Copper Mine, 395
Ubehebe Crater, 18, 19, 112, 309, 327
Ubehebe Crater Road, 308–309
Ubehebe Lead Mine Road, 329
Ubehebe Mine, 329, 411; view, 330
Ubehebe Mining District, 35
Ubehebe Peak Trail, 330

 V

Val Nolan Grave, 305
Valley View Road, 230
Vehicle equipment recommendations: four-wheel drive vehicle, 100–101; high-clearance vehicle, 100; passenger car, 100
Vendian Period, 12
Victor Consolidated Mine, 320
Victory Tungsten Mine, 184
Virgin Springs Canyon Road, 145
Virginia City, Nevada, 393
Virginia Lakes, 328
Volcano Road, 173
Volcanoes, 18, 112, 113, 180, 199, 260, 318, 327, 358

 W

Wade, Harry, and family (49ers), 28, 29, 159, 163, 193
Wagon Wheel History display, 305
Wahguyhe Peak climb, 370
Wanderer of the Wasteland: advertising poster, 40; movie, 39
Warm Spring Camp, 194

Warm Springs Canyon, 194, 302, 385
Warm Springs Canyon Road, 193–194
Warm Sulphur Spring, 293
Water Canyon, 291
Water sources, cautionary note, 102
Waucoba Canyon, 362
Waucoba Mine, 361
Waucoba Mining District, 394, 408, 412
Waucoban Fauna fossils, 362
Waucoba Spring, 362
Waverly Group mines, 394
West Coleman Hills, 237
West Side Road, 173, 180, 181–199
Western Lead Company, 390
Western pipistrel bat, 76
Wheeler Survey, 156, 317
Where Flood Waters Churn display, 307
Whippoorwill Canyon, 362
Whippoorwill Flat, 362
White Cliffs Mine, 359
White Eagle Talc Mine, 191
White Pass, 259
White Sage Flat, 281
White Top Mountain, 336
White Top Mountain Road, 334–338
Wilderness/Backcountry Management Plan, 118
Wild Rose (ghost camp), 276, 399–400
Wildrose (ghost town), 283, 400
Wildrose (plant), 57
Wildrose Campground, 282, 423
Wildrose Canyon Roads, 282–286
Wildrose Charcoal Kilns, 283, *284*, 289, 392, 400
Wildrose Graben, 286
Wildrose Peak Trail, 283; day hike, 113
Wildrose Ranger Station, 282
Wildrose Spring, 285
Wildrose Station Picnic Area, 285
Wildrose Station Spring, 285
Willow Creek (Death Valley), 179

Willow Creek (ghost town), 223, 386, 400
Willow Creek (Saline Valley), 360
Willow Spring (Butte Valley), 197
Willow Spring (Cucomungo Canyon), 319
Willow Springs (Gold Valley), 224, 400
Willow Wash, 319
Wilson Canyon Road, 292
Wilson Spring, 189
Wingate Junction, 299
Wingate Pass, 29, 193, 299, 301, 405
Wingate Road, 298–299
Wingate Wash, 193, 299
Wisconsin Glacial Period, 21
Wollastonite mines, 194, 339, 341
Wood Canyon, 197
Wood Canyon Road, 281
Woodcutter Spring, 368
Wopschau Spring, 352
World Beater Mine, 297
Wright, Thomas, 405

 X

Xanterra Parks & Resorts, 171, 245, 310, 426, 428

 Y

Yucca Flat, Nevada, 258

 Z

Zabriskie, Christian B., 206, 315
Zabriskie Point, 172, 206; short walk, 109
Zebra-tailed lizard, 80
Zinc Hill Road, 269, 270
Zinc mining, 37, 192, 267, 269, 270, 271
Zion National Park, 404; buses borrowed from, 41

Death Valley Wilderness and Backcountry Stewardship Plan of 2013

The new **Death Valley Wilderness and Backcountry Stewardship Plan of 2013** was approved in July 2013. It includes a great many new or altered visitor-use regulations. Many of these have been inserted into the text of this book, but there are more—the full document, including errata and comments, is 94 pages long. The following items are those deemed most of interest to the typical user of this book.

- The park plans to install new vault toilets at the Mosaic Canyon and Darwin Falls trailheads, and near Ubehebe Crater. Additional vault or composting toilets will be installed at other backcountry locations, such as Homestake Dry Camp, Leadfield, and Eureka Dunes group campsites, in the future.

- A permit system for most backcountry and wilderness uses is expected to be in effect by 2015. Permits will be required for all overnight wilderness use and for some overnight backcountry uses including camping at backcountry cabins, in designated roadside camping corridors, and at primitive campgrounds. Permits will not be required for dispersed roadside camping. Permits will be free for the first three years, after which fees may be established. Permits will be available at visitor centers and ranger stations within the park, at the Interagency visitor center in Lone Pine, and via Death Valley's Internet website (www.nps.gov/deva).

- Designated Roadside Camping Corridors (DRCCs) will be gradually phased in along some of the most popular backcountry routes, such as Echo Canyon, Hole-in-the-Wall, Cottonwood Canyon, and Greenwater Valley roads. When these are established, overnight permits will be required.

- Length of stay at backcountry cabins remains 7 consecutive days, except at the Butte Valley and Warm Springs cabins, where the limit is 3 consecutive days. Overnight permits for camping in the cabins will be required by 2015. This is not a reservation system as cabins will still be first come, first served.

- Fires are not allowed inside any backcountry roadside cabins. However, fires are allowed outside of the cabins in metal fire rings if provided by the National Park Service. Cabins can never be locked.

- Overnight camping permits in the wilderness areas are expected to become mandatory by 2015.
- Overnight permits will not be required for backcountry roadside campsites not included within a Designated Roadside Camping Corridor.
- A new primitive dry camp will be established at Salt Well along the southern part of West Side Road. This may be several years in the future, depending on funding; in the meantime, all of West Side Road remains day-use only.
- Overnight group size is limited to 12 people in the wilderness areas.
- Overnight group size at backcountry roadside campsites is limited to 12 people and no more than 4 vehicles.
- Overnight group sizes for horse parties both in wilderness areas and at backcountry roadside campsites is limited to no more than 12 people and no more than 8 pack animals (horses, mules, burros, llamas, or alpacas).
- Backcountry camping is now permitted just 1 mile away from developed areas, paved roads, and "day-use only" dirt roads.
- The southernmost 22 miles of the Big Pine Road/Death Valley Road, between Ubehebe Crater Road and Crankshaft Junction, is now closed to roadside camping.
- Camping is not allowed within 1 mile of Greenwater Canyon. This includes within the canyon itself, which is designated for day-use only.
- Camping is not allowed within 1 mile of any old mine structure or ghost town site.
- Water and food caching is allowed, but such caches may not be left in place longer than 30 days and must be removed whether or not used.
- All mine openings are closed to entry.
- The Eureka, Panamint, and Ibex dune systems are closed to sandboarding and snowboarding.
- The placing of new climbing bolts in wilderness areas is not allowed without permission from the superintendent. Existing bolts and hardware such as webbing can be replaced in kind.
- Permits for canyoneering may be required as early as 2015. Group leaders will be required to register once a year and report the number and locations of trips they have led to the park.
- Commercially guided climbing and canyoneering are not allowed in the park.
- Commercially guided horse trips are not allowed within the wilderness areas.